FACING
PELVIC PAIN

A Guide for Patients and Their Families

EDITORS

Elise J.B. De, MD

Theodore A. Stern, MD

FACING
PELVIC PAIN

A Guide for Patients and Their Families

Facing Pelvic Pain – A Guide for Patients and Their Families

Copyright © 2021 by The Massachusetts General Hospital Psychiatry Academy. All rights reserved. Printed in the United States of America. Except as permitted under the United States Copyright Act of 1976, no part of this publication may be reproduced or distributed in any form or by any means, or stored in a data base or retrieval system, without the prior written permission of the publisher.

ISBN-13: 978-1-951166-22-9 (Print)
ISBN-13: 978-1-951166-24-3 (Ebook)

Cover Design: Falcone Creative Design, LLC
Book Design: Dianne Russell, Octal Productions, LLC
Book Production: Octal Productions, LLC
Managing Director: Jane Pimental, MGH Psychiatry Academy
Program Manager: Heather Giza, MGH Psychiatry Academy
Administrative Coodinator: Alexandra D. Fowler, MGH Psychiatry Academy
Printing and Binding: RP Graphics
This book is printed on acid-free paper.

ABOUT THE EDITORS

Elise J.B. De, MD is an Associate Professor of Surgery at Harvard Medical School, a Staff Urologist at Massachusetts General Hospital (MGH) in the Department of Urology and the Center for Pelvic Floor Disorders, the Director of Urology Training for Female Pelvic Medicine and Reconstructive Surgery, and the Director of Neurourology Services for the Spaulding Rehabilitation Network. She is Chair of The Education Committee for the International Continence Society, has published scores of articles and book chapters on voiding dysfunction, pelvic reconstruction, neurogenic bladder, and pelvic pain, has edited a surgical video atlas on pelvic floor reconstruction, and delivered hundreds of presentations worldwide. Dr. De's current research focuses on pelvic pain and voiding dysfunction. Along with her colleagues she has developed two large networks for the multi-disciplinary care of pelvic pain—at Albany Pelvic Heath Center and at the MGH.

Theodore A. Stern, MD is the Ned H. Cassem Professor of Psychiatry in the field of Psychosomatic Medicine/Consultation, Harvard Medical School and Chief Emeritus of the Avery D. Weisman Psychiatry Consultation Service, and Director of the Thomas P. Hackett Center for Scholarship in Psychosomatic Medicine at the Massachusetts General Hospital in Boston, Massachusetts. Dr. Stern has written more than 450 scientific articles and book chapters and edited more than 40 books, including the *Massachusetts General Hospital Handbook of General Hospital Psychiatry* (4/e–7/e), *Massachusetts General Hospital Comprehensive Clinical Psychiatry* (1/e, 2/e), *Massachusetts General Hospital Guide to Primary Care Psychiatry* (1/e, 2/e), *Massachusetts General Hospital Psychiatry Update and Board Preparation* (1/e–4/e), and *Facing Cancer, Facing Heart Disease, Facing Diabetes, Facing Rheumatoid Arthritis, Facing Immunotherapy, Facing Transplantation, Facing Cystic Fibrosis, Facing Lupus, Facing Osteoporosis, Facing Scleroderma, Facing Eczema, Facing Psoriasis, Facing Vitiligo, Facing Postoperative Pain*, and *Facing Overweight and Obesity*. He is also the Editor-in-Chief of *Psychosomatics*.

DEDICATION

To people facing pelvic pain, their families,
our students, our colleagues, our mentors,
and our families . . .

EJBD & TAS

ACKNOWLEDGMENTS

OUR THANKS

This book would not have come into being if not for members of the pelvic pain community who expressed their need for information and support navigating the experience of diagnosing, managing, and living with pelvic pain. They have been generous in including us in their day-to-day triumphs and struggles. Without the contributions and knowledge of so many dedicated people who have faced pelvic pain, their loved ones, and members of multidisciplinary care teams, this book would never have been completed.

We thank our contributors for their thoughtfulness and gifted writing as well as their tolerance of our deadlines and edits. We thank Melanie Morin, PT, PhD, for her review of Chapter 7. We also thank our teachers and mentors for imbuing in us a sense of responsibility to educate, to write with rigor, and, most importantly, to provide exceptional care to our patients. We would like to thank Sean Mackey, MD, PhD, from Stanford for permission to use the CHOIR body map, and Elsevier for allowing us to reproduce a number of Gray's Anatomy images for the benefit of our readers.

At the Massachusetts General Hospital Psychiatry Academy, we thank Jane Pimental our managing director, Heather Giza our program manager, and administrative coordinator Alexandra D. Fowler for their assistance and support. At Falcone Creative Design, LLC, we thank Lynda Falcone for her thoughtful representation of our message. At Octal Productions, LLC, our thanks go to Dianne Russell for overseeing the production of this book with grace and style.

EJBD
TAS

TABLE OF CONTENTS

Contributors xxi
Foreword xxvii
Preface xxix

CHAPTER 1
What Is Pelvic Pain? 1
Elise J.B. De, MD and Annie Chen, MD

What Are the Symptoms of Pelvic Pain? 2
What Distinguishes Acute from Chronic Pelvic Pain? 2
How Common Is Pelvic Pain? 2
What Causes Pelvic Pain? 4
Why Does Pelvic Pain Have a Relationship to Psychological Health? 4
What Is the Cost of Pelvic Pain? 4
What Can Worsen My Pelvic Pain? 7
When Can Pelvic Pain Indicate a Serious Condition? 7

CHAPTER 2
What Will the Evaluation of My Pelvic Pain Involve? 9
Ngozi Nwaoha, BS; Elise J.B. De, MD; and Jeannette M. Potts, MD

What Parts of My Medical and Surgical History Are Most Meaningful? 10
How Can I Describe My Pelvic Pain to My Health Care Providers? 10
Will My Health Care Providers Need to See My Health Care Records? 11
What Aspects of the Physical Examination Will Help to Clarify the Diagnosis? 12
What Should I Do If I Am Apprehensive About Having a Physical Examination? 12
What Laboratory Tests and Imaging Will Help Identify the Cause of My Pelvic Pain? 12
Who Will Be Members of My Health Care Team? 14
What Causes Pelvic Pain? 14
What Is the Role of My Health Care Provider? 15
What Is My Role in the Evaluation? 16
What If No Cause Can Be Identified or If Something Terrible Is Found? 17

CHAPTER 3
Which Gynecologic Conditions Can Lead to Pelvic Pain? 19
Carey York-Best, MD; Emily Von Bargen, DO; and Erin Crosby, MD

Introduction 20
What Are the Gynecological/Female Anatomy Causes of Acute Pelvic Pain? 20
When Should I Seek Emergency Room Care? 22
What Tests Can I Expect? 22
What Treatments Are Available? 24
What Are Gynecological/Female Anatomy Causes of Chronic Pelvic Pain? 24
Conclusion 35

CHAPTER 4
Which Male Urological Problems Can Lead to Pelvic Pain? 37
Ajay Nehra, MD, FACS; Rachel S. Rubin, MD; and Sijo J. Parekattil, MD

Introduction 38
How Many Men Have Pelvic Pain? Am I Alone? 38
What Prostate Problems May Lead to Pelvic Pain? 39
How Does the Prostate Cause Pelvic Pain? 40
What Are the Epididymis and Vas Deferens, and How Do They Cause 42
    Pelvic Pain in Men?
What Are the Seminal Vesicles and Ejaculatory Ducts, and How Do They Cause Pain? 43
What Are Causes of Chronic Testicular Pain? 44
How Many Men Have Chronic Testicular Pain? Am I Alone? 45
Could Chronic Testicular Pain Be Due to Abnormal Nerves? 46
What Can Be Done to Treat Chronic Testicular Pain? 46
What Causes Pain in the Penis? 47
Why Can Men Have Pain During Intercourse or Other Sexual Activity? 49
Conclusion 49

CHAPTER 5
Which Urogenital Problems Can Lead to Pelvic Pain in Any Gender? 51
Elise J.B. De, MD; Igor Sorokin, MD; and Sarah Mozafarpour, MD

Introduction 52
How Can My Urethra Cause Pelvic Pain? 53
How Can My Bladder Cause Pelvic Pain? 55
How Is Interstitial Cystitis/Bladder Pain Syndrome Diagnosed? 56
What Is Overactive Bladder Syndrome? 59
How Is Overactive Bladder Syndrome Diagnosed? 59
How Is Overactive Bladder Syndrome Treated? 59
What Is Bladder Outlet Obstruction? 60

What Is Underactive Bladder and How Can It Cause Pain?...62
How Is Underactive Bladder Diagnosed and Treated?..62
How Can My Ureters Cause Pelvic Pain?..63
What Signs Might Make Me Think of Cancer As a Cause of My Bladder or...........................64
    Urethra Pain?
What Might Make Me Suspect Infection As a Cause of My Bladder or Urethra Pain?...........65
What Tests Are Used to Evaluate the Urethra, Bladder, and Ureters, and.........................65
    What Can I Expect from Each?

CHAPTER 6
Which Gastrointestinal Problems Can Lead to Pelvic Pain? 75
Chun Hin Angus Lee, MD; Massarat Zutshi, MD; and Barbara Nath, MD

Introduction..76
How Is Gastrointestinal-Related Pelvic Pain Diagnosed? 77
What Parts of My Medical History Are Important to My Doctor?.............................77
How Will I Know If My Pelvic Pain Might Be Related to an Intestinal Problem? 78
What Might the Physical Evaluation Involve?..79
What Tests Might I Need to Evaluate My Pain?...80
Which Intestinal Problems Can Cause Pelvic Pain? 82
If My Pelvic Pain Is Due to Irritable Bowel Syndrome, Is the Pain All in My Head?................83
How Can Traumatic Experiences Early in Life Affect the Gut in Adulthood?.........................83
What Kinds of Questions Might My Doctor Ask Regarding Constipation?............................86
What Tests Might Be Ordered to Evaluate Refractory Constipation?....................................86
How Can Refractory Constipation Be Treated?..86
What Should I Know About Intra-Abdominal Adhesions? 87
How Can a Hernia Cause Pelvic Pain? 87
What Anorectal Problems Can Cause Pelvic Pain?..88
Conclusion 95

CHAPTER 7
Which Musculoskeletal Problems Can Lead to Pelvic Pain? 97
Beth Shelly, PT, DPT, WCS, BCB-PMD; Cynthia E. Neville, PT, DPT, WCS; and
Allison Snyder, PT, MSPT, CLT, CEEAA

What Are Musculoskeletal Problems and How Can They Lead to Pelvic Pain?......................98
What Kind of Evaluation Is Provided by a Pelvic Physical Therapist?..................................106
How Will the Pelvic Floor Muscles Be Examined and Measured?..107
How Should I Prepare for My First Appointment?..108
Will the Pelvic Physical Therapist Examination Be Painful?..108

CHAPTER 8
What Types of Bone and Ligament Problems Can Lead to Pelvic Pain?......... 111
Andrew Dubin, MD, MS and Marilyn Heng, MD, MPH, FRCSC

Why Should I See a Bone or Muscle Specialist for Pelvic Pain? 112
What Should I Know If My Pain Might Be from My Ligaments and Bones? 113
What Kind of Physical Exam Is Needed to Assess Bones and Ligaments? 113
Could My Pelvic Pain Come from My Spine/Hip? 113
What Will Imaging Studies Reveal About My Bones and Ligaments? 118
What Causes Pelvic Fractures? 118
What Tests Are Usually Done to Diagnose a Pelvic Fracture? 119
What Does the Recovery After a Pelvic Fracture Look Like? 120
Do the Long-Term Consequences of Pelvic Fractures Include Pain? 121
Can Injury to Ligaments and Tendons Cause Pelvic Pain? 122
What Bone and Soft Tissue Tumors Occur in or Near the Pelvis? 122
Could My Pelvic Pain Be Coming from My Hip? 123

CHAPTER 9
Which Neurological Problems Can Lead to Pelvic Pain? 125
Antje M. Barreveld, MD; Alexandra R. Adler, MD; and Charles Argoff, MD

How Will I Know If I Have Neurological Pain? 126
What Is Chronic Pain? 127
How Can I Be Evaluated for Neurological Causes of Pelvic Pain? 127
What Are Peripheral Nerves and How Do They Cause Pain? 129
What Is the Autonomic Nervous System? 134
What Is a Peripheral Neuropathy? 134
What Is the Central Nervous System and How Does It Cause Pain? 137
What Do I Need to Do Next? 139
Conclusion 141

CHAPTER 10
What Are Rheumatologic, Neuroinflammatory, and Vascular Pain? 143
Miriam M. Shao, BS; Ruben Peredo-Wende, MD; Charles Argoff, MD; Joseph D. Raffetto, MD; and Jan Alberto Peredes Mogica

Introduction 144
What Is Rheumatologic Disease? 144
What Are the Symptoms of Rheumatologic Diseases? 144
Which Rheumatologic Diseases Can Cause Pelvic Pain? 144
What Other Rheumatologic Conditions Are Often Associated with Pelvic Pain? 149
What Tests Can Be Done to Diagnose Rheumatologic Disease? 151
How Are Rheumatologic Diseases Treated? 151
What Are Neuroinflammatory Conditions and How Do They Affect Pelvic Pain? 151

How Can Blood Vessels Cause Pelvic Pain?	154
What Might Suggest Pelvic Venous Disease?	156
How Are Pelvic Venous Disorders Treated?	159
What Is Vasculitis and How Does It Cause Pelvic Pain?	161
How Would I Know If I Have a Type of Vasculitis?	162
What Is Ischemic Pelvic Disease?	163
How Would I Know If I Have an Ischemic Vascular Condition?	163
Conclusion	165

CHAPTER 11
How Do Physical Therapy, Diet, and Exercise Affect Pelvic Pain? ... 167
Beth Shelly, PT, DPT, WCS, BCB-PMD; Cynthia E. Neville, PT, DPT, WCS; and Allison Snyder, PT, MSPT, CLT, CEEAA

What Can a Physical Therapist Do to Help My Pelvic Pain?	168
What Are the Goals of Physical Therapy?	170
How Can Exercise Help or Worsen Pelvic Pain?	170
What Is Aerobic Exercise and How Can It Help Reduce Pelvic Pain?	171
What Is the Role of Yoga and/or Stretching in Managing My Pelvic Pain?	172
Will Relaxing My Muscles Reduce My Pain?	172
How Do You Relax the Pelvic Floor Muscles?	174
Does Breathing Change Muscle Tension and Pain Levels?	174
What Is Biofeedback and How Does It Help?	175
Will Good Posture and Correct Bending Be Helpful?	176
What Are Healthy Bowel and Bladder Habits?	178
What Else Can Be Done to Decrease Pelvic Pain?	179
How Can I Find a Specialized Physical Therapist?	179
What If There Is No Specialized Physical Therapist Near Me?	180
Summary	181

CHAPTER 12
Which Medications Are Used to Manage Pelvic Pain? ... 183
Joshua Mukalazi Nsubuga, PharmD; Elise J.B. De, MD; Charles Argoff, MD; John Walczyk, PharmD, RPh, FIACP, FACA; Carey York-Best, MD; Peter Cole, MD; Alexandra R. Adler, MD; Antje M. Barreveld, MD; and Annie Chen, MD

Introduction	184
Why Do Medications Have More Than One Name?	184
Does It Matter Whether I Take a Generic or Brand Name Drug?	184
What Is a Compound Medication?	185
What Is Transdermal Pain Management?	185
Which Medication Classes Treat Pain?	186

CHAPTER 13
Which Minimally Invasive Interventions Can Treat Nerve Pain?............ 211
Alexandra R. Adler, MD; Huy Truong, MD; Jianren Mao, MD, PhD; Julie G. Pilitsis, MD, PhD; and Antje M. Barreveld, MD

Introduction..212
What Is a Diagnostic Injection? 212
What Is a Therapeutic Injection?...213
What Are Peripheral Nerve Injections and How and Why Are They Used?.........215
What Risks Are Associated with Peripheral Injections?....................................216
What Is Spinal Cord Stimulation? 218
How Do Spinal Cord Stimulators Work?..218
When Are Spinal Cord Stimulators Helpful? 218
What Is a Spinal Cord Stimulator Trial? 219
Will I Always Have to Feel Tingling with Spinal Cord Stimulators?..................220
What Is Needed Before Spinal Cord Stimulator Implantation Surgery?............220
What Problems May Arise with Spinal Cord Stimulators? 220
What Are Sacral Nerve Stimulators and Pudendal Nerve Stimulators?.............221
What Is an Intrathecal Pain Pump? 221
What Should I Discuss with My Provider Regarding Minimally Invasive 221
   Interventions for Pain?

CHAPTER 14
When Is Surgery Considered for the Management of Pelvic Pain? 223
Miriam M. Shao, BS; Massarat Zutshi, MD; Elise J.B. De, MD; Carey York-Best, MD; Sijo J. Parekattil, MD; Julie G. Pilitsis, MD, PhD; Marilyn Heng, MD, MPH, FRCSC; Huy Truong, MD; Nucelio Lemos, MD, PhD; Peter Cole, MD; and Chun Hin Angus Lee, MD

Introduction..224
What Types of Problems Can Be Fixed with Surgery?.....................................224
What Should I Try Before Undergoing Surgery for Pain Relief? 225
What Should I Learn About Having Surgery?...225
Which Gynecological Conditions (Female Anatomy) Can Be Addressed with Surgery?.......226
How Can Gynecological Problems Be Addressed with Surgery? 226
What Chronic Pain Problems Associated with Male Anatomy Can Be 228
   Treated Surgically?
What Problems with the Bladder, Urethra, or Kidneys Can Be Addressed 229
   with Surgery?...
What Types of Anorectal Problems Can Be Fixed with Surgery?.....................231
How Can Abdominal Hernias Be Fixed with Surgery? 233
What Neurological Pelvic Pain Problems Can Be Corrected with Surgery?......235
How Can Nerve Entrapment Be Fixed with Surgery?.....................................235
How Can a Herniated Disc Be Fixed with Surgery?..235

How Can Other Neurological Pain Problems Be Fixed with Surgery?...................................237
What Musculoskeletal, Bone, and Ligament Problems Can Be Addressed 237
    with Surgery?
What Vascular Problems Can Be Addressed with Surgery? 238
Will I Remain on Medications for Pelvic Pain Around the Time of Surgery? 238
Can Surgery Make My Problems Worse? 238

CHAPTER 15
How Is Pelvic Pain Different in Children and Adolescents? 241
Susan L. Sager, MD, FAAP and Sarah Nelson, PhD

What Causes Pelvic Pain in Children and Adolescents? 242
What Will Be Involved in My Child's Initial Evaluation? 242
Is Pelvic Pain Different in Boys and Girls? 244
Isn't Menstrual Pain a Normal Part of Life, and Don't Most Teenage Girls Have 244
    Irregular Periods?
Will My Daughter Need an Internal Vaginal Exam? 244
Is Endometriosis Different in Adolescents Than in Adults? 245
What Else Can Cause Pelvic Pain in Adolescents? 245
Can Nerve Blocks Help Alleviate My Child's Pain? 246
How Can a Pelvic Floor Physical Therapist Help an Adolescent with Pelvic Pain? 246
Although My Doctor Assures Me That My Child's Condition Is Under Control, ...247
    Why Does He Still Have Pain?
Why Is It Good to Be Young, and What Is Neuroplasticity? 247
What Should I Do If My Child Has Developmental Delay and Pelvic Pain? 247
How Can I Best Support My Child? 248
Should I Worry If Health Care Providers Ask Questions About Sexual Abuse? 249
What Is a Multidisciplinary Approach to Pain Management for Adolescents? 250
How Can a Psychologist Help to Alleviate My Child's Pain? 250
Conclusion 251

CHAPTER 16
How Can Pelvic Pain Be Affected by Physical Disability? 253
Chloe Slocum, MD, MPH and Andrew Dubin, MD, MS

Introduction..254
How Does Mobility Impact Pelvic Pain and Treatment? 254
How Do Neurologic Diseases Affect My Pain and Treatment? 257
What Treatments Are Available for Pain Related to Rheumatologic Diseases? 258
What Treatments Are Available for Neuropathies? 258
Is My Condition Reversible? 259

CHAPTER 17
How Can I Better Cope with Pelvic Pain? 261
Amelia M. Stanton, PhD; C. Andres Bedoya, PhD; and Christina Psaros, PhD

Introduction 262
What Feelings or Thoughts Arise with Pelvic Pain? 262
Which Psychological Factors Are Associated with Pelvic Pain? 263
How Might Pelvic Pain Affect My Relationships? 265
Do Past Experiences Contribute to My Pelvic Pain? 266
Can Psychological Interventions Improve My Ability to Cope with Pelvic Pain? ... 266
Can Mindfulness Diminish Pelvic Pain? 268
What Happens When You Integrate Evidence-Based Treatments for Pelvic Pain? ... 268
Conclusion 269

CHAPTER 18
How Does Sexual Activity Affect Pelvic Pain? 271
Rachel S. Rubin, MD and Talli Y. Rosenbaum, MSc

How Is Pain During Sexual Activity Different for Men and Women? 272
Is Sexual Pain Different Based on My Sexual Orientation or Gender Identity? 272
How Can I Decrease Pain During Sexual Acts, Physically and Mentally? 272
What Alternative Strategies Can I Use to Have an Active Sex Life Despite My Pain? ... 273
Does Persistent Pelvic Pain Mean an End to Intimacy and Sex? 273
How Can Pelvic Pain Affect Sexual Function? 273
How Might I Feel If I Have Pain with Sex? 274
What Can I Do to Manage Living with Sexual Pain? 275

CHAPTER 19
Why Does Pain Persist and Become Chronic? 277
Elise J.B. De, MD and Serge Marchand, PhD

Introduction 278
Am I Predisposed to Pain? 278
How Does Communication Occur Between the Peripheral Nerves and the Brain? ... 279
What Happens When Messages Enter the Spinal Cord? 279
What Is Visceral Pain? 282
How Do the Brain and Emotions Affect Your Gut? 282
How Do the Spinal Cord and Brain Communicate? 282
How Does the Brain Compile and Integrate Pain Messaging? 282
What Is Central Sensitization? 284
How Does Central Sensitization Relate to Small-Fiber Neuropathy? 284
Can My Brain Control My Pain? 284
Conclusion 285

CHAPTER 20
How Do Family Members Typically Respond to Pelvic Pain? 287
Gretchen H. Wilber, PsyD

Introduction 288
Who in My Family and Circle of Friends Is at Risk for Becoming Stressed? 288
What Are Some Indicators That a Family Member Is Not Coping Well? 288
Should I Talk to Family and Friends About the Changes My Body Is Experiencing? 289
How Can I Prevent My Pain from Being a Burden on Those Who Are Important to Me? 290

CHAPTER 21
How Can I Learn More About Pelvic Pain? 293
Jill H. Osborne, MA

Where Can I Turn for More Information About Pelvic Pain? 294
Should I Seek a Second Opinion? 295
Should I Seek Care at a Specialized Center for My Pelvic Pain? 296
How Can My Local Library or the Internet Be of Assistance to Me? 297
What Are the Most Reliable Internet Resources for Me to Use for Information? 297
What Should I Be Concerned About When Using the Internet? 300
What Local, Regional, or National Organizations Provide Information About 300
  Pelvic Pain?
What Articles or Videos Offer Sound Advice or Information? 301
Would It Be Helpful for Me to Speak with Someone Who Has a Similar Condition? 303
What Is the Role of Social Media in Learning About Pelvic Pain? 304

FACING PELVIC PAIN TREATMENT MAP 306

GLOSSARY 317

REFERENCES 389

INDEX 410

CONTRIBUTORS

Alexandra R. Adler, MD
Anesthesia and Pain Management,
Lowell General Hospital;
Lowell, MA

Charles Argoff, MD
Professor of Neurology,
Albany Medical Center;
Albany, NY

Antje M. Barreveld, MD
Assistant Professor of Anesthesiology,
Tufts University School of Medicine;
Medical Director, Pain Management Services,
Director of Education and Outreach,
Substance Use Services,
Anesthesiologist, Commonwealth
Anesthesia Associates,
Newton Wellesley Hospital;
Newton, MA

C. Andres Bedoya, PhD
Assistant Professor of Psychology,
Harvard Medical School;
Clinical Director, Behavioral Medicine Program,
Department of Psychiatry,
Massachusetts General Hospital;
Boston, MA

Annie Chen, MD
Resident in Urology,
Stony Brook Medical Center;
Stony Brook, NY

Peter Cole, MD
Associate Professor of Obstetrics and
Gynecology,
Albany Medical College;
Chief, Division of Gynecology,
Albany Medical Center;
Albany, NY

Erin Crosby, MD
Associate Professor of Obstetrics and
Gynecology,
Albany Medical College;
Residency Director, Obstetrics and Gynecology,
Albany Medical Center;
Albany, NY

Elise J.B. De, MD
Associate Professor of Surgery,
Harvard Medical School;
Staff Urologist,
Department of Urology and the Center for
Pelvic Floor Disorders,
Massachusetts General Hospital;
Director of Urology Training for Female Pelvic
Medicine and Reconstructive Surgery,
Director of Neurourology Services at Spaulding
Rehabilitation Network;
Chair, Education Committee, International
Continence Society;
Boston, MA

Andrew Dubin, MD, MS
Professor of Physical Medicine &
Rehabilitation,
University of Florida Shands Hospital;
Department of Orthopaedics and
Rehabilitation,
Program Director PM&R Residency
Training Program,
University of Florida Shands Hospital and
University of Florida Rehabilitation Hospital;
Gainesville, FL

Marilyn Heng, MD, MPH, FRCSC
Assistant Professor of Orthopaedic Surgery,
Harvard Medical School;
Orthopaedic Trauma Surgeon,
Massachusetts General Hospital;
Boston, MA

Chun Hin Angus Lee, MD
Clinical Associate,
Department of Colon & Rectal Surgery
Digestive Diseases and Surgery Institute,
Cleveland Clinic;
Cleveland, OH

Nucelio Lemos, MD, PhD
Associate Professor of Obstetrics and
Gynaecology,
University of Toronto Faculty of Medicine;
Department of Obstetrics and Gynaecology of
Mount Sinai Hospital and Women's College
Hospital;
Toronto, ON

Jianren Mao, MD, PhD
Richard J. Kitz Professor of Anaesthesia
Research,
Harvard Medical School;
Vice Chair for Research,
Chief, Division of Pain Medicine,
Director, MGH Center for Translational
Pain Research,
Department of Anesthesia, Critical Care and
Pain Medicine,
Massachusetts General Hospital;
Boston, MA

Serge Marchand, PhD
Professor of Surgery, Faculty of Medicine and
Health Science, University Hospital Research
Center, CRCHUS,
Université de Sherbrooke;
Scientific Director, CSO at Lucine,
Digital Therapeutics, DTx;
Specialty Chief Editor, Section Pain
Mechanisms of Frontiers in Pain Research;
Sherbrooke, QC

Sarah Mozafarpour, MD
Resident in Urology,
Massachusetts General Hospital;
Quality and Safety Representative;
Boston, MA

Joshua Mukalazi Nsubuga, PharmD
Massachusetts College of Pharmacy
and Health Sciences,
Worcester, MA;
School of Pharmacy;
Manchester, NH

Barbara Nath, MD
Assistant Professor of Medicine,
Harvard Medical School;
Gastroenterology Associates,
Massachusetts General Hospital;
Boston, MA

Ajay Nehra, MD, FACS
Director of Men's Health and
Male Reconstructive Surgery,
Department of Urology,
Massachusetts General Hospital;
Boston, MA

Sarah Nelson, PhD
Instructor of Psychology,
Harvard Medical School;
Staff Psychologist, Department of
Anesthesiology, Critical Care and Pain
Medicine,
Boston Children's Hospital;
Boston, MA

Cynthia E. Neville, PT, DPT, WCS
Assistant Professor of Physical Therapy,
Mayo Clinic Alix School of Medicine and Science;
Division of Physical Medicine and Rehabilitation;
Jacksonville, FL

Ngozi Nwaoha, BS
Pre-Med Student, Research Assistant,
Department of Urology,
Massachusetts General Hospital;
Boston, MA

Jill H. Osborne, MA
President and Founder Interstitial Cystitis Network;
Healdsburg, CA

Jan Alberto Paredes Mogica
Medical Student,
Anahuac University;
Mexico

Sijo J. Parekattil, MD
Director,
Avant Concierge Urology;
Winter Garden, FL

Ruben Peredo-Wende, MD
Assistant Professor of Medicine,
Albany Medical College;
Chief and Program Director of Rheumatology,
Albany Medical College;
Albany, NY

Julie G. Pilitsis, MD, PhD
Professor, Neurosurgery and Neuroscience and Experimental Therapeutics,
Chair, Neuroscience and Experimental Therapeutics,
Albany Medical College;
Albany, NY

Jeannette M. Potts, MD
Co-founder Vista Urology and Pelvic Pain Partners,
Vista Urology;
San Jose, CA

Christina Psaros, PhD
Associate Professor of Psychology,
Department of Psychiatry,
Harvard Medical School;
Associate Director and Staff Psychologist,
Behavioral Medicine Program,
Massachusetts General Hospital;
Boston, MA

Joseph D. Raffetto, MD
Associate Professor of Surgery,
Harvard Medical School;
Department of Vascular Surgery,
VA Boston Health Care System, and
Brigham and Women's Hospital;
West Roxbury, MA

Talli Y. Rosenbaum, MSc
Individual and Couples Therapist,
Certified Sex Therapist,
Academic Advisor, Merkaz Yahel: The Center for the Jewish Intimacy;
Associate Editor, Sexual Medicine Reviews;
Bet Shemesh, Israel

Rachel S. Rubin, MD
Assistant Clinical Professor in Urology,
Georgetown University;
Urologist and Sexual Medicine Specialist,
IntimMedicine Specialists;
Washington, DC

Susan L. Sager, MD, FAAP
Assistant Professor of Anesthesiology,
Harvard Medical School;
Director, Pediatric and Adolescent Pelvic Pain Program,
Senior Associate, Department of Anesthesiology, Critical Care and Pain Medicine,
Boston Children's Hospital;
Boston, MA

Miriam M. Shao, BS
Fourth-Year Medical Student,
Albany Medical College;
Department of Neuroscience and Experimental Therapeutics;
Albany, NY

Beth Shelly, PT, DPT, WCS, BCB-PMD
Board Certified in Women's Health
Physical Therapy,
Board Certified in Pelvic Muscle
Dysfunction Biofeedback;
Moline, IL

Chloe Slocum, MD, MPH
Instructor in Physical Medicine and
Rehabilitation,
Harvard Medical School;
Staff Physician,
Spaulding Rehabilitation Hospital;
Department of Physical Medicine and
Rehabilitation,
Massachusetts General Hospital;
Charlestown, MA

Allison Snyder, PT, MSPT, CLT, CEEAA
Certified Lymphedema Therapist,
Certified Exercise Expert for the Aging Adult,
Certificate in Achievement-Pelvic Health
(CAPP-Pelvic),
Department of Physical and Occupational
Therapy,
Massachusetts General Hospital;
Waltham, MA

Igor Sorokin, MD
Assistant Professor of Surgery,
University of Massachusetts Medical School;
Division of Urology;
Worcester, MA

Amelia M. Stanton, PhD
Clinical Research Fellow, Department of
Psychiatry,
Behavioral Medicine Program,
Massachusetts General Hospital and
Harvard Medical School;
Boston, MA

Theodore A. Stern, MD
Ned H. Cassem Professor of Psychiatry in the
field of Psychosomatic Medicine/Consultation,
Harvard Medical School;
Chief Emeritus, Avery D. Weisman Psychiatry
Consultation Service,
Director, Thomas P. Hackett Center for
Scholarship in Psychosomatic Medicine,
Massachusetts General Hospital;
Boston, MA

Huy Truong, MD
Resident in Neurosurgery,
Medical College of Wisconsin;
Milwaukee, WI

Emily Von Bargen, DO
Female Pelvic Medicine and Reconstructive
Surgery Associate Fellowship Director,
Associate Obstetrics & Gynecology
Clerkship Director,
Harvard Medical School;
Gynecology Department – Female Pelvic
Medicine and Reconstructive Surgery,
Massachusetts General Hospital;
Boston, MA

John Walczyk, PharmD, RPh, FIACP, FACA
Director, Pharmacy Operations,
Johnson Compounding & Wellness;
Waltham, MA

Gretchen H. Wilber, PsyD
Clinical Psychologist;
Albany, NY

Carey York-Best, MD
Assistant Professor of Obstetrics, Gynecology
and Reproductive Biology,
Harvard Medical School;
Division Director, Benign Gynecology and
Obstetrics,
Associate Director of the Principal
Clinical Experience,
Massachusetts General Hospital;
Vincent Gynecology Service;
Boston, MA

Massarat Zutshi, MD
Associate Professor of Surgery,
Lerner College of Medicine of Case
Western Reserve University;
Staff Surgeon, Department of Colorectal
Surgery,
Cleveland Clinic Foundation;
Cleveland, OH

FOREWORD

THE BEST INFORMATION SOURCE FOR CONFRONTING PELVIC PAIN

Facing Pelvic Pain is for anyone whose life is affected by this condition. Written by leading health care providers, researchers, and advocates in the field, *Facing Pelvic Pain* combines top-tier medical information and compassionate counsel on the diagnosis and management of the condition, with a caring and sensible approach to the physical and emotional aspects of living with pelvic pain and its complications. This book provides easily readable and trustworthy information; it is divided into twenty-one chapters that ask and answer pertinent questions about pelvic pain and its medical and psychiatric/psychological care. A glossary of terms provides important background information to readers (e.g., about medical processes, medications, nutrition, exercise, risk-reduction); online resources and references are also offered; words italicized in the text are defined in the glossary.

Each of the chapters is accompanied by selected references, illustrations, and photographs. The Treatment Map provides a place to log all relevant information in an organized format, facilitating communication with providers and visualization of the next steps for diagnosis and management.

PREFACE

Facing Pelvic Pain employs a user-friendly question and answer format to provide practical information on the medical, surgical, and psychological aspects of pelvic pain. Written in an accessible style, this guide is intended for people facing pelvic pain. Throughout the book, words are italicized to indicate that the terms are defined in a glossary at the end of the book. References, photographs, and a Treatment Map are also provided for interested readers.

EJBD
TAS

WHAT IS PELVIC PAIN?
Elise J.B. De, MD and Annie Chen, MD

CHAPTER

In This Chapter

- What Are the Symptoms of Pelvic Pain?
- What Distinguishes Acute from Chronic Pelvic Pain?
- How Common Is Pelvic Pain?
- What Causes Pelvic Pain?
- Why Does Pelvic Pain Have a Relationship to Psychological Health?
- What Is the Cost of Pelvic Pain?
- What Can Worsen My Pelvic Pain?
- When Can Pelvic Pain Indicate a Serious Condition?

What Are the Symptoms of Pelvic Pain?

Pain in the pelvis (the lower part of the abdomen below the belly button and between the hip bones) (Figure 1-1) can come from any of the structures or organs within the pelvis (including the *bladder, bowel, uterus, vagina, ovaries, prostate, seminal vesicles,* and *appendix*), *muscles, nerves,* and *bones*. Pain from the nerves in the pelvis can be difficult to pinpoint. *Pelvic pain* can be described as sharp, stabbing, crampy, pulling, tugging, burning, dull, or achy. The duration of pain (days, weeks, months, or years), the rapidity of its onset (sudden or gradual), its persistence and its modifying factors (what makes it worse or better, such as lifting, defecating, having a full bladder, ovulating, or having intercourse) can provide important clues to its *etiology* (cause). Pelvic pain can also be associated with conditions outside the pelvis, including (but not limited to) migraine, *neuropathy* in the feet, jaw pain, fibromyalgia, and sciatica. At times, the location of the pain can be difficult to describe (for example, where is it worst, and does it seem to be on the surface or deep inside you)? The *International Pelvic Pain Society* (IPPS) (www.pelvicpain.org) has created a helpful pelvic health history form that you can download and complete to best characterize your *symptoms* and to keep track of them over time (Pelvic Health History Form, 2019). The Treatment Map (page 306), allows you to monitor your evaluations and treatments.

What Distinguishes Acute from Chronic Pelvic Pain?

Acute pelvic pain lasts less than three to six months—regardless of whether a cause is identified. *Chronic pelvic pain* (CPP) persists for three to six months or longer. CPP is defined by the *American College of Obstetrics and Gynecology* (ACOG) as pelvic area pain that lasts for six months or longer. Chronic pain can come and go, or it can be constant (Chronic Pelvic Pain, 2019). The *European Association of Urology* defines chronic pelvic pain as "*chronic* or persistent pain perceived in structures related to the pelvis of either men or women". "It is often associated with negative cognitive, behavioral, sexual, and emotional consequences as well as with symptoms suggestive of lower *urinary tract*, sexual, bowel, pelvic floor, or gynaecological dysfunction." A chronic pelvic pain *syndrome* refers to CPP when there is no proven infection or other obvious local pathology that can account for the pain (Engeler et al, 2016; Engeler et al, 2013).

How Common Is Pelvic Pain?

Fifteen percent of women in the United States have experienced constant or intermittent pelvic pain during the preceding six months (Mathias et al, 1996). Among men, CPP of three months' duration occurs in 8.2% (Magistro et al, 2016; Rees et al, 2015). People who identify as transgender or who were born with ambiguous *genital* anatomy may focus on the primary anatomy present while reading this book, keeping in mind that surgery can also lead to acute pain and CPP.

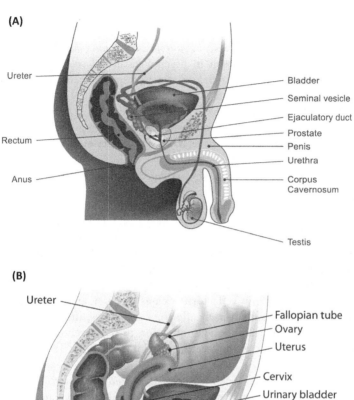

Figure 1-1: Structures present in typical (A) male and (B) female anatomy.

What Causes Pelvic Pain?

Pelvic pain can involve *urologic, gynecologic, gastrointestinal, musculoskeletal, neurologic,* and/or *rheumatologic* causes, and it can result in psychological and social problems. Therefore, multidisciplinary care is often required. Sometimes, a specific cause is not identified, and management of symptoms becomes the goal.

People with CPP sometimes have a difficult time finding providers with expertise in treating their problems. Because the causes of pelvic pain are varied, many providers struggle to diagnose and treat it. Therefore, multidisciplinary evaluations prove beneficial.

Why Does Pelvic Pain Have a Relationship to Psychological Health?

Delaying treatment of pain can lead to heightened pain and involvement of other organs (Engeler et al, 2013). Sometimes, people with pelvic pain undergo needless testing and interventions or are told that their symptoms are "all in the head." These experiences can be invalidating, distressing, irritating, and isolating, and the feelings can lead to anxiety and distress. Moreover, this might interfere with the physician-patient relationship.

Pain is modulated by cognitive factors (such as memory, attention, and context) and emotional experience. Pain can adversely affect our daily lives, affecting mood, sleep, relationships, and activities. Therefore, paying attention to the psychological aspects of pain is crucial to effective assessment and treatment (Flor et al, 1992; Tripp et al, 2013; de C Williams et al, 2018).

Chronic pain in one organ (such as the *bladder [interstitial cystitis]*, uterus *[endometriosis]*, bowel *[irritable bowel syndrome]*, and muscles [tender muscular *trigger points*]) can cause discomfort in neighboring organs. The messages sent from the brain to the organs can contribute to functional changes, such as irritable bowel symptoms, bladder problems, nerve-mediated swelling, and psychological changes, such as anxiety (Fall et al, 2010). These functional changes can result in *central sensitization* (a brain sensitivity to pain), which can be treated with a combination of physical approaches and psychological strategies, such as *Cognitive-Behavioral Therapy* (CBT).

What Is the Cost of Pelvic Pain?

Chronic pelvic pain (CPP) is the most common reason for women to be referred to women's health services in the United Kingdom; it accounts for 20% of all outpatient appointments beyond primary care. In the United States, $881.5 million is spent each year on outpatient management, while an estimated £158 million are spent annually on management in the United Kingdom's National Health Service (Latthe et al, 2006). These costs do not include lost productivity at work, lost opportunities in family life and career, and the overall diminished quality of life experienced by people with CPP.

CPP has multiple causes (see Table 1-1). A deeper review of causes and treatments for pelvic pain make up the remainder of this book.

Table 1-1: Potential Causes of Chronic Pelvic Pain

Location	Potential Explanations
Vulvar pain	• Infection • Exposures (irritants) • *Vulvar atrophy* (low estrogen) • Low *testosterone* (can be caused by *external* oral hormones) • Dermatologic conditions, such as *lichen sclerosis* • Neuropathy
Introital pain	• Low testosterone • Friction from sexual activity or clothing
Urethral pain	• *Vulvovaginal atrophy* • *Urethral caruncle* • Friction • Tight external sphincter muscle or stricture (turbulence) • *Skene's gland* • A stone at ureterovesical junction or urethral diverticulum • Tumor • Infection (ureaplasma/mycoplasma) or sexually transmitted infection • Recurrent urinary tract infections
Pelvic floor muscles	• Dysfunctional voiding • Overactivity of muscles
Gynecological pain	• *Endometriosis (cyclic pain)* • *Endometritis* • *Uterine fibroids* • *Ovarian venous abnormality* • *Ovarian cysts, torsion*, or other growths • *Ectopic pregnancy* • Sexually transmitted infection
Male organ pain	• Prostatitis or epididymitis • Testis mass, torsion, or nerve pain • Ejaculatory duct or vas deferens obstruction • Peyronie's disease • Sexually transmitted infection
Bladder pain	• Interstitial cystitis • *Bladder outlet obstruction* (BOO)

continued

Location	Potential Explanations
Gastrointestinal pain	• Chronic proctalgia • *Levator ani syndrome* • *Proctalgia fugax* • Unspecified functional anorectal pain • Constipation • *Fissures* • Hemorrhoids • *Pruritus ani* • Anal cancer • *Paget's disease* • Warts • Pelvic tumor • *Diverticulitis* • Appendicitis • Adhesions • Inflammatory bowel disease
Vascular pain	• Pelvic venous disorder

Neuromusculoskeletal	• Back, knee, foot, or hip problems
	• Injury to nerves, bones, ligaments, or tendons
	• Inflammation of bone (*osteitis* or *osteomyelitis*)
	• Muscle deficit (myopathy)
	• Upper motor neuron syndrome (upper *spine*/brain nerves)
	   – Spinal stenosis
	   – Herniated disc
	   – Multiple sclerosis
	   – Stroke
	   – Cerebral palsy
	• Lower motor neuron syndromes (lower spinal cord)
	   – *Cauda equina* syndrome
	   – Tethered cord syndrome
	   – *Sacral plexus*
	• Peripheral nerve problem
	   – Pudendal neuropathy or other *nerve entrapment*
	   – Peripheral neuropathy or neuroinflammation

Location	Potential Explanations
Psychological	- *Depression* - Anxiety - History of *sexual abuse*/assault - Poor emotional coping/communication - Personality disorders - Relationship distress
All-over pain	- Fibromyalgia - Small fiber polyneuropathy - Central sensitization - *Neuroinflammatory disease* (e.g., Lyme disease) - Rheumatologic disease - Vasculitis

What Can Worsen My Pelvic Pain?

Few scientific studies have examined what worsens pelvic pain; however, patients report that pelvic pain can be worsened by constipation, diarrhea, pregnancy, exercise (for example, sit-ups or crunches and lifting heavy objects), menstruation, *instrumentation* of the vagina or *penis*, back pain, urinary tract infections, or a full bladder.

When Can Pelvic Pain Indicate a Serious Condition?

Serious symptoms in conjunction with pelvic pain include rapid onset of pain, fever, nausea, vomiting, an inability to drink fluids, severe pain that cannot be controlled by the usual over-the-counter pain medications, altered thought clarity, or sleepiness. These symptoms can indicate a potentially life-threatening condition, such as ectopic pregnancy, a twisted or ruptured ovarian cyst, a serious urinary tract infection, an obstructing ureter stone, appendicitis, a ruptured fallopian tube, diverticulitis, or a herniated disc. These conditions can require an emergency room visit. Less urgent but still serious causes of pelvic pain can be heralded by blood in the urine, a mass or lump, weight loss, a loss of muscle mass, a limp, or blood in the vagina or stool.

Fortunately, most causes of pelvic pain are neither serious nor dangerous. Information provided in subsequent chapters will give you clues about how to diagnose, evaluate, and manage your pain.

WHAT WILL THE EVALUATION OF MY PELVIC PAIN INVOLVE?

Ngozi Nwaoha, BS; Elise J.B. De, MD; and Jeannette M. Potts, MD

CHAPTER

In This Chapter

- What Parts of My Medical and Surgical History Are Most Meaningful?
- How Can I Describe My Pelvic Pain to My Health Care Providers?
- Will My Health Care Providers Need to See My Health Care Records?
- What Aspects of the Physical Examination Will Help to Clarify the Diagnosis?
- What Should I Do If I Am Apprehensive About Having a Physical Examination?
- What Laboratory Tests and Imaging Will Help Identify the Cause of My Pelvic Pain?
- Who Will Be Members of My Health Care Team?
- What Causes Pelvic Pain?
- What Is the Role of My Health Care Provider?
- What Is My Role in the Evaluation?
- What If No Cause Can Be Identified or If Something Terrible Is Found?

What Parts of My Medical and Surgical History Are Most Meaningful?

If you have *chronic* pain, you have probably had to repeat your story numerous times to a variety of health care providers and wondered why they didn't just read what was written in your medical record. However, hearing the story first-hand—as told by you—guides your providers to the source of your *symptoms* and helps to solve your medical mystery. You should maintain organized yet concise records so that you can help your provider to care for you. Because your story might be complicated, your visit might take longer than it was scheduled to last. The Treatment Map (page 306), included in this book, can help you organize what you have had done so that communication will be enhanced. Your medical and surgical histories are essential for your provider to diagnose your condition and treat your *pelvic pain*. Lists of prior therapies and their outcomes will guide the choice of future treatments. Your prior surgical procedures should be reviewed, and the effect on your pain should be noted. Aspects of your medical history that are particularly useful include your obstetric and gynecologic (OB-GYN) history, including the number of pregnancies and the delivery method; gastrointestinal (GI) disease such as hernias, *irritable bowel syndrome* (IBS), *endometriosis, diverticulitis* and *diverticulosis*; genitourinary disease including prolapse, interstitial cystitis, *urinary tract infection* (UTI), and urinary symptoms; and skeletal diseases, including *scoliosis, spinal stenosis,* lumbar disc disorders, and *spondylolisthesis* (Carter, 1999). Pertinent surgical history includes surgery for *urinary incontinence, prolapse, hysterectomy/oophorectomy*, bowel or hernia surgery, and spinal surgery.

How Can I Describe My Pelvic Pain to My Health Care Providers?

A detailed history is crucial to determining the cause of your pelvic pain. Information regarding your pelvic pain covers the following:

- The onset of your pain: When was the first time you noticed the pain?
- The duration of your pelvic pain: How long has it lasted? What is the nature of your pain? Is it continuous or intermittent?
- The quality of the pain: Is it a knife-like sharp pain? Is it a bothersome pressure? Is the pain cramping?
- Whether the pain has changed in quality.
- The severity of the pain.

On a scale from 1 to 10, with 10 being the worst, rate the severity of your pain (Aiken, 1969) and tell your provider if your pelvic pain interferes with your daily activities (such as exercising, lying down to sleep, or enjoying family life). This information will be used to monitor your symptoms with various treatments. It is vital to notify your health care provider if the pain spreads to other body parts, as this will suggest a *neuropathic pain* (pain caused by nerve fibers).

Will My Health Care Providers Need to See My Health Care Records?

Your provider will want to review your health care records to understand your prior treatments and their outcomes. Your records can only be shared after you have signed a *medical release form*. If your story is long, it helps to collect and organize the records such as operative and imaging notes into a binder with their dates. Office notes from prior or current providers are helpful, especially if a diagnostic procedure, such as an *ultrasound* or *cystoscopy*, was performed. Recent lab testing, such as *urine cultures* and *rheumatologic testing*, should be provided. Wherever possible, provide a copy of operative notes relevant to the pelvis or *spine*. Imaging reports, as well as the actual images (provided on a CD from outside healthcare systems), will enhance your provider's ability to be thorough.

What Aspects of the Physical Examination Will Help to Clarify the Diagnosis?

A complete physical examination gives your provider the best chance of finding the source of your problem. Sometimes, a limp or a stiff neck can point to causes of pelvic pain. Examination of your heart, lungs, and neck helps to assess overall health. If a neurological condition is being considered, your health care provider might include an examination of reflexes, gait, and posture.

A pelvic exam is essential to the evaluation of pelvic pain. The exam will involve viewing the skin, touching structures that might otherwise seem unusual (possibly gently pulling up the skin over the clitoris or *penis* to see underneath), performing a testicular exam (for men) or an internal vaginal exam (for women) with or without obtaining a *Pap smear*, and a rectal exam (for both men and women). The examiner will assess the muscle tone, strength, and discomfort of your pelvic area.

What Should I Do If I Am Apprehensive About Having a Physical Examination?

If you are worried about having a *pelvic examination* (due to modesty, pain, a history of trauma [physical or *sexual abuse*], religious concerns, or discomfort because of gender identity), please share your concerns with your health care provider and their staff. Picture what will make you comfortable and communicate this. You can ask for an alternate/unconventional pelvic exam or decline to be examined. Additionally, it is normal to request that a medical assistant or a friend or family member be present during the examination. If you have a history of trauma that you think is making the exam difficult for you, your health care provider can refer you to a therapist to learn strategies to increase your comfort. Because providers are trying to stay on time, they also will feel less stressed during your exam when you communicate your questions and concern at the outset. It is reasonable to schedule additional appointments and to defer an exam until later, if needed.

What Laboratory Tests and Imaging Will Help Identify the Cause of My Pelvic Pain?

Usually, a complete history and thorough physical examination is enough to guide initial thoughts on the cause of pelvic pain. However, the following laboratory tests and exams might be informative (Table 2-1).

Table 2-1: Laboratory Tests to Facilitate the Diagnosis of Pelvic Pain

Urinalysis and culture
Urine cytology
Urine *ureaplasma* and *mycoplasma*
Testing for *genital* infections
Blood tests
Stool test
Completion of a *voiding diary*
Measurement of post-void residual
CT scan of the: • Spine • Head • Abdomen • Pelvis
Ultrasound of the: • Abdomen • Kidneys • Pelvis
MRI of the: • Spine • Head • Abdomen • Pelvis • Spine or Hip X-ray
Other tests: • *Defecography* • Upper GI study • *Cystogram* • Cystoscopy • Urodynamic testing • Colonoscopy • Laparoscopy • *Electromyogram* (EMG) • Autonomic testing (tilt-table testing) • Nerve biopsy (assessing for small fiber polyneuropathy)

Who Will Be Members of My Health Care Team?

Your health care team will consist of your *primary care physician*, possibly a *gynecologist* (a physician who specializes in the female reproductive system and female pelvic anatomy), and a *urologist* (a physician who specializes in the male reproductive system, pelvic anatomy in men and women, and the *urinary tract*). Your health care providers might refer you to other specialists, including a pelvic floor physical therapist, a *neurologist*, a pain management specialist, a *colorectal surgeon*, a GI doctor, an *orthopedist*, a *physical medicine and rehabilitation specialist*, a *psychologist* or *psychiatrist*, or a *rheumatologist*. Providers from different disciplines can offer suggestions for how to treat pain and identify its causes. You should keep a list of your doctors (with addresses and contact information) and sign the release of medical records forms, so your medical records can be shared.

What Causes Pelvic Pain?

Chronic pelvic pain (CPP) and *chronic pelvic pain syndrome* (CPPS) are terms that describe your symptoms; they are not a diagnosis *per se* and do not indicate a cause. Pelvic pain refers to pain below the *umbilicus* (belly button), including the lower back and tailbone. It also refers to pain in the rectum, vagina, the *perineum* (the area between the scrotum and *anus* in men, or the vagina and anus in women), the area above the pubic bone, the groin, and the genitals.

Symptoms in men and women may worsen or be noticeable when urinating, defecating, or having intercourse. In some cases, they can worsen during bladder filling and just prior to voiding. Some exercises can make symptoms better or worse. Some positions, like sitting, can be contributors. Even activities that were previously routine can be uncomfortable.

Syndromes are conditions that have a constellation of symptoms; they can vary from person to person. Each person has his or her own unique conditions, which contribute to the pain. For example, CPPS in men is often diagnosed as prostatitis; however, the vast majority of those with this name given to their syndrome do not have a prostate disorder, much less an infected prostate gland. Often, treatable causes or contributors are identified, and sometimes, treatments focus more on symptoms and coping (Potts, 2016).

Understanding the Diagnostic Process

Effort should be made to clarify how your pain began (for example, suddenly or gradually) and what helps or worsens the symptoms. Pain can be categorized in a variety of ways:

- *Somatic pain*: This type of pain arises from the skin, muscles, and soft tissues because of trauma or inflammation.
- *Visceral pain*: This type of pain arises from internal organs because of stretching. For example, from a blockage (as with bowel distention due to stool impaction) or interruption of blood flow (*ischemia*, or chest pain from a heart attack).

- *Myofascial pain*: The myofascia refers to the lining of *skeletal muscles*. When pain arises from these tissues, it is usually because of muscle shortening or "knots," which can result from de-conditioning or over-training. These knots or trigger points can cause *referred pain*. For example, referred pain occurs when pain is perceived in one place but arises from another, such as the initial pain with an appendicitis often felt around the belly button.

- *Neuropathic pain*: A pain that is caused by an injury or an abnormality in the nervous system. This type of pain can be associated with a spectrum of *sensory symptoms*, ranging from numbness to hypersensitivity in one region of the body corresponding to the *nerves* that *innervate* that body part (such as pain associated with a herniated disc, diabetic neuropathy, or *herpes zoster [shingles] infection*).

- *Small fiber polyneuropathy pain*: This multi-system pain disorder (Chen et al, 2019) might be related to the phenomena of peripheral and *central nerve sensitization*, previously known as a *functional somatic syndrome*.

The significance of the pain's location must also be understood. In some cases, symptoms are perceived in one organ, though the pain originates in an adjacent organ. For example, pain arising from colonic spasms can cause bladder discomfort and an urgency to urinate—this can be described as organ "cross talk." Because these organs share similar *innervation* and *smooth muscle anatomy*, they can each generate symptoms. In *radiculopathy*, the pain might arise from a distant *nerve root*. Some nerves that cause pelvic pain originate in the lower back. Lastly, there is referred pain, such as when a hip problem causes pain in the pelvis.

Similar to the analogy of electrical wiring for understanding neuropathic pain, electrical fuses within a fuse box can be used to explain myofascial *trigger points*. Trigger points in certain muscles can refer pain to areas some distance away. One such "fuse box," the *quadratus lumborum*, can provoke problems in the groin/labia of women or the scrotum of men.

Overlapping conditions, previously called functional somatic syndromes (FSS), are common (Wessely, 1999). In fact, more than 65% of men previously diagnosed with prostatitis do not have a prostate condition; instead, these men meet the criteria for overlapping disorders (irritable bowel syndrome, non-ulcer dyspepsia, non-cardiac chest pain, and fibromyalgia) outside the urinary system (Potts, 2001).

Although people suffering from overlapping syndromes with pelvic pain experience symptoms that arise from other organs, management strategies targeting more than one can ameliorate these seemingly separate conditions.

What Is the Role of My Health Care Provider?

Your physician will seek to rule out reversible causes of pain and rarer but more serious or life-threatening conditions that can arise from the skeletal system, colon, rectum, bladder, and reproductive organs (including the prostate, testicles, uterus, and *ovaries*). The history, assessment of risk factors, and physical examination will help to determine whether further diagnostic testing is necessary. These tests can include blood tests, radiological exams, or minimally invasive diagnostic procedures; however, the history and physical exam are often all that is needed.

Fortunately, serious or life-threatening conditions rarely present as CPP. Life-threatening conditions (such as *appendicitis*, diverticulitis or [infected] *kidney stones*), typically have an abrupt onset of severe pain that is considered as acute, rather than chronic. Of course, there are exceptions. Most cancers are "silent" or *asymptomatic* except in late stages when the cancer has grown or spread. It is important to institute preventive care and adherence to medical screening protocols that are intended to diagnose common malignancies before they become symptomatic and less curable.

Chronic pain is more common in people younger than 50 years old and is not typically associated with malignancies. On the other hand, one must be more suspicious and vigilant for atypical presentations of otherwise acute life-threatening conditions as well as complications of undiagnosed metastatic cancer when examining older patients. Older individuals are more likely to have rheumatologic disorders, such as *polymyalgia rheumatica* (PMR), which is an *inflammatory* disorder that causes muscle pain around the shoulders or hips. It can also be associated with joint stiffness, muscle tenderness, and weakness.

Diverticulitis of the descending colon is a life-threatening disease that is increasingly common among younger individuals because of poor diet. For example, some men in their 30s and 40s who were previously misdiagnosed with prostatitis demonstrated signs and symptoms of acute and chronic diverticulitis. In women, diverticulitis can be misdiagnosed as recurrent *urinary tract infections* (UTIs), pelvic pain, or *interstitial cystitis* (IC). The confusion occurs since the inflamed diverticula can lie against the bladder wall.

Depending on your medical history, family history, and presentation, your doctor might seek to rule out a small kidney stone that can be lodged at the very narrow section of the *ureter* (tube carrying urine from kidney to bladder) as it enters the bladder. This situation can cause referred pain to the scrotum or labia, while provoking severe *urinary urgency*.

Your doctor will review the characteristics of your pain and associated symptoms. You might be asked about sleep, *depression*, anxiety, and your relationships to understand the context in which you are experiencing pain. You will also be asked about your occupation, exercise regimen, and recreational activities, which might reveal factors that predispose you to pelvic pain.

When indicated, the exam will include assessment of the spine, torso, abdomen, and legs. A careful examination of the genitalia should be performed. An internal examination (via the vagina and rectum) is essential to assess pelvic organs, pelvic floor muscles, and nerves that course within these territories.

What Is My Role in the Evaluation?

Your participation in providing the story and your medical records will improve your care. While your history is the most important component of the evaluation, you should be organized and concise. It is of utmost importance that you allow time for your doctor to ask you some straightforward questions. Some aspects of your history are more relevant to medical professionals than you might realize.

You can facilitate the assessment by preparing a one-page timeline that includes the onset or changes in symptoms along with any patterns regarding worsening or improvement, your medications, your tests and interventions. Also, this document should chronicle *psychosocial* events that have occurred during this time. Your doctors will of course have their own information-gathering styles and it is important to try to provide information according to the way they process.

Ask the scheduler about the paperwork that needs to be completed before the visit, and bring all records with you, even if you sent a copy in advance. Be prepared to have a complete physical examination (from head to toe), including the vagina and rectum in women, and internally, via the rectum in men to get the most out of your visit.

During the diagnostic process, it is understandable if you feel frightened and worried. As you prepare for a medical consultation and await the scheduled appointments, you might feel less anxious by taking walks and staying engaged in your daily obligations and pleasures. Catastrophizing (saying things such as, "I can't live like this." "This might be fatal." "I might have to live with this forever!") doesn't help. Instead, imagine the worst-case scenario and reflect on the ways you could problem solve, taking note of your resourcefulness. Living a better life in spite of chronic pelvic pain is a de-escalating technique for patients with pelvic pain that was developed by Dr. Dean Tripp and Dr. Curtis Nickel. Their studies showed benefit with this self-care approach (Tripp, 2011).

What If No Cause Can Be Identified or If Something Terrible Is Found?

Lastly, there are three possibilities when it comes to pelvic pain:

- Something simple will be found that is easy to address; the treatment will cure the pain.
- A combination of contributors will be found that will need to be addressed over time and that will require effort on your part (for example, pelvic floor muscle tension requiring physical therapy, reduction of bladder irritants, and stress reduction).
- No cause will be identified (or a serious cause will be identified) and management will be focused on symptom control, coping, comfort, and "using the brain to treat the pain."

Each of these possibilities can be managed. This book is designed to help you alleviate your symptoms, to refine the diagnostic possibilities, and to navigate and coordinate your subspecialty multi-disciplinary care.

WHICH GYNECOLOGIC CONDITIONS CAN LEAD TO PELVIC PAIN?

Carey York-Best, MD; Emily Von Bargen, DO; and Erin Crosby, MD

CHAPTER

In This Chapter

- Introduction
- What Are the Gynecological/Female Anatomy Causes of Acute Pelvic Pain?
- When Should I Seek Emergency Room Care?
- What Tests Can I Expect?
- What Treatments Are Available?
- What Are Gynecological/Female Anatomy Causes of Chronic Pelvic Pain?
- Conclusion

Introduction

This chapter discusses *pelvic pain* in people born with female anatomy (see Figure 3-1). In this anatomy-based chapter about the internal and *external* genitalia of the female sex, the pronouns used are anatomy based. If you have *gender dysphoria* or identify with a gender other than your anatomy, and pelvic pain, you should communicate your needs and your preferred pronouns to your providers at the beginning of your visit.

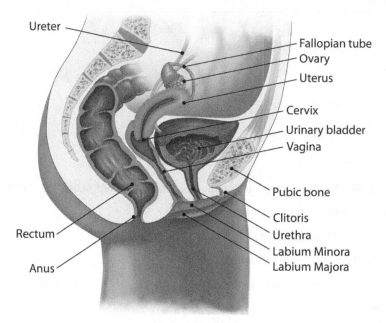

Figure 3-1: The usual anatomy in a person born female. The pelvic organs are positioned side-by-side and can affect one another through direct contact or via shared *nerves*.

What Are the Gynecological/Female Anatomy Causes of Acute Pelvic Pain?

Acute pelvic pain lasts less than three months. It usually begins abruptly and is straightforward to diagnose and treat at the time of presentation. Many of the conditions that can cause *chronic pelvic pain* (CPP) also cause acute pelvic pain, especially when they first appear. However, some specific gynecologic conditions cause acute pelvic pain and require emergent medical or surgical care.

Common causes of acute pelvic pain include:

- *Ectopic pregnancy*: A pregnancy that is located in a *fallopian tube* or outside the *uterus* and that can cause bleeding into the abdomen.
- *Ovarian cyst rupture*: A "functional" ovarian *cyst* (one that develops as part of the menstrual cycle) that can burst with intercourse or other activities and leads to fluid or blood released into the abdominal cavity.
- *Mittelschmerz*: A milder form of ovarian cyst rupture that occurs naturally at the time of *ovulation*.
- *Ovarian* or *fallopian tube torsion* (see Figure 3-2): A condition in which the ovary/tube twists on itself and interrupts the blood supply to that organ.
- *Pelvic inflammatory disease/tubo-ovarian abscess*: An infection of the tubes and *ovaries*, usually caused by *Chlamydia* or *Gonococcus*.
- *Fibroid degeneration* or *torsion*: A *benign* muscle-wall tumor of the uterus that outgrows its blood supply or twists.
- *Endometriosis*: A condition in which endometrial cells from the lining of the uterus implant outside the lining of the uterus in the pelvis, on the surface of the uterus, in the *peritoneum*, and often on the ovaries, which can bleed during the menstrual cycle and can cause severe pain.

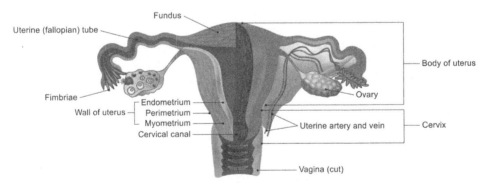

Figure 3-2: Schematic of the anatomy of the female reproductive system.

Non-gynecologic causes of acute pelvic pain include *urinary tract infection* (UTI), *kidney stones, appendicitis, diverticulitis, bowel obstruction, volvulus/intussusception,* or *bowel ischemia.* These should be considered by health care providers when evaluating pelvic pain.

When Should I Seek Emergency Room Care?

Some causes of acute pelvic pain are associated with intra-abdominal hemorrhage, infection, or *acute ischemia* (a state in which organs are deprived of their blood supplies and are in jeopardy of dying). Therefore, these require emergent treatment and possibly surgery. You should seek emergent care if you have severe pelvic pain that does not improve with over-the-counter (OTC) pain medications, such as *acetaminophen* and *ibuprofen,* and is accompanied by any of the following: fever, nausea, vomiting, an inability to stand up, fainting, or near-fainting.

You should also seek care immediately if you are having pelvic pain with or without vaginal bleeding and you have a *positive pregnancy test*, as this could indicate an ectopic pregnancy. An ectopic pregnancy might require surgery to remove the fallopian tube if the tube has ruptured and there is ongoing bleeding. In milder cases, where the tube is not yet ruptured, an ectopic pregnancy could be treated with *methotrexate* (a medicine that dissolves the pregnancy in the fallopian tube).

Taking pain medications and following levels of blood counts for signs of infection or bleeding usually is adequate for ovarian cysts. Usually, the pain resolves on its own unless dropping red blood cell (RBC) counts show significant blood loss and obligate surgery. If the ovary or fallopian tube is twisted, then emergent surgery (usually via *laparoscopy*) is needed to untwist the organ and restore normal blood supply to prevent organ loss. *Torsed uterine fibroids* can also require surgery, but they do not usually pose such an emergency. Endometriosis is usually treated with pain medications and a referral to a gynecologic specialist. In the long run, hormonal treatment can help.

What Tests Can I Expect?

If you have acute pelvic pain, you will have an exam of your abdomen and an *internal pelvic exam* (see Figure 3-3) to determine whether there is an *"acute abdomen."* For example, an acute abdomen would require emergency surgery (such as for hemorrhage, torsion/twisting of ovary or tube, severe infection, or intestinal blockage). You might have a *"FAST"* exam (focused assessment with sonography in trauma), which is a bedside *ultrasound* to look for evidence of bleeding in your abdomen. You will also have blood work (for example, a pregnancy test to rule out an ectopic pregnancy, a blood count to look for evidence of bleeding or infection, and cervical cultures to check for pelvic infection). A pelvic ultrasound (see Figure 3-4) is often performed because it is the best test to look for ovarian cysts, ovarian torsion and blood flow, ectopic pregnancy, or evidence of bleeding into the abdominal cavity. Sometimes, a *computed tomography* (CT) *scan* is needed, especially if a kidney stone or *gastrointestinal* (GI) tract organs (such as the *appendix*) are suspected of being the cause of pelvic pain.

Chapter 3: Which Gynecologic Conditions Can Lead to Pelvic Pain? 23

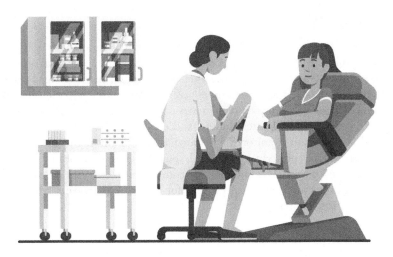

Figure 3-3: The pelvic exam is performed in a comfortable position with drapes to allow privacy. Before the exam, it is normal to tell the examiner what will make you most comfortable.

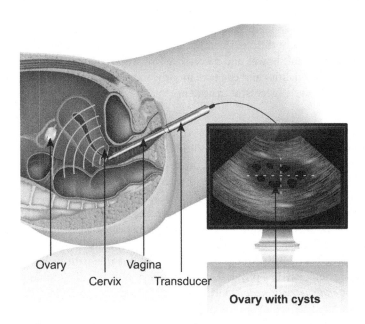

Figure 3-4: Pelvic ultrasound can be performed via the abdominal wall, but better pictures can be obtained with a lubricated sensor in the vagina. The discomfort of this exam, if present, is typically pressure rather than pain. It is acceptable to ask for a break (or to stop the study) if needed.

What Treatments Are Available?

Emergent surgery is generally needed for an intra-abdominal hemorrhage from an ectopic pregnancy, a ruptured ovarian cyst, or in cases of a twisted intra-abdominal organ, such as a torsed ovary or tube. Surgery controls the source of bleeding, untwists organs, or removes acutely infected organs. *Antibiotics*, sometimes given intravenously, will be needed for pelvic infections. Once diagnosed, ectopic pregnancy is often treated with a methotrexate injection. Ruptured ovarian cysts, Mittelschmerz, and endometriosis can usually be followed with serial RBC counts to monitor for hemorrhage, until the pain improves naturally. Pain medications, such as prescription-strength ibuprofen, *ketorolac*, or other *non-steroidal anti-inflammatory drugs* (NSAIDs) are useful to control pain. Narcotics are only used when other pain medications are not strong enough for post-operative pain. Medications are described in detail in Chapter 12.

What Are Gynecological/Female Anatomy Causes of Chronic Pelvic Pain?

By definition, CPP lasts more than three months and involves the territory of the body that is covered when one wears bicycle shorts (i.e., from below the belly button to the upper thighs). Such pain can be distressing and can often interfere with daily activities. If severe, it can cause missed work and social opportunities. Working with medical professionals with relevant expertise can help determine the cause(s) of the pain and the appropriate treatments. Commonly, different conditions co-occur (such as endometriosis, painful bladder syndrome, irritable bowel, and myofascial [muscular] pelvic pain). Treatment often requires a variety of modalities and can take months to be effective. You should not give up, as there is almost always a successful treatment.

Endometriosis

Endometriosis (see Figure 3-5) is a condition in which endometrial cells (those that line the cavity of the uterus) travel out of the uterus through the fallopian tube and then grow on the surface of the uterus, on the ovaries, or elsewhere in the abdominal cavity. Endometriosis is common; it affects about 5% of all women. It is thought to cause pain by causing internal bleeding and scarring and by releasing *prostaglandins* that irritate the lining of the abdominal cavity. Endometriosis can be suspected if one is having severe pain with menses, painful intercourse, or painful bowel movements. Sometimes, people with endometriosis will have CPP throughout the month, but this pain worsens during their menses. It can be detected on a physical examination by findings of endometriosis deposits in the vagina or *endometriosis nodules* felt behind the uterus. It can be seen on pelvic ultrasound as blood filled "chocolate cysts" of the ovaries. Sometimes, it is useful to obtain a pelvic *magnetic resonance imaging* (MRI) *scan*. Many women who have endometriosis will not have any abnormal findings on pelvic imaging studies; in this case, the only way to diagnose endometriosis is to do a laparoscopy, which looks at the pelvic organs directly and takes biopsies when needed. Some women manage the pain of endometriosis with

NSAIDs alone (for example, ibuprofen). However, endometriosis is often treated with a combination of surgery and medication. Most medications that help endometriosis are hormonal in nature (*birth control pills* [BCPs], *progesterone-only birth control* including the *progesterone-releasing intrauterine device* [IUD], *contraceptive implants* or *depo progesterone injections*, and *norethindrone*) and are designed to counteract the effects of estrogen, which stimulates endometriosis to grow. These medications work by shrinking the implants of endometriosis, causing less bleeding and irritation. Other medicines, such a *leuprolide acetate (Lupron Depot®)* and *elagolix (Orilissa®)*, cause a reduction in estrogen production. Even when surgery is used to remove an endometriosis cyst or to burn off all the dots of endometriosis in the abdominal cavity, hormonal treatment is subsequently needed to prevent it from returning. *Menopause*, be it natural, medical, or surgically induced, is the cure for endometriosis. In advanced cases, a hysterectomy (with or without removal of the ovaries) might be the best treatment, but further treatment may still be needed even after those organs have been removed.

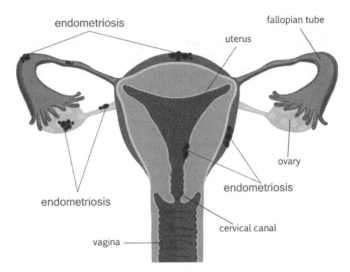

Figure 3-5: Endometriosis is when endometrial (uterine lining) cells implant in an abnormal location. This can lead to cyclic pain with menses and scarring from inflammation.

Adenomyosis

Adenomyosis (see Figure 3-6) is like endometriosis in that the cells that typically line the cavity of the uterus grow into its muscular walls. Each month when a woman has her period, these implants bleed into the uterus' muscular wall, causing blood-filled spaces, like a bruise inside the uterus. Adenomyosis also causes severe pain with menses, but unlike endometriosis, it usually occurs in women who have already had children. It also causes heavy periods because the muscle wall cannot contract normally during menses.

Adenomyosis can cause *chronic* achy pain throughout the month, usually in the middle of the pelvis just above the *pubic bone*. Medicines that help with endometriosis, especially progesterone-releasing IUDs that deliver the progesterone directly into the uterine wall, can also be very helpful with adenomyosis. However, if the pain is severe enough, hysterectomy is the definitive cure because all the adenomyosis is removed with the uterus, and the ovaries can be left in place.

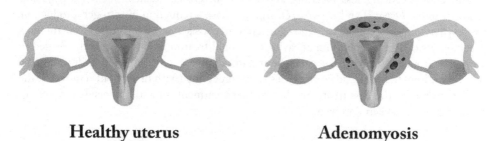

Healthy uterus   **Adenomyosis**

Figure 3-6: Adenomyosis occurs when the inner (endometrial) lining cells of the uterus grow into the muscular wall of the uterus. Bleeding in this abnormal location in response to menses can cause pain.

Ovarian Cysts/Masses

An ovarian cyst is a fluid-filled sac in or on the ovary (see Figure 3-7). Many types of ovarian cysts exist; some of them are painless, although they often cause a persistent low-grade aching pain on one side of the pelvis that flares with certain activities (such as exercise, intercourse, or menses). Fortunately, ovarian cysts are rarely cancerous, especially in women who have not yet reached menopause. However, a full evaluation by a gynecologist might be needed to rule out cancerous ovarian cysts. Because ovarian cysts are common, don't conclude that you have cancer if your doctor discusses ovarian cysts with you! Your providers will tell you if you require further evaluation to address this question. Many women suffer from chronic intermittent pelvic pain related to ovulation, also called "functional" ovarian cysts that are created by the menstrual cycle. In these cases, the ovaries are doing what they are supposed to (making a cyst and then releasing an egg each month). Cysts that develop as a part of this process are called *functional cysts*; they come and go each month with the menstrual cycle. The ovaries usually take turns ovulating, so your pain might alternate sides, and surgery is not helpful because the cyst might be in the opposite ovary the next time. Medicines that stop ovulation (such as birth control pills, progesterone implants, or depo-provera injections) are the best treatments for women who have Mittelschmerz (ovulation pain) or other painful, functional ovarian cysts.

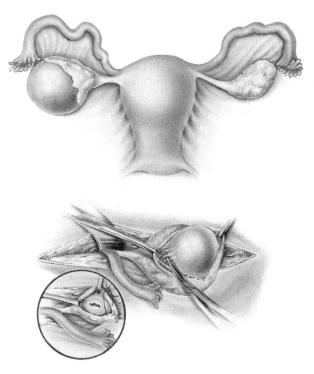

Figure 3-7: Ovarian cyst: An ovarian cyst is a fluid-filled sac in or attached to the ovary. Sometimes, your doctor will recommend surgical removal, which is pictured here.

Benign ovarian tumors are also common and tend to cause chronic aching on one side of the pelvis, although occasionally the pain can become acute in situations in which the ovary twists (torsion). The most common benign cyst is called a *dermoid* or *mature teratoma*, and this contains hair, fatty fluid, and sometimes cartilage or teeth. Other benign cysts are *serous* or *mucinous adenomas*. An ultrasound is the best way to diagnose an ovarian cyst, which can then be removed by performing a laparoscopic ovarian *cystectomy*. *Endometriomas*, the blood-filled cysts from endometriosis, commonly cause CPP, and treatment generally involves surgery. However, they can be followed by ultrasound if they are small and do not cause pain, especially in women who are planning to become pregnant.

Uterine Fibroids

Although uterine fibroids are incredibly common—almost half of women have them by their 40s—they are not a common cause of pelvic pain. If they are located near the cavity of the uterus, they can lead to heavy menses. Pain can occur during menses when the uterus tries to contract around the fibroids. These *submucosal fibroids* can sometimes be scraped out of the uterus through the vagina with a *dilation and curettage* (D&C) and *hysteroscopy*.

Fibroids that grow on the surface of the uterus and twist on a stalk can cause recurrent pelvic pain. Endometriosis or adenomyosis should still be suspected in anyone with pelvic pain who has fibroids on ultrasound. Hormonal treatments, pain control with NSAIDs, or surgery is offered on a case-by-case basis, as appropriate.

Pelvic Inflammatory Disease

Pelvic infections of the uterus, fallopian tubes, and ovaries usually begin with *bacteria* entering the uterus through the vagina. This is often associated with a sexually-transmitted disease, such as *gonorrhea* or chlamydia; however, it can result from other bacteria, such as those that live in the GI tract. Usually, pelvic infections cause acute pelvic pain and fever and require antibiotics. Sometimes, drainage of a pelvic abscess for treatment becomes necessary. The infection can be sub-acute and have a longer duration, which makes diagnosis more difficult. The infection can cause CPP; scar tissue left in the pelvis from the infection can also result in CPP. If you are in a monogamous relationship, it might surprise you if your doctor orders these tests, but testing for a sexually-transmitted infection is a common part of the work-up for pelvic pain.

Myofascial Pelvic Pain

Myofascial pelvic pain is a fairly common cause of pelvic pain because of spasms of pelvic floor muscles (see Figure 3-8). These spasms might be caused by pain from other pelvic structures for example, the bladder, bowel, hip, and back), stress, or musculoskeletal imbalance. Pelvic pain can be caused by tight pelvic floor muscles that can be felt as *trigger points* of pain when pressure is applied during the exam. These muscles support the pelvic floor, which is made up of the vagina, the bladder, and the rectum. Women with myofascial pain often have accompanying symptoms (including pelvic pressure, pain with intercourse, pain with urination, or pain with bowel movements). The best way to diagnose myofascial pain is to perform a pelvic exam in which the provider can feel a tight (painful) band of muscle. Sometimes there are distinct trigger points that cause pain to the touch. There are no blood tests or imaging studies to make the diagnosis of myofascial pain, and people often worry that something has been missed; however, the physical findings are quite distinct. The best treatment for this condition is pelvic floor *physical therapy* that releases these trigger points and teaches you how to relax your pelvic floor muscles. Sometimes medications, such as muscle relaxants, trigger point injections with *botulinum toxin*, *steroids*, or *local anesthetics* are used. For many, recognition of early signs and learning to relax the pelvic floor decreases the number of flares.

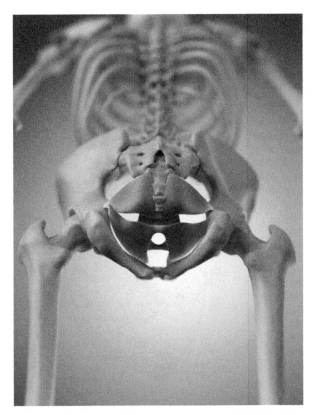

Figure 3-8: The organs of the pelvis are supported and surrounded by muscles. The muscles pictured here are more surface level, but there are deeper layers, as well as muscles stabilizing the *spine* and passing through the pelvis to the legs. These muscles can be a source of or contributor to pain.

Pelvic Organ Prolapse

Prolapse (see Figure 3-9) occurs when the walls of the vagina are relaxed, causing the bladder, bowel, or uterus to bulge through the vaginal opening. This is not an uncommon cause of pelvic pain. Women with prolapse usually describe a sensation of pelvic pressure or a palpable vaginal bulge. Pelvic organ prolapse is diagnosed by a health care provider who performs a careful pelvic exam. Treatment options for symptomatic prolapse include pelvic floor physical therapy, use of a pessary, or surgery.

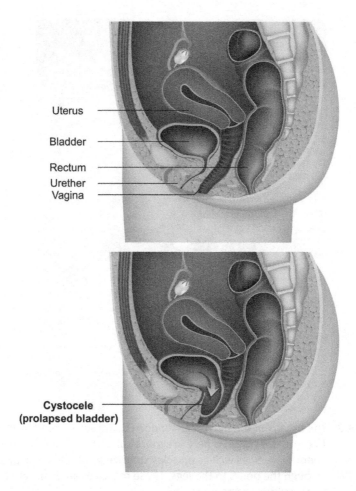

Figure 3-9: Prolapse (dropping or herniation) of the pelvic organs, pictured here with a bladder prolapse, can lead to a feeling of pelvic pressure and stretching. In some cases, the bladder or rectum can be kinked, which can lead to pelvic pain from difficulty emptying.

Vaginal and Vulvar Pain

Common causes of vaginal pain include vaginal atrophy, myofascial pain, inflammation or pain disorders of the surrounding organs surrounding the vagina (such as endometriosis and painful bladder syndrome). Rarely, a woman can be born with a vaginal *septum* (a tissue bridge in the center of the vagina) or a *Gartner's duct cyst* (a benign vaginal cyst originating from the *Mesonephric duct*), which has to do with sex determination as we develop *in utero*. These anatomic variants, scarring of the vagina from prior surgery, or even rarely a chronically inflamed appendix can lead to vaginal pelvic pain, especially during intercourse or tampon usage. The best ways to diagnose causes of vaginal pain include performing a speculum exam (where *vaginal swabs* or cultures might be obtained) and an *internal digital exam*. Vaginal pain can be treated with topical creams or suppositories, vaginal injections, pelvic floor physical therapy, or treatment of the conditions that affect the surrounding organs. Because vaginal pain can be associated with difficulties with sexual intercourse, individual or couples therapy with a certified sex therapist can be helpful.

Vulvar Pain

The vulva (see Figure 3-10) make up most of the external portion of the female genitalia. There are the labia majora (the fatty hair bearing "lips"), the labia minora (the thin velvety inner "lips"), and the clitoral prepuce (the hood of the clitoris). They cover the vaginal opening (the introitus or vestibule, which include the hymen or hymenal remnant), the urethral opening (where the urine comes out), and lubricating glands. Vulvar pain can be caused by chronic infections, *inflammatory* skin conditions, scarring from childbirth or skin conditions, or it might be nerve pain as seen in *vulvodynia*. The diagnosis of these conditions often requires a careful external vulvar exam and internal vaginal exam. Cultures should be performed as part of your initial assessment and if there is a significant change to your usual pain. Sometimes, a biopsy of the vulva is performed to aid in diagnosis. Vulvar pain is treated with topical ointments, oral medications, and physical therapy. Sometimes, a vulvar irritant can be identified (see Table 3-1), and avoidance can improve symptoms significantly. Vulvovaginal atrophy (a lack of natural vaginal estrogen after menopause or while on *hormone* medications) can cause burning and even urinary tract infections (UTIs). You might be a candidate for a surface cream with estrogen in it. Surgery is rarely used to treat vulvar pain. Sometimes people respond differently to medications, so several may be tried before one that works is found. If an inflammatory skin condition like *lichen sclerosis* is diagnosed, then prescribed topical ointments can be effective. Continuing topical treatments even after the symptoms improve prevents progressive scarring and decreases the risk of a cancer in this area. This is another condition in which treatment by a sexual health therapist can be helpful.

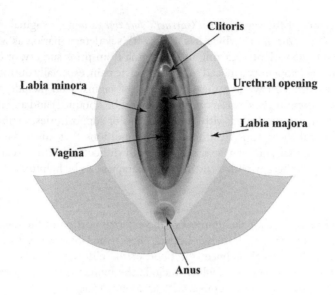

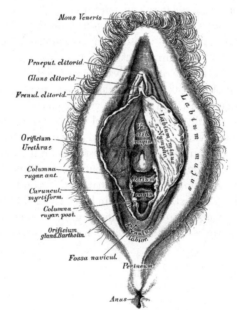

Figure 3-10: Schematic and anatomic diagrams of the female external genitalia. The vulva form a protective seal at the vaginal entrance. They have a high concentration of nerves as part of natural sexual function and therefore, can be more vulnerable to painful stimuli.

Table 3-1: Vulvar Exposures

Avoid
Perfumes, bleach, scented laundry detergents, or softeners
Colognes, perfumed lotion, or cleansers on partner
Feminine wipes, powders, creams, or other over-the-counter vulvar products
Harsh soaps or cleansers (such as antibacterial or perfumed soaps)
Douching or washing the vulva (if you feel like you need to wash, do not scrub)
Filamentous toilet paper or pads (such as recycled brands)
Vigorous wiping
Lace or other abrasive clothing (tight jeans)
Horseback or bicycle riding
Spermicidal lubricants or even particular condoms
Certain lubricating jelly or petroleum jelly for intercourse (can lead to chafing)
Infections that can cause vulvar symptoms
Tea tree oil, witch hazel, menthol talc powder, or magnesium sulfate salts
Over-the-counter yeast treatments used without talking to your provider first

Consider Using
Cotton underwear (or no underwear when possible)
Soft, non-shedding toilet paper (some have aloe)—pat rather than wiping
Squirt water bottle rather than soap or toilet paper
Hypoallergenic soap (consider you may have an allergy to sodium laurel sulfate)
Sanitary napkins with a plastic rather than fibrous top (still can irritate)
Olive oil, coconut oil for comfort or intercourse (avoid with condoms)
Certain lubricants for sex are less irritating
Petroleum jelly (as barrier) after cleaning to protect from irritation (e.g., urine, chlorine)
Nighttime zinc oxide paste as a barrier after cleansing
Trial of a low-oxalate diet (there is not a great deal of evidence for this)
Lidocaine gel as needed
Compounded ointment, such as amitriptyline, gabapentin, or *baclofen*
Oral medications such as amitriptyline, gabapentin, or *duloxetine*
Sitz bath (sitting in a few inches of lukewarm water) once or twice a day
Ice or cool compresses to soothe the area (avoid excess)
Sleep with gloves or socks on your hands if you scratch in your sleep

continued

Consider Using
"Soak and seal" a few times a day to keep the skin hydrated and protected (this means getting the area moist—in the shower, or by sitting in a lukewarm sitz bath, or by using a cool compress—and then applying something to trap the moisture in [for example, petroleum jelly, coconut oil]). You can do this as many times a day as needed.
Vaginal estrogen cream, insert, or ring: prior to use, stay up-to-date on mammograms and seek advice on abnormal estrogen or a history of breast cancer (hypoallergenic creams can be created at an affordable price at compound pharmacies).
Non-estrogen vaginal moisturizers can be found over the counter and at compound pharmacies, as well as through some of the larger breast cancer centers nationwide (for example, Haylo GYN, Biafene, Replens, or sodium hyaluronate Pluronic Gel [consider compound 10% hydrocortisone with advice from a physician]).

Vulvar Irritants

Vulvar skin can be quite sensitive—it can react to products that you tolerate well in other parts of the body. Also, products you have used for years may suddenly cause irritation. Once the vulva is irritated, a cycle of itching and scratching can develop. Where the vulva is concerned, less is more: less clothing, fewer products, less washing, and less scratching will all help the skin heal.

Clitoral Pain

The *clitoris* (see Figure 3-10) is located at the top of the vulva under the edge of the pubic bone. It is the sensitive protrusion that becomes erect during sexual stimulation. It has long stalks that originate deep within the pelvis (along the inferior pubic rami). Therefore, it is still present in women who have undergone female *genital* mutilation/cutting (an illegal culturally based female "circumcision" practice). Clitoral pain can result from a straddle or sharp injury; from a hair or other object caught under the hood (prepuce); from vulvar atrophy; from dilated veins; or from a nerve problem. There is a condition called persistent genital arousal syndrome that involves persistent unwanted genital arousal that can become painful. It has a variety of causes including vessels, nerves, and medications.

Pelvic Congestion Syndrome

Pelvic congestion is a term used to describe dilated veins in the pelvis that cause pooling of blood in pelvic organs. This is similar to *varicose veins* found elsewhere in the body (such as in the legs). Classically, the pain is aching, throbbing, pressing, or cramping. It increases with menses and occurs with prolonged standing or with intercourse or *orgasm*; it occurs most often in women who have given birth. The diagnosis can be suspected when pelvic varicosities (dilated veins) are seen on pelvic ultrasound. Pelvic MRI is considered as the diagnostic test of choice when dilation of the left gonadal (ovarian) vein is seen because this is a sign of more significant back-up of blood in the pelvis. In women who no longer desire to be fertile, a hysterectomy is a treatment option, although use of birth control pills and other hormonal therapies can be helpful. Surgery on the vessels is appropriate in certain situations. *Interventional radiology* specialists can also treat this condition by placing a coil in the dilated ovarian vein to stop blood from running back into the pelvis. Chapter 10 provides more in-depth information on pelvic venous congestion.

Gynecologic Cancer

Almost every woman who faces pelvic pain is afraid that her pain is caused by a gynecologic cancer. However, cancer is actually a rare cause of pelvic pain, except in advanced cases of cervical, uterine, and vulvar cancer (when abnormal vaginal bleeding and dysfunction of bowel and bladder are present). Ovarian cancer, which is considered to be a silent killer, can lead to abdominal bloating and distension and to non-localized pelvic pain, even early in the disease. Often, new *urinary frequency*, loss of appetite, and constipation are present. Fortunately, cancer can be ruled-out early in the course of CPP by the routine steps that are taken during a gynecologic exam (such as a *Pap smear* and internal pelvic exam), a pelvic ultrasound, and when needed, a biopsy of the lining of the uterus, cervix, or vulva. If you are worried about your diagnosis and prognosis, you should ask your gynecologist if a cancer diagnosis has been ruled out. Almost certainly, they will be able to reassure you.

Referred Pain to Gynecologic Organs

Referred pain is when the pain is felt at a site, but the cause of pain lies somewhere else. Referred pain to gynecologic organs could originate in the lower back, hips, abdominal muscles, bladder, or bowel. Treatment of those other areas with physical therapy or medication can alleviate the pain in the gynecologic organ. A common cause of pelvic pain can be damage to the *ilioinguinal* or *iliohypogastric nerves* of the abdominal wall by prior surgery, usually laparoscopy or *pfannenstiel*/horizontal *Cesarean section incisions*. This pain can be experienced in the area of the ovaries and can be treated with NSAIDs or by trigger point injections, if needed.

Conclusion

Usually, when CPP is caused by a gynecologic organ, it can be identified. At first, this can feel discouraging if your physical exam and diagnostic tests do not identify one of the female anatomic structures. However, there are many other structures or interactions of organs and nerves that can lead to pain. Even when the gynecologic organs are involved, these other contributors to pain can be important. The combined approach explored in the rest of this book will most likely help you and your providers find a path to improve your pain.

WHICH MALE UROLOGICAL PROBLEMS CAN LEAD TO PELVIC PAIN?

Ajay Nehra, MD, FACS; Rachel S. Rubin, MD; and Sijo J. Parekattil, MD

CHAPTER 4

In This Chapter

- Introduction
- How Many Men Have Pelvic Pain? Am I Alone?
- What Prostate Problems May Lead to Pelvic Pain?
- How Does the Prostate Cause Pelvic Pain?
- What Are the Epididymis and Vas Deferens, and How Do They Cause Pelvic Pain in Men?
- What Are the Seminal Vesicles and Ejaculatory Ducts, and How Do They Cause Pain?
- What Are Causes of Chronic Testicular Pain?
- How Many Men Have Chronic Testicular Pain? Am I Alone?
- Could Chronic Testicular Pain Be Due to Abnormal Nerves?
- What Can Be Done to Treat Chronic Testicular Pain?
- What Causes Pain in the Penis?
- Why Can Men Have Pain During Intercourse or Other Sexual Activity?
- Conclusion

Introduction

Urologists are *surgeons* of the *genitourinary* systems of both men and women and the reproductive organs, specifically in men. This includes problems with *kidneys*, ureters, bladders, *prostates*, and *genitals*. People with *pelvic pain* might find a consultation with a urologist helpful to help determine what is causing their pelvic pain and learn about possible treatments. Pain in the male anatomy organs (prostate, *epididymis*, *seminal vesicles*, *testis*, and *penis*) as well as some of the pelvic structures with common anatomy (such as the pelvic floor muscles, which are covered elsewhere in this book) can be a significant issue with substantial health care implications. A urologist with an interest and expertise in pain is a key specialty provider for evaluation and work up.

How Many Men Have Pelvic Pain? Am I Alone?

Pelvic pain is a common problem for both men and women, but it is rarely talked about in routine office visits. Male pelvic pain is often caused by musculoskeletal, neurological, or *inflammatory*/infectious problems, but it also can be caused by male anatomic organs (Figure 4-1), which are discussed in this chapter. (People who identify as transgender might have been born with male genitalia but identify as female gender, so this chapter would still be relevant to anyone born with male anatomy.) Male pelvic pain can cause sexual problems, such as erectile dysfunction, ejaculatory problems, or changes in *orgasm* quality, which can lead to further distress. If you are a male with pelvic pain, you are not alone. Men like you are facing similar symptoms and quality of life challenges. This book is designed to put tools for diagnosis and treatment in your hands.

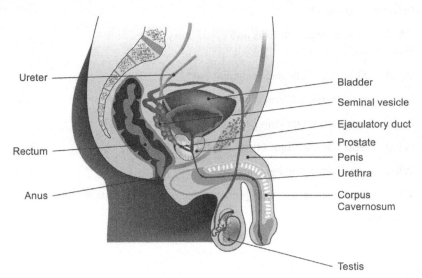

Figure 4-1: Typical male pelvic organ anatomy. The *nerves*, vessels, *bones*, and muscles are not pictured here, but they also can be important in pelvic pain.

What Prostate Problems May Lead to Pelvic Pain?

The prostate is an organ that is located at the base the bladder and surrounds the urethra, the tube that expels urine. The prostate contributes to the fluid contents of *semen* and contains nerves that aid in sexual pleasure. The prostate can be the source of numerous health problems, including cancer, urinary blockage problems, and pelvic pain (Figure 4-2).

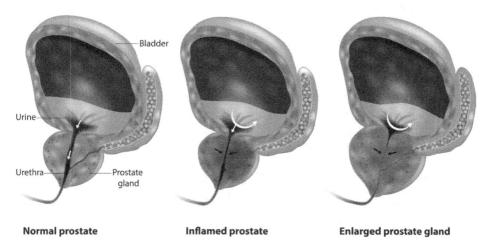

Normal prostate **Inflamed prostate** **Enlarged prostate gland**

Figure 4-2: The male prostate. When it becomes inflamed or blocked, pain, urinary problems, or true infection can ensue.

Enlarged Prostate (Benign Prostatic Hyperplasia [BPH])

As men age, their prostates can become enlarged or the muscles of the prostate and bladder neck can become tight. This can lead to urinary symptoms including weak stream, *urinary frequency*, urgency, incomplete emptying, and increased nighttime urination. While these symptoms are not typically painful, bothersome urinary symptoms can severely affect quality of life and potentially, can be a factor that worsens pelvic pain. Urinary blockage by the prostate can lead to pain as the bladder works hard to pass the urine or if the bladder does not empty completely. It should be noted that the prostate does not need to be enlarged to cause these symptoms. The inner channel of the prostate where the urethra passes can be narrowed by increased prostate and bladder neck muscle tone or by inward growth of the prostate tissue.

Acute Prostatitis/Infection

There are numerous inflammatory disorders that can affect the prostate and contribute to pelvic pain. *Bacteria* can infect the *urinary tract* and prostate and lead to "acute or bacterial prostatitis." Prostatitis can cause symptoms such as pelvic pain, pain in the lower abdomen, testicular or penile pain, urethral pain, difficulty urinating, pain with urination, painful ejaculation, and pain between the scrotum and the *anus* (the perineum). *Acute prostatitis* can also cause fever, nausea and vomiting, and is considered a medical emergency. If you have these symptoms, you need urgent evaluation by a doctor and you might need treatment with a course of antibiotics.

Chronic Pelvic Pain Syndrome (CPPS)

Chronic male pelvic pain, previously referred to as "Chronic Prostatitis," can present with symptoms similar to those of acute prostatitis (prostate inflammation) or sexual complaints, but in this case, no source of infection is found in the prostate (Magistro et al, 2016). Sexual complaints can include urethral pain, ejaculatory pain, and erectile dysfunction. This condition is often treated with *anti-inflammatory* medications, muscle relaxants, other medications, and special forms of physical therapy directed to the pelvic floor muscles. Reading the other chapters in this book will help you consider what might be causing your pain other than your prostate.

How Does the Prostate Cause Pelvic Pain?

Over the past two decades, a panel of experts at the *National Institutes of Health* (NIH) have worked to agree on a categorization of prostatic syndromes. The syndromes are classified as acute (sudden, limited in time), chronic (long term or recurrent), or asymptomatic (no symptoms experienced). Recurrent urinary tract infections can be an issue. The pelvis is surrounded by muscles that comprise the pelvic floor. When the prostate is irritated, infected, or inflamed, this can cause generalized muscle guarding with irritation and pain, burning, urinary frequency/urgency, and sexual symptoms. A tight or painful pelvic floor can also cause symptoms like constipation, pain with bowel movements, pain with sex, or even pain with sitting. When these symptoms occur, the problem has become more complicated than just a prostate problem.

To determine whether your prostate is the cause of pain, physicians might check your urine for infection and perform a physical exam (Figure 4-3). A physical exam will usually consist of a digital rectal exam. Typically, a finger placed in the rectum should not cause a great deal of pain if it is placed carefully, with adequate lubrication, and allowing the anal sphincter to relax. However, this exam can be uncomfortable if there are prostate inflammation, tight muscles in the pelvic floor, anal *fissure*, or even hemorrhoids. A staged urine test can be performed systematically to evaluate the urethral specimen, bladder specimen, and prostatic specimen at stages of the prostate exam. Additional testing can be performed to diagnose prostate problems including ultrasounds (of the prostate and bladder), cystoscopy (in which a camera is inserted inside the bladder to evaluate the size and shape of the prostate), and specialized bladder testing to look for abnormal bladder contractions and blockage of urinary stream (urodynamics). If a *radiology* test is required, then a pelvic/prostate CT or MRI might be recommended.

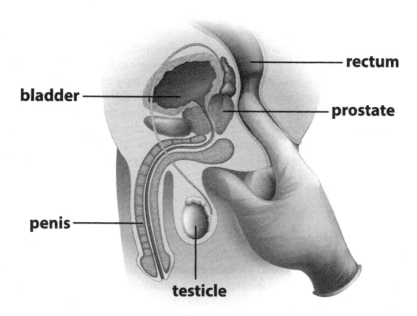

Figure 4-3: The digital (finger) rectal exam. This exam allows your provider to check for prostate cancer, anal or *rectal cancer*, an inflamed prostate, or tight pelvic floor muscles.

Treatment for Prostate Problems

1. **Medication:** It is important to establish a diagnosis before starting medications (see Chapter 12). When the pain is thought to be related to enlargement of the prostate, medications called "alpha blockers" might be recommended. These are very common medications that relax the internal muscles of the prostate and bladder neck, allowing the urine to flow more easily. For men with changes in the tone of the pelvic floor musculature, pelvic floor muscle physical therapy also will be recommended (Chapters 7 and 11). If prostatic inflammation is suspected, a course of antibiotics is commonly prescribed. The course of antibiotics will run for a few weeks and might be prescribed with or without identifying bacteria because bacteria are believed to live deep within the tissues. However, antibiotics should only be tried once, and follow-up cultures should be obtained. For chronic prostate pain and inflammation a few different types of therapies may need to be tried: for example, medications, pelvic floor physical therapy, and avoidance of caffeine. A definitive cure might not be attained. Looking beyond the prostate is important, especially if you have pain in other regions of the body.

2. **Surgery:** Surgical therapy might be recommended for men with chronic/relapsing bacterial inflammation *(microcolonies)* of the prostate if a specific area of the prostate is suspected of harboring bacteria—especially if prostate stones are identified. Success rates for relieving symptoms in this way range from 30%–70%. Surgery to open the inside of the prostate channel is even more likely to help if the cause of pain is more consistent with bladder outlet obstruction (blockage by the bladder neck or prostate), especially if the alpha-blocker medications helped to a degree. Unfortunately, no intervention is a guarantee! Often after surgery, medications are used (or retried given the new anatomy) to address the pain. Further diagnostic testing or referrals to other specialties with expertise in pain might be recommended.

What Are the Epididymis and Vas Deferens, and How Do They Cause Pelvic Pain in Men?

The epididymis is a delicate, winding tube through which semen traverse as they exit the testis, maturing as they proceed. The vas deferens is the tube that carries *sperm* from the epididymis to the ejaculatory ducts and prostate. Epididymal pain is most often secondary to urinary and lower urinary tract infections and inflammation. Multiple factors can play a role, including an increased pressure in the prostatic segment of the urethra, increased bladder pressures during voiding that prevent vas deferens-urethral closure, or *urethral instrumentation*.

Acute (relatively sudden onset) epididymal infection requires urgent medical intervention. The most common bacteria involved are sexually transmitted bacteria (C. Trachomatis) in men younger than 40 and naturally occurring bowel bacteria (lactose positive *colibacillus*) in older men. Typically, symptoms include swelling and pain of the epididymis and testes (scrotum), which can be associated with fever, chills, groin pain, and even flank discomfort. Also, there might be urethral pain/burning during voiding and pain above the pubic bone caused by bladder inflammation or infection. Diagnosis of epididymal infection is established by a urethral swab, a urine culture (mid-stream), and a scrotal ultrasound. Treatment includes scrotal elevation, pain control, possibly fever management, and appropriate antibiotic treatment. Complications can include abscess formation, secondary infertility, and chronic scrotal pain; rarely, testes infarction (interruption of blood flow) can occur. It is important to know that epididymal pain takes six weeks to resolve after treatment for infection. Anti-inflammatory medications (NSAIDs) can help.

Chronic epididymal and vas deferens pain are more challenging to treat. Their pain can be confused with the pain of a varicocele, which is a dilated set of veins serving the testis (Figure 4-4). Historically, chronic epididymitis has been treated with surgery. However, with improved diagnostic techniques and therapeutic options, chronic epididymitis is rarely treated with surgery now. Pain and relapses are managed conservatively, with inciting factors being addressed. If symptomatic, men might question whether their vasectomies could have led to pain in the testes or epididymis. Additionally, cysts associated with testicular enlargement might be associated with pain/discomfort. Management of these men is based on their individual clinical signs and symptoms.

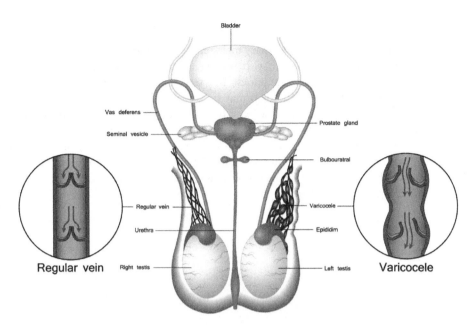

Figure 4-4: Diagram of varicocele. Dilation of the veins draining the testis, which also shows the vas (ductus) deferens, seminal vesicles, and prostate.

What Are the Seminal Vesicles and Ejaculatory Ducts, and How Do They Cause Pain?

The seminal vesicles (SVs) are located at the base of the bladder, and, along with the vas deferens, form the ejaculatory duct. The ejaculatory ducts connect to the urethra within the prostate at the *verumontanum*. Differences in how the seminal vesicles developed (congenital anomalies) along with cysts along the ejaculatory duct can cause urethral pain and decreased urine flow. In the presence of prostate infections, the seminal vesicles can become enlarged and tender. Chronic infections, such as *tuberculosis* or *schistosomiasis* (more common outside of the United States) are associated with chronic infection of the SVs.

Seminal vesicle and ejaculatory duct abnormalities are rare but expected when pain occurs with or following ejaculation or if there is a low ejaculate volume. Pelvic floor muscle dysfunction is a more common cause of pain associated with ejaculation. A physical examination, urine culture (midstream), and radiologic diagnostic tests (ultrasound or pelvic MRI) can be useful in establishing a diagnosis. For patients with a suspected ejaculatory duct obstruction, a low semen volume and transrectal ultrasound showing dilation of the ejaculatory ducts are used to diagnose this issue.

What Are Causes of Chronic Testicular Pain?

The testes are the male *gonads*—the primary male reproductive organs (Figure 4-5). Acute (sudden) testicular pain is an emergency. If you have testicular pain that arises quickly, immediate urological evaluation is required. The testis can twist on its blood supply (referred to as testicular torsion). The pain may be associated with nausea, and the testis may ride high in the scrotum or lay sideways. If not addressed urgently, the testis tissue can be lost because of lack of blood flow. A very rare cause of chronic testicular pain is intermittent torsion in which the testis rotates and constricts its blood supply and then reverts to its normal position. Other urgent testis diagnoses include fracture (experienced after an injury such as a straddle fall), a palpable mass (usually painless), and testis infection (*orchitis*, which can be accompanied by redness, enlargement, and fever).

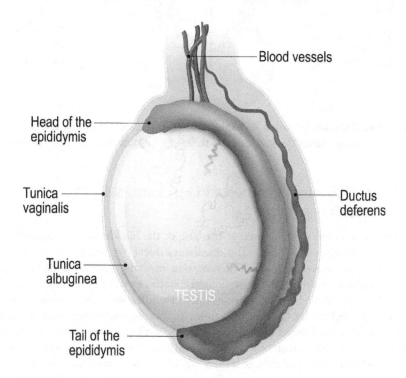

Figure 4-5: Anatomy of the testis, the male gonad where sperm is made; the testes are located in the scrotum.

If acute testis pain is not of concern, your provider can focus on the causes of chronic testis pain. A scrotal ultrasound is usually performed first to make sure there are no immediate identifiable problems with the testicle. If the ultrasound is negative (meaning that

Chapter 4: Which Male Urological Problems Can Lead to Pelvic Pain? 45

there is good blood flow in the testicle, and there's no mass or evidence of abscess), then the most likely cause of pain would be an infection or inflammation in the testicle or the epididymis. Most men who suffer from chronic testicular pain are likely to be treated for a possible infection with antibiotics and anti-inflammatory medications. If these methods do not resolve the pain, then there is a possibility that the pain could be from nerve hypersensitivity. The physician also will perform a physical exam and ultrasound, if one hasn't already been done, to determine if there are structural problems in the scrotum, such as varicose veins or any testicular masses, to explain the pain.

Sometimes, men develop chronic testicular pain after a surgical procedure, such as a *vasectomy* (Figure 4-6), inguinal hernia, abdominal surgery, or any other type of pelvic surgery. Again, this could indicate some type of nerve injury or nerve hypersensitivity after such procedures.

Some men develop testicular pain without seeming to have a specific cause, which might indicate some sort of nerve problem.

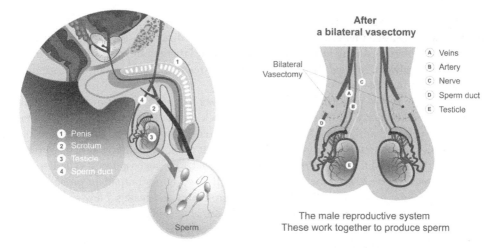

Figure 4-6: Vasectomy. During male surgical sterilization, the vas deferens are cut. This interrupts passage of sperm out of the testes. Vasectomy is a rare cause of testicular pain.

How Many Men Have Chronic Testicular Pain? Am I Alone?

Fewer than 1% of men suffer from chronic testicular pain. Chronic testicular pain is defined as pain in the testicle or groin area that lasts for more than three months and fails to respond to conservative treatment options.

Could Chronic Testicular Pain Be Due to Abnormal Nerves?

One study compared 56 men who had chronic testicular pain and 10 men who had no pain but were being operated on for other reasons. Biopsies were performed of the *spermatic cord* (the cord that provides blood supply to the testicle and runs down the groin into the scrotum). It was found that 84% of the men with chronic testicular pain had some changes in the nerves in the cord compared to only 20% of the men who had no pain (Parekattil et al, 2013). This was the first study to show that there was a difference in the spermatic cord nerves in men who had pain compared to men who have no pain. The changes in the nerves were found in three specific locations in the cord. This could explain the cause for pain in some men. The type of nerve changes found could make these nerves hyper-sensitive. This could explain why there are usually no visible abnormalities on imaging studies even though these patients still feel pain.

What Can Be Done to Treat Chronic Testicular Pain?

Initially, conservative, low-risk, and reversible treatments are best. One should try antibiotics, anti-inflammatories, or nerve-calming medications such as gabapentin (Chapter 12). Nerve-calming techniques, such as physical therapy and possibly *acupuncture*, should almost always be tried. If these conservative treatment options fail, then surgical techniques can be explored.

The first step is to perform a spermatic cord *anesthetic block* to determine if the pain could be caused by nerve hypersensitivity. If the block creates temporary pain relief, then this would suggest that there could be a nerve hypersensitivity problem. The next possible option would be some type of surgical technique to cut or block the nerve signal (without damaging the testicle) to provide long-lasting pain relief. One such option is called *microsurgical targeted denervation* of the spermatic cord. This is a minor outpatient procedure in which the surgeon makes a small incision in the groin area and makes a few specific cuts in the cord tissues in the three areas where the abnormal nerve changes were noted in the above study. It is a precisely targeted technique that preserves the bulk of the spermatic cord to avoid long-term effects on the testicle. Such a targeted nerve cutting procedure also does not affect the penis or its function. Overall, about 83% of patients have a significant reduction in pain after this procedure (Calixte et al, 2018).

If patients still have pain after a targeted denervation of the spermatic cord, the next option is targeted perispermatic cord cryoablation. This is a minimally invasive technique in which a small needle is inserted through the scrotal skin on either side of the spermatic cord as it exits the groin; the nerves around the outside of the cord are frozen, killing them. Overall, about 70% of patients achieve a significant reduction in pain after this procedure (Calixte et al, 2019).

If patients still have pain after cryoablation, the next option is a nerve block with botulinum toxin. This is a minimally invasive procedure in which an anesthetic cord block is performed with the addition of botulinum toxin. The idea is to create a block that can provide pain relief for a few months. Most men only achieve pain relief for three to six months and then might need to have another procedure performed.

Some men may have persistent pain even after all these treatments. There are a few cases in which removal of the testicle has been considered. However, there is a 10%–15% risk of developing phantom pain, which is when the person feels like the testicle is still there even though it has been removed. Thus, this procedure is usually only performed as a last resort.

If pain is still present after removal of the testicle or temporary relief in pain is seen with an anesthetic block in the groin area, your physician might suggest cutting the spermatic cord nerves higher inside the abdomen. This is called intra-abdominal targeted denervation. This can be performed using key-hole surgery (laparoscopy or robotic-assisted laparoscopy). Overall, about 70% of patients get significant reduction in pain with this approach.

Men who have post-vasectomy testicular pain can have a vasectomy reversal. The theory is that the pain could be caused by a blockage of the vas tube (the tube carrying the sperm from the testicle to the ejaculatory duct inside the body). Overall, vasectomy reversals provide about 70%–85% significant reduction in pain in these patients (Edwards, 1997; Nangia et al, 2000).

What Causes Pain in the Penis?

The penis (Figure 4-7) can be associated with significant pain and discomfort caused by infections (sexually or non-sexually transmitted) or non-infectious factors. Infectious factors can cause urethral discharge, penile ulcerations, blood in the urine, or urethral pain, which manifests as penile/urethral pain. Non-infectious factors can be divided into Peyronie's disease (a scarring of the elastic sheath surrounding the erectile tissue, which is called the *tunica albuginea* and usually is secondary to penile trauma) or direct penile injury. Pain associated with Peyronie's (non-infectious) disease is usually a dull throbbing pain caused by inflammation of the tissues that are in proximity to the nerves on the penile shaft. This pain can worsen with erection or sexual activity. Injuries to the penis can be associated with pain at the skin level or the tissues of the penile shaft. Pain in the penis, especially the tip, can be referred from inflamed prostate nerves as well.

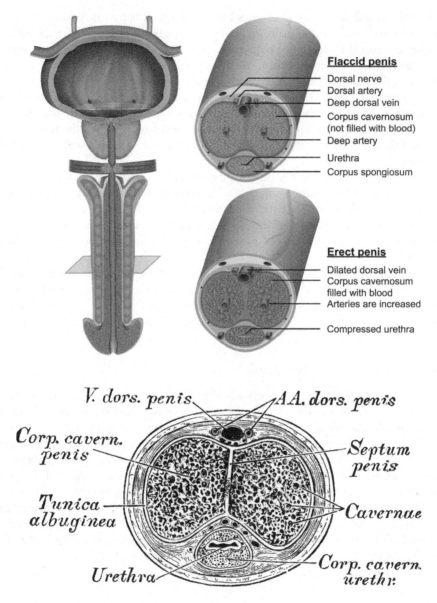

Figure 4-7: Male penile anatomy in English and Latin terms. The sheath surrounding the corpus cavernosum is called the tunica albuginea. This structure is the site of Peyronie's disease, where penile scarring occurs.

Why Can Men Have Pain During Intercourse or Other Sexual Activity?

Pain associated with intercourse can be caused by Peyronie's disease and recurrent trauma of the inflamed nerves enveloping the penis. Pain during intercourse can also be secondary to seminal vesicle inflammation or prostatitis affecting the ejaculatory ducts. Ejaculatory duct obstruction can cause penile pain and is discussed above. Diagnosis is based on the suspected cause. Pain with orgasm/ejaculation has been reported in 1%–10% of men and can be localized to any part of the genitals and perineum. Conditions commonly associated with ejaculatory pain include pelvic floor muscle dysfunction, chronic pelvic pain syndrome (CPPS), ejaculatory duct calculi, BPH, prostatitis, and prior hernia repair, among other causes (Shoskes et al, 2004). Suspected sexually transmitted infections should be *evaluated* by blood tests as well as by swabs, as indicated. Often, local county Health Departments or Hospital-Based Infectious Disease Departments have excellent resources for testing for sexually transmitted infections. The diagnosis of Peyronie's disease is established by a physical examination showing a lump within the penile shaft and with a penile ultrasound. Direct injuries to the penile shaft can occur, primarily during sexual activity, and are referred to as a "penile fracture." These are sudden events rather than a source of chronic penile pain, but rarely, there can be a delay in diagnosis causing prolonged pain. You should suspect a fracture if a "pop," comparable to a tire blowing out, is felt during sexual activity that bends the penis. Because of the physics of the bending, these events occur more commonly in men with mild erectile dysfunction. Diagnosis requires an ultrasound or a penile MRI, and intervention involves semi-urgent surgery when the diagnosis is made in time.

Treatment provides pain relief as well as treatment of the causative factor. Patients who have penile, prostate, bladder, or perineal pain may benefit from pelvic floor therapy if the pelvic floor muscles seem tight or tense during a physical exam. Sometimes, the dorsal nerves of the penis may be involved in inflammation or injury, and a penile anesthetic block may help. Patients with Peyronie's disease might not always need treatment. However, injection of the scar tissue with *collagenase clostridium histolyticum (Xiaflex™)* can be helpful for pain. Surgery for Peyronie's disease is usually not intended to directly relieve pain; instead, it is intended to correct curvature that is severe enough to impair sexual activity. If ejaculatory duct obstruction is identified, surgical treatment and transurethral resection of the duct can be performed in hopes of relieving of pain after ejaculation.

Conclusion

Different areas of the pelvis can cause pain. Identifying possible causes and then treating those specific areas is the key to success when pain is from a particular organ. Chronic pelvic pain is more difficult to treat, but a careful evaluation and identification of all contributors is likely to lead to a successful strategy for pain reduction.

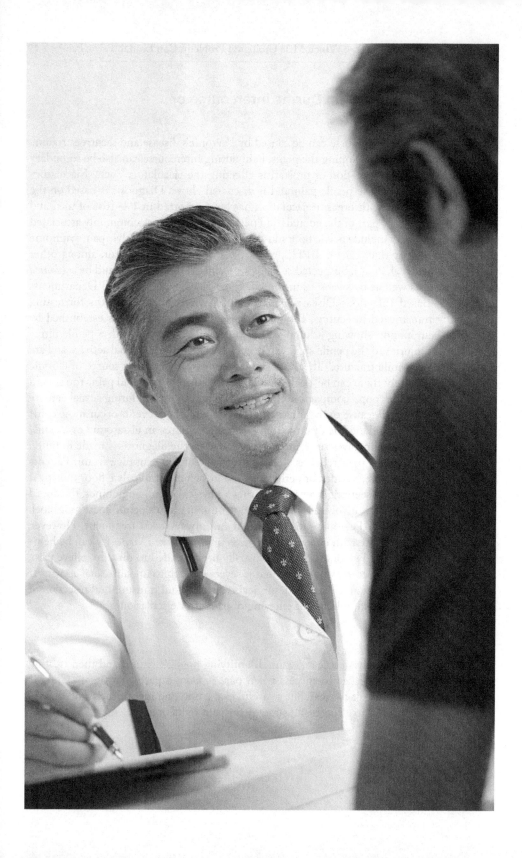

WHICH UROGENITAL PROBLEMS CAN LEAD TO PELVIC PAIN IN ANY GENDER?

Elise J.B. De, MD; Igor Sorokin, MD; and Sarah Mozafarpour, MD

CHAPTER

In This Chapter

- Introduction
- How Can My Urethra Cause Pelvic Pain?
- How Can My Bladder Cause Pelvic Pain?
- How Is Interstitial Cystitis/Bladder Pain Syndrome Diagnosed?
- What Is Overactive Bladder Syndrome?
- How Is Overactive Bladder Syndrome Diagnosed?
- How Is Overactive Bladder Syndrome Treated?
- What Is Bladder Outlet Obstruction?
- What Is Underactive Bladder and How Can It Cause Pain?
- How Is Underactive Bladder Diagnosed and Treated?
- How Can My Ureters Cause Pelvic Pain?
- What Signs Might Make Me Think of Cancer As a Cause of My Bladder or Urethra Pain?
- What Might Make Me Suspect Infection As a Cause of My Bladder or Urethra Pain?
- What Tests Are Used to Evaluate the Urethra, Bladder, and Ureters, and What Can I Expect from Each?

Introduction

While Chapters 3 and 4 specifically discuss female (gynecologic) and male (*prostate*, *testis*, *seminal vesicle*, and *ejaculatory duct*) anatomy causes of *pelvic pain*, this chapter focuses on structures that are present in people regardless of gender: the *bladder*, *urethra*, and *ureter*, as shown in Figure 5-1 (noting that *bladder exstrophy* and *agenesis* are rare diagnoses in which the bladder and/or urethra may be absent).

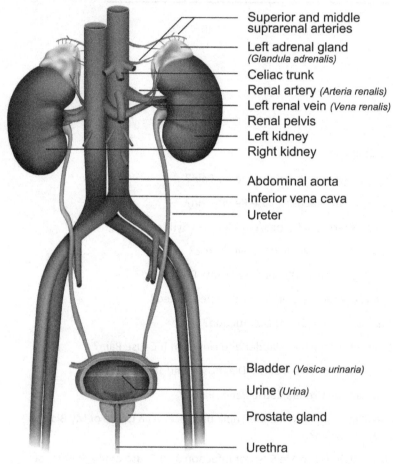

Figure 5-1: Kidneys, ureters, bladder, urethra, and major blood vessels (pictured here in a male).

Chapter 5: Which Urogenital Problems Can Lead to Pelvic Pain in Any Gender?   53

How Can My Urethra Cause Pelvic Pain?

The urethra (Figure 5-2) is a narrow tube made of muscles, *connective tissue*, and vessels that conducts urine from the bladder to the tip of the *penis* or to an opening between the vagina and the clitoris.

Urethral pain is typically perceived as originating within this structure (rather than referred elsewhere). It usually is felt when voiding and often is associated with increased daytime and/or nighttime frequency. It can be combined with dull pressure, and sometimes, it can *radiate* toward the groin, *sacrum*, and perineum, which are the soft tissues in the bicycle seat area (Doggweiler et al, 2017).

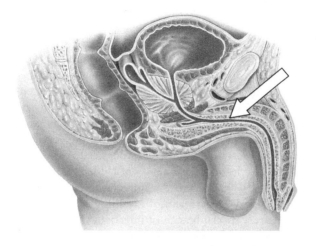

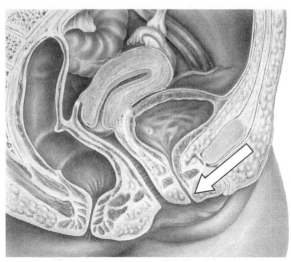

Figure 5-2: A side view of the male and female urethra in the pelvis.

Urethral Conditions Associated with Pelvic Pain

Urethritis

Urethritis is a common condition that affects people of all ages. Urethritis simply means "inflammation of the urethra". The most common cause of urethritis is a *urinary tract infection* (UTI), which can be identified using a urine test and can be treated with appropriate *antibiotics*. Typically, a voided urine specimen is thought to represent a true UTI when the culture shows more than 100,000 colonies of one strain of *bacteria* and there are more than 10 white blood cells (WBCs) (pus cells) seen with a *microscopic exam (urine sediment)*. If the specimen is a catheterized specimen, a culture with more than 10,000 colonies of bacteria is considered to represent a true infection. Interpretation becomes more subtle outside these parameters, including those with indwelling tubes *(catheters)* in the bladder. Discussion of symptoms with your provider in reference to the lab results is recommended. *Sexually transmitted infections* (STIs) account for a large percentage of non-UTI urethritis. Some of the organisms associated with STIs have specific findings on the physical exam, such as rash-like lesions in the genitalia or a *vaginal discharge*, which will often be evident on the exam. STIs can also be diagnosed with a swab obtained from a vaginal discharge in women or from a urethral discharge in men and they can be treated with antibiotics or anti-viral agents. The most common causes of STIs in the general population are *Chlamydia* and *Gonococcus*. However, if your tests are negative and your health care provider still suspects a STI, you might be tested for less common causes of UTI/STI, including *Ureaplasma* and *Mycoplasma genitalium*. If you are concerned you might have been exposed to an STI, it is often best to call your County Department of Health or to seek local clinics specifically focused on STIs. STIs are a special branch of infectious disease, and the providers who work in these clinics may be most skilled in diagnosing the infections—as well as handling the emotions associated with them (Ulmer et al, 2014).

Urethral Diverticulum

A *urethral diverticulum* is an out-pouching in the urethra (Rovner, 2008). It is a rare cause of urethral pain, and it is much more common in females. (In males, a urethral diverticulum tends to be caused by a scarred narrowing called a stricture or by an injury from a catheter placement.) Based on autopsy studies, the overall incidence in females is between 1%–6%, but far fewer women have *symptoms*. When present, the *diverticuli* typically occur in the *distal* two-thirds of the urethra, which is closest to the tip called the *meatus*. You could have a urethral diverticulum and not even notice it, and it may never cause a problem. However, if it causes symptoms, you might notice a painful vaginal mass, pain during vaginal penetration, *chronic pelvic pain* (CPP), urinary blockage or *stress urinary incontinence*, intermittent passage of pus or bloody material, and recurrent UTIs. A diverticulum might be suspected if a mass is found with a physical exam. Urethral fluid might be expressed by pushing on the urethra, and a *cystoscopy* might reveal an opening *(ostium)* in the wall of the urethra. *Magnetic resonance imaging* (MRI) is the most sensitive imaging modality to diagnose this condition. A diverticulum is considered if the symptoms mentioned above are present and the physical exam is suspicious. Also, a diverticulum might be suspected if the more straightforward diagnoses for urethral pain and UTI have been treated, and the symptoms persist. It is otherwise unreasonable to look for a urethral diverticulum before investigating other causes of urethral pain.

Urethral Caruncle and Urethral Mucosal Prolapse

These diagnoses are relevant to women. A *urethral caruncle* is a non-cancerous outgrowth of the posterior surface of the urethra, which is the side closest to the vagina (Conces et al, 2012). *Urethral mucosal prolapse* is a circumferential loosening and slippage of the lining of the urethra, like the lining of a pant leg elongating and stretching beyond the pant leg. It usually affects *post-menopausal* women or very young girls and has to do with changes in the tissue in the absence of *estrogen*. Often, there are no symptoms and no treatment is required. Some women present with blood in the urine, vaginal bleeding, and (potentially severe) pain. If symptoms occur, the initial treatment is with estrogen cream. Most cases resolve with this intervention alone. Urethral masses that have an unusual appearance, that are large and non-tender or enlarging, or those that do not resolve with estrogen should be *evaluated* by a physical exam and sometimes by a cystoscopy or *biopsy* to make sure they are not actually cancerous growths. If you have been diagnosed with a caruncle or urethral mucosal prolapse, you should monitor its appearance over time and let your provider know if it is not getting smaller with use of vaginal estrogen (Schreiner et al, 2013).

Bladder Outlet Obstruction

A blockage of urine flow that is caused by tight *pelvic floor muscles* (PFMs), a tight bladder neck, the prostate, scar tissue (aka a stricture), a sling placed for incontinence, or a stone lodged in the urethra can all cause pain because turbulent flow results in high pressures in the urethra. The jagged edges of the stone also can cause urethral pain as it passes along the sensitive tissues. Bladder outlet obstruction is discussed below.

Nerve Causes of Urethral Pain

Nerve sensitivity can cause urethral pain in both men and women. Nerve conditions, such as *nerve entrapment* or *small fiber polyneuropathy*, can cause pelvic pain. In women, vaginal atrophy can affect the urethra because of the presence of *estrogen receptors* (ERs) in that location, and vaginal estrogen will resolve the discomfort after many weeks of usage. Chemical irritants (such as bleached underwear or cleansing wipes, soaps, toilet paper, or rough clothing) can irritate the tip of the urethra. Lastly, some people, especially those with *interstitial cystitis*, can have sensitivities to foods such as spices or citrus, and the pain can be felt in the urethra.

How Can My Bladder Cause Pelvic Pain?

Bladder Symptom Complex

The *bladder symptom complex* includes a large group of people with bladder, and/or urethral, and/or pelvic pain, and lower *urinary tract* symptoms, many of whom have *specific identifiable causes*.

Interstitial Cystitis/Bladder Pain Syndrome

Interstitial Cystitis (IC)/Bladder Pain Syndrome (BPS) is a subset of the bladder symptom complex. The *American Urological Association* (AUA) definition is: "An unpleasant sensation (pain, pressure, discomfort) perceived to be related to the urinary bladder, associated with lower urinary tract symptoms of more than six weeks' duration, in the absence of infection or other identifiable causes" (Hanno et al, 2011).

Symptoms of IC/BPS overlap significantly with other causes of bladder and pelvic pain.

Pain (including sensations of pressure and discomfort) above the pubic bone related to bladder filling might also be felt in the urethra, *vulva*, *vagina*, *rectum*, lower abdomen, and lower back. Pain or discomfort that worsens with specific foods or drinks and/or worsens with bladder filling and improves with urination is typical of IC/BPS (Tincello and Walker, 2005; Fitzgerald et al, 2005; and Warren et al, 2008).

Urinary urgency and frequency (often to avoid pain) are present in most people with IC/BPS but do not distinguish IC from other conditions.

How Is Interstitial Cystitis/Bladder Pain Syndrome Diagnosed?

This is confusing because IC/BPS is a "diagnosis of exclusion," based primarily on history and the initial evaluation. It can only exist if no other explanation (such as bladder outlet obstruction) is found. According to the American Urological Association Guideline, the basic assessment that should be performed when suspecting IC/BPS should include a history (including use of pain-focused *questionnaires*), a physical exam, a *voiding diary*, measurement of *post-void residual* (the amount of urine in the bladder after voiding, measurable by *ultrasound* or a quick passage of a catheter), laboratory testing of the urine (urinalysis and culture and *cytology* if the patient has a history of smoking) (Hanno et al, 2011). For straightforward symptoms of IC/PBS, treatments begin with education and changing habits (for example, drinking too much coffee). Next, *physical therapy* (PT) and light medications are tried, followed by *hydrodistention* (a stretching of the bladder using fluid under *anesthesia* with *fulguration* of a *Hunner's ulcer*, if found). Other treatments include botulinum toxin, nerve stimulation (*neuromodulation* using a sacral nerve stimulator), higher-impact medications, such as the immune-based *cyclosporine A*, and finally, surgery to remove the bladder or at least divert urine away from it. Diagnostic testing should be considered for those with more-complicated symptoms of IC/PBS, such as blood in the urine, *urinary incontinence*, *gastrointestinal* (GI) symptoms, or infections. Testing and off-pathway treatment require a dialogue with an experienced provider who can help you sort out whether your symptoms are caused by IC/PBS or an underlying cause. A cystoscopy might identify a Hunner's ulcer (Figure 5-3), which is an *inflammatory* or ulcerated patch on the wall of the bladder and is further suggestive of IC/PBS. Your provider also might point out *glomerulations* (little capillary bleeds), which can be seen with IC/PBS but also in other conditions or in people with normal bladders; glomerulations are not fully helpful in the diagnosis. Cystoscopy can also help to identify non-IC/PBS causes of symptoms, such as an obstructing bladder neck, an irritating tumor or bladder stone, or irritation from inflamed bowel or *endometriosis* tissue.

Chapter 5: Which Urogenital Problems Can Lead to Pelvic Pain in Any Gender?   57

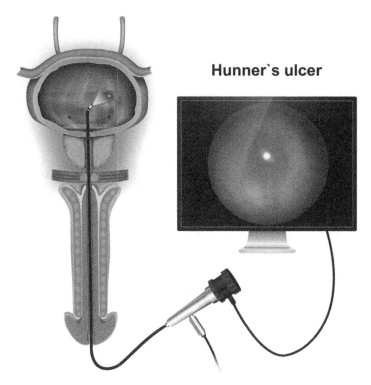

Figure 5-3: Cystoscopy, using a thin flexible camera, shows your urologist what is happening on the surface of the bladder. In this case, an ulcerated patch called "Hunner's Ulcer" was found in a person with interstitial cystitis.

Fortunately, whether you have IC/PBS or something else, many of the treatments overlap, and it is common for your health care provider to start you on several treatments to help with your symptoms while setting up a timeline and algorithm for testing. Most of these options will be found in the Treatment Map (page 306), where you can keep track of what you have tried and what might make sense in the future.

A wide variety of treatment options is available for management of IC/BPS. Your provider usually starts with non-invasive or conservative options and progresses through the American Urological Association algorithm (Figure 5-4) to options that require higher decision-making (Hanno et al, 2015).

It is important to follow your provider's advice if you have IC/PBS or an overlapping condition. Try not to be disappointed early in the treatment course if one treatment does not work because there are lots of other options that might work for you.

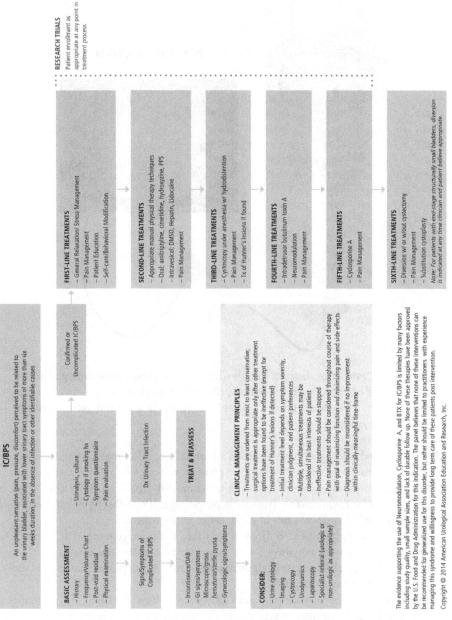

Figure 5-4: The American Urological Association Guideline on Interstitial Cystitis and Painful Bladder Syndrome. This guideline is followed by urologists when taking care of people with bladder pain. (Reproduced with permission. Hanno et al, 2015.)

What Is Overactive Bladder Syndrome?

Overactive bladder syndrome (OAB) is a urinary diagnosis which is made based on symptoms (in the absence of infection or other explanation). It occurs when you experience urinary urgency (sudden compelling desire to pass urine that is difficult to put off). This urgency is accompanied by daytime frequency (urinating what you consider to be too often—up to seven times per day is considered to be normal—and/or *nocturia* [waking up to urinate one or more times per night]). You might or might not have urgency urinary incontinence, which is involuntary leakage of urine, accompanied by or immediately preceded by urgency (Abrams et al, 2002). People with OAB share many symptoms with those who have IC/PBS. However, urinary urgency—rather than pain—is the most bothersome symptom in those with OAB (Fitzgerald and Brubaker, 2003).

How Is Overactive Bladder Syndrome Diagnosed?

According to the American Urological Association Guideline, the basic assessment should include a history (including completion of a pain-focused questionnaire), a physical exam, and laboratory testing of the urine (urinalysis and culture). Like in the management of those with IC, these authors always assess how empty the bladder is after voiding by using a small ultrasound on the lower abdomen or with a brief urethral catheterization. You might be asked to fill out standardized questionnaires at your visit, which screen for your urinary symptoms. You might be asked to complete the questionnaires again at each follow-up visit, so you can help monitor your symptoms and your responses to different therapies (Gormley et al, 2015; Lightner et al, 2019).

How Is Overactive Bladder Syndrome Treated?

Your provider usually starts with the non-invasive options, such as education, dietary modification, pelvic physical therapy, and *bladder re-training*. Bladder re-training involves increasing the amount of time between emptying your bladder and the amount of fluids your bladder can hold. It requires following a fixed-voiding schedule, regardless of whether you feel the urge to urinate. If the urge to urinate occurs before the assigned interval, muscular and distraction urge suppression techniques are used. The techniques include relaxing or counting to 10, deep breathing, focusing on relaxing all other muscles, sitting down until the sensation passes, and waiting five minutes, then slowly making your way to the bathroom.

If symptoms persist, there are further treatment options. These include certain medications that suppress the contractions of the bladder *(detrusor)* muscle or relax the bladder muscle to accommodate more fluid before starting to squeeze.

Your provider starts from a smaller dose and will adjust the dose based on your symptoms. Therefore, it is important to follow-up with your provider to monitor your response to the treatment. If you continue to have symptoms, your provider might consider advanced options including stimulation of the nerve going to the bladder (*tibial nerve stimulation* or *sacral nerve stimulation*), or cystoscopy and injection of *botulinum toxin* into the bladder muscle. Please refer to the Algorithm from the Guidelines on Overactive Bladder (Figure 5-5) published in 2019 by the American Urological Association/Society of Urodynamics, Female Pelvic Medicine, and Urogenital Reconstruction below (Lightner et al, 2019).

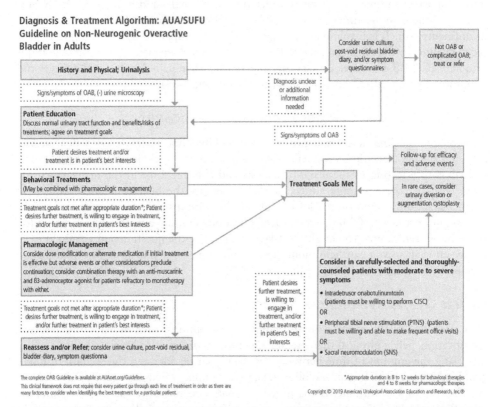

Figure 5-5: The American Urologic Association Guideline on Overactive Bladder. This guideline is followed by urologists when taking care of people with overactive bladder. (Reproduced with permission. Gormley et al, 2015.)

What Is Bladder Outlet Obstruction?

Bladder outlet obstruction (BOO) occurs when there is a blockage at the neck (exit) of the bladder or the urethra. Such a blockage reduces or stops the flow of urine out of the bladder or urethra, preventing it from leaving the body. Bladder outlet obstruction is suspected if:

- The post-void residual is high (the amount remaining in the bladder after voiding).

- You have a hard time starting your stream.
- You have an intermittent or weak stream.
- You have urinary retention (inability to void).
- There is pain during voiding.

Blockage can cause a wide variety of urinary symptoms, and pain can result from hard squeezing of the bladder (detrusor) muscle or incomplete emptying.

The causes of BOO can be divided into two main groups: *anatomical* and *functional*. *Anatomical obstruction* in males is usually caused by a tight or enlarged prostate (Figure 5-6); in females, it usually is caused by a *"prolapse"* or *"cystocele,"* in which the bladder kinks over the urethra, due to a urethral diverticulum, or due to a prior sling or bulking injection placed for incontinence. In both genders, blockages can be caused by a urethral narrowing (scarring called a *stricture*, which is more common in men). These anatomic issues are usually treated surgically.

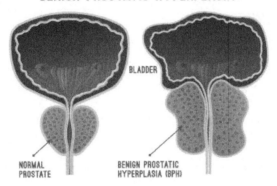

Figure 5-6: Benign prostatic hyperplasia is a common cause of bladder outlet obstruction in men. Inward compression on the urethra slows the urine stream and puts strain on the bladder muscle. In some cases, bladder emptying is impaired.

Functional obstruction is more common in females (85% of female BOO) or younger males and can only be found during voiding while undergoing a *video urodynamic study*. Functional obstruction can be caused by a tight muscle at the bladder neck (primary bladder neck obstruction, the involuntary sphincter) or by a non-relaxing *external* urethral sphincter (this more voluntary sphincter is related to the levator muscles in the pelvic floor and is often under voluntary control) (Malde et al, 2019). Typically, functional obstruction will be treated with a trial of an *alpha blocker medication* (see Chapter 12) or injection of botulinum toxin to relax the muscles at the bladder exit.

Neurological obstruction of the urinary tract caused by *detrusor sphincter dyssynergia* can be the first clue that leads to a diagnosis such as multiple sclerosis, and is often present after spinal cord injury. If the external sphincter muscle is non-relaxing or even activates during the voiding attempt, suspicion will be raised, especially if you have had other neurological symptoms. Your provider might suggest physical therapy first, or your provider might refer you for neurological evaluation, depending on the subtleties of your exam.

What Is Underactive Bladder and How Can It Cause Pain?

Underactive bladder (UAB) is lesser-recognized compared to overactive bladder (OAB). According to the *International Continence Society* (ICS) terminology report, UAB is characterized by prolonged urination time, with or without a sensation of incomplete bladder emptying; this prolonged urination time is usually accompanied by hesitancy, reduced sensation on filling, and a slow urinary stream. With underactive bladder, you might have the following problems (Chapple et al, 2018):

- You might be unable to completely empty your bladder.
- You might have to push or strain to urinate.
- You might hesitate to urinate.
- You might have dribbling at the end of urination.
- You might feel you did not completely empty your bladder after you urinate.

This condition can stretch the bladder over time, which can cause further problems with emptying or incontinence. Also, it can lead to incomplete emptying (accumulation of urine in the bladder) and a buildup of bacteria and recurrent UTIs. Any of these outcomes can result in lower urinary tract (bladder) symptoms, including pelvic pain.

How Is Underactive Bladder Diagnosed and Treated?

A diagnosis of *underactive bladder* (UAB) is based on symptoms, an elevated post-void residual, and urodynamic testing. Your provider might perform a cystoscopy and *uroflowmetry/urodynamics* to confirm the diagnosis and rule out other causes for your symptoms, such as an obstruction.

The treatment options for incomplete bladder emptying are less broad than in OAB or IC/PBS. The available options include *behavior modification therapy*, *pelvic floor physiotherapy* and *biofeedback*, medications to relax the bladder outlet (alpha blockers), and catheterization.

If you have incomplete bladder emptying syndrome, you are **encouraged** to perform timed voiding (voiding on a schedule) and double voiding (remaining on the toilet after you urinate the first time, waiting anywhere from 20 to 30 seconds, and leaning slightly further forward and urinating again). You also should avoid constipation because it affects your bladder-emptying ability. If these conservative techniques are not effective, your provider might recommend *clean intermittent catheterization* (CIC) to ensure adequate bladder emptying. In severe cases in which a patient has limited self-care ability, surgical options are available in which an *indwelling suprapubic catheter* is placed or the urine is diverted away from the bladder surgically (Hoag and Gani, 2015).

How Can My Ureters Cause Pelvic Pain?

The ureter (Figure 5-7) is the tube that carries urine from the *kidneys* to the bladder. Pain along the entire upper urinary tract is *complex*. The upper urinary tract consists of the kidneys that make the urine and the ureters than carry the urine to the bladder. Most people have one ureter on each side, but some people are born with a "duplicate" or double ureter, and some people only have one. The ureters are an uncommon source of pelvic pain. When they are blocked, the kidney can dilate and pain is often felt in the flank (the midback under one of the shoulder blades). The innervation is non-specific and can be felt in the pelvis. If the kidney did not develop in a normal manner when you were *in utero*, an abnormal and rare pelvic or "horseshoe" fused kidney can be located in the pelvis. A *ureterocele* is another developmental (congenital, *in utero*) abnormality that can lead to blockage of the kidney or of the bladder neck with resulting pain. This would be an extremely rare cause of pelvic pain, especially in adults. Another rare condition is *ureteral endometriosis*. Active endometrial cells are deposited in areas inside or outside the ureter, which can lead to obstruction and dilation of the ureters. Ureters can cause pelvic pain when there is a kidney stone lodged within the last part of the ureter before it enters the bladder, passing within the wall of the bladder. A stone is the most common reason the ureter might cause pelvic pain.

The entire ureter is lined with *alpha receptors* that regulate the ureter's smooth muscle tone. Typically, a *kidney stone* blocking the ureter would lead to increased ureteral peristalsis (increased spasms of the ureter's smooth muscle). The alpha receptors are concentrated in the part of the ureter that is in the pelvis. These receptors only have an indirect role in pain. For example, using an alpha blocker, such as the drug *tamsulosin*, would cause smooth muscle tone relaxation. In the case of a blockage or a stone, this translates to *mechanoreceptors* sensing less pressure and therefore, less pain. As a reference, normal pressure in the kidneys is somewhere between 0–10 millimeters of mercury (atmospheric pressure is 760). Exceeding that pressure would increase pain in the flank, which would radiate down to the groin. *Non-steroidal anti-inflammatory drugs* (NSAIDs) and alpha blockers help with ureteral pain in this situation because they decrease the abnormal ureteral peristaltic activity.

Hyperalgesia, or hypersensitivity in which pain thresholds are decreased, can persist in muscles for months to years after a stone has passed (Pedersen et al, 2010). Anatomic studies on human cadavers also reveal that women have a significantly greater density of *nerves* than men in the very last two centimeters of the ureter as it enters the bladder (Vernez et al, 2017). This can make evaluation of ureter-related pelvic pain challenging.

All the above ureteric causes of pelvic pain would be found by ultrasound, MRI, or CT scan. A CT scan is most likely to pick up stones in the ureter.

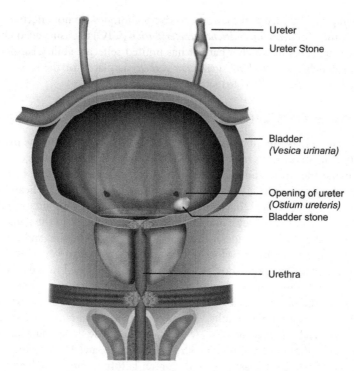

Figure 5-7: Stone in the ureter and the bladder; the ureter is the tube that drains urine from the kidney. The blockage from the ureter stone can cause pain in the kidney and in the pelvis or urethra as it passes through the ureter within the wall of the bladder and out through the urethra. If your pain started suddenly, a stone might be the culprit.

What Signs Might Make Me Think of Cancer As a Cause of My Bladder or Urethra Pain?

You should be evaluated for cancer in the urinary tract if you have blood in the urine that you can see with the naked eye. This is referred to as *gross hematuria* because it is visible without a microscope. Be mindful of what you have eaten because beets or certain synthetic dyes can lead to red urine. If you were injured with a difficult urinary catheter placement, this could also explain visible blood. Visible blood can come from hemorrhoids, vaginal sources, or a urethral caruncle, so it is helpful to look at your genital area with a mirror—and even take a picture—if you see blood in the toilet or on the toilet paper. *Microscopic hematuria* is defined as the presence of at least three *red blood cells* (RBCs) per 40x magnification under a microscope in the absence of a UTI. Blood in the urine that is not definitively explained by another cause requires a work-up for cancer. Never fear, however, as usually the work-up is negative and no cancer is present! Often, the findings include infections, stones, blockage, stress on the bladder, or stress on the kidney. Sometimes, no cause is found (Davis et al, 2012).

Another scenario in which cancer of the bladder is considered is when refractory lower urinary tract symptoms are present. When initial measures do not help with bladder urgency, frequency, or pain, the inside of the bladder can be visualized with a cystoscope to make sure that the wall of bladder is unaffected. Rarely, a growth irritating the wall of the bladder is found. More often, a blockage, stones, infection, or signs of bladder overactivity are detected. Often, there is no visible explanation for the symptoms. Based on your situation, a special urine test called "cytology" might be ordered to look for cancer.

What Might Make Me Suspect Infection As a Cause of My Bladder or Urethra Pain?

UTI symptoms can include pain or a burning sensation with urination, pain with intercourse, a frequent need to urinate, an urgent need to urinate, feelings of incomplete bladder emptying, blood in the urine, and discomfort in the lower abdomen. In severe cases where the infection involves the kidneys, you will have fever, flank pain, nausea, or vomiting.

What Tests Are Used to Evaluate the Urethra, Bladder, and Ureters, and What Can I Expect from Each?

Some of these details are discussed in Chapter 2, but more specific information is provided below.

Questionnaires

Standardized questionnaires are the best way to objectively measure your symptom severity and your progress with treatment. They are tiresome, but they allow your provider to focus on your outcome and next steps more effectively.

Voiding Diary

A bladder diary (Table 5-1) is a tool used by you and your health care provider to better understand your bladder symptoms. It tracks when and how much fluid you drink, when and how much you urinate, how often you have that "gotta go" urgency feeling, and when and how much urine you leak. You will be asked to complete the diary for at least 48 hours. It will show your 24-hour volumes, whether your nighttime volumes are normal, and how much your bladder holds in your daily life outside the clinic. For the diary following, please collect, measure, and discard ALL urine for two days, including nighttime voids. To identify nighttime voids, circle all voids AFTER falling asleep including 1st AM void.

Table 5-1: Bladder Diary

TOTAL Day #1: 24-hour voided volume: _____
Nighttime voided volume: _____

TOTAL Day #2: 24-hour voided volume: _____
Nighttime voided volume: _____

Mark Time Up for Day & Bedtime	Time	Voided Volume Oz/Ml/Cc	Failed Void	Volume Liquids Drunk Oz/Ml/Cc	If Leak: Wet	If Cathing: Cath Volume	If Meds: Diuretics
"Awake" "In Bed"		Each void: (e.g., 30 cc/145 cc)	Mark if tried and unable	Record type: (e.g., coffee)	Yes or no	Amount catheterized	Mark water pills if taken
	5 AM – 7 AM						
	7 AM – 9 AM						
	9 AM – 11 AM						
	11 AM – 1 PM						
	1 PM – 3 PM						
	3 PM – 5 PM						
	5 PM – 7 PM						
	7 PM – 9 PM						
	9 PM – 11 PM						
	11 PM – 1 AM						
	1 PM – 3 AM						
	3 AM – 5 AM						

Mark Time Up for Day & Bedtime	Time	Voided Volume Oz/Ml/Cc	Failed Void	Volume Liquids Drunk Oz/Ml/Cc	If Leak: Wet	If Cathing: Cath Volume	If Meds: Diuretics
	5 AM – 7 AM						
	7 AM – 9 AM						
	9 AM – 11 AM						
	11 AM – 1 PM						
	1 PM – 3 PM						
	3 PM – 5 PM						
	5 PM – 7 PM						
	7 PM – 9 PM						
	9 PM – 11 PM						
	11 PM – 1 AM						
	1 AM – 3 AM						
	3 AM – 5 AM						
	5 AM – 7 AM						
	7 AM – 9 AM						
	9 AM – 11 AM						

Pelvic/Genitourinary Examination

Having a full examination is always your choice, but to get the best information to help both men and women, the provider will recommend a respectful examination of your private areas. Let your provider know what will make you most comfortable during the exam; for example, you might want to have a loved one or staff in the room or to use a specific draping for privacy. Your provider will perform a pelvic exam to assess for signs of vaginal atrophy, pelvic organ prolapse, and penile abnormalities (such as tight foreskin, large prostate, pelvic floor muscle strength, or a cystic urethral diverticulum), that might be the underlying cause of your symptoms.

Urinalysis

This is a simple "dip" test strip of your urine that takes minutes to analyze. It checks for multiple parameters in the urine, such as inflammatory cells, blood, overall appearance, concentration, and the sugar and protein content of your urine. An abnormal urinalysis might be caused by an infection, inflammation, stone, malignancy, dehydration or other baseline condition, such as diabetes.

Urine Sediment

This is a microscopic analysis of the actual types and number of cells and content of your urine. It takes several hours for the sample to be transported to the lab and processed. The sediment is the best way to know if there is truly blood or pus in the urine. The presence of >10 pus cells (WBCs) per high power field suggests infection.

Urine Culture (Including Mycoplasma and Ureaplasma)

A urine culture is a test that can detect bacteria in your urine. It takes two to three days for the result to come back (the bacteria need to grow in the lab environment before the information can be interpreted). This test will also help your provider choose the best antibiotics in case of an infection. If you have recurrent infections and if you have access to your results, you can compare the antibiotic you are prescribed to the susceptibilities reported by the lab.

Sexually Transmitted Infection Testing

These tests look for sexually transmitted infections (STIs). They include blood tests, urine tests, and sometimes swab specimens taken from the genitals or suspicious lesions in the urogenital area. If you have been sexually active within the past two years and suspect there may be a risk of STI (no matter how unlikely), there is a chance that your pelvic pain is due to sexually transmitted disease. The more experienced the provider is in STIs (for example, those who work in the Department of Public Health or in specialized clinics), the more accurately these tests will be chosen and interpreted.

Urine Cytology

This is a urine test to look for cancer cells in urine. An abnormal test might be a reason to do further diagnostic studies (such as looking into your bladder, getting biopsies, or having advanced imaging). A negative test does not rule out cancer completely, but it is reassuring.

Straight Catheterization

This is a way to empty the bladder, to get a sterile urine sample, and to determine how tight the urethra and its sphincter muscles are. A small tube called a *"straight catheter"* is inserted in the urethra by the clinic staff, provider, or patient/caregiver *(self-catheterization)*. In *straight catheterization*, the catheter is removed after the bladder is emptied.

Indwelling Urethral Catheter

This catheter also helps to empty the bladder (Figure 5-8) by insertion of the catheter through the urethra into the bladder; however, the catheter is left in place while the patient is not able to urinate effectively. The catheter is held in place by a soft balloon; it should be changed monthly if needed for an extended period of time. *Indwelling urethral catheters* are not recommended for long-term bladder management because of the risk of dilating or eroding the urethra. Securing the catheter with a minimum of tension is key, so it does not pull; this technique should help prevent pain and other complications.

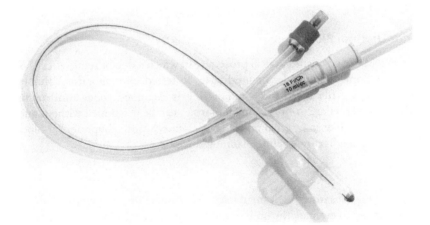

Figure 5-8: An indwelling urethral catheter is a soft, flexible tube placed to drain the bladder, that is held in place by a soft balloon. If you have need for a catheter for more than one month, ask your provider about a suprapubic catheter, which enters the bladder above the pubic bone—it is more comfortable and is safer in the long run.

Indwelling Suprapubic Catheter (SP Tube)

This is also a way to empty the bladder through a urinary catheter. However, the catheter is inserted through your lower abdomen above the pubic bone and then directly into your bladder rather than through the urethra. The *SP Tube* is widely used in those who are unable to empty their bladder because of underlying medical problems, such as multiple sclerosis and spinal cord injury. This modality avoids erosion of the urethra, and therefore, it can be used for long-term management of bladder-emptying problems. It is still recommended that the SP Tube be changed every four weeks and be secured off-tension. The stiffness of the catheter, the length of the tip beyond the balloon, and the way it is secured all affect pain. Overactive bladder medications and other interventions can help with comfort. Diameters 18 French and larger tend to drain most effectively.

Cystoscopy

This is a procedure that involves inserting a small telescopic camera into the urethra and the bladder. It allows your doctor to examine the bladder, urethra, ureter openings, and prostate (in males). It is mostly performed awake in an outpatient setting, and most patients report that it is completely tolerable. However, if a more invasive procedure is anticipated, such as obtaining multiple biopsies, it will be performed in the operating room after sedation or general anesthesia. Many people undergoing this procedure worry unnecessarily about discomfort. The procedure can be stopped if the discomfort is too great, as long as no biopsy has been performed.

Bladder or Urethral Biopsy

A *bladder biopsy* is a diagnostic surgical procedure in which a doctor removes cells or tissue with a grasper from your bladder or urethra to be tested in a laboratory. This typically involves cystoscopy. After the tissue is removed, it is examined under a microscope. The pathology results can take 2–14 days. Small biopsies can be performed without anesthesia in the clinic and feel like an internal pinch. If you are on aspirin, ibuprofen, or blood thinners, discuss these medications before planning the biopsy.

Ureteroscopy

This procedure involves inserting a small telescopic camera into the urethra and the bladder. It is performed to evaluate the ureters and the lining of the kidney (the renal pelvis or "collecting system"). In this procedure, the provider visualizes the inside of the ureters to look for stones, abnormal growths, or strictures by using a very small telescopic camera. The procedure is performed in the operating room under anesthesia.

Uroflowmetry

In a private room, you will be asked to sit on a special toilet and urinate as you usually do. The toilet will record how much urine you pass and how strong your stream is. It is best to come for this test with a full bladder. The results will be interpreted by your provider when you meet afterward. The results show how much you void and the strength of the urinary stream.

Urodynamic Evaluation

This test is performed in a specially equipped private room in the voiding dysfunction clinic. You will meet the technician and go over the procedure. After you change and sit comfortably in position, a tiny catheter is placed in your bladder, and another is placed in the rectum or vagina (or rarely a stoma) to balance the pressures. Your bladder is slowly filled with a sterile liquid, you are asked to report bladder sensation, and then you empty your bladder (urinate) while measurements are made. Video urodynamics include X-rays, so it is important to tell the staff if you could be pregnant.

Urethral Swab

This is a laboratory test performed in males to check for infection-causing germs in the urethra. To collect the sample, a cotton swab is gently inserted into the urethra. It can be uncomfortable. To obtain a good sample, the test should be done at least two hours after last urinating.

Vaginal Swab

This is a laboratory test in females to check for infection-causing germs in the vagina. To collect the sample, a cotton swab is gently inserted into the vagina. This is typically not painful beyond the typical discomfort of a pelvic exam.

Ultrasound

This is a painless, non-invasive, low-risk imaging modality that uses high-frequency sound waves to assess different organs. It is thought to be safe during pregnancy. Sometimes, transrectal or transvaginal ultrasound provides better images, in which case the discomfort that is typical of an extended pelvic or rectal exam is possible. In this case, be sure to let your technician know that you have pelvic pain before you start. Ultrasound is usually not the most accurate way to see the ureters.

Computed Tomography Scan

Computerized tomography (CT) *scans* (Figure 5-9) are imaging modalities using multiple *X-ray* films. They offer much more detailed images compared to a single X-ray, and although they are safe, they do use more radiation. Based on the information needed (for example, if you have had blood in the urine and it is important to see the inside of the ureters), a special form of iodine-based dye might be used to better delineate fine details. Some people with pelvic pain are offered a CT scan every time they visit the emergency room. To prevent unnecessary radiation, try to attend the same emergency room every time there is an urgent issue, bring your records and CDs of prior imaging to new institutions and providers, and try to plan your care with a thorough primary care doctor who coordinates your specialists.

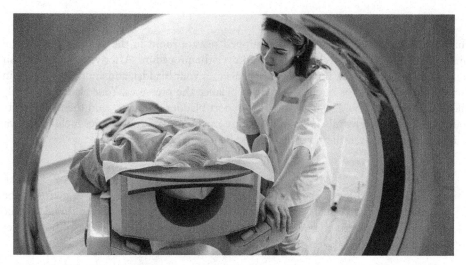

Figure 5-9: Computed tomography (CT) scan is a short, painless imaging study that provides detailed images of the area studied.

Magnetic Resonance Imaging

Magnetic Resonance Imaging (MRI) is an advanced imaging study using strong magnetic field and radio waves to create detailed images of the organs and tissues within the body. The contrast sometimes recommended in this study is gadolinium, and it is different from the contrast used in a CT scan. The tube for MRI is smaller and can sometimes lead to *claustrophobia*. If you need this test, strategize how best to manage your claustrophobia. For example, ask the technician if you can enter the machine foot-first, leaving your head and shoulders out. The MRI is the most accurate imaging modality for urethral diverticuli.

Urethrogram

This is a special X-ray in which *iodinated contrast* is injected through the urethra to show urethral abnormalities. Primarily, it is used for characterizing urethral strictures or injuries in men. Because the contrast is not administered intravenously, it is usually well tolerated, even by people with a contrast allergy, so long as there is no urethral injury.

Cystogram/Voiding Cystourethrogram

Cystogram/Voiding Cystourethrogram (VCUG) are special imaging studies to specifically assess the bladder and urethra, and sometimes the ureters. Plain *cystograms* are performed by a radiologist, urologist, or *urogynecologist* and their technicians, and CT cystograms are performed by *radiology* departments. In this study, iodine-based contrast (a liquid that is visible on X-rays) is injected to the bladder through a urethral catheter. Sometimes, you will be asked to empty the contrast by urinating while pictures are taken. These studies can demonstrate holes in the bladder, urethral diverticula or strictures, abnormal *reflux* of urine up the ureters, and abnormal muscular changes of the bladder called trabeculation. Since the dye is only touching the bladder surface, it is often safe to use in people who have reacted to IV contrast, but this should be discussed with your doctor on a case-by-case basis ahead of time.

Retrograde Pyelogram

This is a procedure performed by your urologist or urogynecologist in the operating room. In this procedure, contrast is injected into the ureter, allowing an "inside X-ray" of the ureter. The contrast allows the ureters and kidneys to be more easily seen on the X-ray. This test helps your provider assess the ureters and kidneys without having to pass a telescope to directly visualize them.

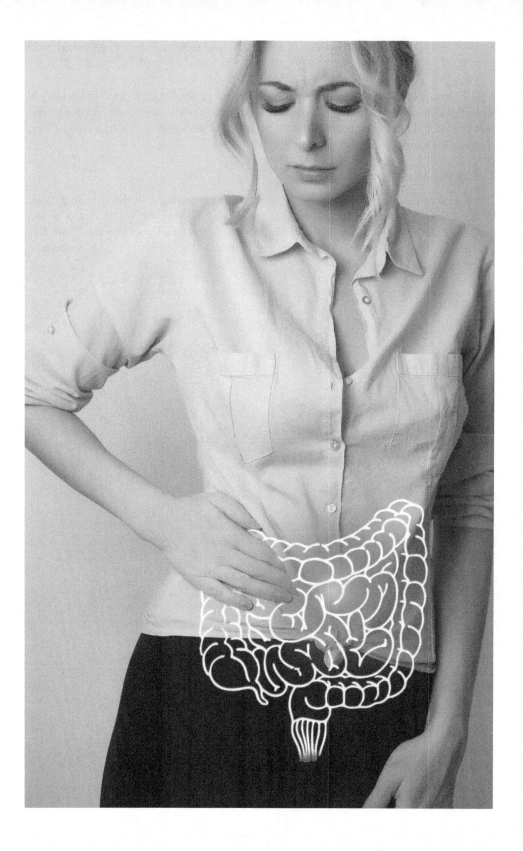

WHICH GASTROINTESTINAL PROBLEMS CAN LEAD TO PELVIC PAIN?

Chun Hin Angus Lee, MD; Massarat Zutshi, MD; and Barbara Nath, MD

CHAPTER

In This Chapter

- Introduction
- How Is Gastrointestinal-Related Pelvic Pain Diagnosed?
- What Parts of My Medical History Are Important to My Doctor?
- How Will I Know If My Pelvic Pain Might Be Related to an Intestinal Problem?
- What Might the Physical Evaluation Involve?
- What Tests Might I Need to Evaluate My Pain?
- Which Intestinal Problems Can Cause Pelvic Pain?
- If My Pelvic Pain Is Due to Irritable Bowel Syndrome, Is the Pain All in My Head?
- How Can Traumatic Experiences Early in Life Affect the Gut in Adulthood?
- What Kinds of Questions Might My Doctor Ask Regarding Constipation?
- What Tests Might Be Ordered to Evaluate Refractory Constipation?
- How Can Refractory Constipation Be Treated?
- What Should I Know About Intra-Abdominal Adhesions?
- How Can a Hernia Cause Pelvic Pain?
- What Anorectal Problems Can Cause Pelvic Pain?
- Conclusion

Introduction

Pelvic pain can be caused by a variety of *gastrointestinal* (GI) disorders that affect the intestines and anorectal region. Also, pelvic pain can be caused by gynecologic, urologic, *musculoskeletal*, rheumatologic, psychologic, and neurologic problems (Stein, 2013). Frequently, more than one cause exists for the pain. Although anorectal problems often go unreported because of embarrassment, they can be diagnosed based on the medical history and examination without performing any invasive procedures.

Conditions that can create anal pain include prolapsed *hemorrhoids*; an *anal fissure* (a split in the skin and muscle that line the *anus*); an *abscess*; prolapse of the rectum through the anus; *proctalgia fugax* (Latin for fleeting rectal pain); and *anal cancer*. By performing a rectal exam and an exam with an *anoscope*, your doctor can begin to sort out which condition might be causing your *symptoms* and which symptoms require more testing.

Your pain can also arise from your small bowel and/or large intestine (Figure 6-1), which are located partly in your pelvis. Intestinal conditions that can cause pelvic pain include *irritable bowel syndrome* (IBS); *inflammatory bowel disease* (IBD) (such as *Crohn's disease* and *ulcerative colitis* [UC]); severe constipation; a *stricture* (an intestinal narrowing) that causes obstruction; colon cancer; and problems related to *diverticulosis* (pockets forming on the colon).

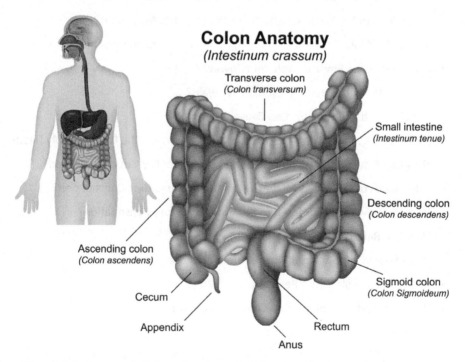

Figure 6-1: Anatomy of the colon (large intestine), with the small intestine and remainder of the gastrointestinal tract in the background.

How Is Gastrointestinal-Related Pelvic Pain Diagnosed?

A thorough history by your clinician will narrow down the diagnostic possibilities to a few conditions (Table 6-1).

Table 6-1: A Brief List of Gastrointestinal (GI) Causes of Pelvic Pain

• Diverticular disease
– *Diverticulitis*
– *Stricture*
– *Fistula*
• Inflammatory bowel disease
– *Crohn's disease*
– *Ulcerative colitis*
• Irritable bowel syndrome
• Levator ani syndrome
• Proctalgia fugax
• Anal fistula and abscess
• Pruritis ani
• Hemorrhoids
• Rectal prolapse
• Anogenital warts
• Malignancy
– *Anal cancer*
– *Rectal cancer*
– *Perianal Paget's disease*

What Parts of My Medical History Are Important to My Doctor?

Your doctor will want to know several things about your pelvic pain:

- Its characteristics (e.g., sharp, burning, or dull)
- Its severity
- Its aggravating and alleviating factors (such as what triggers it and what makes it better)
- How long you have had pain
- How often pain occurs

- How long each episode lasts
- Whether it is related to your bowel habits
- If it is related to eating and if so, whether it is triggered by specific foods
- If it followed a specific event in your life
- Whether it is accompanied by changes in your bowel habits (such as constipation or diarrhea)
- Whether it is associated with discharge, itchiness, or rectal bleeding
- Whether there is difficulty in emptying your bowels and/or difficulty in holding on to your stool *(fecal incontinence)*

Some symptoms are crucial; you should tell your doctor if you have had rectal bleeding, black stool, fever, nausea, vomiting, or weight loss. Sometimes, symptoms that appear to be unrelated to your pelvic pain (such as red or swollen joints, skin rashes, severe fatigue, and even eye pain or irritation) can be a key to the problem.

You should tell your doctor if:

- You have had similar symptoms, even if they occurred years ago
- You have had a prior diagnosis of a GI problem
- There are problems with other organs in your pelvis (for example, some people with fecal incontinence have *urinary incontinence* or a *vaginal prolapse*)

A complete obstetrical history is relevant. Also, because traumatic experiences early in life can lead to symptoms of bowel irritation later in life, your doctor needs to know if you ever had an eating disorder or experienced a traumatic event, such as physical or psychological abuse. Although these topics can be difficult to discuss, they will help your doctor develop a more complete understanding of your symptoms and how best to help you. Your medical and surgical history might be relevant when determining your surgical options. You should bring copies of your operative notes. If you've had a recent *colonoscopy*, bring your colonoscopy report to your appointment, as conditions such as bowel cancer and inflammatory bowel disease can be excluded by these test results.

How Will I Know If My Pelvic Pain Might Be Related to an Intestinal Problem?

Your pelvic pain might be intestinal or anorectal if:

- **The pain is associated with bowel habits**. For example, is the pain relieved by a bowel movement or is it worsened by a bowel movement? Individuals with irritable bowel syndrome often report that pain is worse just before a bowel movement and goes away after it. Those with constipation—even if they are unaware that they are constipated—can have pelvic pain when they haven't moved their bowels for several days.

- **The pain returns when you are eating.** Sometimes this association can include a benign condition, such as IBS. It can also indicate a more serious problem, such as an insufficient blood supply to the intestine or an obstruction in your small or large intestine.

- **You are can identify specific foods that cause your pain.** People with lactose intolerance might notice more abdominal bloating and pain when they eat foods containing dairy. People with *celiac disease* (a sensitivity to wheat that results in damage to the small intestine) or people with wheat intolerance but no celiac disease will develop abdominal bloating and discomfort when they eat *gluten-containing foods*, such as bread, pasta, pastries, and crackers. Some people are sensitive to foods that ferment easily in the small and large intestine, such as apples, avocado, watermelon, and certain types of beans.

- **There has been a recent change in your bowel habits, such as new constipation or diarrhea that began at the same time as your pain.** A change in your bowel habits might be temporary and might not indicate a problem. But if the change persists, you should discuss it with your doctor. This change could be related to IBS, or the change could indicate something more serious, such as bowel inflammation, bowel obstruction, or even colon cancer. Some symptoms might indicate a more concerning problem and should prompt you to call your doctor immediately. These "red flag" symptoms include fever, severe pain (that does not resolve), bloody diarrhea, unexplained rectal bleeding, pelvic pain associated with nausea and vomiting, and unexplained weight loss.

- **The pain is easily provoked.** Some conditions, regardless of whether they are related to anal or intestinal problems (especially if they are *chronic*) can cause you to be hypersensitive to even small changes, such as increased intestinal gas or abdominal bloating. If your doctor believes that some of your symptoms are caused by hypersensitivity, he or she might prescribe a medication that might reduce your pain, such as gabapentin, *nortriptyline*, or *duloxetine*.

- **The pain gets progressively worse and is associated with fever and/or weight loss.** These *signs* and *symptoms* could indicate an inflammatory bowel disease or diverticulitis, or they could indicate something more serious, such as abdominal cancer.

What Might the Physical Evaluation Involve?

Physical examinations can be intimidating, but a complete exam is paramount in diagnosing anorectal problems. The examination should be performed in a well-lit room with adequate privacy. Chaperones are commonly used to reduce your anxiety and to provide emotional support. You should feel comfortable telling your provider what you need. Your clinician will start by inspecting the anorectal region. The condition of the skin around the anus can provide useful insights into an underlying problem. For example, irritated and inflamed skin due to chronic itching can lead to significant pain. *Lesions* (such as anal fissure, *anal fistula, external* hemorrhoids, and anal warts) can often be visualized. You might be asked to bear down or strain to raise your intra-abdominal pressure, revealing rectal prolapse and determining its severity. You might be examined in the seated position.

Clinicians should conduct the internal examination, such as a *digital rectal examination*, using a well-lubricated and gloved finger. This will help to rule out lesions (such as anal and rectal tumor) and assess your *anal sphincter* tone and function. If you experience pain during palpation of the pelvic floor muscles (such as the *levator ani muscles*), this might indicate *levator ani syndrome*.

What Tests Might I Need to Evaluate My Pain?

Specialists, such as *colorectal surgeons* and *gastroenterologists* (GI doctors), are well-equipped for office-based investigations (such as *proctoscopy* and flexible *sigmoidoscopy*, which can be readily performed in a clinic setting without causing significant discomfort). These procedures allow clinicians to directly visualize the anatomy of the anal canal and lower rectum. Further investigation might be required depending on symptoms (Table 6-2). Examination under *general anesthesia* might be warranted to allow for more detailed examination (if a detailed exam is too painful in the office) or if a *biopsy* is required.

Table 6-2: Investigations for GI-Related Pelvic Pain

Useful Investigations	Conditions Investigated
Colonoscopy	• Colorectal cancer • Inflammatory bowel disease
X-ray or magnetic resonance imaging (MRI) defecography	• Rectal prolapse • Rectocele, *enterocele*
Endoanal ultrasound	• Anal fistula
CT scan	• Tumor • Intestinal blockage
Anorectal manometry	• Obstructive defecation • Rectal prolapse • Anal fissure*
Sitzmark study	• Intestinal transit problems

*An anorectal manometry is not routinely performed for anal fissure unless it's unresponsive to medical and surgical management.

By far, colonoscopy (Figure 6-2) is the most important procedure for detection of abnormalities of the bowel wall within the colon and rectum. It is indicated in chronic abdominal pain, rectal bleeding, changing bowel habits (such as constipation or diarrhea), and fecal incontinence. Your doctor might conduct a colonoscopy to determine whether there is inflammation, such as might occur with ulcerative colitis or Crohn's disease. If it appears that your pelvic pain is related to constipation, he or she might order an *anorectal manometry*, which is a test that looks at your pelvic floor function in relation to whether it is helping or hindering a bowel movement. Your doctor might also order a *Sitzmark study*, which is a test that indicates whether you could have a sluggish colon as the cause of the constipation. You might also have blood tests performed to screen you for a thyroid disorder, celiac disease, and inflammation. Your doctor might order a *stool test* called a *fecal calprotectin*, which is another screen for inflammation. These tests are designed to help your doctor better understand your symptoms. He/she might order an ultrasound of your pelvis, a *computed tomography* (CT) *scan* of your abdomen and pelvis, or a *magnetic resonance imaging* (MRI) *scan* of your pelvis.

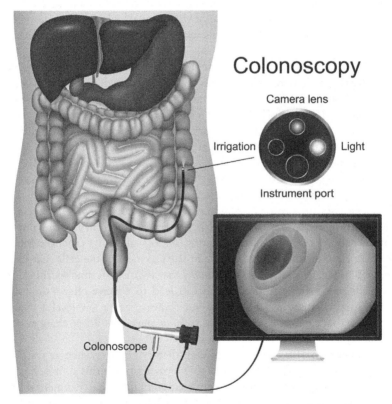

Figure 6-2: A colonoscopy is a direct camera diagnostic test of the colon, rectum, and anus. It is performed with a flexible thin camera, typically under sedation in case there is discomfort.

Which Intestinal Problems Can Cause Pelvic Pain?
Irritable Bowel Syndrome

Irritable bowel syndrome (IBS) is a condition that causes chronic abdominal and pelvic pain (often described as cramping in the lower abdomen and pelvis) in association with changes in bowel habits. The pain is usually associated with defecation, and it can be better or worse after a bowel movement. Changes in bowel habits include diarrhea, constipation, or a combination of both, meaning there is a change in both stool consistency (hard or loose) and stool frequency (fewer or more frequent bowel movements). These changes can be accompanied by abdominal bloating and distention. IBS is considered a *functional disorder*, meaning that all other causes of these symptoms have been excluded by appropriate testing, including inflammatory bowel disease, celiac disease, severe constipation, ovarian cancer, and colon cancer. Your doctor will know which tests to order to ensure that there are no other causes for the pain. This testing is especially important if you are more than 50 years old.

Although IBS can result in significant abdominal pain, it is a *benign* condition. Food triggers (such as high-fiber foods, high-fat foods, spicy foods, dairy, gluten [wheat], alcohol, and poorly absorbed carbohydrates which cause increased fermentation and gas) are commonly reported by those with IBS. Even if a specific food trigger cannot be identified, the initial treatment for IBS is usually diet restriction, such as avoiding dairy, gluten, and fermentable carbohydrates. IBS is also associated with hypersensitivity, which means people with IBS are more sensitive to gas and distention of the colon. People with IBS often have other disorders associated with hypersensitivity (such as *fibromyalgia*, *migraine headaches*, and chronic fatigue). They are also more likely to be anxious and depressed.

IBS can be associated with stressful life events that date back to childhood. Traumatic experiences early in life or in adolescence (such as separation from a parent, physical abuse, and emotional abuse) cause biochemical and neurological changes that contribute to IBS. Some of these changes include an increase in the leakiness of the cells that line the large intestine, which is called increased *intestinal permeability*. Intestinal permeability affects the nerve cells lining the intestine, which can lead to adverse effects on colon muscle (motor) function, changes in the kinds of gut *bacteria*, and a low-level activation of the immune system that can increase activity of *inflammatory* cells. These changes can begin in childhood and persist through adulthood.

The treatment for IBS usually starts with dietary changes, such as restricting dairy, gluten, fatty foods, and/or foods that are highly fermentable. If this approach is unsuccessful and depending on whether you have constipation or diarrhea, treatment might include medications that help hypersensitivity, such as gabapentin and certain antidepressants. Your doctor can tailor the treatment to your symptoms.

If My Pelvic Pain Is Due to Irritable Bowel Syndrome, Is the Pain All in My Head?

No, it is not. There is an *enteric nervous system* that is responsible for managing all aspects of digestion. This explains why, for example, some people get diarrhea from stress and why many people with anxiety and *depression* have problems with their digestive tracts. The nervous system of the gut resides within the walls of your *esophagus, stomach, small intestine*, and *large intestine*. Like the brain, the gut's nervous system relies on connections among individual *nerves* as well as on chemical signaling among these nerves via *neurotransmitters*. These are often the same neurotransmitters that are active in the brain. For example, *serotonin* is a brain neurotransmitter involved in depression. Drugs like fluoxetine, which are called *selective serotonin reuptake inhibitors* (SSRIs), lead to more serotonin in the brain. However, 95% of the body's serotonin *receptors* are in the gut. Too much serotonin in the gut can cause diarrhea. Conversely, high levels of serotonin in the gut can cause the serotonin receptors to shut down—the result can be constipation!

How Can Traumatic Experiences Early in Life Affect the Gut in Adulthood?

Traumatic experiences (such as illness, separation from a parent, physical abuse, and emotional abuse) early in life or in adolescence can disrupt an important hormone system (the *hypothalamic-pituitary-adrenal* [HPA] *axis* in the body that regulates the body's response to stress (Fuentes and Christianson 2018). The *adrenal gland* produces "fight and flight" *hormones* like *adrenaline*. Early disruption of this system by traumatic experiences can cause overactivity of this hormone axis; it can be permanent and is often associated with chronic pain (for example, IBS) later in life. In addition to its effect on *pain signaling*, overstimulation of the emotional-arousal circuit can result in biochemical changes in the body and the brain by causing certain cells in the body to produce high levels of inflammation.

This means if someone has a history of physical or emotional trauma—regardless of whether pain is caused by intestinal, gynecological, or urinary problems—it is often helpful to include psychological interventions when treating pelvic pain (Palsson and Whitehead, 2013). These supportive interventions include *cognitive-behavioral therapy* (CBT) as well as medications that address the chronic overstimulation of the nervous system caused by these stress reactions.

Inflammatory Bowel Disease

There are two forms of inflammatory bowel disease (Figure 6-3): ulcerative colitis and Crohn's disease. These are more severe bowel disorders than irritable bowel syndrome (IBS). The symptoms of ulcerative colitis include severe diarrhea, sometimes bloody diarrhea, crampy abdominal pain, and often fever, weight loss, and generalized fatigue (Moelski and Choudhary, 2011; Feagins and Kane, 2016). If you describe symptoms such as these, your doctor will likely order a colonoscopy to see if inflammation exists.

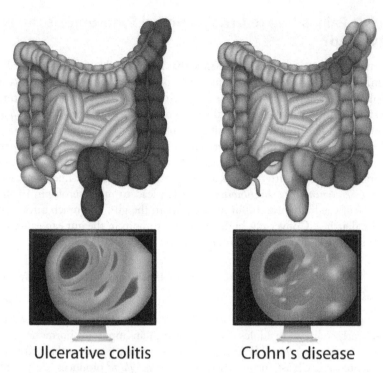

Figure 6-3: The two types of inflammatory bowel disease (IBD), which is not to be confused with irritable bowel syndrome (IBS). Crohn's disease affects both the small and large intestine, and the inflammation can involve the full thickness of the bowel. Ulcerative colitis affects the innermost lining of just the large intestine, including the rectum.

Crohn's disease causes pelvic pain more commonly than ulcerative colitis. The reason for this difference is that Crohn's disease can affect both the large and small intestine (ulcerative colitis involves only the large intestine, including the rectum) and Crohn's can cause inflammation that traverses all layers of the bowel, not just the intestinal lining that is affected in ulcerative colitis. It can result in strictures (scars in the bowel that can cause partial obstruction), abscesses in the anus and rectum, and fistulas (inflammatory tracts between neighboring organs, such as the colon and anus or the colon and vagina). To see if you have Crohn's disease or ulcerative colitis, your doctor will order a colonoscopy as well as a CT scan of the abdomen and pelvis. Blood tests and a stool test called a fecal calprotectin can screen for an inflammatory condition. Symptoms of Crohn's disease and ulcerative colitis are rarely confused with those of IBS because they tend to be more severe and point to underlying inflammation.

The treatment for Crohn's disease depends upon how extensive and severe the disease is. Treatments can include *prednisone*—which suppresses inflammation—as well as drugs that manipulate the immune system (such as *azathioprine, infliximab [Remicade®], adalimumab [Humira®], ustekinumab [Stelara®],* and *vedolizumab [Entyvio®]*). When treating severe ulcerative colitis, all these medications might be used; however, at times, lesser symptoms can be managed with simple *anti-inflammatory* medications, such as *mesalamine*.

Refractory Constipation

Severe constipation (Figure 6-4) can cause pelvic pain. Sometimes, people with constipation-related pelvic pain are not aware that they are constipated. Constipation can be caused by disorders of the colon (such as an anal fissure, a colon stricture, rectal inflammation, or colon cancer) as well as neurologic disorders (such as *Parkinson's disease* and spinal cord injuries). More commonly, however, constipation is caused by slow colon transit (a sluggish colon), or pelvic floor issues whereby the *pelvic floor muscles* and the anal sphincter don't coordinate and relax as they should during defecation—or both.

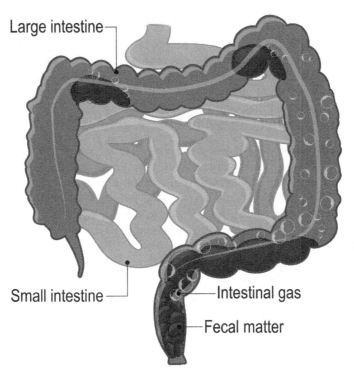

Figure 6-4: Constipation can occur anywhere in the colon because of a blockage, nerve problems, slow muscles of the colon, or non-relaxing pelvic floor muscles.

What Kinds of Questions Might My Doctor Ask Regarding Constipation?

These questions include:

- How long has the constipation has been a problem?
- How frequently do you move your bowels?
- What is your stool consistency (for example, hard, semi-formed, loose, or watery stools)?
- Do you strain with bowel movements?
- Do you have a sense of incomplete evacuation?
- Do you need to perform manual maneuvers to help evacuate the stool?
- Do you have normal stool or diarrhea and constipation?

Your doctor might ask what dietary changes you have made or laxatives you have used to treat constipation. Because some *connective tissue disorders* (such as *Ehlers-Danlos syndrome* [EDS], a disorder characterized by joint and pelvic floor laxity) are associated with constipation, your doctor might also ask about joint and muscle pain.

What Tests Might Be Ordered to Evaluate Refractory Constipation?

A colonoscopy should be done if you are over age 50 or have any "red flag" symptoms such as blood. To study your pelvic floor function, you might have an *anorectal manometry* that involves placing a thin catheter into your rectum to measure the pressures in your anal sphincter, the coordination between your pelvic floor muscles and your anal sphincter when you bear down, a test of your rectal sensation thresholds, and a *balloon expulsion test* (a functional test where the balloon is a flexible test replacement for stool). In addition, you might have a Sitzmark study where you swallow a pill that contains 24 tiny pellets that show up on an X-ray. Six days after you have taken the pill, you will have an abdominal X-ray. If five or more pellets (Sitz markers) remain, this indicates that you have slow transit constipation. To see if there are any internal problems in your pelvis causing constipation, your doctor might order a *defecography* (defecating with barium under X-ray or MRI).

How Can Refractory Constipation Be Treated?

If your anorectal manometry shows that you have a problem with the function of your pelvic floor muscle, you might be referred for *pelvic floor physical therapy*, a highly specialized form of physical therapy that can address and usually correct disorders of pelvic floor function. If you have slow transit constipation, you could be offered a variety of dietary changes as well as laxatives. Several different types of laxatives are often used in combination. If you have both slow transit constipation and pelvic floor issues, the first intervention would be to correct the pelvic floor muscle problem with pelvic floor physical therapy and then add laxatives if the slow transit constipation persists (Bharucha et al, 2013).

What Should I Know About Intra-Abdominal Adhesions?

Intra-abdominal adhesions from prior surgery or inflammation (such as *endometriosis*) can lead to restrictions of bowel transit or irritation of the *peritoneum*, the lining of the abdomen. These are suspected based on history and are diagnosed by performing diagnostic *laparoscopy* or an open surgical procedure, if needed.

How Can a Hernia Cause Pelvic Pain?

In a *hernia* (Figure 6-5), an abnormal opening or weak spot in the peritoneum, the lining of the abdominal cavity, and the surrounding muscular supports, exists through which abdominal organs or tissue can protrude. Hernias can develop in both genders and are a potential source of pelvic pain that can be treated with surgery. Hernias are worsened when intra-abdominal pressure is increased, and stretching of tissues occurs, such as during coughing, straining for bowel movement, or lifting heavy objects (Perry and Echeverri, 2006).

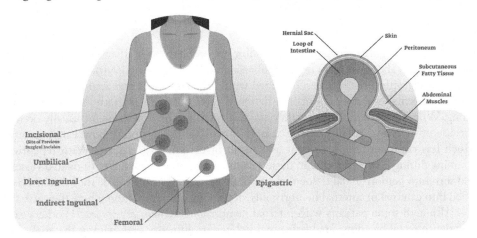

Figure 6-5: A hernia is like a tire bubble, in which the normal supports weaken and bulge. If internal structures enter this bulge, there can be pain.

Common types of hernias associated with pelvic pain are *inguinal* and *femoral hernias*. In an inguinal hernia, abdominal contents bulge from the lower abdominal wall through the *inguinal canal* (located in the groin on either side of your pubic bone). In males, the inguinal canal serves as a passageway for reproductive structures to travel from the abdominal cavity to the pelvic region. Inguinal hernias more commonly occur in men than women because of the differences in the development of reproductive structures between the two genders—*testes* in men but not *ovaries* in women—descend through the inguinal canal into their final destination in the *scrotum* during embryological development. This can create gaps that can develop into openings or weak spots that can lead to hernias. In a femoral hernia, tissue protrudes through the *femoral canal* (located under the crease between your leg and your trunk) from the abdomen into the upper inner thigh region. Femoral hernias are rare, but they are more common in women because they tend to have wider hips. If you have a painful bulge in these locations that balloons with straining, a hernia should be suspected, and you should be *evaluated* by a colorectal or general *surgeon* who performs hernia surgery.

Hernias become a medical emergency if they become *incarcerated* and/or *strangulated*. In incarceration, the herniated contents are trapped and cannot be pushed back into the abdominal cavity. Incarcerated hernias can become strangulated if blood flow to the herniated contents is cut off, thereby causing tissue death. Symptoms of a strangulated hernia include sudden pain, a hernia bulge that turns red or purple, loss of bowel movement, fever, and vomiting. These signs indicate that you need to be taken to the emergency room and prepared for surgery.

What Anorectal Problems Can Cause Pelvic Pain?

Hemorrhoids

Hemorrhoids (Figure 6-6) are common anorectal problems that affect more than half of the population above 50 years of age (Johanson and Sonnenberg, 1990). They arise from blood vessels within the soft tissue located within the anal canal and anal opening. These veins are normal and are present in a flattened form below the surface of the intestinal lining. When these veins enlarge, they can cause symptoms. Enlargement usually occurs because of increased rectal pressure associated with straining during bowel movements. Much less common is enlargement as a result of chronic liver disease. With repetitive straining during bowel movement, these soft tissues become engorged with dilated vessels and turn into hemorrhoidal tissue that can prolapse from the anal canal. They can be classified into external or internal hemorrhoids, depending on the location where they arise.

Although some patients with internal hemorrhoids remain *asymptomatic*, others can experience rectal bleeding, anal pain, anal itching, or difficulty with wiping the anal area clean. The most common symptom of internal hemorrhoids is painless rectal bleeding (do not assume that rectal bleeding is from a hemorrhoid; discuss any rectal bleeding with your doctor.) Pain associated with *internal hemorrhoids* is associated with a clot *(thrombosis)*, prolapse (extrusion outside the anus), and with strangulation (when the blood supply is disrupted). *External hemorrhoids* occur in the part of the anus below the pectinate line, where sensitivity is greater. If they form a blood clot (thrombosis within hemorrhoidal tissue), pain can be excruciating and occurs suddenly, often after lifting weights, moving furniture, running, or straining to have a bowel movement. Your doctor can tell you if you have hemorrhoids by performing a rectal exam and *anoscopy* exam in the office. Anoscopy involves insertion of a small tube that makes it possible to see the area just above the anus. Anoscopy does not require any preparation or *intravenous sedation*. If there is concern that the bleeding might not be coming from hemorrhoids, your doctor will recommend that you have a colonoscopy. Other causes of rectal bleeding include bleeding from a *diverticulum*, from a *polyp*, or even from a cancer.

Chapter 6: Which Gastrointestinal Problems Can Lead to Pelvic Pain? 89

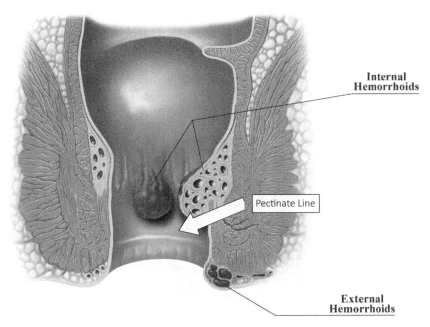

Figure 6-6: Hemorrhoids are dilated blood vessels in the anus. They are distinguished as either internal or external based on their location above or below the pectinate line, which has to do with the way the gut develops in utero. The pectinate line divides sensitive from non-sensitive surfaces.

The key element in managing hemorrhoids is to avoid constipation, because regular bowel movements interrupt the vicious cycle of chronic straining and hemorrhoidal tissue vein congestion. Constipation avoidance strategies include hydration, dietary changes to increase fiber intake, and use of soluble fiber supplementation. Also, toilet positioning can help, such as positioning your feet on a step stool during a bowel movement. This maneuver straightens the angle between the rectum and anus which helps stool pass through the rectum. If you have constipation because of a problem with the way your pelvic floor moves, pelvic floor physical therapy can also be effective. Sitz baths, topical preparations, and suppositories that contain hydrocortisone are often helpful. Most of the time, hemorrhoids will resolve with these conservative measures. If not, you will likely be referred to a surgeon for consideration of several different options.

Depending on the severity and extent of hemorrhoids, several procedural options are available, including placing tight bands (rubber band ligation) around the hemorrhoids, so they get strangled, scarred, and then fall off. Also, hemorrhoids can be *cauterized* (burned off, including use of infra-red coagulation) or injected with a medication that will cause them to scar and contract *(sclerotherapy)*. Occasionally, the doctor will need to remove them surgically. Formal surgical treatment includes ligation of the hemorrhoidal artery with or without *mucopexy* (excision of anal lining tissue that has moved outward with the hemorrhoids) and the traditional *hemorrhoidectomy* (surgical excision of hemorrhoids) (Davis et al, 2018). Thrombosed hemorrhoids are managed by evacuating the clot in the office under local anesthesia; if the procedure will be too painful, the clot can be excised under anesthesia. Prolapsed thrombosed hemorrhoids can be treated by reducing the prolapse and waiting for the clot to dissolve (within three weeks). If they are strangulated, they might need surgical excision.

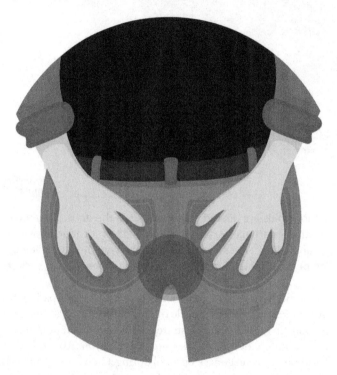

Anal Skin Irritation

Exposure of anal skin to excessive moisture and irritants (such as feces) results in skin erosion or *erythema*, which is scaly damaged skin with poorly defined borders. This skin condition is referred to as *irritant dermatitis* from exposure to feces. Because of its known rapid onset, the skin damage occurs within hours after exposure (McNichol et al, 2018; Doughty et al, 2012). Irritant dermatitis is confined to the contact area and leads to complaints of burning and itching. A fungal infection presents as a diffuse red rash with defined margins and/or yeast (Candida) infection, which presents as a rash with satellite *papules* and *pustules*. Often, these infections are seen with irritant dermatitis caused by exposure of skin to feces (McNichol et al, 2018).

The normal skin flora stays in balance when the skin pH remains within the usual acid range (4 to 6). Repeated exposure of skin to moisture and feces causes the skin pH to move into an alkaline range—greater than seven (McNichol et al, 2018). The pathologic bacteria multiply in the alkaline environment and the skin becomes vulnerable to breakdown. Wet skin is more susceptible to mechanical trauma from aggressive cleansing and excessive friction. As the skin ages, its function deteriorates and has increased tendency toward alkalinity. This means older adults are at higher risk for developing perianal skin irritation from moisture and passage of frequent loose stools. Soaps and cleansers with preservatives, fragrances, and dyes increase the chance for skin irritation in people who are susceptible. Identifying the causes of irritant dermatitis and differentiating them from other skin conditions is imperative to guide prevention and treatment (Colwell et al, 2011).

The skin should be washed daily with a pH-balanced cleanser to maintain its acidity, and it should be dried using a soft cloth to reduce friction and the risk for breakdown from trauma. In addition to cleansing the skin and keeping it dry, the anal skin needs to be protected from exposure to feces and moisture. Skin-barrier products containing zinc oxide, petrolatum, or dimethicone provide a physical barrier to irritants and moisture (McNichol et al, 2018). Before choosing the *skin barrier* product, clinicians should review the ingredients, learn the ease of application, investigate the product availability in the patient's community, and investigate the form in which it is supplied (cream, lotion, ointment, or liquid). The skin barrier product must be reapplied to the skin after each bowel movement. Excessive wiping with tissue paper should be avoided. A better choice is to wipe with a moistened tissue (with plain water) to reduce friction. A soft toilet paper without filamentous components (a non-recycled paper) is preferable. Topical anti-fungals, such as clotrimazole and miconazole, are recommended if fungal and/or yeast infection is suspected. The medication should be applied first to the clean skin, followed by the protective barrier (McNichol et al, 2018; Doughty et al, 2012).

In addition to proper cleaning and protection of anal skin, other measures should be considered, such as dietary modifications and the use of *bulking agents* and bowel stoppers.

Foods to bulk-up your stool include apple sauce, bananas, pasta, smooth peanut butter, and potatoes. Avoid greasy and spicy foods and foods high in simple sugars that make the stools looser, more irritating to the skin, and harder to control. Bulk-forming fiber *supplements* (such as psyllium products), improve stool consistency and reduce the frequency and leakage. Anti-diarrheal medications slow bowel motility and decrease stool frequency. These agents need to be balanced with a desire to prevent constipation because constipation can lead to hemorrhoids. Clinicians should keep close contact with you and adjust the plan of care as indicated.

Anal Fissure

Anal fissures (Figure 6-7) are tears of the inner lining of the anal canal. They are usually caused by baseline high anal sphincter tone. Also, anal fissures can be exacerbated by chronic constipation and anal trauma. Typically, people with anal fissures report sharp anal pain that gets worse during bowel movements and is often described as "passing razor blades or shattered glass." Associated features include minor bleeding, discharge, burning, and itching. Given the unique characteristics of pain caused by an anal fissure, the diagnosis can often be made based on your history. This can be confirmed by gently spreading and flattening the perianal skin around the anus with Q-tips. It is common to have a soft anal skin tag associated with the anal fissure (a sentinel tag, which is a benign lesion). Further internal examination can be limited by pain, so your clinician might need to perform a more thorough examination under anesthesia (EUA) to rule out other pathologies. Again, treating constipation and avoidance of straining are the primary goals.

Topical agents to relax the anal sphincter muscles are efficacious in improving fissure healing (Nelson et al, 2012). These agents include nifedipine, diltiazem *(calcium channel blocker)*, and glyceryl nitrate (GTN). The downside of using GTN is that it can cause headache as a side effect. Other minimally invasive approaches include *botulinum toxin*, which can be injected during the EUA and is an option to reduce anal sphincter tone and to allow the fissure to heal. Typically, the effects start 10 days after injection and last for three months. Repeat procedures may be needed if the fissure is unhealed. A *fissurectomy* (surgical cleaning up of the fissure floor and walls) might be done simultaneously if the fissure needs extra help healing. The most effective way to treat a chronic anal fissure is a lateral internal *sphincterotomy* (partially dividing the internal sphincter muscles under anesthesia), although this carries a small risk of impairment in fecal and gas continence (Nelson et al, 2012; Hyman, 2004).

Pruritis Ani

Chronic anal itching can lead to perianal skin irritation, bleeding, and pain, called *pruritis ani*. Although its underlying mechanisms are not well understood, anal itching can be triggered by food, fecal soiling, contact dermatitis (skin irritation), *psoriasis*, and infection (Siddiqi et al, 2008). Perianal dermatological skin growths (such as Paget's disease or cancer) need to be considered as possibilities and can be excluded with a skin biopsy.

Other than treating the underlying cause, supportive therapy (such as perianal hygiene and the use of barrier creams) can provide significant relief of itching. Perianal skin should be kept clean and dry. After each bowel movement, the perianal region should be cleaned with water and patted dry with toilet paper. Perfumed paper or wipes should be avoided because they can cause further chemical-related skin irritation. Try to avoid wearing tight clothing in the summer and consider wearing clothing made with cotton because it has better breathability for moisture control. Corn starch can be used to prevent moisture build-up in the perianal region in the hot summer. After showering, allow the area to dry in open air prior to dressing. Barrier creams such as zinc oxide cream (diaper cream) can be used sparingly to prevent excessive dryness in winter.

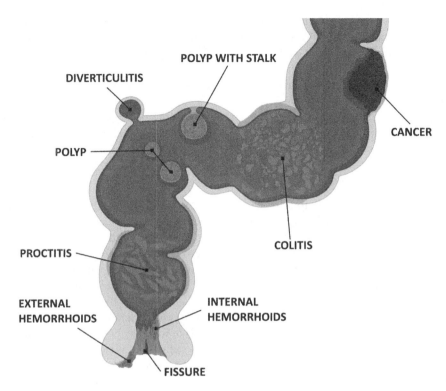

Figure 6-7: Rectal bleeding. Most sources of rectal bleeding are benign, but because of the possibility of cancer, it is important to speak with your doctor to determine whether medical tests are necessary.

Rectal Prolapse

Rectal prolapse refers to full-thickness protrusion of the rectum through the anus. It is more common in women and in those with increasing age. Rectal prolapse can be more likely in people with weakness of the pelvic floor muscles, the rectal attachments, and a redundant (long) *sigmoid colon*. It often co-exists with other urogynecological disorders (such as bladder, recto-vaginal, and utero-vaginal prolapse). Symptoms of a rectal prolapse include pelvic discomfort, rectal bleeding, and mucous discharge. The rectum can prolapse while straining during a bowel movement, and it might have to be manually pushed back in through the anus. You might have a sensation of incomplete bowel emptying after the movement because of the physical feeling of the rectal prolapse tissue. Occasionally, a rectal prolapse can extrude and remain out, with inability to place it back inside. This would require urgent evaluation in case the blood flow to the tissue is compromised (strangulation).

Diagnosis can be made based on the history and physical examination, but further work-up is usually required prior to surgical treatment. At times, it can be difficult for clinicians to visualize a rectal prolapse in the clinic, so patients are encouraged to bring photos of their rectal prolapse when straining. A colonoscopy is usually required to rule out other obstructive problems. A defecography can demonstrate the severity of the rectal prolapse, and it can also identify pelvic organ prolapses. An anorectal manometry can assess the anal sphincter function objectively, which can alter surgical management of rectal prolapse.

Rectal prolapse can be helped by improving the stool consistency, but for the most part, it is treated surgically.

Levator Ani Syndrome and Proctalgia Fugax

Levator ani syndrome is thought to be secondary to a levator ani (pelvic floor muscle) spasm. It is characterized by recurrent dull pelvic or rectal pain lasting for 30 minutes or longer each time. Typically, the rectal pain is worse when sitting compared to lying down or standing, and tenderness will be experienced during palpation of the puborectalis or other pelvic floor muscles. Levator ani pain can be associated with or worsened by defecation and might start even without a history of surgery in the anal area. For rectal pain associated with levator *muscle spasm*, treatment aims to relax the pelvic floor muscles. Options include digital rectal massage; biofeedback; physical therapy for pelvic girdle pain (if present); Sitz bath; application of heat (preferred) or ice (may help temporarily but can increase tension in the muscle); use of an albuterol/salbutamol inhaler; muscle relaxants; botulinum toxin injection; gabapentin; and pain blocks. In conjunction with psychological counseling, biofeedback has been more effective than a historic treatment called *electrogalvanic stimulation* and standard massage (Chiarioni et al, 2010). Pelvic floor physical therapy (internal vaginal or rectal massage) has been shown to help pelvic pain referable to the levator ani muscles (Weiss 2001; Oyama et al, 2004; Anderson et al, 2005; Fitzgerald et al, 2013). Injection of botulinum toxin into the pelvic floor muscles is a valid option with variable response based on small studies in the medical literature (Ooijevaar et al, 2019; Rao et al, 2009; Bibi et al, 2016).

The prevalence of levator ani syndrome and proctalgia fugax are estimated to be 7% and 8%, respectively (Drossman et al, 1993). Although they are both considered as benign conditions, pain can be debilitating enough to interfere with daily living; approximately 10% of those with these conditions had to take time off work or school (Drrossman et al, 1993). Proctalgia fugax refers to sporadic episodes of severe rectal pain that can last from a few seconds to a maximum of 30 minutes. Typically, it is not related to defecation. People are often pain-free between episodes. Attacks are not frequent, with most patients having fewer than five attacks per year. Proctalgia fugax is thought to be caused by abnormal smooth muscle contraction of the *anal sphincter complex* and it is associated with stress, anxiety, depression, and other mood disorders. After excluding other causes of anorectal pain, supportive care is the mainstay treatment. Unfortunately, because of the fleeting nature of the attacks, it is impracticable to intervene surgically to prevent further attacks. Nonetheless, there are several topical (surface) agents available to relax the anal sphincter muscle for symptomatic relief during the event, such as diltiazem and glycerol nitrate. Inhaled salbutamol can be considered to shorten the duration of each attack (Eckardt et al, 1996).

Conclusion

Many GI and anorectal diagnoses can lead to pelvic pain. If you carefully detail your history and symptoms for your provider, a targeted physical exam and work-up should help sort out the causes. You and your providers might target a few pain triggers, even during the diagnostic work-up. Many treatments and interventions—including lifestyle changes, behavior modification techniques, medications, physical therapy, and psychological therapy—can singly or in combination contribute to improvement of your symptoms.

WHICH MUSCULOSKELETAL PROBLEMS CAN LEAD TO PELVIC PAIN?

Beth Shelly, PT, DPT, WCS, BCB-PMD;
Cynthia E. Neville, PT, DPT, WCS; and
Allison Snyder, PT, MSPT, CLT, CEEAA

CHAPTER

In This Chapter

- What Are Musculoskeletal Problems and How Can They Lead to Pelvic Pain?
- What Kind of Evaluation Is Provided by a Pelvic Physical Therapist?
- How Will the Pelvic Floor Muscles Be Examined and Measured?
- How Should I Prepare for My First Appointment?
- Will the Pelvic Physical Therapist Examination Be Painful?

What Are Musculoskeletal Problems and How Can They Lead to Pelvic Pain?

Musculoskeletal problems are problems with *muscles*, *bones*, joints, *connective tissue*, skin, or *nerves* that lead to altered movements, which adversely affect the body's function. Several different musculoskeletal conditions can lead to *pelvic pain*. Musculoskeletal problems differ from medical or surgical problems such as infections or tumors in that they relate more to functional usage than to disease. However, medical problems can lead to musculoskeletal problems, such as when a woman with a painful *urinary tract infection* (UTI) develops *muscle spasms* in the *pelvic floor muscles* (PFMs). What follows are categories of musculoskeletal problems and how they can lead to pelvic pain.

Pelvic Floor Muscle Dysfunction

The PFMs (Figure 7-1) extend from the tailbone in the back to the pubic bone in the front, surrounding the openings of the *urethra* (where urine is expelled), the *anus* (where bowel movements are eliminated), the *prostate* (in men), and the *vagina* (in women). They support the pelvic organs and allow for normal bladder and bowel function. The PFMs also contribute to the control of posture, breathing, support of the *spine* and pelvis (including the lower back), and sexual function. When the PFMs are too weak, there might be urinary leakage, pelvic organ prolapse, and/or pelvic instability. When the PFMs are too tight, there may be pelvic pressure, urinary or fecal urgency, bowel irritation, constipation, painful intercourse, painful ejaculation, or lumbo-pelvic-hip pain. Pelvic pain is usually associated with PFM pain. Muscle pain can be caused by muscle spasms, increased muscle tone, increased muscle tension, or muscle overactivity in which the muscle has difficulty relaxing fully. There are many names for PFM pain dysfunctions. The most common are reviewed here.

PFM pain (also called *myalgia*) is pain on *palpation* (or touching) of the muscle inside or outside the vagina and rectum. A painful "knot" in a muscle can be referred to as a *trigger point*. A trigger point is tender to the touch and might be tense, or it can refer (send) pain to other areas of the pelvis. For example, a trigger point in the PFMs might cause pain in the bladder, vulva, *penis*, or the sacrum. PFM myofascial pain is a broader term that indicates pain in the PFMs and surrounding connective tissues of the pelvis.

PFM spasm (tension) can be related to PFM pain or can occur separately. All the muscles in the body should be able to contract and relax. Emotional stress, fear of pain, or fear of leaking urine can result in excess tension in the PFMs and lead to increased activity and tone of the muscles. You might not realize that you are tensing your muscles when they should be relaxed. A muscle spasm involves increased tension that you are unable to relax voluntarily. In both cases (muscle spasm and muscle overactivity/tension), the PFMs remain contracted and they have difficulty relaxing when they are supposed to. Pain can develop when muscles do not relax because not enough oxygen and nutrients can get to the muscle tissue when it is in the contracted state. As a result, the muscles can become shortened and tight. *Levator ani syndrome* is another name for PFM myofascial pain, spasm, and dysfunction.

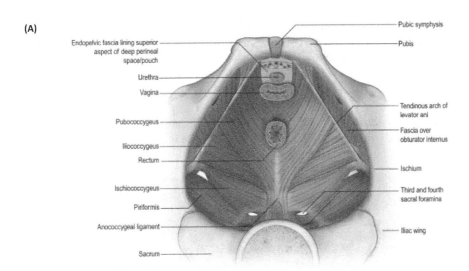

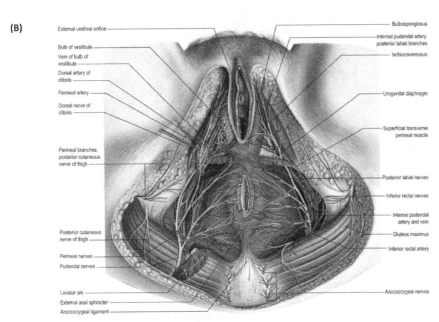

Figure 7-1: Muscles of the pelvic floor (in a female) including the levator ani muscle group, which includes the puborectalis, ileococcygeus, and pubococcygeus muscles. (A) Top (internal) view with organs not pictured. (B) Bottom view, including nerves and vessels. (Reproduced with permission: Standring S, ed.: A) Figure 73.3. Muscles of the female pelvis viewed from above. B) Figure 77.4. The muscles, vessels and nerves of the female perineum: inferior view. In: Gray's Anatomy: *The Anatomical Basis of Clinical Practice*. 41st Edition. Philadelphia, PA: Elsevier Limited. 2016; A) 1221–1236.e1. B) 1288–1313.e1.)

Vaginismus involves strong muscle tension of the surface-level (superficial) or deep PFMs in women; it leads to painful constriction of the vaginal opening and pain during vaginal penetration (such as with a *gynecological examination* or intercourse).

Proctalgia fugax is a sharp pain in the muscles that feels like it occurs around the anus and lasts for a few seconds to a few minutes before subsiding. It is thought to be caused by a PFM spasm.

Non-bacterial *prostatitis* (or *prostatodynia*) is pain in the area of the prostate; it usually involves PFM pain dysfunction (Figure 7-2). In fact, the pain might not come from the prostate; instead, the muscles mimic prostate pain.

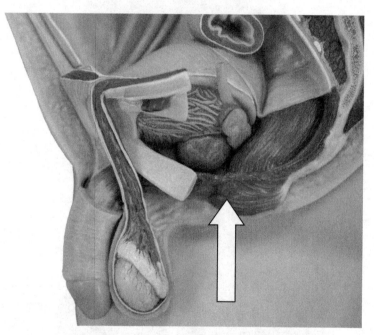

Figure 7-2: Model of the male pelvis, which shows how close the pelvic floor muscles are to the prostate.

Pudendal neuralgia is pain from the pudendal nerve, which supplies the PFMs and travels near the bones of the buttock. It can be injured during labor and delivery, during surgery, or due to sitting injuries, such as from bicycling.

Lumbo-Pelvic-Hip Pain

The joints of the lower (lumbar) back, pelvis, and hips work together to provide stability, mobility, and protection of the organs. This region of the body is called the "lumbo-pelvic-hip complex" because all these body parts interact with each other (Figure 7-3). These structures share nerves and form the attachments for the muscles of the trunk, pelvis, and hips.

Problems that affect the lower back or the hip might also affect the pelvis—and *vice versa*. Movement of the joints in one area affects the movement of the joints in another area. In this way, problems with the lower back and hips can cause or contribute to pelvic pain. For example, when your hip is stiff and painful, you might alter the way you walk. After a while, the change in your walking pattern might strain the pelvic joints.

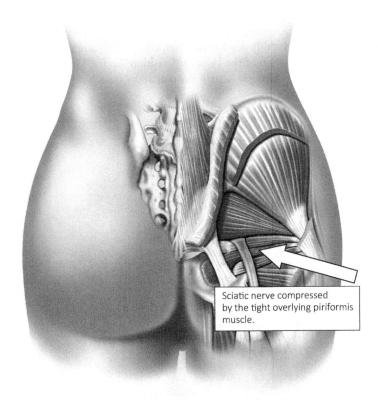

Sciatic nerve compressed by the tight overlying piriformis muscle.

Figure 7-3: The muscles of the lower back and hip work together with the pelvic floor and abdominal muscles. Here, the piriformis muscle is pictured compressing the sciatic nerve.

Pain that originates from the lower back can cause or contribute to bladder and bowel symptoms through their shared nerves. The PFMs attach to the pelvis and tailbone very close to the hip muscles. The PFMs can become tense in response to pelvic joint pain or instability, contributing to PFM pain. Non-specific low-back pain (LBP) is the term used for generalized LBP attributed to degeneration of the structures of the spine or to an undefined cause. Specific LBP is caused by a known condition, such as *scoliosis* (curvature of the spine) or a *herniated disc*.

Muscles of the hip (Figures 7-4 and 7-5) can contribute to pain when they have become tight because of a lack of flexibility, muscle spasms, or trigger points. Muscles, such as the hip flexor muscles (*iliopsoas*, which originate near the *kidneys* and travel to the thigh) or hip rotator muscles (*piriformis* or *obturator internus*) can directly cause pelvic pain or can indirectly contribute to symptoms by referring pain to the pelvic region. Dysfunction of the muscles of the hips can also cause bladder urgency and frequency. *Femoral acetabular impingement* (FAI) *syndrome* occurs when a structure within the hip joint (such as a ligament or the lining called the labrum) becomes pinched or impinged upon between bony structures. FAI can be difficult to diagnose, and pelvic pain might be the chief complaint. *Bursitis* is *inflammation* of the bursa or "cushion" on the lateral (outside) surface of the hip. The main sign of bursitis is pain on palpation (touching) the hip or pain while lying on your side.

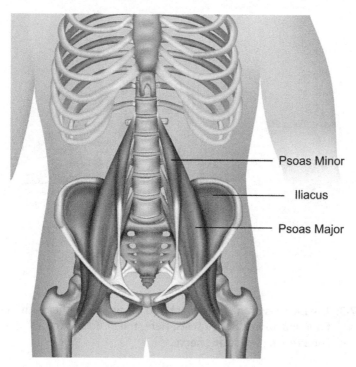

Figure 7-4: The iliopsoas muscle group (the psoas muscle and iliacus muscle) can cause pelvic and inner-leg pain and can even mimic the flank pain associated with a kidney stone.

Chapter 7: Which Musculoskeletal Problems Can Lead to Pelvic Pain?   103

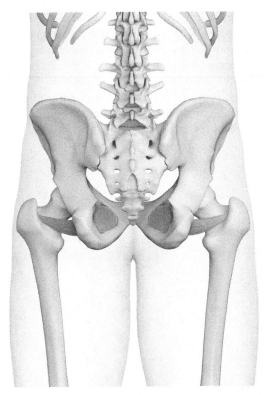

Figure 7-5: Obturator internus muscle (pictured inside the pelvic bone) and obturator externus muscle (extending from the pelvic bone) can both cause pelvic pain. The obturator internus can easily be examined during a vaginal or rectal exam.

The *pelvic girdle* is the combination of bones, joints, and ligaments of the pelvis. The *anterior* (front) joint of the pelvis is the *pubic symphysis*. The large wing-like bone of the pelvis is called the *ilium* and connects to the *sacrum* (the area above the tail bone) in the back at the *sacroiliac joint* (SIJ) (Figure 7-6). You have a right ilium and SIJ and a left ilium and SIJ. The *coccyx* is the tailbone located below the sacrum near the rectum. The pelvic girdle controls the distribution or "transfer" of body weight or "load" to and from the lower body, spine, and upper body. This is called "load transfer." When the transfer of load is disrupted or ineffective, joint pain can occur. *Pelvic girdle pain* (PGP) caused by impaired load transfer across the pelvic joints is usually a "sharp" and sudden pain that occurs during movement (such as rolling over in bed, moving from sitting to standing, standing on one leg, or stepping up or down). PGP can feel like aching and soreness underlying sharp pains that occur with different movements. PGP includes pubic symphysis dysfunction (PSD), sacroiliac joint, or sacrococcygeal joint dysfunction. PSD is a localized pain in the pubic region with possible shooting pain into the groin or inner thigh. SIJ dysfunction feels like a sharp poking or stabbing pain in the very low back and/or in the upper buttocks. PGP can occur by itself, or it can occur along with pain from the lumbar spine. Pelvic girdle pain is often associated with PFM spasm or tension.

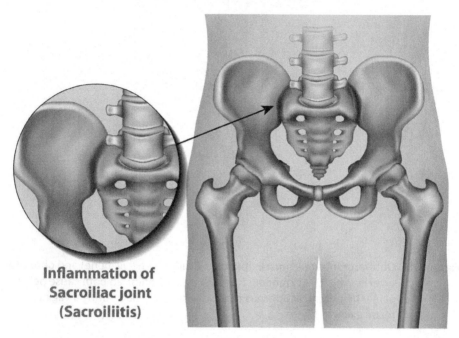

Figure 7-6: The sacroiliac joint can be a source of pain, as can the coccyx, the tip of the tailbone.

Abdominal Wall Dysfunction and Nerve Entrapment

The abdominal wall is another musculoskeletal structure that can cause or contribute to pelvic pain (Figure 7-7). The abdominal wall is made up of muscles, nerves, blood vessels, and connective tissue. The major functions of the abdominal wall include maintaining the position and protection of the internal abdominal organs from trauma/injury and assisting in breathing, coughing, and vomiting by increasing intra-abdominal pressure. Also important is the role that abdominal muscles play in stabilizing the trunk, protecting the spine, and allowing you to be active at work, leisure, and sports activities.

Chapter 7: Which Musculoskeletal Problems Can Lead to Pelvic Pain? 105

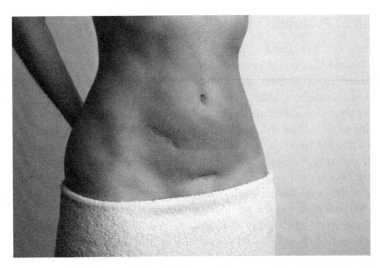

Figure 7-7: This person has a right-sided appendix scar and a midline C-section scar. These common scars can be a source of tight muscles, trapped nerves, or hernias.

Abdominal and pelvic surgery normally leads to the development of scar tissue; this scar tissue allows for complete healing. Many nerves course through the abdominal wall and associated structures, such as its muscles and *ligaments*. Nerves can become trapped in the tissues and scars of the abdominal wall. They can create and contribute to annoying and bothersome (irritative) bowel and bladder symptoms. The abdominal muscles can cause pelvic pain if they have myalgia or trigger points with pain referral to the groin, the front of the thigh, or the back. It is possible for the abdominal muscles to become too tight, tense, or spasm. This can be caused by or result in pain and poor posture. Weak abdominal muscles and lack of muscular trunk stability can contribute to low back pain and PGP. Identifying whether the abdominal muscles are too weak or too tight is the key to treatment success.

Common symptoms of *nerve entrapment* include burning, tingling, increased sensitivity *(hyperesthesia)*, or numbness *(hypoesthesia)* in the body part supplied by the nerve. The body can be painful to the touch in the area where the nerve is trapped or embedded in a scar. Symptoms can occur immediately after a surgery or injury, or symptoms can arise many months or years later. Pain caused by nerve entrapment can cause pain in any part of the abdominal and pelvic region. Nerve entrapment can cause pain and problems with sexual activity, including pain during or after intercourse, sexual activity of any kind, or *orgasm*. In some cases, the persistence of pain for a longer period results in alterations or modifications of the nervous system responsible for carrying *pain signals*. The altered nervous system then abnormally maintains a pain sensation even though the initial source of pain is no longer present or active.

What Kind of Evaluation Is Provided by a Pelvic Physical Therapist?

Physical therapy (PT) is aimed at identifying structures (nerves, muscles, ligaments, and connective tissues) that could be the source of or contribute to pelvic pain, movement patterns that contribute to pain, and muscle dysfunction. Your first visit for physical therapy is called the "initial evaluation." Most *pelvic floor* physical therapists are women. First, you will meet your physical therapist for an interview to discuss your medical history and *symptoms*. This could include information about what makes your pain better or worse, how your bowels and bladder work, and information about your sexual function. Your physical therapist will determine which physical procedures will be performed based on your interview. It might take several sessions to complete all portions of the examination. Different components of the evaluation might include examination of the lumbo-pelvic-hip connection, the abdominal wall, and the pelvic floor.

During the lumbo-pelvic-hip examination, your physical therapist might examine your spinal posture (Figure 7-8) and your ability to bend forward, backward, and laterally. The therapist might palpate (or touch and feel) your hip and pelvic bones and muscles, feeling for position or tenderness. Your therapist might perform maneuvers (such as pushing on your bones, muscles, and joints), to diagnose different conditions. The therapist will lift each of your legs and move your hips and knees to check their motion, mobility, and flexibility. The therapist will check your muscle strength and might watch you walk, bend, sit, balance, or perform other movements that you find difficult.

The abdominal wall examination starts with observation of your abdomen. Your physical therapist will look at your entire abdomen (from your ribcage to your *pubic bone*). If you have any scars from childbirth or surgery, the therapist might feel them to determine whether they are restricted or painful. The therapist might test your abdominal muscle strength and may press and feel for any tension and tenderness in the muscles.

An important component of the initial examination is the PFM examination. Your physical therapist will explain the exam to you and make sure that you understand the procedures.

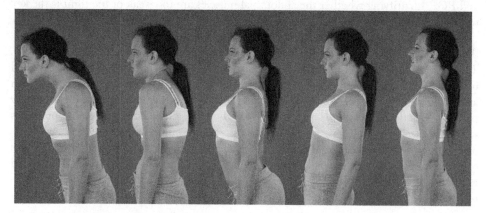

Figure 7-8: Four abnormal postures your physical therapist might notice, followed by normal posture.

How Will the Pelvic Floor Muscles Be Examined and Measured?

Your physical therapist might decide to use any number of exam techniques. Your opinion is important. If there is an examination procedure that you do not wish to have performed, you should discuss your preferences with your physical therapist prior to the examination. If you are concerned about your ability to tolerate the internal exam, discuss your concern with your physical therapist—you will not be the first person to voice concerns. Most physical therapists do not use stirrups or a speculum and measurement of the PFMs are not as deep as measurements of the organs (like the uterus or prostate). Some treatment can begin with the results of the *external* examination only. However, internal measurements and treatment are often needed for full recovery. You might find that after some time using external treatments, you might be comfortable progressing to an internal exam and treatment. Psychological factors, especially a history of trauma, are important to address and can sometimes be straightforward to address for the purpose of a specific health concern.

During an external palpation of PFM contraction, you may keep your underpants or clothing on. Your physical therapist will palpate or feel your PFMs as you contract (squeeze or clench) and relax them through your underwear or clothes by placing the fingertips near the anus in the buttock region. This examination allows your physical therapist only to determine if the PFMs can contract.

For an external PFM exam, your physical therapist will give you a gown or sheet to cover you as you remove your underwear. The therapist will then observe your *genital* region, including the vagina and or the anus, while you contract and relax the muscles. The therapist will put on gloves to check your reflexes and sensation, and she or he will palpate your body parts (including the skin, bones, and muscles on the outside the vagina and anus). Your physical therapist will ask if you have tenderness on palpation of the muscles or skin on the outside. Sometimes, it is helpful to watch the movement on the outside with a mirror. Normally, when the PFMs contract, the muscles and skin move toward your head. During PFM relaxation, the muscles and skin move toward your feet.

The internal PFM exam is the procedure that allows your physical therapist to measure your PFM function and to identify specific structures in the pelvis that may be causing pain. Your physical therapist will put on gloves and perform an external PFM exam. The therapist will apply lubricant and insert a finger into your vagina and/or anus to feel the PFMs internally. The therapist will check your sensation, palpate the muscles and structures for pain and tenderness, and test your muscle function (including your ability to both contract and relax your PFMs). The therapist might feel the tailbone (coccyx) and test how it moves.

A non-invasive option for diagnosis of PFM function is an assessment using *surface electromyography* (sEMG). sEMG PFM assessment allows your physical therapist to measure the electrical activity of your muscles. The therapist will place small sensors on the muscles around the anus or (with your permission) place a sensor-probe inside the vagina or anus. When you contract and relax the muscles, the therapist will be able to measure the amount of muscle activity on a computerized system.

Ultrasound imaging is a technique to view muscles and body structures while they contract and relax. Ultrasound uses sound waves to create an image. Physical therapists do not perform ultrasound inside the vagina. Your physical therapist will place some gel on your body and then put the ultrasound probe on the gel on your abdomen or the *perineum*. The perineum is located between the anus and testicles in men and between the vagina and anus in women. The ultrasound provides a picture of your muscles or bladder. Your physical therapist will look at the images to see how the structures move when you contract and relax the PFMs and bear down as if moving your bowels.

How Should I Prepare for My First Appointment?

You can prepare for your first appointment with a pelvic physical therapist by bringing previous records and tests relevant to your condition with you. It can be helpful to jot down a history of your pain, including when your pain started and what type of pain you are primarily experiencing (sharp, dull, constant, intermittent, or provoked). You can also include what activities seem to make your symptoms better or trigger your pain. For example, you should note if sitting increases your pain or if your pain is provoked only by sexual activity. You might find it helpful to identify a few treatment goals that you would hope to be able to accomplish with a course of PT.

When you arrive (or even before your first appointment), your physical therapist will ask you to complete *questionnaires* about your history and symptoms. This assists the therapist in identifying your key symptoms and potential pain triggers.

You should plan to wear comfortable clothing in which you can bend and move to your pelvic floor physical therapy evaluation. Clothing that is easy to remove is also advisable. It might be helpful to bring a support person with you to your first visit. This person could help to ease some of your anxiety, remind you of questions you may have, and help you remember key points after the visit. However, this is only an option, and many patients come to the PT sessions alone.

Will the Pelvic Physical Therapist Examination Be Painful?

Ultimately, pelvic PT should reduce your pain and improve the quality of your life. The evaluation might include both internal and external measurements. You and your physical therapist will decide which tests would be helpful. You might have some increased pain during or after the initial exam and even after the first few PT sessions as your therapist identifies how sensitive your muscles, tissues, and nerve endings are to movement, pressure, and/or stretching. You might have had a back massage that led to soreness, but you knew it was going to be helpful. Muscles of the pelvic floor can act the same way. You should feel comfortable communicating with your physical therapist and share how you are feeling during and after the exam and each treatment session. Your physical therapist will offer recommendations for pain-reduction strategies after the exam that could include use of a cold pack to the perineum, the use of any previously prescribed medication that your physician has recommended, or different positions for sitting or lying to reduce your pain.

After the examination, your physical therapist will discuss important contributing aspects that were identified during the exam. You should understand how these components contribute to your symptoms. This helps you understand why the therapist might include various treatment strategies, exercises, and lifestyle recommendations. You might receive some written material to better understand your condition. You might be given initial recommendations from your physical therapist to start you on the path to feeling better. You will discuss with your therapist the plan for PT, which often includes discussion of:

- The frequency and duration of pelvic floor PT sessions
- The estimated length of course of pelvic floor PT
- The various treatment options that may be included during your course of PT
- The goals of PT

Remember, the best way to manage your pelvic pain is via a team approach where you are the most important part of the team. The best results come when you work together with the other team members and follow recommendations as best as you can.

WHAT TYPES OF BONE AND LIGAMENT PROBLEMS CAN LEAD TO PELVIC PAIN?

Andrew Dubin, MD, MS and Marilyn Heng, MD, MPH, FRCSC

CHAPTER 8

In This Chapter

- Why Should I See a Bone or Muscle Specialist for Pelvic Pain?
- What Should I Know If My Pain Might Be from My Ligaments and Bones?
- What Kind of Physical Exam Is Needed to Assess Bones and Ligaments?
- Could My Pelvic Pain Come from My Spine/Hip?
- What Will Imaging Studies Reveal About My Bones and Ligaments?
- What Causes Pelvic Fractures?
- What Tests Are Usually Done to Diagnose a Pelvic Fracture?
- What Does the Recovery After a Pelvic Fracture Look Like?
- Do the Long-Term Consequences of Pelvic Fractures Include Pain?
- Can Injury to Ligaments and Tendons Cause Pelvic Pain?
- What Bone and Soft Tissue Tumors Occur in or Near the Pelvis?
- Could My Pelvic Pain Be Coming from My Hip?

Why Should I See a Bone or Muscle Specialist for Pelvic Pain?

Chronic pelvic pain (CPP) is a common and often vexing problem for patients and their providers. Many patients have had extensive work-ups by *urologists, obstetric/gynecologists* (OB-GYN), *colorectal surgeon*s, *gastroenterologists*, and *urogynecologists*, but the *musculoskeletal system* is often neglected. In many instances, the cause of CPP goes undiagnosed and becomes a source of frustration (Dubin, 2018). The dilemma facing those with CPP is understanding the interplay of multiple organ systems.

Many individuals undergo multiple tests and *invasive procedures* before the musculoskeletal system is considered in the *differential diagnosis*. However, it can be a significant source of pain. The musculoskeletal system is made up of *bones, muscles, cartilage* (connective tissue), *tendons* (that connect muscles to bones), *ligaments* (that connect bones to bones, Figure 8-1), and *joints* (where bones connect to each other). A *bursa* lies between a tendon or muscle and an adjacent bone, acting as a cushion. Many types of practitioners, such as *physiatrists* (physical medicine and rehabilitation doctors), *orthopedists* (bone and joint doctors), osteopaths, and *physical therapists*, care for bones and ligaments.

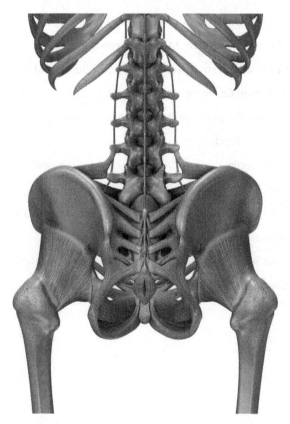

Figure 8-1: The pelvis and ligaments viewed from behind.

What Should I Know If My Pain Might Be from My Ligaments and Bones?

You might be reluctant to discuss issues of CPP, and your physicians might not be inclined to delve into the topic, particularly if you have been disappointed by prior conversations. This can lead to dissatisfaction and helplessness when trying to address the *symptoms*. Consequently, many people with CPP delay their evaluations until the issues can no longer be avoided.

Complaints of CPP are often non-specific. The vague nature of these complaints raises diagnostic challenges. You should note whether walking, bearing down, prolonged sitting, prolonged standing, and lumbar (low-back) flexion and/or extension negatively affect your *pelvic pain*. These activities can cause pain by itself, or they can cause pain in combination with urinary urgency or frequency, bowel dysfunction, *perineal* sensory problems, and sexual problems; in males, *erectile dysfunction* can develop (Neville et al, 2012). Communicating the pattern of your symptoms guides your provider to the cause. The duration of symptoms and the timing of the relationship to activities or trauma are of paramount importance. Factors that exacerbate or relieve your pain should be noted. Interventions and medication trials should be explored, with focus on the response to the interventions.

What Kind of Physical Exam Is Needed to Assess Bones and Ligaments?

A focused history and a detailed physical exam that emphasizes the neuromusculoskeletal system (Figure 8-2) is essential. Your provider should observe and examine your musculoskeletal system. Observing you while taking your history is critical: how you sit, stand, and walk, change position from sitting to standing, and move about the exam room will provide clues to the cause.

Could My Pelvic Pain Come from My Spine/Hip?

The work-up for CPP should include a detailed evaluation of the *lumbosacral spine* as well as observation of gait. If a "*Trendelenburg gait*" is noticed, your doctor will determine which of the two types are presenting:

1. A classic Trendelenburg-compensated gait is typically caused by *intra-articular hip joint dysfunction*, which presents with groin pain caused by muscle compensation for the joint problem.

2. A painless Trendelenburg gait can be seen in disorders that result in weakness of the *gluteus medius* (buttock) musculature. This pattern can be a result of an underlying muscle disorder *(myopathy)* that should be considered when the gait is *asymmetric*.

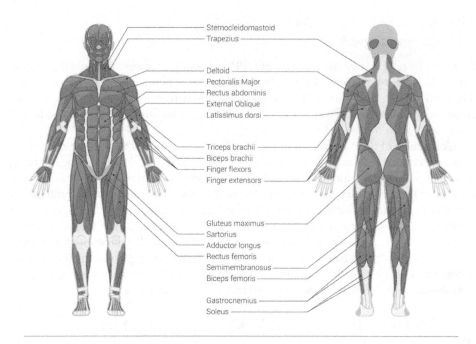

Figure 8-2: The muscular system.

Over distances, heel walking might reveal subtle weakness of the ankle dorsi flexors. This can manifest as an old low-back (fifth lumbar nerve) *radiculopathy* with incomplete *reinnervation* as the cause of a painless Trendelenburg gait. This can transform into a painful gait over long distances when fatiguing musculature causes cramping and pelvic region discomfort.

Similarly, weakness of sacral (sacral first nerve root) *innervated* musculature can be evoked by long-distance toe-walking (Figure 8-3) during the physical exam and might explain deep gluteal (buttock) pain with prolonged ambulation (Neville at al, 2010).

Assessment of reflexes is also critical (Figure 8-4). Merely noting their presence or absence is not enough. Appreciating the significance of the findings is key. Weak reflexes *(hypo- or areflexia)* can be a manifestation of a *peripheral neuropathy* (problems with the small peripheral *nerves*), or *polyradiculopathy* (problems with pinched nerves at multiple levels of the spine) that is secondary to lumbar *spinal stenosis*. A loss of the *Achilles (heel) reflexes* is commonly seen in both scenarios. It is important to note that impaired sacral sensation (sensation of the *genitals* and anal area) is not typical with peripheral neuropathy or *polyradiculopathy*. The combination of a loss of an Achilles reflex in concert with impaired sacral sensation—especially if it is on one side—can be observed in sacral *Tarlov cysts*. These are naturally occurring fluid-filled structures in the sacral spine that often don't cause symptoms (Figure 8-5). *Electrodiagnostic* (EDX) *testing* with pelvic floor reflex testing and anal/urethral sphincter needle testing *(electromyogram)* can find the location and extent of nerve involvement.

Chapter 8: What Types of Bone and Ligament Problems Can Lead to Pelvic Pain? 115

Figure 8-3: An exam involving toe walking (walking on one's toes) and heel walking can identify weakness from nerve problems.

Figure 8-4: Reflex testing can identify reflexes that are either dull or too brisk.

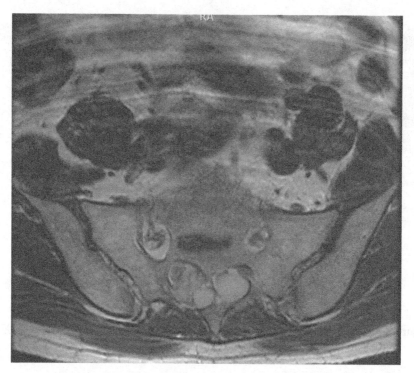

Figure 8-5: Tarlov cysts—fluid filled structures—present in the sacrum are often asymptomatic but *can* cause pain or injury from nerve compression. (Reproduced with permission.)

Loss of reflexes and symmetric sensory difficulty in the "seat" (*saddle dysesthesias* or *anesthesia*) can be seen in *cauda equina syndrome*. The cauda equina is the area in the lower spinal cord that has loose nerves (like a horse's tail). If saddle (seat) sensory abnormalities arise, *magnetic resonance imaging* (MRI) of the lumbosacral spine should be obtained to assess compression of the nerves coming from the lower sacrum either at the level of the cauda equina (where the nerves are traveling loosely from the lower spine) or the sacral foramina (the exit sites from the bony spine).

Leg hyper-reflexia (overactive reflexes) should raise suspicion of thoracic or *cervical myelopathy*. In the case of cervical myelopathy (nerve impairment in the neck), upper-extremity hyper-reflexia and altered sensation should be present. Loss of a specific nerve root level reflex in the upper extremities with hyper-reflexia below the level of *hyporeflexia* is consistent with the diagnosis of *cervical radiculomyelopathy*. A cervical or *thoracic radiculomyelopathy* can result in pelvic pain that is either secondary to altered sensation as a result of an incomplete spinal cord injury or secondary to spasticity of pelvic floor musculature. (Neville et al, 2018).

Physical examination of the hip should include an assessment of the *range of motion*, looking for asymmetry of motion and pain with internal or *external* rotation. Pain (groin pain) with internal rotation is typical for internal derangement of the joint. Pain with external rotation may be *labral* in etiology (coming from the "lip" or lining of the hip joint), but it also can be seen in *psoas dysfunction*. The psoas is a muscle that runs from the inner mid-back to the inner thigh (see Figure 7-4).

True joint-derived hip joint pain can be distinguished from *extra-articular* (outside the joint) pain by administering an ultrasound-guided hip joint anesthetic injection. If there is immediate reduction in pain with a local anesthetic, this points to a joint (intra-articular) cause.

Many additional maneuvers can be helpful in the assessment of CPP. The goal is to localize the source of the pain and strive for internal consistency amongst the test maneuvers.

The forced FABERs (Flexion, Abduction, External Rotation) Test (Figure 8-6) allows the examiner to evaluate the role of the *sacroiliac joint* (SIJ) in the pelvic pain. In the forced FABER test, you are placed on your back with one leg placed in the FABERS position (hip bent, opened, and turned outward). (Note that this test can also be performed in the seated position.)

While in this position, extra pressure is applied to the inner knee of the rotated leg while holding the opposite hip to the exam table. This results in a distracting force placed throughout the pelvis. This test places stress on the SIJ. A positive test produces pain in the SIJ, though it can replicate pain without having SIJ pathology, especially if you have dysfunction/*dystonia* of the *iliopsoas muscle*. As such, other tests to assess psoas function in isolation (resistive hip flexion, lower abdominal palpation) might need to be included in the exam to help isolate SIJ from psoas issues.

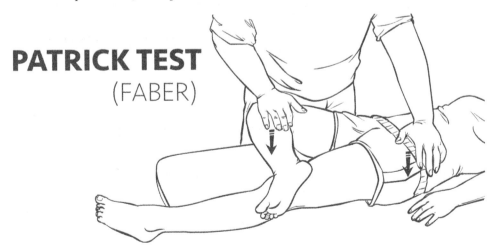

Figure 8-6: The FABER (Flexion, Abduction, External Rotation) test stretches the pelvis to open somewhat. It can diagnose sacroiliac joint discomfort and might uncover tightness of the iliopsoas muscle.

The *Posterior Pelvic Pain Provocation Test* is performed while lying on your back (the supine position). The hip is flexed to 90 degrees on one side with a direct line of force applied through the *femur* (the large bone in the thigh). This compresses the *femoral acetabular joint*, which applies force to the *ipsilateral* (same-sided) SIJ. A positive test involves pain in the ipsilateral SIJ (Neville et al, 2018; Silvis et al, 2011).

Reproducing the pain by pressing on the pelvic floor muscles and ligaments can happen when examining people with CPP. In women, palpation of the pelvic floor can be carried out trans-vaginally with firm digital pressure to the right and left sides of the vaginal vault. Tension and trigger points in the *pubococcygeus muscles* can be noted on palpation. In men, surface palpation behind the scrotum to the right and left of the mid-line is useful, as the *bulbocavernosus muscles* are easily palpated in this manner. Symmetry of bulbocavernosus muscle bulk can be assessed as can sensitivity to palpation. In both men and women, a *digital rectal exam* will allow for palpation of the puborectalis and pubococcygeus muscles as well as the deeper layers of the *anal sphincter*. An assessment of anal sphincter strength and endurance can also be ascertained during a digital rectal exam (Neville et al, 2018; Silvis et al, 2011). Your examiner might ask you to squeeze this muscle as part of the exam.

What Will Imaging Studies Reveal About My Bones and Ligaments?

Abnormalities of the bones ligaments and joints noted on a *magnetic resonance imaging* (MRI) *scan* might correlate with the history and physical exam. In all instances, the results of imaging studies need to be reviewed in context with your history and physical exam. (Kokubo et al, 2017). Findings on the physical exam and a response to intra-articular (joint) injection will allow providers to assess the significance of the MRI findings.

Posterior pelvic pain is common in those with hip problems, such as a labral tear or early arthritis.

Similar to the hip, an MRI scan of the lumbar spine often reveals lumbar spine pathology in asymptomatic individuals (Neville et al, 2012). Therefore, your MRI scan must be interpreted in the context of your symptoms and a careful physical exam.

What Causes Pelvic Fractures?

Typically, pelvic fractures occur in one of two scenarios. Elderly people with *osteoporosis* can sustain low-energy pelvic fractures after a relatively innocuous event, such as a fall from a standing height. At times, the pelvis breaks during regular day-to-day activities; this is called an *insufficiency fracture* (the bone was insufficiently able to withstand the stresses of normal activities). At the other end of the spectrum, people who are involved in high-energy trauma, such as a motor vehicle collision or a fall from a height, sustain high-energy *traumatic pelvic fractures* that can be life-threatening because of bleeding and associated injuries.

Pelvic fractures can be categorized by the part of the pelvic bone that is broken. The pelvis can be thought of as a ring that is formed by two bones—the right hemi-pelvis and the left hemi-pelvis. These bones are held together with strong, thick, ligaments

Chapter 8: What Types of Bone and Ligament Problems Can Lead to Pelvic Pain?

(Figure 8-7). When either the bone or the ligaments of the ring are disrupted, a *pelvic ring fracture* develops. The pelvis connects the torso to the legs via the *sacrum* at the end of the spine and then through the hip joints. Fractures of the sacrum can occur as part of a pelvic ring fracture or can be isolated to the sacrum. The tip of the sacrum (also known as your "tailbone") is the *coccyx*, and it also can be fractured. The socket of the hip joint is the *acetabulum* of the pelvis, and fractures through this bone are called *acetabular fractures*. Fractures that break off small parts of the bone that are attached to tendons and ligaments are called *avulsion fractures*.

Fractures of the pelvis can range from being non-displaced (still in line with the other side of the break) to being severely displaced. The amount of displacement is often correlated with the energy involved in injuring the pelvis.

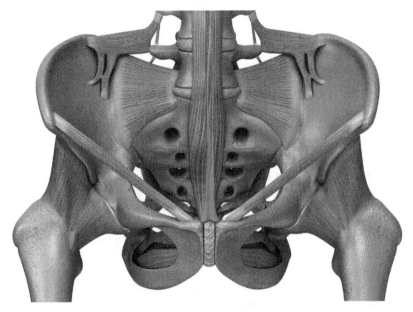

Figure 8-7: Front view of pelvis with its ligaments connecting to the hips and lower spine.

What Tests Are Usually Done to Diagnose a Pelvic Fracture?

Usually, an *X-ray* is the first test performed to diagnose a pelvic fracture. X-rays are painless *radiology* imaging studies that take less than a minute once you are on the X-ray table. Your doctor might order anywhere from one to three different X-ray views, looking at different angles of the bone. Sometimes, non-displaced pelvic fractures are not obvious on an X-ray. If you have significant pain even though no fracture is seen on an X-ray, your doctor might order a more sensitive imaging test. A *computed tomography* (CT) *scan* of the pelvis is a test that is more powerful and uses more radiation than X-rays to see more bone detail.

It allows for a two-dimensional view of the bone, and it is especially useful for identifying fractures at the back of the pelvis in the sacrum. In general, a CT scan takes several minutes to complete, and your X-ray bed passes through the open circular machine.

An MRI scan is an imaging study that uses magnetic waves instead of radiation to image the pelvis. MRIs offer a greater-detail view of the soft tissues, tendons, and ligaments. An MRI scan can detect an occult fracture of the pelvis, which is a fracture that is there but was not seen on the X-ray or CT scan. Often, MRI scans are reserved for when the X-rays and CT scans do not reveal a fracture, but you are still having significant pain or your doctor thinks something else (other than bone) is causing your pain. During an MRI scan, you are required to lie still inside of a large tubular machine for approximately 30–60 minutes. If you worry that you might feel claustrophobic, you can ask the technologist whether it is possible to position you with your face outside the machine. Because it is a strong magnet, tell the imaging center if there is concern that you might have metal or metal fragments in your body.

What Does the Recovery After a Pelvic Fracture Look Like?

The time required to heal a bone is never exact. It depends on the bone and your body. If you have risk factors (such as being a smoker or having poor nutritional health), then your fracture might take longer to heal. In rare cases, your fracture might not heal at all, which is called a *non-union*. However, in general, a fracture of the pelvis takes at least three months to heal. In the case of insufficiency or stress fractures, healing might proceed very slowly and take up to a year for complete healing. Fortunately, the pain you experience from a pelvic fracture will begin to improve well before healing is apparent on X-rays. Most people note a lessening of their pain after the first 2–4 weeks, with pain continuing to decrease as the fracture heals. Healing of a fracture can be judged by decreasing pain (despite stress or pressure on the fracture site) and by radiographic bridging of bone that can be seen on X-rays.

Treatment decisions regarding fractures are often based on an assessment of the stability of your fracture (Figure 8-8). A stable fracture is one that is not expected to move even if some stress or pressure is placed on the fracture. If you have a stable fracture of the pelvis, your doctor will allow you to *weight-bear as tolerated* (WBAT). This means that you are allowed to put as much weight on the leg as your pain allows. Depending on which side of the pelvis your main fracture lies, you might be WBAT on the right, the left, or both legs. When a fracture appears unstable or it is not clear whether it is stable, your doctor will restrict you to being *touchdown weight-bearing* (TDWB) on the one leg. This means that you can put your foot on the ground for balance, but no weight should be placed through that leg. To do this, you will need to use either crutches or a walker. For unstable fractures located on both sides of the pelvis, you might be non-weight-bearing on both legs and require a wheelchair until your fractures start healing. If you are placed on a weight-bearing restriction because of your pelvis fracture, it generally takes 10–12 weeks from the time of your fracture to when your doctor will allow you to become weight-bearing. After any of the above scenarios, you might benefit from *physical therapy* (PT)—or specialized *pelvic floor physical therapy*—to help normalize the muscle function again.

Chapter 8: What Types of Bone and Ligament Problems Can Lead to Pelvic Pain? 121

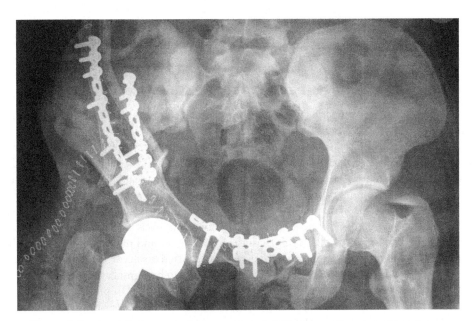

Figure 8-8: A pelvic fracture that required stabilization with surgical hardware. Also, note that there has been a hip replacement.

As your fracture heals, you will be seen in follow-up by your doctor for X-rays to ensure that the fracture is staying in place and that it heals. Your first follow-up appointment is generally about two weeks after the fracture for repeat X-rays (and also to remove staples or *sutures* if you had a surgery). Then you can expect to follow-up every 4–6 weeks to three months for repeat X-rays to monitor healing. Recovery from a pelvis fracture can take upward of a year to return to your prior levels of function.

Do the Long-Term Consequences of Pelvic Fractures Include Pain?

A pelvis fracture is a major injury; despite satisfactory bony healing of your fracture, it can have significant long-term consequences. CPP occurs in some people. The prevalence of *chronic* post-traumatic pelvic pain increases with the severity of the fracture pattern; in the worst type of pelvis fracture, up to 90% of people experience long-term pain (Gerbershagen et al, 2010).

Genitourinary disease (prolapse, *interstitial cystitis*, *urinary tract infection* [UTI], and urinary symptoms) and sexual dysfunction might occur after pelvic fractures in both men and women. Even in the absence of direct injury to your bladder or *urethra*, dysfunction can occur. The chances of genitourinary dysfunction or pain are related to the specific type of fracture; for example, it is higher in sacroiliac joint fractures in men and *pubic symphysis diastasis* (widening) in women. If you have a nerve injury from your pelvis fracture, this predicts a higher likelihood of poor long-term functional outcome (Kokubo et al, 2017).

If you have pain after a pelvic fracture, ask your orthopedist and primary care provider whether they would recommend consultation with a pelvic floor physical therapist and an interventional pain specialist.

Can Injury to Ligaments and Tendons Cause Pelvic Pain?

A ligament is tissue connecting bone-to-bone, and a tendon is a collagen-based tissue connecting muscle to bone.

Pubic symphysis diastasis describes a widening of the pubic symphysis (which is in the front of the pelvis where the right and left hemi-pelvis meet). On X-rays, there is normally a space of approximately 5–10 mm that represents the symphyseal ligaments holding the bones together. Widening of this space can occur traumatically with a high-energy pelvis fracture that causes the symphyseal ligaments to tear and the pelvis to open like a book (hence the term "open-book pelvis fracture"). Pubic symphysis diastasis can also occur during vaginal delivery. Normally, this diastasis is temporary and resolves after childbirth. However, persistent postpartum pubic diastasis is reported to occur rarely in anywhere from 1 in 300 to 1 in 30,000 births. In these cases, there can be significant pain at the front of the pelvis, especially with attempted walking after childbirth. On physical exam, pain can be evoked if the examiner applies pressure on both the *trochanters* (outer hips) or by lifting your straight legs to flex the hip.

Another *soft tissue* (non-bone) injury that can occur in the pelvis is a hamstring tendon rupture (Figure 8-9). The hamstring muscles are located at the back of the thigh and attach to the *ischial tuberosity* (the sit bones, located in the region of the crease of the buttocks) of the pelvis. Injury to the hamstrings can range from a mild muscle strain in which the muscle and tendon are just stretched but not torn, to a partial tear of the tendon, to a complete rupture in which the entire tendon is pulled away from the ischial tuberosity. This is called an avulsion fracture if a piece of the ischial tuberosity is torn away with the tendon. Complete hamstring tendon ruptures can cause severe pain in the buttocks and down the back of the thigh. This will be accompanied by swelling, bruising, and weakness in the back of the thigh. Hamstring injuries might heal with rest or might need surgery depending on their severity.

What Bone and Soft Tissue Tumors Occur in or Near the Pelvis?

An abnormal growth, such as a *tumor*, arising from the bone or soft tissues of the pelvis is a rare cause of pelvic pain. Tumors of bone can be *malignant* (cancer) that can spread to other parts of the body, or they can be *benign*, which might grow in the pelvis but do not have the potential to spread. Both malignant and benign tumors can cause pain. Lastly, cancers that start somewhere else in the body can spread to bones. These *metastatic lesions* of bone are most common in lung cancer, breast cancer, prostate cancer, renal cell cancer, and thyroid cancer. Cancer is an uncommon cause of pelvic pain. Bone or soft tissue tumors are investigated with X-rays, CT scans, or MRIs. Evaluation of pelvic pain involves imaging, usually after initial investigations and treatments are unrevealing or if there are specific findings leading to the imaging request.

Chapter 8: What Types of Bone and Ligament Problems Can Lead to Pelvic Pain? 123

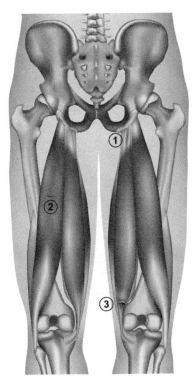

Figure 8-9: Hamstring injury, viewed from behind.

Could My Pelvic Pain Be Coming from My Hip?

Often, pain that comes directly from the hip joint feels like groin or pelvic pain. Pain from other structures of the pelvis is more often described along the front, side, or back of the hip region.

Hip arthritis is a common cause of pain. It occurs when the cartilage lining of the hip joint wears down and the space in the joint becomes narrower until the bone of the femoral head grinds against bone of the acetabulum. Symptoms of hip arthritis include groin pain and stiffness of the hip. Pain can also be referred to the buttocks, down the thigh, and to the knee. Pain from hip arthritis tends to worsen with activity and prolonged weight-bearing. Stiffness is often worse when rising from a prolonged sitting position.

The *labrum* of the hip is a ring of cartilage around the bony edge of the acetabulum that serves to deepen the hip joint and make it more stable. A hip labral tear can cause symptoms of groin pain, hip stiffness, and mechanical symptoms of locking or catching with hip motion. In addition to a thorough physical exam of the hip, an MRI scan is often done to diagnose a hip labral tear. The decision to have surgery will be affected by the cause of the tear (such as injury versus wear and tear) and how stable the joint remains.

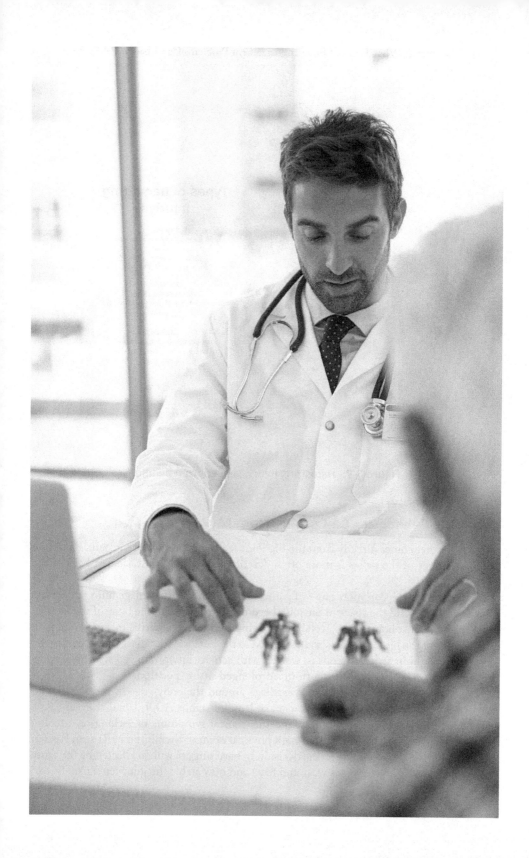

WHICH NEUROLOGICAL PROBLEMS CAN LEAD TO PELVIC PAIN?

Antje M. Barreveld, MD; Alexandra R. Adler, MD; and Charles Argoff, MD

CHAPTER

In This Chapter

- How Will I Know If I Have Neurological Pain?
- What Is Chronic Pain?
- How Can I Be Evaluated for Neurological Causes of Pelvic Pain?
- What Are Peripheral Nerves and How Do They Cause Pain?
- What Is the Autonomic Nervous System?
- What Is a Peripheral Neuropathy?
- What Is the Central Nervous System and How Does It Cause Pain?
- What Do I Need to Do Next?
- Conclusion

How Will I Know If I Have Neurological Pain?

Pain is an unpleasant physical and emotional experience that is transmitted by the nervous system (Figure 9-1). Therefore, all pain can be thought of as neurological. The *central nervous system* (CNS) is composed of the brain and *spinal cord* (the control centers), while the *peripheral nervous system* (PNS) involves the *nerves* that exit the spinal cord and form both large nerves (for example, the *sciatic nerve*) as well as the tiny nerves, such as those that serve the fingertips (somatic) and the pelvic organs (autonomic). *Pelvic pain* is an especially *complex* syndrome with many contributing factors. It can occur as the result of a variety of medical conditions such as *endometriosis* and injuries to various parts of our bodies (including organs and nerves in the periphery, spinal cord, and brain). Pelvic pain involves *psychosocial* and psychological contributors to pain. Pelvic pain can be short-lived or *acute*, such as from a recent surgery. In many instances, *acute pain* resolves after less than a week as the injured tissue heals. However, in certain instances, *chronic pain* develops. In other words, pain that might have started after a normal pain-producing event can persist beyond the time of normal healing. This is how chronic pain is defined.

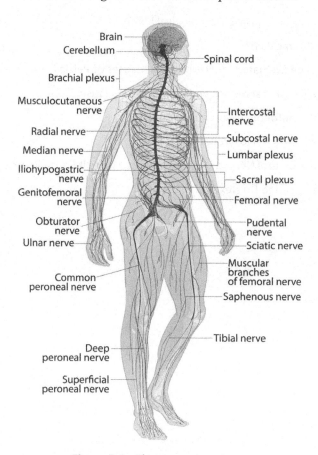

Figure 9-1: The nervous system.

What Is Chronic Pain?

Chronic pain is pain lasting longer than three to six months. Chronic pain can lead to actual *anatomical* and *physiological* changes in our nervous systems, the PNS (the nerves outside of our spinal cord and our brain) as well as the CNS (the spinal cord and brain). Because changes arise in your nervous system with chronic pain, chronic pain can affect all aspects of your life. *Chronic pelvic pain* (CPP) is especially challenging to diagnose and to treat completely. As your providers search for a primary cause of pelvic pain, you can also work with a team to provide treatments that make the pain as manageable as possible. This unified approach can restore quality of life, even without a named cause for the pain.

Pain can present in distinct peripheral nerve pathways. For example, a nerve injury or compression that results from trauma or pelvic or abdominal surgery (such as a *hysterectomy*, prostate surgery, uterine or bladder prolapse repair, bladder suspension, Caesarean section, *laparoscopy*, anal fissure repair, or inguinal hernia repair) can contribute to your pelvic pain. Recognizing peripheral nerve pathways and nerve injuries can guide treatment of acute pain and prevent chronic pain. New guidelines for pain management following surgical procedures emphasize the importance of proactively treating acute pain following procedures with a *multi-modal* (more than one treatment type) approach to help prevent acute pain from becoming chronic pain.

The onset of pain triggers mechanisms in our nervous systems to make our bodies more sensitive to pain. Think of how sensitive your ankle can be after an ankle sprain—this is a natural protective process that has been called *peripheral sensitization*. If the mechanisms of pain persist, chronic pain can arise as the result of a process known as *central sensitization* (see Chapter 19). This refers to the state in which the CNS responds to pain at a lower pain threshold than normal. This might sound counterintuitive. "Why should my nervous system respond to pain more easily, and why doesn't it know to stop the pain?" The truth is that the nervous system might respond to what it experiences in an overly adaptive manner and might try to facilitate the experience (even pain) if it becomes chronic. This is quite literally how some of us are wired!

How Can I Be Evaluated for Neurological Causes of Pelvic Pain?

The first step in the assessment of neurological conditions associated with pelvic pain is evaluation. This can begin with any of a variety of medical specialists from *primary care*, *urology*, *obstetrics/gynecology*, *neurology*, and pain management. The point is to undergo a thorough evaluation to identify neurological and organ-based (such as prostate or ovary) causes of the pain.

When a specialist assesses pelvic pain, he or she will ask about your "pain story" as well as your medical, surgical, and *psychosocial history*. Specialists can use a simple *mnemonic* (or memory aid), such as "OPQRST".

- **O—Onset:** When did the pain start? What was happening at that time?
  - Obtain a clear timeline as to when the pain started. For example, did the pain develop immediately after a surgical procedure? If so, this might indicate a peripheral nerve injury that might require another operation.
- **P—Palliative and provocative factors:** What makes the pain better or worse?
  - Include specific activities, treatments tried and their results, as well as pain with sexual activity, eating, or diet-induced factors.
- **Q—Quality:** Is the pain burning, sharp, shooting, stabbing, aching, throbbing, or spasmodic?
- **R—Region and radiation:** Where is the pain? Does it spread to other areas?
  - Illustrate on a diagram (Figure 9-2) where you feel your pain. This might lead to skin surface *(dermatomal)* clues to corresponding peripheral nerve injuries.
- **S—Severity:** How bad is the pain?
  - Rate the average, least, and worst pain score and its effect on function and *activities of daily living* (ADLs), such as dressing.
- **T—Timing:** When does the pain occur?
  - Has it changed since it began? If so, how? Does the pain arise with certain movements or activities, or is it constant?

The information obtained from these above questions helps the specialist focus on neurological causes and to complete an appropriate physical/neurological examination. Keep in mind that an examination is a crucial part of the assessment. It is often helpful for you to indicate on a diagram (see Figure 9-2) the areas that are painful and to note the severity of the pain (in the shaded location[s]). This information should correspond to what the provider knows about the nerves that serve these areas.

When you are being *evaluated* for neurological conditions associated with CPP, in addition to a pelvic and rectal examination, the physical exam might focus on:

- The specific area of your pain.
- A skin exam looking for surgical scars, evidence of nerve injury, or other lesions. Areas of nerve injury might feel numb, even if painful, and surprisingly, after the injury of a peripheral nerve, the involved area might become more sensitive rather than dulled. Pain that occurs with a normally non-painful sensation (such as touching) is known as *allodynia*. When **more** pain than normal results from a painful sensation, *hyperalgesia* is diagnosed.
- Reflexes (including reflexes of the *penis*, clitoris, or anal sphincter).

Chapter 9: Which Neurological Problems Can Lead to Pelvic Pain? 129

- A *musculoskeletal* exam with an emphasis on the hips and back and the *muscles* of the abdomen and pelvis, which may also be contributors to pelvic pain (Gyang et al, 2013). Tightened muscles related to *myofascial dysfunction* (areas of *trigger points*) are commonly noted because of nerve injury.

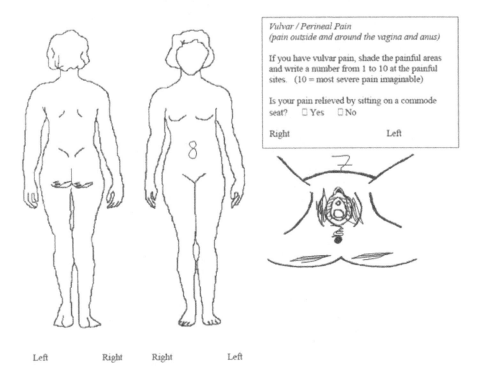

Figure 9-2: Example of a pain diagram completed by a patient demonstrating both the painful areas and the pain score from 1 to 10. © April 2008, The International Pelvic Pain Society.

What Are Peripheral Nerves and How Do They Cause Pain?

Peripheral nerves can be implicated in pelvic pain and provide clues to management. Single nerves that service a body part can be compressed (such as via an *inguinal* or *obturator hernia*, or compression that can be caused by riding a bicycle) or injured (such as during gynecologic surgery or childbirth). Descriptions of peripheral nerves, as well as their distributions, are presented in Table 9-1 as well as Figures 9-3, 9-4, and 9-5. The skin *innervated* by peripheral nerves are named *dermatomes*, and the sets of muscles controlled by nerves are called *myotomes*.

Table 9-1: Peripheral Nerves of the Pelvis and Typical Associated Pain Patterns

Peripheral Nerve	Area or Pattern of Pain
Ilioinguinal nerve	Pain, numbness and/or allodynia* on the groin and/or lateral waist with or without radiation to vulva, penis, or scrotum.
Iliohypogastric nerve	Pain, numbness, or allodynia in the lower abdominal wall or pubic region, sometimes hip and lateral thigh.
Genitofemoral nerve	Pain, numbness and/or allodynia on the groin, urethra, clitoris, anterior vulva in females; in males, symptoms are felt on the groin/crotch, scrotum, and base of the penis.
Obturator nerve	Pain, numbness and/or allodynia on the inner thigh. Also, can cause some hip instability.
Anterior abdominal cutaneous nerves	Pin-point abdominal pain, often lateral to the rectus sheath (Applegate, 2002).
Pudendal nerve (rectal, perineal, vaginal, scrotal/penile branches)	Pain, numbness and/or allodynia on the *anus*, vulva/scrotum, penis, and perineum. Usually associated urinary and bowel urgency and frequency, pain on passing urine or stool. Genital arousal disorders, erectile dysfunction, and/or lack of vaginal lubrication may be present. May be described as knife-like pain or like a foreign-body sensation in the rectum, vagina, or perineum as well as an inability to sit; pain is often relieved by lying down. The Nantes Criteria is used as a diagnostic tool for pudendal nerve pain, also known as *pudendal neuralgia* (Labat Riant and Robert, 2008).
Lateral femoral cutaneous nerve	Pain and numbness of the lateral thigh is seen more frequently in those with obesity, wearing tight pants or belts, or with impingement secondary to prolonged hip flexion.
Sciatic nerve	Pain and numbness or allodynia on the buttocks, going down the back of the thigh, calf, and leg, to the sole of the foot. Sciatic *nerve entrapments* can cause difficulties walking and a foot drop.
S1 nerve root	Pain and numbness on the *external* aspect of the posterior thigh, calf, and leg and the exterior aspect of the foot. S1 nerve root entrapments can cause gait disturbances and loss of ankle stability.
S2 nerve root	Pain and numbness on the internal half of the posterior thigh, calf, and leg; internal surface of the foot; the vulva and clitoris (female); and penis and scrotum (male). Usually associated with urinary urgency and frequency. Genital arousal disorders, erectile dysfunction, and/or lack of vaginal lubrication might be present.
S3/4 nerve root (usually entrapped together because of proximity)	Pain and numbness on the buttock, anus, perineum, vulva, and clitoris (female), and penis and scrotum (male). Usually associated urinary and bowel urgency and frequency, pain on passing urine or stool. Often associated with vaginal and/or rectal foreign-body sensation.
Posterior femoral cutaneous nerve and *inferior cluneal nerves*	Inferior gluteal (buttocks) pain.

*Allodynia is when a stimulus that is usually sensed as gentle/subtle is perceived as a painful/unpleasant sensation; for example, underwear touching the skin or the touch of a cotton swab can be perceived as scratching, burning, or shocking.

Chapter 9: Which Neurological Problems Can Lead to Pelvic Pain? 131

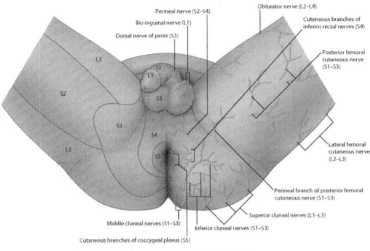

Dermatomes and cutaneous nerves of perineum in men

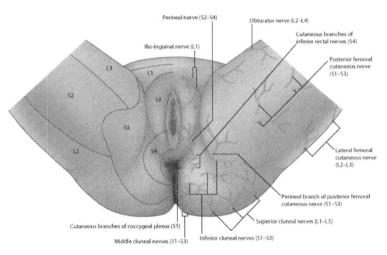

Dermatomes and cutaneous nerves of perineum in women

Figure 9-3: The distribution of select nerves of the pelvis that can contribute to chronic pain. (Reproduced with permission: Drake RL, Vogl AW, Mitchell A, eds.: Dermatomes and cutaneous nerves of perineum in men. Dermatomes and cutaneous nerves of perineum in women. In: Gray's Atlas of Anatomy. Philadelphia, PA: Elsevier Limited. 2021; 213–292.)

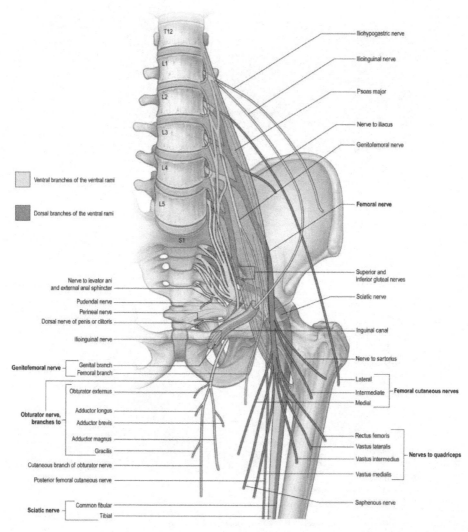

Figure 9-4: The pathways of individual nerves (the ilioinguinal, pudendal, obturator, and genitofemoral nerves) are demonstrated in an anatomical drawing of the pelvis. One can imagine how pelvic surgery might occur close to these nerves. (Reproduced with permission: Standring S, ed.: Figure 62.15. The lumbar plexus and its branches. In: Gray's Atlas of Anatomy. *The Anatomical Basis of Clinical Practice*. 41st ed. Philadelphia, PA: Elsevier, Limited. 2016; 1083–1097.e2.)

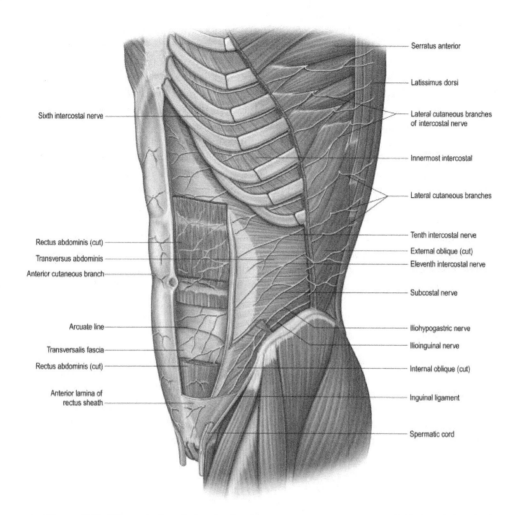

Figure 9-5: The anterior abdominal cutaneous nerves can cause pinpoint abdominal pain, which is often felt along the outer edge of the rectus sheath (the 6-pack muscles in the middle of the abdomen). Surgical incisions can be located in the paths of these nerves. (Reproduced with permission: Standring S, ed.: Figure 61.5. The cutaneous branches of the lower intercostal and lumbar nerves. In: Gray's Atlas of Anatomy. *The Anatomical Basis of Clinical Practice*. 41st ed Philadelphia, PA: Elsevier Limited. 2015; 1069–1082.e2.)

Peripheral nerves can be injured during peri-operative positioning because when anesthetized, you cannot feel discomfort and move when a bent leg or leg leaning against a support bothers you. Compression injuries include those to the nerves that innervate the lower extremity, such as the femoral, tibial, peroneal, and sciatic nerves. Lastly, you might hear the term *radiculopathy*, which refers to irritation or injury of a *nerve root* emanating from the spinal cord that can cause pain, numbness, or weakness in a specific distribution.

Although commonly believed to cause CPP, nerve entrapments usually cause pudendal, gluteal, or sciatic pain, as can be understood from the figures earlier in this chapter. Pelvic pain is usually a secondary complaint and is most often caused by pelvic floor muscle dysfunction because these muscles are innervated by some of these nerves. The only nerve entrapments that will primarily cause CPP are the ilioinguinal and iliohypogastric nerve entrapments, which will cause pain on only one side of the pelvis.

Understanding the nerve supply of the abdominal wall and pelvis provides diagnostic clues and treatment targets. Interventional approaches that target the suspected nerves, such as peripheral *nerve blocks* (injecting a numbing medication with or without an *anti-inflammatory* medication), can aid in the diagnosis and provide symptomatic relief. Post-operatively, if a nerve might have been sutured in a fixed location, early removal of the suture can take place.

What Is the Autonomic Nervous System?

The nerves discussed so far in the chapter are considered part of the *somatic nervous system*, which involves mainly external perceptions (from the skin, muscles, and so on). The *autonomic* or *visceral nervous system* (Figure 9-6) involves *sympathetic* and *parasympathetic nerves*, which sense internal conditions (such as pressure in the blood vessels, airways, bladder, or digestive tract). The *enteric nervous system* serves the *gastrointestinal* (GI) and is part of the autonomic nervous system but has some independence from the sympathetic and parasympathetic nerves.

What Is a Peripheral Neuropathy?

A *peripheral neuropathy* (Figure 9-7) is not a single disease (Foundation for Peripheral Neuropathy, 2019). It is a general term used for a series of disorders that result from damage to the peripheral nervous system (PNS), as can occur with *diabetes*, for instance. Typically, peripheral neuropathy refers to a diffuse set of somatic and autonomic nerve endings, rather than injury to the central nervous system (CNS) or a specific peripheral nerve (Figures 9-6 and 9-7).

Chapter 9: Which Neurological Problems Can Lead to Pelvic Pain? 135

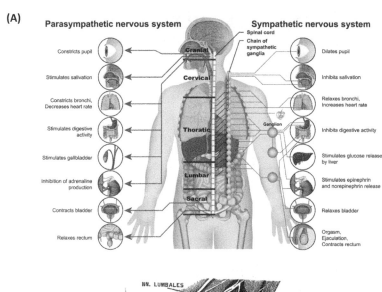

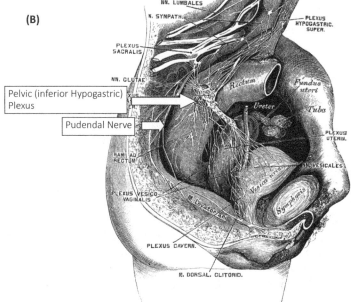

Figure 9-6 (A) and (B): The autonomic or visceral nervous system involves sympathetic and parasympathetic nerves, which sense internal conditions (such as pressure in the blood vessels, airways, bladder, or digestive tract). The delicate autonomic (organ-based) nerves of the pelvis that converge in the pelvic (inferior hypogastric) plexus can be affected by surgery or peripheral neuropathy. Also pictured here are the pudendal nerve and the levator ani muscle.

PERIPHERAL NEUROPATHY
NERVE DAMAGE

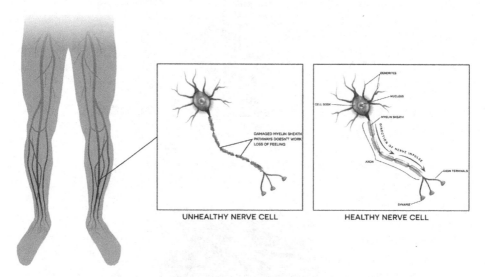

Figure 9-7: Schematic of peripheral nerve damage.

A peripheral neuropathy of certain nerves, called *small fiber polyneuropathy* (SFPN), can be associated with *complex pelvic pain* (non-resolving pain or pain in multiple systems within the body). SFPN occurs when specific, small-diameter nerve fibers of the PNS are damaged. A major function of these fibers is to relay pain information. When they are damaged and/or malfunctioning, abnormalities of sensation, such as increased pain, can arise. This can affect somatic nerves, making them more sensitive to pain. Because the autonomic nervous system also has small-diameter fibers and serves the bladder, bowel, and blood vessels, difficulty with bowel and bladder function frequently develops. In one study, nearly two-thirds of people who presented to a pelvic health center experienced complex CPP and a SFPN (Chen et al, 2018). Many of those who were diagnosed with complex pelvic pain and SFPN had other chronic pains, such as *migraine headache, irritable bowel syndrome* (IBS), and *fibromyalgia*. The observation that many people with complex pelvic pain are experiencing SFPN might lead to a new understanding of CPP and assist in the development of new treatments. Causes of SFPN include diabetes, untreated *thyroid disease, Lyme disease, sarcoidosis, systemic lupus erythematosus* (SLE), vitamin B_{12} *deficiency, amyloidosis,* some genetic disorders, and certain medications (including *chemotherapeutic* agents). Some causes of SFPN are reversible, such as gluten allergy. If you think you might have SFPN, talk to your doctor about seeing a *neurologist* for evaluation, including a possible skin biopsy and autonomic nerve testing to evaluate the small nerve fibers.

What Is the Central Nervous System and How Does It Cause Pain?

The CNS is made up of the brain and the spinal cord (Figure 9-1) and coordinates the activities of the entire nervous system you read about above. Specific neurologic causes of CPP following injury to the CNS can be difficult to determine, but in one study, approximately one-fourth of people had CPP following a spinal cord injury (Modirian et al, 2010). Less is known about CPP that follows injury to the brain. Increased muscle tone *(spasticity)* is also common following spinal cord injury, and this can be associated with pelvic pain.

Your pelvic pain providers might not have considered a CNS cause for your pain. If you have any of the following symptoms or physical exam findings (Table 9-2), you might want to discuss this possibility with a specialist. In some cases, he or she might consider radiologic imaging to evaluate other diagnoses.

Table 9-2: Relationship Among Signs, Symptoms, and Neurologic Injuries

Spine Diagnosis	Symptoms	Physical Exam Finding
Herniated disc—Occurs when a spinal disc protrudes and causes nerve compression, irritation, or a radiculopathy of a spinal nerve root.	Back pain, shooting pain, numbness that follows a specific dermatomal pattern (for example, a T10 through L1 disc herniation can *radiate* into the skin of the groin or abdomen); or sciatic symptoms in the leg. Persistent genital arousal disorder has also been attributed to the *spine*.	Abnormal gait, pain with provocative maneuvers (such as pain with low back flexion; positive straight leg test that radiates pain with spine range of motion); and possible increased or decreased reflexes.
Tarlov cysts—Fluid-filled nerve root cysts found most often at the sacral level of the spine; small cysts can be a normal variant and are present in 5%–10% of people.	Symptoms vary but can present with pain over the buttocks and sacrum or with bowel, bladder, or sexual dysfunction.	Pain with sitting, standing, or walking; might have increased sensitivity or loss of sensitivity to touch over the sacrum and buttock; and might present with lower extremity weakness.
Spina bifida occulta—Occulta means "hidden." This occurs when the spine does not fully form in a developing fetus and there is a gap in the spine, usually discovered when the spine is imaged. More severe versions of spina bifida exist with exposed membranes over the lower spine at birth.	The mild forms of spina bifida occulta can be *asymptomatic* but might cause lower extremity symptoms, including weakness, as well as urinary, sexual, or bowel symptoms, pelvic pain, and impaired sensation of the genitals, bladder, or bowels. Sometimes, symptoms begin during growth spurts because of associated *tethered spinal cord*.	Might present with lower extremity weakness, and the skin over the spine might present with an abnormal tuft of hair, dimple, or birthmark.

continued

Spine Diagnosis	Symptoms	Physical Exam Finding
Tethered spinal cord—Caused by tissue attachments that limit the movement of the spinal cord within the spinal column; these attachments cause an abnormal stretching of the spinal cord; associated with spina bifida.	Back pain or shooting pain in the legs; weakness or numbness in the legs; lower extremity spasms; and bowel or bladder dysfunction (over or underactive).	Lower extremity weakness, abnormally low or high reflexes, and diminished lower extremity sensation.
Cauda equina syndrome—caused by central spine nerve compression, such as stenosis in the lumbar region from a large herniated disc (or tumor).	Symptoms might include severe lower extremity weakness and/or pain; decreased sensation in the legs and/or the lower pelvic region (*"saddle anesthesia"*); new-onset difficulty urinating or sudden *urinary incontinence*; and sudden stool incontinence. If the above symptoms are sudden, they might require emergency care.	Lower-extremity weakness or reduced or absent reflexes in the legs.
Sacral tumor—Benign (non-cancerous) or malignant (cancerous) growths around the sacral nerve roots.	Might present with symptoms similar to Tarlov cysts and herniated discs, such as back pain, lower extremity pain, lower extremity weakness, numbness or tingling, rectal dysfunction, urinary retention or incontinence, or erectile dysfunction. If the symptoms have arisen quickly, timely evaluation is required.	Might present with tenderness over the sacrum or lower extremity weakness. A mass might be felt in the sacral area.

An expedited MRI scan of the lower spine should be considered if you have the following symptoms or findings:

- New or rapid-onset lower extremity weakness or severe lower extremity pain
- Sudden onset of numbness, urinary retention or incontinence, or stool incontinence

Brain Diagnoses

The brain is part of the CNS and is always involved in any kind of pain. When one has prolonged or chronic pain, the brain must process that information; central sensitization can be one outcome of that processing, leading to amplification of pain.

Central sensitization can be thought of as though your pain perception "volume control setting" is turned up too high. A person without chronic pain would interpret the same *pain signal* at a lower "volume" setting. Chapter 19 discusses pain processing—and how to improve it—in more detail.

What Do I Need to Do Next?

In summary, a stepwise approach to the diagnosis and treatment of neurological conditions associated with CPP begins with a pain history and physical/neurologic exam. Based on this foundation, your provider will help you choose among multimodal pain management strategies:

- Observe over time.
- Engage in standard physical therapy or pelvic physical therapy (internal pelvic and external abdominal wall myofascial treatment, nerve desensitization, education).
- Employ standard behavioral-medicine strategies (with a focus on coping skills, *cognitive-behavioral therapy* (CBT), *meditation, mindfulness techniques*, and treatment of *depression* and anxiety).
- Consider use of medications:
  - Oral medications that can help decrease nerve pain, such as *tricyclic antidepressants* (TCAs)—for example, amitriptyline or *nortriptyline*, serotonin-norepinephrine reuptake inhibitors (SNRIs), *duloxetine*, and anti-seizure medications (such as gabapentin or pregabalin).
  - Oral medications (such as *tizanidine*, cyclobenzaprine, or baclofen) that can relax muscles and reduce pain associated with *muscle spasm*.
  - Topical medications, such as those that can be applied to the skin (lidocaine 5% ointment, lidoderm patches, and pelvic floor muscle relaxants) or rectally administered agents like suppositories.
  - Intravenous (through a vein) medications, such as lidocaine.
- Consider alternative treatments, such as:
  - Appropriate use of meditation and relaxation.
  - Anti-inflammatory foods and *supplements*.
  - Heat (or limited ice).
  - Specialized cushions to relieve pudendal nerve compression.
  - Support groups and education.
  - Massage, *acupuncture*, and chiropractic manipulation.
- Testing:
  - Blood tests to assess for systemic medical conditions associated with pelvic pain and more widespread pain, such as autoimmune and infectious conditions.
  - Electromyography to assess for nerve response (Figure 9-8).

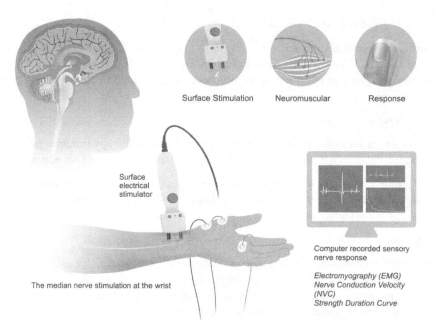

Figure 9-8: Electromyography can help determine if a peripheral nerve is functioning normally.

- Imaging (MRI, CT scan, ultrasound, and X-rays) to assess for specific neurological conditions that can cause pelvic pain.
- Recognize possible peripheral nerve insults and neural pathways and consider:
  - Surgical revision if there is an acute post-surgical injury.
  - Diagnostic peripheral nerve blocks, if appropriate, such as frequently performed by a pain management specialist or interventionalist) to guide the diagnostic work-up and provide therapeutic relief. For diagnostic purposes, a small amount of local anesthetic (such as bupivacaine 0.25% or lidocaine 1%–2%) can be injected at the target nerve, like what your dentist would use to numb your gums. Relief can last for the local anesthetic's duration of action (for example, one or more hours), but the duration of relief can also be quite variable and pain reduction might persist beyond this period (perhaps explained by muscle spasm release or "nerve reset"). If duration of relief is brief with local anesthetic alone, a local anesthetic with a *steroid* can be injected to possibly prolong relief. Frequent repeat injections of steroids can lead to systemic side effects, muscle or tendon breakdown, or infection; therefore, the total steroid dose should be monitored and limited.

- Stimulators and pain pumps:
  - Spinal cord or peripheral nerve electrical stimulation.
  - Placement of an internal medication pump to more directly provide medication for pain relief.
- Consider SFPN and central sensitization of pain when CPP does not resolve with conservative measures or when multiple pain syndromes exist (such as *trigeminal neuralgia*, heartburn, and foot sensitivity).

Conclusion

Recognizing peripheral nerve injuries and therapeutic targets may have a profound impact on decreasing pain and improving function, allowing for a meaningful recovery. Finding a CNS cause of pain, such as a tethered spinal cord, allows the opportunity to prevent worsening of neurologic function along with treatment of pain with surgery. A stepwise approach to diagnosis and treatment of pelvic pain can guide management. If the above approaches do not succeed and specific nerve problems are not identified, other nerve-based contributors can be explored (such as central sensitization, SFPN, systemic neurologic, rheumatologic, or psychologic disorders). A team-based, multi-modal approach to improve your function will best help manage any complexities to your pain.

WHAT ARE RHEUMATOLOGIC, NEUROINFLAMMATORY, AND VASCULAR PAIN?

Miriam M. Shao, BS; Ruben Peredo-Wende, MD; Charles Argoff, MD; Joseph D. Raffetto, MD; and Jan Alberto Peredes Mogica

CHAPTER

In This Chapter

- Introduction
- What Is Rheumatologic Disease?
- What Are the Symptoms of Rheumatologic Diseases?
- Which Rheumatologic Diseases Can Cause Pelvic Pain?
- What Other Rheumatologic Conditions Are Often Associated with Pelvic Pain?
- What Tests Can Be Done to Diagnose Rheumatologic Disease?
- How Are Rheumatologic Diseases Treated?
- What Are Neuroinflammatory Conditions and How Do They Affect Pelvic Pain?
- How Can Blood Vessels Cause Pelvic Pain?
- What Might Suggest Pelvic Venous Disease?
- How Are Pelvic Venous Disorders Treated?
- What Is Vasculitis and How Does It Cause Pelvic Pain?
- How Would I Know If I Have a Type of Vasculitis?
- What Is Ischemic Pelvic Disease?
- How Would I Know If I Have an Ischemic Vascular Condition?
- Conclusion

Introduction

This chapter discusses a mix of diagnoses, such as *systemic diseases* that affect *inflammation*, *nerves*, and the blood supply to the pelvic structures, as well as specific anatomic diseases of the blood vessels to the pelvis, that are all less commonly considered when *pelvic pain* is addressed.

What Is Rheumatologic Disease?

Rheumatologic disease refers to medical conditions of the joints, *muscles*, ligaments, and tendons, such as *arthritis* or systemic lupus erythematosus (SLE) or lupus. Most rheumatologic diseases present with pain caused by inflammation. Inflammation refers to processes in which your immune system responds to any perceived irritant or harmful substance. Inflammation can facilitate the repair and healing of damaged tissue from irritants (such as harmful chemicals, disease-causing *bacteria*, viruses, fungi), and physical injuries (such as a scraped knee or sprained ankle).

Inflammation associated with rheumatologic disease is usually low-grade and persistent. Often, abnormal inflammation is facilitated by an *autoimmune disease processes* in which the body's own cells are perceived as foreign irritants and are therefore attacked by the *immune system*. As a result, the inflammation associated with rheumatologic disease can cause significant harm to the body in the form of a variety of medical conditions.

What Are the Symptoms of Rheumatologic Diseases?

Because the joints, muscles, ligaments, and tendons affected by rheumatologic disease are present throughout the body, rheumatologic disease can be manifest in different ways. *Symptoms* include fever, weight loss, and fatigue. However, localized *signs* of inflammation, such as swelling, redness, heat, loss of function, and/or pain, can occur in any body part. Rheumatologic disease can present as pelvic pain when the joints, musculature, and other components of the pelvis are involved. In the context of pelvic pain, symptoms that differentiate rheumatologic disease from other conditions include pain that occurs at night, alternates between the *gluteus* (buttock) muscles, improves with activity throughout the day, and is relieved with *non-steroidal anti-inflammatory drugs* (NSAIDs). Morning pelvic stiffness that lasts more than one hour also suggests rheumatologic disease.

Which Rheumatologic Diseases Can Cause Pelvic Pain?

Common rheumatologic diseases include *osteoarthritis* (OA), *rheumatoid arthritis* (RA), systemic lupus erythematous (SLE, "Lupus"), *Sjögren's syndrome, scleroderma*, a group of diseases known as *seronegative spondyloarthritis*, and crystal-associated arthritides, such as *gout*.

OA and RA are common forms of arthritis, which involve inflammation of joints and tissue surrounding the joints. OA is the most common type of arthritis; it is caused by joint degeneration from mechanical wear and tear that accumulates over years. Risk factors for

OA include increased age, prior injury to the affected joint, and *obesity*. Because OA results from mechanical degeneration rather than an autoimmune disease process, its symptoms present differently from other rheumatologic diseases. Pain in OA occurs at the end of the day and improves with rest, and OA is not associated with fever, weight loss, or fatigue.

RA (Figure 10-1) is another form of arthritis, but it is a body-wide autoimmune disorder in which the tissue that lines the joints, also known as the *synovium*, is attacked by the immune system. Blood tests called *rheumatoid factor* (RF) and *antinuclear antibodies* (ANA) are elevated in this diagnosis. It is known to present with many other signs and symptoms other than joint pain. These include lung disease and *rheumatoid nodules*, which are firm lumps that form beneath the skin.

Other autoimmune disorders (affecting the whole body) associated with joint pain include SLE, scleroderma, and Sjögren's syndrome. Rheumatoid factor and ANA can be elevated in these conditions.

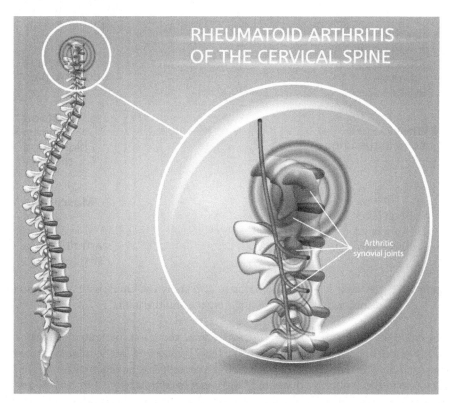

Figure 10-1: Rheumatoid arthritis affects the lining of the joints, called the synovium, as well as other areas of the body.

Systemic lupus erythematous (SLE) (Figure 10-2) is commonly associated with fever, joint pain, and a red "butterfly" facial rash, which you may hear referred to as a *malar rash*. Other symptoms include sensitivity to light, *kidney* dysfunction, neurologic dysfunction in the form of seizures and/or mood disorders, mouth ulcers (that are generally painless), and inflammation of the membranes that line the heart and lungs.

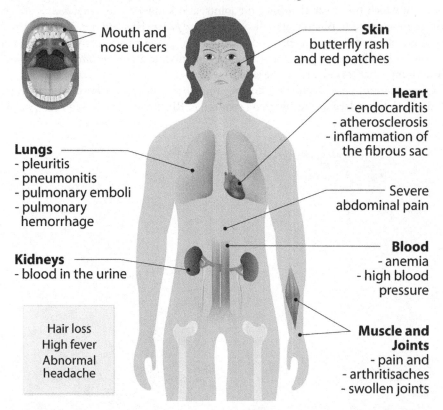

Figure 10-2: Systemic lupus erythematosus, also known as lupus, is an autoimmune disorder that affects multiple organs and the joints.

Scleroderma (Figure 10-3) affects *connective tissue* and results in tightening of the skin, especially of the fingers. It happens when the body is triggered by the immune system to produce and deposit too much *collagen*, which is a protein that provides structural support and is found in the connective tissue and skin; it is related to scarring. Other symptoms of scleroderma include kidney dysfunction, lung disease, difficulty swallowing (from esophageal [throat] dysfunction), red, thread-like lines in the skin from dilated blood vessels, and *Raynaud's phenomenon*. In Raynaud's phenomenon, the fingertips and/or toes change in color from white to blue and then to red in cold temperatures (or stress). These color changes occur as a result of blood vessel constriction, which results in painful decreased blood flow to the skin.

Chapter 10: What Are Rheumatologic, Neuroinflammatory, and Vascular Pain? 147

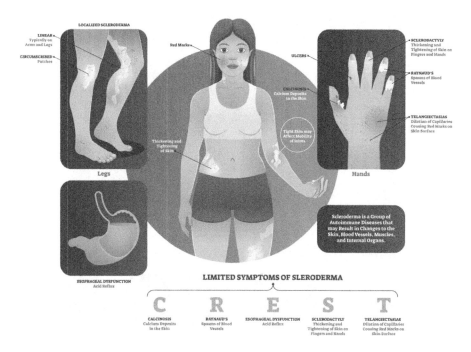

Figure 10-3: Scleroderma affects connective tissue (collagen) throughout the body and can cause tightening of the skin of the hands.

Sjögren's syndrome refers to autoimmune destruction of the *lacrimal* and *salivary glands*, which are responsible for producing tears and saliva, respectively. In this disorder, the immune system can also attack joints, the thyroid gland, kidneys, liver, lungs, skin, and nerves. In addition to dry eyes and mouth, symptoms can be present in any of these organs. Vaginal dryness is common, as is nerve pain *(neuropathy)*, both of which can affect pelvic pain (see Figure 10-4).

Seronegative spondyloarthritis refers to the following diseases: *ankylosing spondylitis, psoriatic arthritis, enteropathic spondyloarthritis, reactive arthritis (Reiter's syndrome), axial,* and *peripheral spondyloarthritis*. These are a family of rheumatologic diseases that cause arthritis and are distinguished from other arthritic diseases because they involve inflammation of the location where ligaments and tendons attach to *bones*. They are called "seronegative" because the blood *(serum)* tests are negative for rheumatoid factor and ANA.

Ankylosing spondylitis (Figure 10-5), the most common of these, refers to arthritis involving the *spine*. The conditions are all associated with lower back pain, peripheral arthritis, *enthesitis, dactylitis,* and *uveitis*. (Enthesitis, dactylitis, and *uveitis* refer to inflammation of the tendon insertion sites, fingers, and eye membrane, in that order.)

Psoriatic arthritis commonly presents with dactylitis and *psoriasis* (which appears as red, itchy, and scaly skin patches). It often affects the hands and spine.

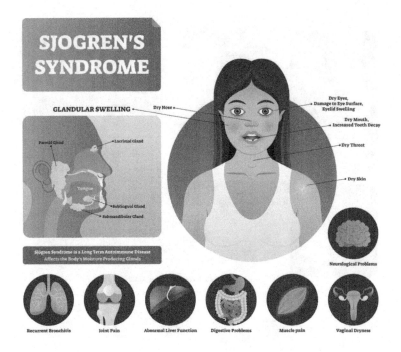

Figure 10-4: Sjögren's syndrome can affect glands, joints, organs, and nerves, and it is known for dry eyes and mouth.

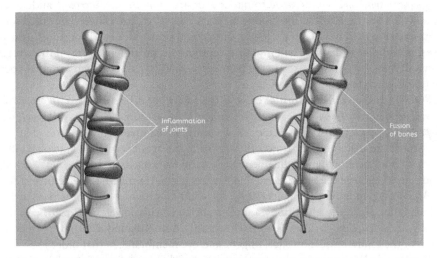

Figure 10-5: Ankylosing spondylitis is the most common of the seronegative spondyloarthritis family and involves inflammation of the connective tissue of the spine.

Enteropathic spondyloarthritis occurs with *inflammatory bowel diseases* (IBD), which are comprised of *Crohn's disease* and *ulcerative colitis* (UC). Along with lower back and pelvic pain, IBD presents with inflammation of the *gastrointestinal* (GI) *tract*, diarrhea, rash, eye inflammation, and kidney stones.

Reiter's syndrome is a *reactive arthritis*, which is usually triggered by a bacterial infection. It presents with a classical triad of inflammation in the eyes, joints, and urethra (the channel from which urine is expelled from the bladder). Signs and symptoms of urethritis include painful urination, blood in the urine, and a feeling of needing to urinate more frequently.

Axial spondyloarthritis is the seronegative spondyloarthritis that is very commonly associated with pelvic pain. Disease in the *sacroiliac joint* (SIJ), spine, and pelvis is the hallmark of axial spondyloarthritis. The SIJ is part of the pelvis, and it is the point in which the spine connects to the left and right pelvic bones, where the lowest part of your back contacts a chair. The most common symptoms include chronic pain and stiffness, predominantly involving the pelvis and lower back; this chronic pain and stiffness improves with exercise. Other common symptoms include enthesitis (inflammation of the tendon insertion sites where the tendons attach to the bones), arthritis in limb joints, and eye inflammation. Axial spondyloarthritis usually starts in the third decade of life, and unlike most other rheumatologic diseases, it affects predominantly men (Sieper and Poddubnyy, 2017).

Peripheral spondyloarthritis affects mostly the arms and legs. This might lead to pelvic pain if a gait abnormality led to *pelvic floor muscle* (PFM) tension.

Gout is a crystal-induced arthritis that can present with hip pain. In gout, pain occurs after high levels of uric acid concentrate in the blood and form crystals in the joints. High uric acid levels result from certain medications, such as thiazide diuretics, as well as from a diet that is rich in red meat, alcohol, and seafood. Other risk factors include obesity, *hypertension (high blood pressure)*, *diabetes*, and being born male.

What Other Rheumatologic Conditions Are Often Associated with Pelvic Pain?

Other rheumatologic conditions that often present with pelvic pain include *Schnitzler syndrome*, *polymyalgia rheumatica* (PMR), *synovitis acne periostitis hyperostosis and osteitis* (SAPHO), *osteitis condensans ilii*, and *bursitis*.

Schnitzler syndrome often presents with *hives* (big flat rashes), joint pain, fever, and enlarged *lymph nodes*. Lymph nodes are glands that are found throughout the body and contain important components of the immune system that ward off infection. On a *molecular level*, Schnitzler syndrome is associated with *monoclonal gammopathy*. Monoclonal gammopathy refers to the dysfunctional overproduction of *antibodies*. Antibodies are important protein products of the immune system that aid in recognizing irritants as foreign and targeting them for attack by the immune system. Complications of monoclonal gammopathy include *amyloidosis* (Gellrich and Gunther, 2019). Amyloidosis refers to the deposition of abnormally formed proteins throughout the body; such protein deposition often leads to dysfunction in the kidneys and heart but can also cause nerve pain from neuropathy.

Polymyalgia rheumatica (Figure 10-6) is common among the elderly, and it often presents with another disease called *giant cell arteritis* (GCA). Polymyalgia rheumatica presents with pain and stiffness in the pelvis and shoulders (and therefore, pelvic pain), as well as fever and weight loss. Fortunately, polymyalgia rheumatica does not usually cause muscle weakness, but the stiffness may lead to difficulty rising from a chair. Symptoms of GCA include headache, jaw pain, and difficulty chewing (Camellino et al, 2019). CGA can lead to vision loss due to loss of blood flow to the optic nerve and therefore is a medical emergency.

Synovitis acne periostitis hyperostosis and osteitis (SAPHO) often presents between the third and fifth decades of life, but it can occur at any age. This syndrome includes five different entities: synovitis (inflammation of the joint lining), acne (blemishes that occur when dead skin cells and oil from the skin clog hair follicles), pustulosis (blister-like inflammation of the skin), hyperostosis (excessive growth of bone), and osteitis (inflammation of bone). It presents with joint pain and a variety of skin lesions, such as *acne*. The joint pain in SAPHO is primarily of the central skeleton and pelvis rather than the extremities (Rukavina, 2015) and can cause pelvic pain.

Osteitis condensans ilii also commonly presents with *chronic pelvic pain* (CPP) and low back pain. It is thought to result from mechanical stress across the pelvic joints causing inflammation and usually presents in women before and/or after childbirth. Fortunately, the condition is self-limiting and resolves on its own (Biswas et al, 2019).

Bursitis refers to inflammation of the *bursa*, which are fluid-filled sacs that line joints of the entire body to provide cushioning and minimize friction across joints. Bursitis can present as pelvic pain if bursas of the pelvic joints are involved.

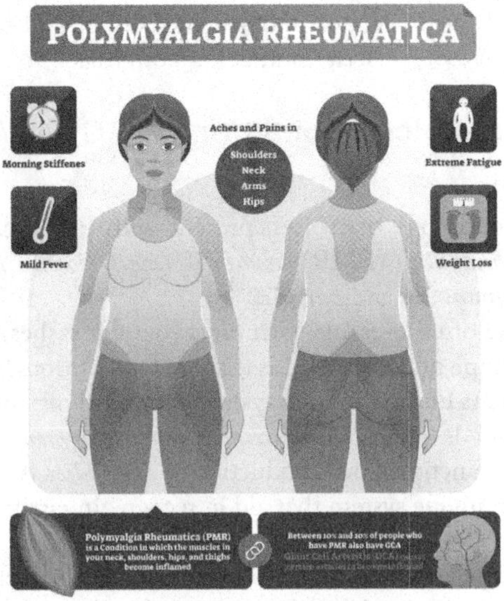

Figure 10-6: Polymyalgia rheumatica involves inflammation of the muscles of the shoulders, neck, hips, and thighs, therefore, someone with polymyalgia rheumatica might have stiffness causing trouble getting up from a chair.

What Tests Can Be Done to Diagnose Rheumatologic Disease?

For rheumatologic conditions, health care providers often rely on your presenting symptoms and the history of your condition to help them make a diagnosis. Therefore, you might be asked many questions to determine if your pain improves throughout the day with exercise, if you have pain at night, and if your pain is relieved by NSAIDs; these three categories increase the chance that your pelvic pain is rheumatologic. Blood tests can also aid in the diagnosis. Because rheumatologic conditions involve inflammation, elevations in markers of increased inflammation, such as *erythrocyte sedimentation rate* (ESR) and *C-reactive protein* (CRP), suggest rheumatologic involvement. Blood tests that are positive for *HLA-B27* (a protein that might be present on the surface of *white blood cells* [WBCs], which are important components of the immune system) suggest seronegative spondyloarthritis. High levels of a certain type of *antibody* suggest monoclonal gammopathy and point toward Schnitzler syndrome. For ankylosing spondyloarthritis, imaging with *magnetic resonance imaging* (MRI) scan is especially helpful in diagnosing the disease (Braun et al, 2018). Often, ankylosing spondyloarthritis appears on an MRI scan as bone erosions in the pelvic and spinal joints. Although MRI scans are useful, they can still fail to visualize ankylosing spondyloarthritis. Therefore, your doctor may still diagnose you with ankylosing spondyloarthritis even with a negative MRI scan.

How Are Rheumatologic Diseases Treated?

Treatment for rheumatologic diseases is largely centered around decreasing inflammation. Therefore, people with rheumatologic diseases are often treated with *anti-inflammatory* medications, such as NSAIDs and *corticosteroids*. Because rheumatologic conditions involve dysfunction in the immune system, *immunomodulators* (medications that control the immune system) such as *blockers of interleukin-1* (IL-1), *interleukin-17* (IL-17), and *tumor necrosis factor-alpha* (TNF-α) have also been used. IL-1, IL-17, and TNF-α are proteins that facilitate inflammation; they do this by binding to receptors on cell surfaces and by activating *cell signaling pathways* that lead to inflammation. IL-1 and IL-17 blockers are medications that bind to the cell surface receptors for IL-1 and IL-17; this prevents them from activating cell signaling pathways for inflammation. TNF-α blockers bind to the TNF-α protein itself and prevent it from connecting to cell-surface receptors. IL-1, IL-17, and TNF-α blockers are synthesized in the lab and are modeled after proteins that naturally exist in the human body, functioning to thwart inflammation cell signaling pathways. IL-17 and IL-1 blockers have proven to be especially helpful for ankylosing spondyloarthritis and Schnitzler syndrome, respectively (Tahir, 2018).

What Are Neuroinflammatory Conditions and How Do They Affect Pelvic Pain?

Neuro-inflammation can be defined as inflammation of the nervous tissue, especially within the brain or spinal cord, also known as the *central nervous system* (CNS). This inflammation can occur secondary to nerve injury, infection, trauma, autoimmune disorders, or toxic agents (DiSabato et al, 2016; Ji et al, 2018; Crean and Tirupathi, 2019). The *peripheral nervous system* (PNS)—the nervous structures outside the CNS—also can be affected.

Neurons are the primary cells within the nervous system, and they transmit electrical and chemical signals via projections of their own body called *axons*. Axons communicate by forming *synapses* with other neurons, muscle fibers, and a range of different structures. The *neuromuscular junction* is where the communication between a neuron's axons and the target muscle takes place (Rutkove, 2018).

Among the most common diseases that affect neurons and/or axons are: *multiple sclerosis* (Figure 10-7); *sensory neuropathies*, such as *diabetic neuropathy* (Figure 10-8); *toxic neuropathies* (secondary to use of *chemotherapeutic agents*, such as platinum, taxans, bortezomib, and vinca alkaloids); nutritional deficiencies (such as *vitamin B_{12} deficiency*); and *chronic demyelinating neuropathies* (CIDP) and infections (such as *cranial nerve palsy* due to *Lyme disease*). The neuromuscular junction can also be affected: *Myasthenia gravis* and *Lambert Eaton Syndrome* are diseases that affect this functional structure (Rutkove, 2018).

Chronic pain, including CPP, from these conditions can arise in response to harmful stimuli. Different cells within the CNS (*microglia* and *astrocytes*) produce molecules called *cytokines*, which among other molecules, affect the *inflammatory* response. When the inflammatory response gets activated within the CNS, immune cells are recruited, causing swelling, tissue damage, and even cell death (DiSabato et al, 2016).

Neuro-inflammation has also been linked to the development and maintenance of chronic pain, in part because of the sensitization of certain sensory pathways and receptors, which facilitate the transmission of nerve impulses that get identified as pain within the CNS (Ji et al, 2018).

Diagnosis

The diagnosis of pelvic pain due to a neuroinflammatory condition relies largely on the medical background of the person. Because many disorders of the nerves, neuromuscular junction, or the muscle itself can present similarly, a comprehensive neurological exam is warranted. The examination should be focused on the distribution of muscle weakness and sensory abnormalities, while also testing for tendon reflexes.

Electrodiagnostic testing (EDX), which includes both *electromyography* and *nerve conduction studies*, can help make a diagnosis. Also, *genetic studies* and *muscle biopsies* can be used in *complex* patient presentations (Rutkove, 2018).

Treatment

Treatment varies depending on the underlying condition. If the underling condition, such as multiple sclerosis, can be treated directly with disease-modifying therapy (and multiple therapies exist), then treatment should include optimizing management of the underlying condition. Another example is peripheral and/or CNS dysfunction caused by nutritional deficiencies, such as of vitamin B_{12}, which can be treated with its respective *supplementation*. In contrast, other conditions might be best treated with symptomatic treatment, using medications such as *carbamazepine* and *pregabalin* (Crean and Tirupathi, 2019).

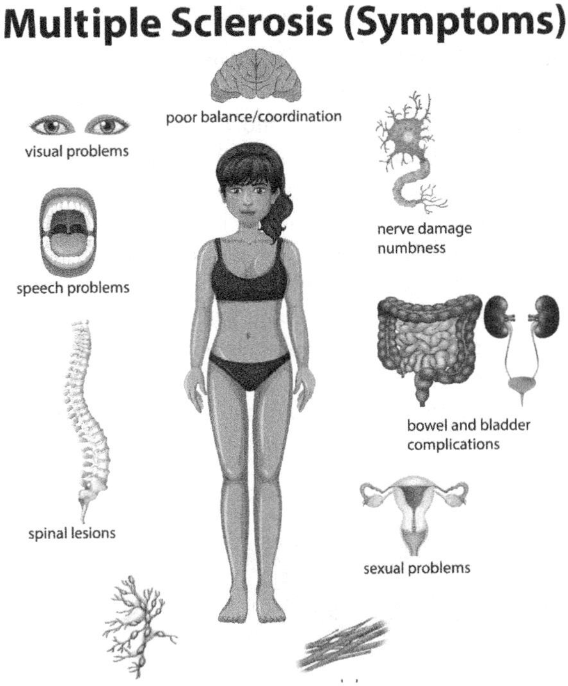

Chapter 10: What Are Rheumatologic, Neuroinflammatory, and Vascular Pain? 153

Multiple Sclerosis (Symptoms)

- visual problems
- poor balance/coordination
- speech problems
- nerve damage numbness
- spinal lesions
- bowel and bladder complications
- sexual problems

Figure 10-7: Multiple sclerosis is an autoimmune central nervous system disease in which the immune system attacks the protective sheath surrounding the nerve fibers, making it difficult for the cell to transmit its messages with the brain.

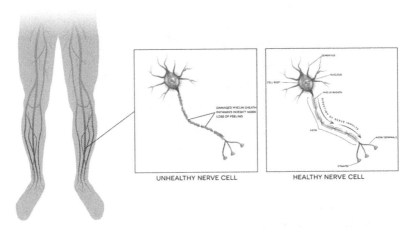

Figure 10-8: Peripheral neuropathy refers to damage of the peripheral nerves; there can be many causes, such as diabetes.

How Can Blood Vessels Cause Pelvic Pain?

Pelvic pain of venous vascular (blood vessel) origin is referred to, collectively, as *pelvic venous disorders*. The *veins* (Figure 10-9) are the vessels returning blood to the heart after it has circulated through the body, and *arteries* move *oxygenated blood* from the heart to the body. Pelvic venous disorders include *pelvic congestion syndrome* (PCS) (the general word for dilated pelvic veins causing pain, including that caused by poor function of the valves in the veins); *nutcracker syndrome* (blockage and/or stretching of the *left renal vein* by anatomic compression of the superior mesenteric artery against the aorta, which is the largest artery in the body); and *May-Thurner Syndrome*, which is the *external* compression of the pelvic (iliac) veins between the pelvic (iliac) arteries and bones (the bony pelvis or lumbar-sacral bones). Pelvic venous disorders are usually associated with vague or complex signs and symptoms from the swollen vessels. This can confuse practitioners, and the symptoms are often mistaken for other disease processes, such as *endometriosis, adhesions, uterine fibroids, adenomyosis, malignancy, uterine prolapse*, and *inflammatory bowel disease* (IBD) (Meissner and Gibson, 2015).

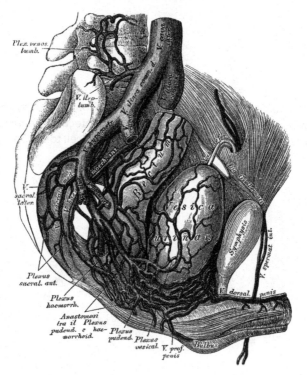

Figure 10-9: The venous blood supply of the pelvis involves a complex network of interconnecting tubes that drain blood from the pelvis back toward the heart.

Pelvic venous disorders are common disorders that are affected by levels of female *hormones*. Therefore, they are usually seen in women of child-bearing age, but they might occasionally arise in postmenopausal women who are on *hormone replacement therapy* (HRT). The pain is caused by *pelvic venous hypertension* (increased venous pressure) that is either caused by blockage (obstruction) or poor venous drainage (pelvic venous insufficiency). The veins dilate because of poor drainage and cause pain. Pelvic congestion syndrome might account for up to one-third of women with pelvic pain, second only to endometriosis (Meissner and Gibson, 2015). For pelvic venous congestion to be diagnosed, pelvic pain must be present for at least six months, with variable complaints of *dyspareunia* (pain with or after intercourse), *dysuria* (painful urinary symptoms), and *dysmenorrhea* (pain during menses). Gastrointestinal symptoms might be present. The pain is usually non-cyclic, meaning that it is present throughout the menstrual cycle, but might become more intense during menses. Pain is typically better in the morning and worse when in an upright position throughout the day as the veins stretch. Up to one-third of women with pelvic venous congestion have vulvar-vaginal varicose veins, and up to 90% will have lower extremity *varicose veins* (Figure 10-10). However, only 5% of women who present with symptomatic lower extremity varicose veins have pelvic venous disorders, and nearly half of women might be completely asymptomatic but present with varices in the vulva, *perineum*, and lower extremities (Meissner and Gibson, 2015; Labropoulos et al, 2017). These distinctions are important because treatment differs based on symptoms and presentation. Lower extremity symptomatic varicose veins only require varicose vein treatment, while pelvic varicosities require more invasive pelvic vein (internal iliac, gonadal, para-uterine) obliteration. Pelvic varicosities found by chance on CT or MRI scans do not necessarily equate with pelvic symptoms or a diagnosis of a venous disorder. An exception is *iliac venous outflow obstruction* from external compression of the pelvic iliac vein (May-Thurner syndrome). This leads to internal iliac vein high venous pressure (hypertension), and it is strongly associated with pelvic venous congestion symptoms (Hernandez-Rodriguez et al, 2009; Obara, 2018).

Nutcracker syndrome is a rare entity that results from the compression of the left renal (kidney) vein between two major arteries: the superior mesenteric artery and the aorta (Figure 10-11). This is the most common pathology, but it can also occur when the left renal vein courses behind the aorta and is compressed between the aorta and the *vertebral body*. Those with Nutcracker syndrome can present with flank (upper back) pain, blood in the urine from high pressure in the *renal vein* (renal hilum varicose veins), and pelvic pain. Often, there is associated ovarian vein dilation (greater than 6 mm) with left renal vein compression because the left ovarian vein drains into the left renal vein. Ovarian vein *reflux* into the uterine venous plexus near the uterus can result in pelvic venous varicosities and pelvic pain. Similar findings of ovarian reflux and internal iliac venous insufficiency with high venous blood pressures can also occur on the right side, but not due to Nutcracker syndrome here. (The right ovarian vein drains into the inferior vena cava, the largest vein in the body passing back to the heart, so right sided reflux is typically due to faulty valves within the vein.) Therefore, both sides warrant careful evaluation during diagnostic testing. The male counterpart to pelvic venous congestion in women is a *varicocele* (Figure 10-12), which is gonadal vein reflux in the testicular vein that leads to varicosities of the scrotum. Typically, this is not associated with pelvic pain, but it is a cause of infertility.

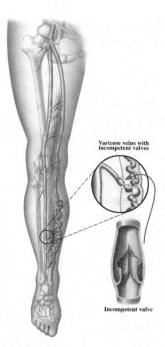

Figure 10-10: Varicose veins seen in the lower extremities rarely suggest pelvic venous congestion; varicose veins on the vulva sometimes suggest the possibility of pelvic venous congestion. Therefore, these findings should be discussed with your provider.

What Might Suggest Pelvic Venous Disease?

Your doctor should suspect a pelvic venous disorder if he or she takes a thorough history of your symptoms and finds dilated veins, leg swelling, and pain when pushing on your lower abdomen near the *ovaries* during the internal manual exam. Because of the venous connections between the internal iliac pelvic veins and the *saphenous-femoral junction* (the external system), if you have a pelvic venous disorder, you might be able to see external varicose veins in the labia, vulva, perineum (the area in front of the *anus*), groins, buttocks, inner thighs, and lower extremities. If you have pelvic pain with lower leg symptoms (swelling, pain, and varicose veins), this suggests the possibility of pelvic (iliac) vein obstruction, which is seen more commonly (2–3:1) on the left iliac venous system and lower extremity compared to the right (see Figure 10-13). If you do not have any visible varicosities, but you are a woman with pelvic and/or flank pain, there is still a possibility of having *ovarian vein reflux* with poor drainage or *left renal vein compression* (nutcracker syndrome) with obstruction of the ovarian vein leading to internal vein dilation. Internal pelvic varicosities can only be seen on radiologic imaging or might be noticed during surgery (Meissner and Gibson, 2015; Labropoulos et al, 2017; Daugherty and Gillespie, 2015).

Chapter 10: What Are Rheumatologic, Neuroinflammatory, and Vascular Pain?   157

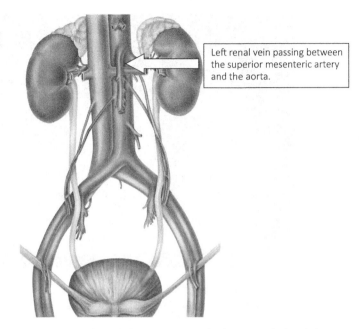

Figure 10-11: Normal anatomy of the left renal vein, which passes behind the superior mesenteric artery and in front of the aorta.

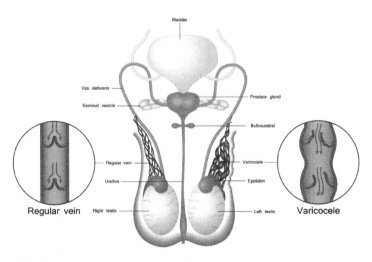

Figure 10-12: The left gonadal vein, which drains into the left renal vein, can have varices and can dilate within the scrotum, forming a noticeable varicocele.

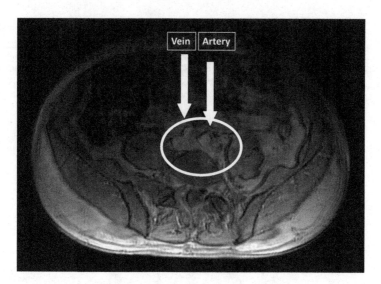

Figure 10-13: May-Thurner syndrome, a cause of pelvic venous disease, in which the stiffer *iliac artery* compresses the softer iliac vein against the spine.

Testing

Imaging is usually obtained with *venous duplex ultrasound*, which can evaluate the surface (superficial) and internal (deep) veins of the lower extremity, the varicose vein connections to these superficial and deep venous systems, and the iliac veins (evaluating for patency and flow). Abnormal flow in the *common femoral vein* and *external iliac vein* can indicate venous obstruction in the upstream common iliac vein and/or further up in the inferior vena cava. Vulvar, perineal, and gluteal varicose veins should be *evaluated* and traced to a pelvic source with *ultrasound*; however, following the surface level varicose veins to where they terminate might not be possible because communications with the internal iliac venous complex is outside of the window of ultrasound view, located deep within the pelvis. Vaginal ultrasound can be performed and can demonstrate varicosities and abnormal flow patterns near the uterus. Ovarian vein duplex is possible to perform transabdominally, and measurement of an enlarged diameter (greater than 6 mm) and identification of poor drainage (retrograde flow insufficiency) is helpful in the diagnosis of a pelvic venous disorder. Left renal vein imaging can be performed with external abdominal ultrasound, demonstrating compression of the vein or abnormal flow (peak velocities). The majority of people with PCS will undergo cross-sectional imaging of the body with either a *computed tomography* (CT) *scan venogram* or magnetic resonance (MR) scan venogram, which are excellent at evaluating venous anatomy, pelvic varicose veins, compression, obstruction, and dilated segments of gonadal (ovarian or testicular) veins. Invasive imaging includes entering the venous system and performing *venography* with dye or *intravascular ultrasound* (IVUS) (Labropoulos et al, 2017; Daugherty and Gillespie, 2015). Venography is important while considering treatment. Imaging the inside of the veins directly helps determine the volume of clotting agents *(sclerosants)* needed to treat, to provide directed road maps for the treatment of varices in the pelvic, internal iliac veins, and ovarian veins. IVUS is used to determine intraluminal (inside the vein) obstruction from external compression or intravascular webs and scarring. For patients with iliac vein outflow obstruction, IVUS is extremely important for identifying the cause and location of obstruction and for guiding treatment and placement of *stents* or for performing surgery that will keep the vein open.

How Are Pelvic Venous Disorders Treated?

Treatments for pelvic venous congestion include medication (pharmacologic), surgical, and *endovascular* approaches. For patients with *pelvic congestion syndrome* (PCS), medications that can blunt the *estrogen* stimulus by the ovaries might be effective. However, results with, e.g., *medroxyprogesterone acetate* (MPA) or the *gonagotropin-releasing hormone analog, goserelin* might provide only short-term relief of symptoms, and improvement is often not sustained. Furthermore, the side effects (weight gain and bloating) with MPA and pseudo-menopausal symptoms (including hot flashes and bone loss with goserelin), are not favored in the long term as a treatment option. Surgical management with *hysterectomy* and *oophorectomy* can accomplish symptom relief, but the consequences of increased complications because of bleeding risk, and the young age and child-bearing potential of most people with pelvic congestion syndrome precludes such an aggressive approach (Meissner and Gibson, 2015). In addition, the surgical management does not correct the underlying venous hypertension. Surgical resection of the ovarian vein where it meets the left renal vein or right inferior vena cava, down to the ovarian tributaries in the pelvis, can correct venous hypertension. However, this approach has a high bleeding risk and has been replaced by *endovascular techniques* that are equally effective and less invasive. Endovascular techniques involve approaching the problem from inside the vein using radiographic guidance and isolating the area of the veins to treat.

If there is reflux, meaning the venous blood is flowing the wrong direction, your doctor can inject a variety of clotting or scarring materials (sclerosants) to block the flow from refluxing. These materials include simple *metal coil embolization*, glue, and *gel foam embolization*, and they include a combination of *sclerotherapy* (usually foam) and coil embolization. (Embolization is a minimally invasive technique used to interrupt blood flow to an area of the body). Access to the venous pathology requires entering either one or both common femoral (groin) veins and jugular (neck) veins. Usually, embolization/sclerotherapy of both the left and right (bilateral) internal iliac vein and ovarian vein are required to achieve success. Complete or partial symptom improvement occurs in most people (68% to 100%) (Meissner and Gibson, 2015). If you have superficial varicosities from a pelvic source causing limb symptoms, in the absence of pelvic congestion syndrome-associated pelvic pain, your superficial varicosities can be treated at the site without pelvic venous interventions. Close follow-up is required to evaluate for progression, but many people are satisfied with this less invasive approach that often has excellent outcomes.

Nutcracker syndrome has been treated with both open surgical left renal vein transposition (moving the left renal vein from the native inferior vena cava to a more inferior position of the inferior vena cava away from the vessel compressing it) or with endovenous stents placed through endovascular approaches within the compressed left renal vein. Surgical correction of the compression is favored and remains the treatment of choice because of more reliable data and likely lower complication rates. About 20% of those undergoing left renal vein transposition require additional procedures to increase the outflow at the time of the new reconnection *(anastomosis)* of the left renal vein to the *inferior vena cava*. Furthermore, close follow-up is required because an additional 30% of patients might need re-interventions to keep the re-connection functioning. The early results of *endovenous stents* in the left renal vein appear promising, but long-term success has not been well defined. Stent complications including migration, embolization to the right heart, and thrombosis (clotting off) have created concerns about offering these options. Resolution of symptoms in formal surgical approaches is excellent with complete symptom-free resolution occurring in 87% of patients during a mean follow up of 37 months (Velasquez et al, 2018; Erben et al, 2015).

In some series identifying patients with May-Thurner Syndrome, opening of the vein at the site of blockage with a cylindrical balloon (angioplasty) and then placing stents to maintain patency might be considered as the first treatment option before any attempts at embolization of dilated pelvic veins (O'Brien and Gillespie, 2015). The premise is that the venous hypertension within the pelvic veins is a result of blockage of the large-caliber common iliac veins, and relieving this obstruction would correct the drainage and high pressure. Treating the iliac venous system requires needle access, usually in the common femoral (groin) veins, but it might also require access of the *internal jugular* (neck) *veins*. Because the pathology is compression of the iliac (pelvic) venous outflow, IVUS confirms the diagnosis and guides treatment in determining stent diameter and placement location. Stent placement results in increased internal vein channel diameter and relief of the venous obstruction and venous hypertension. Following iliac venous stenting, 80% of those with pelvic venous congestion symptoms from May-Thurner syndrome reported pain resolution one year after the procedure (O'Brien and Gillespie, 2015). Open surgical approaches are an option, but they are less commonly employed given the newer minimally invasive technologies available.

Currently there are no good guidelines with regards to *antiplatelet therapy* or blood-thinning medication *(anticoagulation)* following interventions for pelvic venous disorders, and usually this is directed by the physician caring for the patient. However, people with a history of a venous clotting *(thromboembolism)* and/or a propensity to clotting (a *hypercoagulable* disorder) are likely to be placed on a blood-thinning regimen after the procedure. This might include aspirin and/or an oral anticoagulant, such as *warfarin* or the newer direct oral anticoagulants.

What Is Vasculitis and How Does It Cause Pelvic Pain?

Vasculitis (Figure 10-14) is a term used to encompass a range of disorders characterized by inflammation of the blood vessels. Infiltration of immune cells within the vessel wall causes inflammation and can even destroy its cells (Roane, 1999). Vasculitis is a rarely identified cause of pelvic pain; it can be difficult to diagnose because of the non-specific signs and symptoms it presents, and because it can affect any blood vessel in the body. These disorders might present as a primary disease or as a reaction to another process (Roane, 1999; Merkel, 2019). Usually, the cause is unknown, but different factors (such as medications, infections, rheumatoid, and autoimmune disorders) can play roles in its development (Bhatt, 2017). The classification of vasculitis is still an ongoing effort, but it usually depends on the size of vessels that are involved, as well as the cell-level *(histopathologic)* features of each disease (Bhatt, 2017; Luqmani et al, 2011).

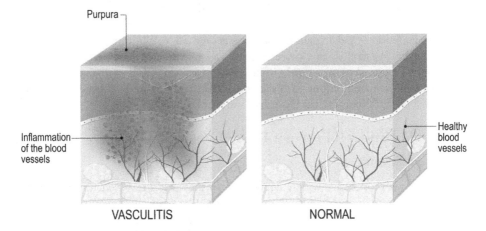

Figure 10-14: Vasculitis refers to inflammation of the blood vessels.

What follows is a quick overview of classification, according to the size of the vessels affected.

Large Vessels

Takayasu's arteritis: A large-vessel vasculitis that affects the aorta, its major branches to the extremities, and sometimes, internal organs. It usually occurs in young women (under age 50 years).

Giant temporal cell arteritis: Affects mostly the *temporal artery*. It can manifest with headache, jaw *claudication*, scalp tenderness, and visual disturbances. It is a medical emergency because it can cause blindness, and is often associated with polymyalgia rheumatica (PMR).

Small and Medium Vessels

Granulomatosis with polyangiitis (GPA) (formerly known as *Wegener's*): A systemic disease that involves the lungs, kidneys, upper respiratory tract, and other organs. It is associated with the *autoantibody* known as antineutrophil cytoplasmic antibody (ANCA).

Eosinophilic granulomatosis with polyangiitis (EGPA) (formerly known as *Churg Strauss syndrome*): Associated with asthma, nasal polyps, sinusitis, elevated eosinophil counts, and vasculitis. EGPA tends to involve lungs, peripheral nerves, skin, kidneys, and heart.

Microscopic polyangiitis: A systemic vasculitis affecting small– and medium–sized blood vessels associated with the autoantibody ANCA.

Polyarteritis nodosa (PAN): The prototype of systemic vasculitis involving many different organ systems, such as the intestines and kidneys.

The presentation of pelvic pain in vasculitis is unusual, so clinicians must have a high level of suspicion. Vasculitis, as a cause of pelvic pain, can occur as a part of an isolated process (such as *Gynecologic vasculitis*) or one of the vasculitides discussed above; giant-cell arteritis is the most common one (Traisak et al, 2016; Hernandez-Rodriguez et al, 2009; National Institute of Neurological Disorders and Stroke, 2020).

How Would I Know If I Have a Type of Vasculitis?

Signs and Symptoms

The signs and symptoms vary widely depending on the vessels involved, so the diagnostic approach can remain a challenge. Vasculitis should be suspected when someone with systemic (body-wide) symptoms also has evidence of organ dysfunction.

Some of the key symptoms include: fever, fatigue, weight loss, joint pain, eye inflammatory conditions, upper and lower airway manifestations (such as cough and nose bleeding), absent or diminished pulses, and the appearance of skin lesions called *purpura* (Merkel, 2019; National Institute of Neurological Disorders and Stroke, 2020).

Tests

Because of the association between the formation of autoantibodies and vasculitis, laboratory tests that identify the most common antibodies, ANAs, and *antineutrophil cytoplasmic antibodies* (ANCAs), are often helpful in diagnosis.

Other tests, such as a chest X-ray, vascular imaging, or even biopsy can further help your physician establish a diagnosis (Merkel, 2019).

Treatment

Once a diagnosis is established, pelvic pain caused by vasculitis is usually is treated with *glucocorticoids* and/or *immunomodulatory* therapies, which minimize the autoimmune and inflammatory responses, which play a major part in the disease (Roane, 1999).

What Is Ischemic Pelvic Disease?

Oxygen is necessary for virtually all body cells to survive and perform their respective functions; it is transported in the blood via *hemoglobin* within the *red blood cells* (RBCs). *Ischemia* refers to a lack of blood flow (and thus oxygen) to anywhere in the body, which can lead to cell injury and even cell death (American Heart Association, 2019). Ischemia can present as both an acute or chronic entity, with the latter being most common in ischemic pelvic disease and mostly caused by *atherosclerosis* (Obara, 2018; Antunes-Lopez et al, 2019). Atherosclerosis refers to the formation of plaques within the arteries; these are usually made from *cholesterol*, fat, inflammatory cells, and calcium (National Heart, Lung and Blood Institute [NHLBI], 2019). These plaques restrict the internal diameter of blood vessels, reducing blood flow. In chronic pelvic ischemia, the main abdominal artery (the *aorta*) and its branches (the *common and internal iliac arteries*) are the most common places for *atherosclerotic plaques* to form (Antunes, 2018).

How Would I Know If I Have an Ischemic Vascular Condition?

Risks

There are several identified risk factors for the formation of atherosclerotic plaques within the body's blood vessels: smoking (the most important risk factor), high blood pressure *(hypertension)*, *diabetes mellitus*, high cholesterol *(hyperlipidemia)*, and physical inactivity are major risk factors for the development of the disease (National Heart, Lung and Blood Institute, 2019; Davies, 2019).

Signs and Symptoms

Ischemic pelvic disease is a rare cause of pelvic pain. Your signs and symptoms might include numbness, tingling, cramps, and aches in the pelvis, buttocks, thighs, legs, or feet. Other signs and symptoms include muscle atrophy, poor hair growth or wound healing, as well as formation of *distal* (such as the foot or ankle) skin ulcers, which happens because these structures are further away from the heart and receive less blood flow because of this condition. The signs and symptoms of ischemic vascular disease appear most often during periods of physical effort and stress, which is largely caused by the increased demand of oxygen by body cells during these activities. On the other hand, pain and other symptoms are likely to get better with rest because of the decreased oxygen demand. The combination of limb and/or pelvic pain that worsens with activity and improves with rest is called *intermittent claudication*, a hallmark of *chronic ischemic vascular disease* (National Heart, Lung and Blood Institute, 2019).

Tests

The diagnosis is usually made by identifying the signs and symptoms described above and usually in people with major risk factors. Following are additional tests that can be used to identify the disease.

Ankle-Brachial Index: The blood pressure at the ankle is compared to blood pressure at the arms to test for arterial insufficiency. This can be done at rest or after doing some physical activity.

Penile-Brachial index: Indicative of internal iliac artery disease (but rarely performed).

Imaging: Ultrasound is the preferred imaging modality to assess for vascular disease because it is non-invasive and provides valuable data about blood flow. In some circumstances, other tests such as *computed tomography angiography* (CTA), *magnetic resonance angiography* (MRA), and even invasive vascular imaging procedures are needed if the diagnosis is equivocal (National Heart, Lung and Blood Institute, 2019; Davies, 2019).

Treatment

Treatment usually revolves around lifestyle changes and medication. Among the changes that can be made, smoking cessation, lipid-lowering medical therapy, blood sugar and hypertension control are the most important interventions to consider. Other changes include the introduction of a supervised exercise program that gradually increases the amount of physical activity that can be done before developing symptoms (Davies, 2019). Medications that reduce cardiovascular mortality and morbidity should probably be taken by people with ischemic pelvic disease or *peripheral artery disease*; these include aspirin and *clopidogrel*. Cilostazol is the most effective medication for symptom control because it helps with vasodilation and, in turn, blood flow, which diminishes symptoms. In cases where conservative management fails, *revascularization* (procedures improving the flow of blood) is warranted. It is usually accomplished via *endovascular* intervention or surgical revascularization.

Conclusion

This chapter provided information on the "everything else" of pelvic pain. If you think you may have one of the above conditions, write a list of the reasons why and discuss it with your providers. Many of these diagnoses are rare, so your provider might prefer to start with the more common diagnoses.

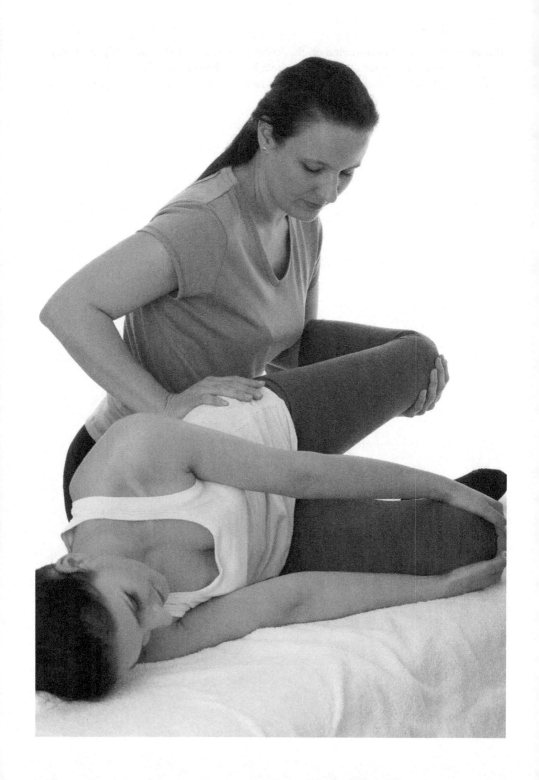

HOW DO PHYSICAL THERAPY, DIET, AND EXERCISE AFFECT PELVIC PAIN?

Beth Shelly, PT, DPT, WCS, BCB-PMD;
Cynthia E. Neville, PT, DPT, WCS; and
Allison Snyder, PT, MSPT, CLT, CEEAA

CHAPTER 11

In This Chapter

- What Can a Physical Therapist Do to Help My Pelvic Pain?
- What Are the Goals of Physical Therapy?
- How Can Exercise Help or Worsen Pelvic Pain?
- What Is Aerobic Exercise and How Can It Help Reduce Pelvic Pain?
- What Is the Role of Yoga and/or Stretching in Managing My Pelvic Pain?
- Will Relaxing My Muscles Reduce My Pain?
- How Do You Relax the Pelvic Floor Muscles?
- Does Breathing Change Muscle Tension and Pain Levels?
- What Is Biofeedback and How Does It Help?
- Will Good Posture and Correct Bending Be Helpful?
- What Are Healthy Bowel and Bladder Habits?
- What Else Can Be Done to Decrease Pelvic Pain?
- How Can I Find a Specialized Physical Therapist?
- What If There Is No Specialized Physical Therapist Near Me?
- Summary

What Can a Physical Therapist Do to Help My Pelvic Pain?

Most people are familiar with *physical therapy* (PT) for back pain, for recovery from a *stroke*, or after knee surgery; but how can a physical therapist help my *pelvic pain*? A small number of physical therapists have specialized training in providing therapy to patients with pelvic pain. Such a therapist will evaluate the *muscles* and *bones* in your pelvis, including the *pelvic floor muscles* (PFMs) (Figure 11-1). The PFMs are a group of muscles that stretch like a hammock from the tailbone in the back and to the pubic bone in the front. These muscles surround the urethra, vagina, and *anus*, and they span the area underneath the pelvis. The pelvic muscles can become tense and uncoordinated, which causes or contributes to pelvic pain, just the way a "Charlie-Horse" can in other areas of the body. After a thorough assessment, the therapist will develop a treatment plan specifically for you—because every person is different. This treatment might include the following modalities, all of which will be discussed later in this chapter:

- Education, exercise, hands-on treatments, and a variety of modalities to best address the underlying orthopedic and pelvic floor dysfunction identified during your *physical therapy* (PT) *exam*.

- *Surface electromyography* (sEMG), *PFM biofeedback,* and *ultrasound imaging biofeedback* can help you learn how to relax and contract your muscles.

- *Therapeutic ultrasound* uses sound waves to increase circulation, relax muscles, and loosen scar tissue.

- *Transcutaneous electrical nerve stimulation* (TENS) and other forms of electrical stimulation are often used to calm *nerves* and decrease pain. If you already have a TENS unit, you should bring it with you to your PT visit.

- The physical therapist may perform a specialized massage called "*myofascial release*" to stretch scars, muscles, and skin.

- Joint mobilization techniques can loosen tight joints that could be related to your pain.

- A specialized pelvic physical therapist can advise you about the activities or behaviors that should be encouraged (or avoided) to decrease your pain.

This chapter provides an overview of the goals of pelvic floor PT (also referred to as *physiotherapy*) and explains common exercises. A pelvic physical therapist can be a crucial member of your health care team and your recovery.

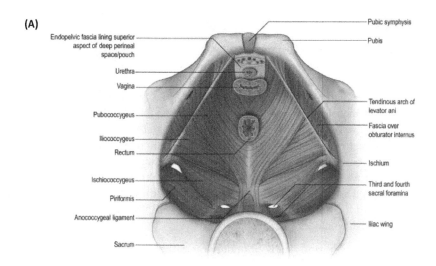
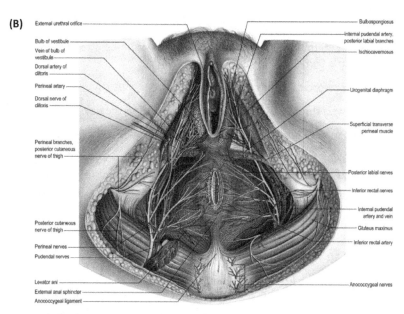

Figure 11-1: Muscles of the pelvic floor (in a female), including the piriformis and the levator ani muscle group, which includes the puborectalis, ileococcygeus, and pubococcygeus muscles. (A) Top (internal) view with organs not pictured. (B) Bottom view, including nerves and vessels. (Reproduced with permission: Standring S, ed.: A) Figure 73.3. Muscles of the female pelvis viewed from above. B) Figure 77.4. The muscles, vessels and nerves of the female perineum: inferior view. In: Gray's Anatomy: *The Anatomical Basis of Clinical Practice*. 41st Edition. Philadelphia, PA: Elsevier Limited. 2016; A) 1221–1236.e1. B) 1288–1313.e1.)

What Are the Goals of Physical Therapy?

You and your therapist will work together to set goals, such as to reduce your *symptoms* and improve your quality of life. Pain is usually a useful sensation that is meant to alert your brain of potential danger or tissue damage. It allows your body to withdraw from damaging situations, to protect a damaged body part while it heals, and to avoid similar experiences.

PT is aimed at identifying structures (such as nerves, muscles, ligaments, or *fascia*) that could be the source of or contribute to your pain. One goal of therapy is to correct the structures responsible for your pain. With persistent pain, you might experience pain long after the initial source of pain is resolved. In this case, PT targets the sensitive nervous system and the pain itself. PT is also focused on restoring function. Before going to the physical therapist, you should consider what you hope to gain. What tasks are you unable to do or are very hard for you to do?

Goals of PT might include:

- Being able to put on pants, jeans, or underwear without triggering pain
- Being able to sit at your desk for 30 minutes or more with only a minimal increase in pain
- Participating in 60 minutes of an exercise class or swimming 30 minutes with no more than a little pain
- Engaging in comfortable intercourse
- Being able to wait three hours between urinating during the day
- Having bowel movements three to six times per week without straining

Another goal of PT is to develop a comprehensive home program that will give you the knowledge and tools to care for your condition. This is crucial in your recovery. You could see the "best" pelvic physical therapist once, twice, or even three times per week, but if you are doing the wrong things between PT visits, your recovery will occur much more slowly.

How Can Exercise Help or Worsen Pelvic Pain?

Exercise has many benefits. Frequently, exercise can reduce your pelvic pain. However, the type, frequency, and intensity of your exercise program should be appropriate for your symptoms, problems, and goals. For example, pelvic floor muscles (PFMs) are often tight in those with pelvic pain. Therefore, the goal is to teach you how to relax your muscles. Intense PFM-strengthening exercises such as *Kegels* were developed to treat *urinary incontinence*. They are not generally recommended for those with pelvic pain, and they might make your symptoms worse because they focus on PFM contraction without consideration for adequate relaxation. PFM control and relaxation can be achieved by a personalized PFM program that includes gentle contraction and most importantly, sufficient relaxation. Performing range-of-motion and stretching exercise to target the muscles of the pelvic floor and hip muscles also can help to restore normal function and decrease pain. An ideal exercise program can improve symptoms and help you by:

- Increasing blood flow to the restricted muscles and fascia of the pelvic floor
- Increasing muscle elasticity and length
- Improving muscle strength
- Mobilizing tightened tissue including fascia, ligaments, and tendons
- Allowing nerves to slide more easily within the pelvis

Exercise also improves muscle balance so that you can stabilize your core without over-compensating and over-tensing your PFMs. Exercise is an additional tool to help you alleviate pain. By including a few simple stretches and movements into your daily routine, you can help to decrease your pelvic pain and improve your function.

What Is Aerobic Exercise and How Can It Help Reduce Pelvic Pain?

It is widely recognized that *aerobic exercise* improves *cardiovascular* (heart) health. But, did you know that there is also research to support the benefits of aerobic exercise for pelvic pain? When you participate in aerobic exercise, your heart rate increases and pumps more blood and oxygen through your body, which can help to calm nerves and improve healing of muscles, tissues, and bones. Moreover, aerobic exercises reduce pain by targeting the messaging that occurs in the *central nervous system* (CNS) of someone who has persistent pain. Exercises help to improve the capacity of the nervous system to calm *pain signals*, also called the *endogenous* pain modulatory pathway (Vandyken and Hilton, 2012). Furthermore, the *endorphins* that are released by your brain during aerobic exercise are the strongest pain medicines known to science. Some call this the "runner's high," which is the light feeling you get after an aerobic workout. For many people, this can be achieved by continuous movement for at least 10 minutes, which results in an increased heart rate. Most people start with walking. Aerobic exercise should not exacerbate your pain. Here are some strategies and guidelines to begin an exercise program:

- Start small. Even a few minutes (for example, start with a 5-minute brisk walk) can be a great way to start. Then, add a minute every other day until you reach 20–30 minutes of regular exercise.
- Include aerobic exercise in your daily schedule.
- Exercise with a friend or family member or with music to help motivate you.

- Begin with low-impact forms of exercise, such as walking, swimming or pool exercise, riding on a recumbent bike (avoid a standard narrow bike seat), or elliptical training. (Note that pool exercise might irritate the skin of the perineum.)
- If you are already an avid exerciser, you might try to reduce the intensity or frequency of your aerobic exercise. Consult with the physical therapist to determine the correct intensity and type of exercise for your condition.

What Is the Role of Yoga and/or Stretching in Managing My Pelvic Pain?

Yoga can be a great technique to add to your self-management program. Yoga can increase the pliability of muscles and *connective tissue*, and it can increase the flexibility of the soft tissues in the pelvis and trunk. This allows your nerves to move freely and not get irritated as easily. After months of pain, the brain might be conditioned to expect that movement will be dangerous or harmful. By practicing yoga, you can improve your body-awareness and your ability to move in pain-free motions. An additional benefit of yoga is the inclusion of conscious breathing, or *"pranayama,"* which helps to decrease your heart rate and blood pressure and to relax your PFMs.

Several different styles of yoga are often offered at your gym or a local yoga studio. It is best to start with a gentle form of yoga, such as Hatha, or restorative styles, in which the movements are slower and stretches and breathing are emphasized. Also, you might benefit from the support of props and pillows to aide in the yoga practice. If you don't have access to a yoga studio or if you prefer to practice yoga in your home, you can also find gentle restorative yoga DVDs or online modules. In any class, you should listen to your body and not push yourself beyond your ability. Work hard, but don't hurt yourself.

It is also helpful to add daily stretching at home. Your physical therapist will tell you which stretches are best for you. Yoga and self-stretch exercises are held for 10 to 15 seconds (or longer) while relaxing, breathing, and slowly easing into the stretch. As your condition improves, you might be able to stretch longer (up to 30 seconds for each stretch). The stretches should be repeated three times each, and they should be done every day. Below are some commonly used stretches for pelvic pain (see Figure 11-2 [A–D]).

Will Relaxing My Muscles Reduce My Pain?

Muscle spasms, cramps, and tight muscles can decrease blood flow and cause pain. Even a small amount of extra tension over months, days, or even hours can be problematic. Sometimes, a spasm results in a *trigger point*, which is a small painful nodule in the muscle. Up to 75% of those with pelvic pain have painful, tense, and tight muscles (Fitzgerald et al, 2011). When this is the case, relaxing the muscles will decrease pain. In addition, tight and short muscles pull on joints and compress nerves, contributing to pain in other areas. Relaxing your muscles can decrease the strain on joints and nerves, allowing them to heal more completely. In some cases, muscle tension develops in response to something else, like a painful rash or an irritated colon. In any situation, tight muscles should be relaxed and loosened.

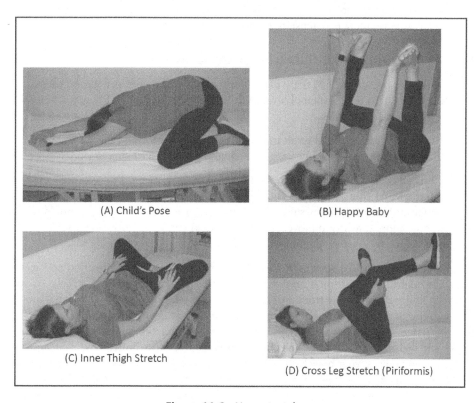

Figure 11-2: Yoga stretches.

At times, you might notice muscle tension, while at other times, others might notice your tension by the way you sit, stand, or walk. You should become aware of your body's tension, such as in the abdominals, buttock, inner thigh, and neck. Notice which situations create tension and which positions or situations decrease your tension. Practice releasing your muscles in all positions and situations. Mindfulness is the practice of being aware, and it can inform you about your muscle tension level. This will help you gain control over your tension. Some spasms are more resistant to stretching; specialized therapy might be needed.

Meditation is a practice of relaxation that encourages focus and quieting. Focus can be on breathing, an image, a phrase, a relaxing location, or other focal points. Meditation calms muscles and nerves and can reduce pain if practiced consistently over time. Many meditation resources exist (in books, on the internet, and even apps). You might find that it is difficult to meditate on your own, and you might have better results working with a professional or in a group. The key is to persist. Meditation usually does not result in an immediate decrease in pain or tension; it takes time and practice.

How Do You Relax the Pelvic Floor Muscles?

The pelvic floor muscles (PFMs) are particularly hard to relax; you cannot see them, and sometimes, it is hard to feel them. However, it is helpful to understand how your muscles move during certain activities.

- PFM contraction should result in the PFMs moving up and in toward the head. This is important during sneezing and coughing to avoid leaking urine.
- PFM relaxation should result in the PFMs moving downward toward the feet. After a PFM contraction, you should feel the tissue release and move slightly downward. Bearing down, such as releasing gas or moving the bowels, should result in even more downward movement if performed gently. Vigorous bearing down can stimulate a guarding reflex with unwanted contraction of the PFMs.

With pain and PFM spasms, it might be difficult to feel the contraction and relaxations. It might help to sit on a firm chair and notice the way the perineum feels: As you contract, it lifts slightly away from the chair, and as you relax or gently bear down, it moves closer to the chair. You might also try to place your index finger lightly on the rectum and feel the tissue move up away from your finger with contraction and down toward your finger with relaxation. This works best lying on your side. Also, notice how your muscles feel when you release your bowels. If you have normal bowel release, you are relaxing your PFMs. It is important to avoid repeated bearing down. Once you are aware of PFM relaxation, you should gently release and relax it without bearing down frequently during the day, especially if you have pain or stress. If you are unable to feel this movement, you should consult with a pelvic physical therapist specialist who can teach you.

Does Breathing Change Muscle Tension and Pain Levels?

The functioning of the PFMs is closely related to the *diaphragm* and the abdominal wall muscles. Tension in the abdominal wall and PFMs can restrict breathing, and improper breathing can affect the abdominal wall and PFMs. Normal diaphragmatic breathing results in movement of the PFMs and the belly.

Chapter 11: How Do Physical Therapy, Diet, and Exercise Affect Pelvic Pain? 175

- Inhaling with the diaphragm results in outward expansion of the belly, and downward relaxation of the PFMs
- Exhaling results in inward movement of the belly and upward movement of the PFMs

Diaphragmatic breathing helps to relax the PFMs as well as facilitate overall relaxation of the nervous system. This type of breathing is often used in meditation, relaxation, and *mindfulness training*, and it can decrease pain. You should practice sitting or lying down with your hand on your belly, while noticing a small outward movement of the belly as you breathe in. Don't let your chest rise a large amount. It takes practice—and at first, is not relaxing. Keep trying until you can breathe easily with a belly bulge, and then notice the change in the PFMs as they relax downward as you breathe in.

What Is Biofeedback and How Does It Help?

Sometimes, it is difficult to find the PFMs and to feel their contraction or relaxation. *Biofeedback* refers to training that increases the awareness of muscle activity (Figure 11-3). This might include using a hand mirror to watch the outside of the perineum, a therapist giving verbal feedback, or a machine. Surface electromyography (sEMG) PFM biofeedback and ultrasound imaging biofeedback are tools that can help you visualize the PFM activation and learn how to contract and relax them. While you are watching the display, you can more easily recognize the small changes in sensation that show relaxation and realize what you must do to accomplish it. sEMG PFM biofeedback can be performed with a sensor inside the vagina or rectum, but often in those with pelvic pain or a history of trauma, the sensors are placed on the skin outside the rectum, which avoids internal application. This device gathers information from the muscles and displays it graphically on the screen. When the PFMs contract, the line rises; when they relax, the line is lower.

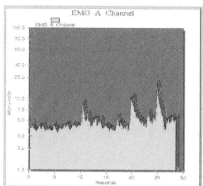 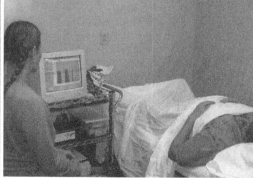

Figure 11-3: Biofeedback display.

Ultrasound imaging biofeedback uses a probe on the lower belly or perineum (the area between the vagina or testicles and the rectum) to visualize movements. Pelvic structures move toward the head during contraction and toward the feet during relaxation.

Will Good Posture and Correct Bending Be Helpful?

Posture has a significant effect on many bodily functions. Slouched posture can place stress on the back, cause compression and pain in the tailbone, decrease breathing capacity, and increase downward pressure in the abdominal cavity. In some cases, correct posture results in decreased pain. In all situations, correct posture helps facilitate good joint alignment, relaxed muscle function, and enhance effective breathing patterns. Correct sitting posture is especially important for health of the pelvic joints and tailbone (Figures 11-4 and 11-5). When you are sitting on a chair, it is best to place your low back way back in the chair, sitting up tall with a small arch in your lower back. A small towel roll at your low back can help (usually, a pillow is too big). Having even pressure on both buttocks helps as well. Side shifting can strain pelvic joints, especially if you side shift routinely to the same side. You should experiment with having seating surfaces with different firmness. Sometimes, it is better to have a firmer (though not too hard) chair instead of the soft cushion. Many types of cushions are available. It might be helpful to have several types of cushions for different surfaces, including one that has a cut-out that spares the tailbone.

Correct bending technique helps to decrease strain on the muscles and joints. When you bend, take a wide stance around the object. Then bend your knees and bend at the hips (sticking your buttocks out and keeping a small inward curve in your low back). Keep your chest open; do not round-down and drop your chest toward your pelvic area. As you engage the weight, tighten your belly inward and your PFMs upward to support the trunk. It might be helpful to practice with your side to the mirror so you can see the line of your back and chest.

Chapter 11: How Do Physical Therapy, Diet, and Exercise Affect Pelvic Pain? 177

Hip Hinge	Golfer's Lift
	 Maintain a neutral spine. • Bend at the hip and knee, lean body forward, and extend the opposite leg at the same time. • Avoid twisting the body. • Useful for retrieving very light objects.
Maintain neutral spine. • Separate your feet for a wider stance. • Bend forward at the hips. • Useful for lifting larger or heavier objects at or below waist level.	
Deep Knee Bend	Good Sitting posture with a Lumbar Roll
	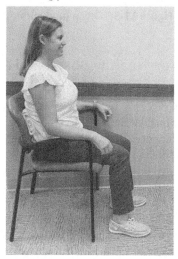
Maintain a neutral spine. • Bend down on one or both knees. • Useful for lifting objects from the floor.	

Figure 11-4: Healthy positioning.

Figure 11-5: Office (and commuting) ergonomics can affect pelvic pain.

What Are Healthy Bowel and Bladder Habits?

Sometimes, the primary condition that causes pelvic muscle dysfunction involves a bladder or bowel problem. In this case, you might require a specialist to help with correcting the bowel or bladder function. In all cases, it is good to understand healthy, normal bowel and bladder function. Bad habits might be random or learned from others, and these bad habits may contribute to your pain.

Normal urine output is related to several factors, including normal fluid intake. Health care professionals typically suggest 64 ounces of fluid intake per 24 hours; this includes all the fluid you drink. Ask your therapist how many ounces you should drink per day. Some fluids, such as caffeine, certain teas, and artificial sweeteners are irritating to the bladder. Not everyone has these sensitivities, but you might consider avoiding or eliminating these substances after a taper for three to five days to see how your bladder functions and pain changes. If they do not change, then the substance could be consumed in moderation. It is also helpful to understand that caffeine can excite nerves, and this might increase your pain if your pain is related to a sensitive nervous system. Other types of fluid, such as acidic fluids, can also increase bladder pain; milk products might result in intestinal cramps or diarrhea. Water is always the best fluid. Ask your medical professional and check trusted websites for types of fluids you should avoid. If you are taking in the correct amount and type of fluid, you should be urinating fewer than seven times in a 24-hour period. Normal bladder function should not feel urgent, nor should it require pushing to empty your bladder.

Similarly, normal bowel function is related to good food intake. Dietary Guidelines for Americans outlines a normal healthy diet (https://health.gov/dietaryguidelines/2015/guidelines/). Eat regular meals that are high in vegetables and low in processed food. Food sensitivities, such as *lactose intolerance* or *gluten allergies*, can affect bowel function and might require testing. Be mindful of the type of food you are eating and its result on your bowel function and pelvic pain. With normal food intake, you should be emptying your bowel between one to three times per day to every third day. Most people fall within this range, so for example, it can be normal to move your bowels every other day. It is important to relax while sitting on the toilet, with your feet on the floor, leaning slightly forward, even resting your forearms on your thighs. Gentle downward pressure with bearing down and belly contraction is usually needed to empty the bowels. Straining too much can irritate muscles and nerves, increasing pain and dysfunction. You can practice relaxation and breathing while sitting correctly on the toilet. Speak to your medical professional if moving your bowels is painful, if you are straining a lot, or if certain foods cause significant bowel changes.

What Else Can Be Done to Decrease Pelvic Pain?

Smoking decreases blood flow and healing capacity throughout the body. It is a stimulant to nerves, and it can increase the feeling of pain. It also results in coughing, which puts excessive pressure on your bladder, bowels, and PFMs. Smoking cessation is important for full recovery from pelvic pain.

Emotional stress increases pain. This is especially true if you are scared or worried about the pain. Pain also seems to be worse when the onset was related to an upsetting event, such as a car accident, surgery, or divorce.

How Can I Find a Specialized Physical Therapist?

Not all physical therapists can provide treatment for pelvic pain. Ideally, the therapist will be *board-certified* or have a certification. Here are the most common certifications:

- *WCS (Women's Health Clinical Specialist)*: Board certification with high level of knowledge and experience in all areas of women's and men's health, including pelvic pain. http://www.abpts.org/FindaSpecialist/.

- *CAPP* (Certificate of Achievement in Pelvic Physical Therapy): Issued through the Section on Women's Health (SOWH) of the American Physical Therapy Association (APTA). http://aptaapps.apta.org/findapt/default.aspx?navID=10737422525&UniqueKey=.

- *PRPC (Pelvic Rehabilitation Practitioner Certification)*: The Herman and Wallace Institute pelvic therapy certification. Find a practitioner at https://www.pelvicrehab.com.

- *BCB-PMD (Board Certified Biofeedback Pelvic Muscle Dysfunction)*: Certified through the Biofeedback Certification International Alliance, which specifically certifies therapists in the use of all forms of biofeedback. https://www.certify.bcia.org/4dcgi/resctr/search.html.

If there is no therapist near you with any of these qualifications, you should ask your physical therapist what course work they have taken. The main education for pelvic physical therapy is provided through the SOWH and the Herman and Wallace Institute. Therapists should be able to answer a variety of questions, such as:

- How long have you been treating pelvic pain?
- Do you have machines to measure the muscles?
- Do you examine the muscle inside the vagina or rectum?
- How often do you see patients with pelvic pain?
- Will I be seeing other therapists?
- Do you work with assistants or technicians?

There are many ways to treat pelvic pain. If you start off with a physical therapist and do not feel you are receiving knowledgeable or experienced care for pelvic pain, you should search for another physical therapist. It is always good to ask questions and to feel comfortable with the therapist you have chosen, and this physical therapist might even be able to help you find a colleague with more experience with pelvic pain. In some cases, the best physical therapist for your condition might be one hour or more away.

What If There Is No Specialized Physical Therapist Near Me?

Unfortunately, many small cities and towns do not have specialized pelvic physical therapists. It is a good idea to communicate with the nearest pelvic physical therapist to establish your options. Maybe there is a physical therapist who works closer to you and has some experience. Sometimes, the specialized physical therapist can work with a local physical therapist to provide parts of the treatment so that your long trips to the specialized physical therapist are less frequent. Telemedicine is another option that is gaining popularity.

This involves confidential web-based treatment, although there are limitations to any care in which a hands-on exam cannot be performed. Some people with pelvic pain might find these practitioners also helpful:

- OCS *(orthopedic certified specialist)*: A board certification in orthopedic PT; this physical therapist has advanced knowledge and experience and would be able to address most *external* pelvic dysfunctions. http://www.abpts.org/FindaSpecialist/.
- *Osteopath*: A medical doctor whose training focuses on how body structure influences function.
- *Chiropractor*: Some patients find a local chiropractor who can provide external treatment of pelvic joints.
- *Massage therapist*: General relaxation massage or loosening of certain external hip and trunk muscles. Ask if the therapist treats gluteus muscles and make sure you are able to see the same therapist each time. https://www.ncbtmb.org/.
- *Acupuncturist*.
- Meditation or *relaxation therapist*.
- *Pain specialist* or *pain psychologist*.

Summary

PT for pelvic pain comes in many forms and can be very helpful in your overall recovery. Start now by using some of the suggestions described in this chapter, and work toward putting together the best treatment team for you based on the parts of this chapter—and book—that apply to you.

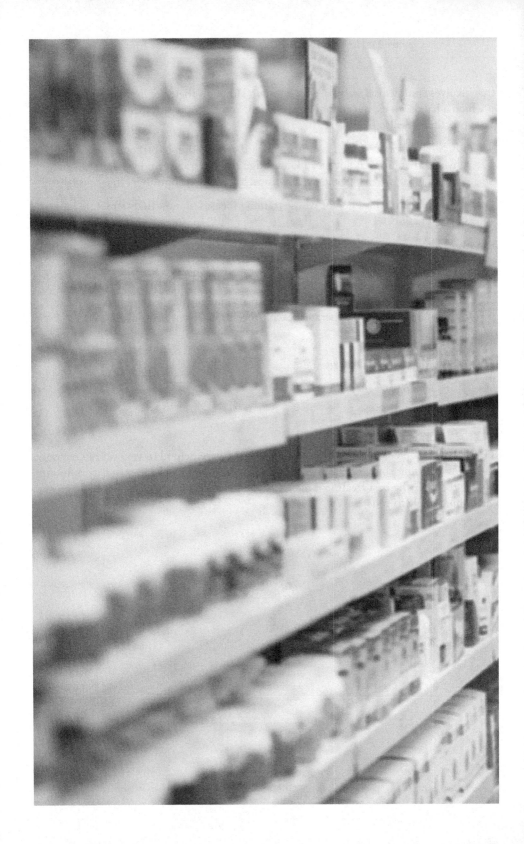

WHICH MEDICATIONS ARE USED TO MANAGE PELVIC PAIN?

Joshua Mukalazi Nsubuga, PharmD; Elise J.B. De, MD; Charles Argoff, MD; John Walczyk, PharmD, RPh, FIACP, FACA; Carey York-Best, MD; Peter Cole, MD; Alexandra R. Adler, MD; Antje M. Barreveld, MD; and Annie Chen, MD

CHAPTER

In This Chapter

- Introduction
- Why Do Medications Have More Than One Name?
- Does It Matter Whether I Take a Generic or Brand Name Drug?
- What Is a Compound Medication?
- What Is Transdermal Pain Management?
- Which Medication Classes Treat Pain?

Introduction

Medications are commonly used as part of a management program for *pelvic pain*. *Multimodal therapy* is often employed, which involves taking advantage of the properties of different classes of medications (in combination with behavior changes, *physical therapy* [PT], and/or procedures if indicated) to target pain. Frequently-used medications that help with nerve pain, muscle pain, and *inflammatory* pain include *anticonvulsants*, *antidepressants*, *muscle relaxants*, *non-steroidal anti-inflammatory drugs* (NSAIDs), and *local anesthetics*. The aim of medication therapy is to reduce (but not necessarily eliminate) pain to allow you to improve your daily functioning and your quality of life. Given that your symptoms can change over time, your medications might also need to be adjusted. You should know your medications and their doses (past and current) and report to your health care providers any side effects that you experience. Side effects might be less bothersome at lower doses. Sometimes, taking two classes of medications allows you to lower your overall doses. When co-administered, certain medications can cause more side effects and these should be discussed with your prescriber. Your pharmacist can run queries of your medication list to double check for medication interactions and allergies. Therefore, it is important that your provider and all your pharmacies have up-to-date lists of your prescriptions, over-the-counter (OTC) medications, and medication allergies. Some medical conditions are important for drug metabolism, such as *kidney (renal)* or *liver insufficiency*, *myasthenia gravis* (an *autoimmune disorder* that affects nerve and muscle connections), or *glucose-6-phosphate dehydrogenase* (G6PD) *deficiency* (an enzyme disorder that affects *red blood cell* [RBC] function), and they should be on file.

Why Do Medications Have More Than One Name?

Medications have both *generic* and *brand names*. The generic name is an approved scientific or medical name that is decided by expert scientists to classify the drug. The brand name, also known as a trade name, is created by the pharmaceutical company as a marketing name. If more than one company markets the drug, there will be more than one brand name. It is helpful if you know both the generic and brand names of your medications.

Does It Matter Whether I Take a Generic or Brand Name Drug?

Most medications contain two types of ingredients—active (the generic drug) and inactive (the material in which the drug is mixed to make a tablet, capsule, or cream). The *inactive ingredients* are responsible for things such as its color and whether the medication takes 1, 8, or 24 hours to be absorbed and metabolized. For most medications, generic and brand name compounds have no differences you can perceive because the *active ingredient* is the same. Sometimes, the difference in formulation can be important. For example, a woman might experience irritation from a commercial estrogen cream.

What Is a Compound Medication?

It can be important when you are experiencing side effects, for example vulvovaginal irritation with creams, to determine what might be the cause of the undesired effect. The active ingredient of the medication can be one source of intolerance, but oftentimes, it is the *"vehicle"* (the cream base or whatever holds a tablet together) that carries the medication, which might be the offending agent. Commercial medication often contains allergens and/or irritants, including *propylene glycol, parabens,* preservatives, and alcohols. These additives can irritate, for example, the vaginal tissue. The *compound pharmacist* identifies the known potential allergens and/or irritants and creates a dosage form of the medication with drug concentrations that can facilitate pain management without introducing unwanted additives. These combinations and concentrations can be custom-made as a *compound medication*. In addition to avoiding known allergens/irritants, compound medications can expand the way a medication is taken. For example, certain commercial products might not be intended for internal use or use on sensitive tissue types, such as the vaginal or anal entrance. The compound pharmacist can mix the drug into a vehicle that is safe for these sensitive sites. Lastly, certain medications, such as *benzodiazepines* (an example of this class would be diazepam [Valium®]), can be compounded and inserted into or applied to the vagina or rectum. Because the medication is not being ingested by mouth and is being applied directly to the irritated site, there can be a more direct approach to treating the pain with fewer side effects impacting the body as a whole.

What Is Transdermal Pain Management?

Transdermal or *topical* pain management is the delivery of medication by applying it to the skin and having it absorb and work directly on the site where it is needed. With more patients and prescribers understanding the risks associated with opioids, we have seen a radical shift from heavy *opioid* use to a modality that focuses more on what is causing the pain and looking at treating at the underlying conditions as opposed to masking the pain with an opioid. A good example is if your knee hurts and is inflamed, you can apply a medication like *ibuprofen, diclofenac, ketoprofen,* or *naproxen* (a NSAID) directly to your knee to decrease the inflammation. This concept also works for other types of medications. Transdermal *baclofen* or *cyclobenzaprine* can be used as a muscle relaxant/antispasmodic, while *gabapentin, pregabalin,* and *amitriptyline* work on *neuropathic pain*. Drugs like *lidocaine, tetracaine,* and *bupivacaine* help as an *anesthetic* agent to numb the area, while transdermal *piroxicam* and *tramadol* work on general pain. Those using transdermal pain management tend to see fewer side effects—which makes them more appealing. An advantage in transdermal pain management is the ability to combine multiple medications at lower concentrations to treat a specific condition. For example, if you have neck or shoulder pain and are experiencing sharp nerve pain as well as inflammation, a combination formula like gabapentin/ketoprofen/lidocaine can be used to work on both aspects of the pain. Most of these formulations would be compounded by a compounding pharmacy; certain single ingredient creams, like diclofenac or lidocaine, can be found at a regular pharmacy.

Which Medication Classes Treat Pain?

When some of us think of needing a "pain medication," we think of opioids. The word opioid comes from "opium," as this class of prescription medications stimulates the same receptor on brain cells as *opium* and *heroin*. Prescribed opiates include *oxycodone (OxyContin®), hydrocodone (Vicodin®), codeine, morphine, hydromorphone, tramadol, fentanyl,* and many others. The use of opioids in the management of *chronic* pain is controversial. Although opioids might provide excellent relief from acute pain, such as pain after surgery, their efficacy with long-term use in chronic pain is less well defined. There is little evidence for functional improvement with higher doses of opioids, and there is clear evidence of harm, including significant side effects as well as the risk of misuse or addiction. In other words, opiates are typically not effective in chronic pain as one's body gets used to them. If opioids are considered as part of your plan, you should speak to your health care provider regarding the risks and benefits of using opioids both in the short-term and long-term before starting them (Steele, 2014; Chou et al, 2009; Els et al, 2017).

Fortunately, opioids are only a small part of what can be used to treat pain. Most people can find effective pain relief without any opioids at all! Based on what is causing your pain, you and your provider will be able to choose among *barrier creams*, *hormones*, *bladder-relaxing medications*, antidepressants, *allergy medications*, anticonvulsants, antidepressants, muscle relaxants, NSAIDs, local anesthetics, and many more classes of medication listed below. Table 12-1 provides basic information about these medication classes. You should also speak with your health care provider and pharmacist.

Table 12-1: Medications Commonly Used in the Treatment of Pelvic Pain (Organized by Class)*

	Medication and Daily Dose Range	Medication Class	Therapeutic Effect	Side Effects	Contraindications	Main Drug Interactions
Bladder-relaxing medications	• Oxybutynin (Ditropan®) 5–15 mg ER • Oxybutynin Gel (Gelnique®) transdermal sachet daily • Oxybutynin Transdermal Patch (Oxytrol®) 3.9 mg • Hyoscyamine (Levsin®) 0.375–0.75 mg	• Anticholinergic	• Decreased sensitivity of the bladder surface • Less vigorous contractions • Decreased bladder spasms	• Dizziness • Drowsiness • Dry mouth • Constipation • Urinary retention • Pruritis (patch)[1,2]	• Hypersensitivity • Patients at risk of uncontrolled narrow-angle glaucoma, urinary and gastric retention, severely decreases gastric motility[1,2] • Use cautiously if over age 65	• Revefenacin • Tiotropium • Umeclidinium • Potassium citrate • Secretin[1,2]
	• Tolterodine (Detrol®) 2–4 mg ER, 4–8 mg IR • Fesoterodine (Toviaz®) 4–8 mg • Trospium (Sanctura®) 60 mg ER • Darifenacin (Enablex®) 7.5–15 mg • Solifenacin (Vesicare®) 5–10 mg			• Constipation • Urinary retention • Xerostomia (**dry mouth**)[1,2]	• Gastric retention • Uncontrolled narrow-angle glaucoma • Urinary retention • Hypersensitivity	• Mesoridazine Drugs (CI) • Tiotropium • Umeclidinium • Aclinidium • Conivaptan • Eluxadoline • Fusidic acid[1,2]
	• Mirabegron (Myrbetriq®) 25–50 mg	• Beta-3 agonist	• Decreased sensitivity of the bladder surface • Less vigorous contractions • Decreased bladder spasms	• Hypertension	• Hypersensitivity[1]	• Eligustat • Metoprolol (strong CYP 2D6 inhibitors) • Thioridazine[1]

Continued

	Medication and Daily Dose Range	Medication Class	Therapeutic Effect	Side Effects	Contraindications	Main Drug Interactions
Medications that open bladder outlet	• Terazosin (Hytrin®) 1–10 mg • *Tamsulosin* (Flomax®) 0.4–0.8 mg • Doxazosin (Cardura®) 2–4 mg • Alfuzosin (Uroxatral®) 10 mg • Silodosin (Rapaflo®) 8 mg	• Alpha-adrenergic blocker	• Relaxation of the bladder neck and prostate • Easier initiation of void and better emptying • Decreased burning with void in some cases	• Orthostatic hypotension • Headache • Dizziness • Rhinitis • Ejaculation occurring retrograde into the bladder (safe and reversible)[1,2]	• Hypersensitivity[1]	• Conivaptan • Idelalisib[1,2]
Bladder pain medications	• Pentosan Polysulfate Sodium (Elmiron®) 200–300 mg	• Heparin-like molecule	• Coating of bladder surface in interstitial cystitis • Low efficacy rates above placebo	• Alopecia • Nausea • Diarrhea[1] • Some reports of vision change See a retina specialist if long-term usage is planned (Jain et al, 2019)	• Hypersensitivity	• Anticoagulants • Antiplatelets (NSAIDs, SSRIs, P2Y12 inhibitors)[1]
	• Phenazopyridine (Pyridium®) 100–600 mg	• Analgesic	• Urinary anesthetic • Decreases bladder pain	• Headache[1]	• Hypersensitivity • Renal insufficiency[1]	
	• Amitriptyline (Elavil®) • *Nortriptyline* (Pamelor®) See below in general pain medications	• *Tricyclic antidepressants*				

	Medication and Daily Dose Range	Medication Class	Therapeutic Effect	Side Effects	Contraindications	Main Drug Interactions
Bladder pain medications (*continued*)	• Methenamine (Uribel®) 118 mg • Sodium phosphate monobasic 40.8 mg • Phenyl salicylate 36 mg • Methylene blue 10 mg • Hyoscyamine sulfate 0.12 mg	• *Antihistamine*	• Urinary anesthetic • Decreases bladder pain	• Rapid heartbeat • Blurred vision • Dizziness • Drowsiness • Difficult urination • Urinary retention • Dry mouth • Nausea • Vomiting • Shortness of breath • Trouble breathing	• Hypersensitivity to any component of the product	• Urinary alkalizers • Thiazide diuretics • Antimuscarinics • Antacids/*antidiarrheals* • Anti myasthenics • Ketoconazole • Monoamine oxidase (MAO) inhibitors • Opioids • Sulfonamides
	• Hydroxyzine (Atarax®) • Diphenhydramine (Benadryl® Genahist®, Sominex®, Unisom®) • Cimetidine (Tagamet®) • Cetirizine hydrochloride (Zyrtec®) • Fexofenadine (Allegra®) • Loratidine (Claritin®)	• Various • Antihistamine		• Flushing • Dyspnea • Dizziness • Blurred vision[1,2]	• Nursing mothers • Hypersensitivity to diphenhydramine • Other similar antihistamines	• Alcohol • Aclidinium • Atomoxetine • Atropine[1,2]

Continued

	Medication and Daily Dose Range	Medication Class	Therapeutic Effect	Side Effects	Contraindications	Main Drug Interactions
Bladder pain medications (*continued*)	• Bladder instillations (heparin, lidocaine, sodium bicarbonate, antibiotic)	• Sterile compound mixture instillation	• Decreased bladder pain over time with repeat instillations	• Can cause local irritation, absorption of lidocaine • Could be dangerous at higher doses	• Blood in the urine • *Urinary tract* infection	
	• Bladder instillations • Dimethyl sulfoxide, DMSO (Rimso-50®)	• Other • Used as a solvent in manufacturing • Used for instillation with sterile compound mixture in bladder	• Decreased bladder pain over time with repeat instillations	• Can cause severe bladder irritation, paradoxically	• Blood in the urine • Urinary tract infection	• DMSO can increase uptake of other medications
	• Cyclosporine A (Gengraf®, Neoral®, Sandimmune®)	• Immunosuppressive	• Interstitial cystitis	• Hypertension • Stomach pain • Tremor • Kidney damage		
Local anesthetic	• Lidocaine (Xylocaine®), bupivicaine (Marcaine®, Sensorcaine®)	• Local anesthetic for nerve block or instillation	• Depends on mode of administration (bladder instillation, skin surface, intravenous [IV])	• Possible drug class side effects: metallic taste in the mouth, ringing in the ears, dizziness, and sedation • These are not administered orally and are generally used for diagnostic and therapeutic injections • IV administration can have cardiac risk	• Cardiac arrythmia	

Medication and Daily Dose Range	Medication Class	Therapeutic Effect	Side Effects	Contraindications	Main Drug Interactions
Injected Steroids	• Steroid injected near nerve				
Injected Irritants	• *Dextrose*				
Injected Growth Agents	• *Platelet-rich plasma* (PRP)	• *Growth factors* • Collected from your own blood	• Variety of uses		
Injected *Neurolytic*	• Alcohol (ethanol)	• Substance injected to damage overactive nerves			
Injected Botulinum Toxin	• OnabotulinumtoxinA (Botox®) • RimabotulinumtoxinB (Myobloc®) • AbobotulinumtoxinA (Dysport®)	• *Chemodenervation of muscles or nerves*	• Chemodenervation	• Distant spread of toxin effect	• Hypersensitivity to any botulinum toxin preparation • Diagnosis of myasthenia gravis

Continued

	Medication and Daily Dose Range	Medication Class	Therapeutic Effect	Side Effects	Contraindications	Main Drug Interactions
Penile Injections	• *Collagenase clostridium histolyticum* (Xiaflex®)	• Peyronie's disease • Dupuytren's contracture, with a palpable cord			• Peyronie plaques involving the penile urethra • Hypersensitivity to collagenase clostridium histolyticum • Avoid concomitant use of anticoagulants • Avoid use in patients with coagulation (bleeding) disorders	• Concomitant use of anticoagulants
Urinary Tract Infection Management	• Oral or IV antibiotics (doses and # days) • Antibiotic instillation in the bladder • Proanthocyanidins (Ellura®, Theracran®) or other cranberry extract • D-Mannose (a simple sugar, monosaccharide)		• Inhibits the adherence of P-fimbriae of *E. coli* to uroepithelial cells (Howell et al, 2010) • Thought to work by blocking type 1 fimbriae, inhibiting *bacterial* adherence to urothelial cells (Altarac and Papes, 2014)	• Nephrolithiasis[2]	• Difficult to know which brands actually contain therapeutic concentrations of cranberry product	• H$_2$ blockers • Proton pump inhibitors • Warfarin[2]

Chapter 12: Which Medications Are Used to Manage Pain? 193

	Medication and Daily Dose Range	Medication Class	Therapeutic Effect	Side Effects	Contraindications	Main Drug Interactions
Urinary Tract Infection Management (*continued*)	• Methenamine (Hiprex®, Mandelamine®, Urex®)	• *Organic compound*	• Works by converting to formaldehyde in acidic urine, which then exhibits non-specific antiseptic activity (dependent on dwell time)			• Vitamin C increases efficacy by making urine more acidic
	• Probiotics	• *Supplement* • Look for multi-strand bacteria count of lactobacillus, rhamnosus, and reuteri	• Healthy bacteria can theoretically naturally suppress unwanted bacteria • Data is limited			
GI and Anal Pain	• Loperamide (Imodium®)	• Antidiarrheal	• Antidiarrheal	• High blood sugar • Abdominal pain • Nausea • Vomiting • Xerostomia • Dizziness • Fatigue	• Abdominal pain in the absence of diarrhea	• Venetocla • Lasmiditan • Simeprevir
	• Nifedipine, diltiazem rectal ointments often compounded with lidocaine to help with pain Applied 3 × per day nifedipine 0.2% or 2% with lidocaine 2% Diltiazem 2% with lidocaine 1%	• Calcium channel blocker	• Anal fissure—relaxes and dilates blood vessels and increases circulation to the area	• Headache (dilute with Vaseline® if this occurs) • Lightheadedness, flushing, dizziness, and nausea	• Low blood pressure • Severe anemia • Heart failure • Recent heart attack • Exposure to nitrates	• Cough cold products • Migraine drugs • Ergotamine, diuretics, and some medications for high blood pressure and erectile dysfunction

Continued

Medication and Daily Dose Range	Medication Class	Therapeutic Effect	Side Effects	Contraindications	Main Drug Interactions
GI and Anal Pain (*continued*)					
• Nitroglycerin (Rectiv®) rectal ointment often compounded with lidocaine to help with pain • Nitroglycerin 0.2% with lidocaine 2%	• Nitrates	• Anal fissure • Relaxes and dilates blood vessels and increases circulation to the area	• Low blood pressure • Flushing • Dizziness • Headache • Anaphylactoid reaction • Methemoglobinemia • Raised intracranial pressure	• Severe anemia or heart failure • Methemoglobinemia • Low blood pressure • Brain hemorrhage • High pressure in the skull • Allergy	• Tadalafil • Vardenafil • Sildenafil • Beta blockers • Calcium channel blockers • Aspirin • Heparin • Alcohol • Ergotamine
Stool softeners					
• Docusate sodium (Colace®), Psyllium (Metamucil®) or other fiber	• Bulking and softening agents for stool	• Helps with constipation • Drink plenty of water	• Must be titrated to effect • Can lead to diarrhea		
• Psyllium (Metamucil®) or other Fiber	• *Bulking agent* for stool	• Helps with diarrhea			
Skin Barriers					
• Zinc oxide • Dimethicone • Petroleum	• Skin Barrier	• Helps coat the skin to allow healing			
Antifungals: Perianal and Vaginal					
• Clotrimazole (Lotrimin®), miconazole (Monistat®)	• Topical antifungal (anti-yeast)	• Decreases vaginal or perianal yeast on skin surface			
• Nystatin powder (Nystop®) or cream (Mycostatin®)	• Topical antifungal (anti-yeast)	• Skin folds (non-mucous membranes)			

Chapter 12: Which Medications Are Used to Manage Pain? 195

	Medication and Daily Dose Range	Medication Class	Therapeutic Effect	Side Effects	Contraindications	Main Drug Interactions
Antifungals: Perianal and Vaginal *(continued)*	• Fluconazole (Diflucan®) oral	• Oral antifungal (anti-yeast)	• Used for vaginal or systemic yeast infection, such as yeast in urine	• Headache • Diarrhea • Nausea • Dizziness • Rash • Taste change	• Low magnesium or potassium • Some abnormal heart rhythms • Pregnancy • Problems with liver or kidney function	• Clopidigral • Pimozide • Quinidine • Macrolide antibiotics (such as erythromycin)
	• Nystatin Oral (Mycostatin®)	• Oral antifungal (anti-yeast)	• Best for perianal and bowel-related yeast infection as Fluconazole does not enter the GI tract as well	• Diarrhea • Nausea • Stevens-Johnson syndrome (severe rash)	• Allergy	
Vulvar/Vaginal Treatments for Atrophy, Inflammation or Infection	• Vaginal estrogens (creams, tablet, ring, insert) • Compounded Estradiol or Estriol Estradiol dosages: range between 0.04–100 mcg dosing, two to three times a week after a two-week, daily loading dose Estriol dosages: range between 0.5–1 mg dosing, two to three times a week, after a two-week, daily loading dose	• Estradiol or conjugated estrogens	• Changes pH and promotes a healthy microbiome • Can decrease frequency of UTI by changing pH, cell structure, ability of bacteria to adhere, and by creating better urethral seal	• Headache[1] • Temporary hot flashes • Breast pain All are addressed by decreasing the number of grams applied Irritation can occur on skin surface, which is addressed by compounding in a different hypoallergenic base	• Angioedema • Prophylactic reaction[1] • Use with permission from breast doctor if personal history of breast cancer or suspicious mammogram • Data regarding the small risk of breast cancer, stroke, and other risks is based on estrogen oral ingestion	• *Aromatase inhibitors*, such as anastrozole, which is used for breast cancer

Continued

Medication and Daily Dose Range	Medication Class	Therapeutic Effect	Side Effects	Contraindications	Main Drug Interactions
Vulvar/Vaginal Treatments for Atrophy, Inflammation or Infection (continued) • Boric acid 600 mg vaginal suppository (compounded) Directions: insert 1 suppository vaginally at night for either 14 or 28 nights Suppository form decreases local site reactions	• Vaginal antibacterial and anti-yeast medication	• Changes pH and hospitality to bacteria and yeast	• Local site irritation, redness, burning, watery vaginal discharge • Toxic if taken by mouth		• Idoxuridin[2]
• Metronidazole (Metrogel®), clindamycin (Cleocin®)	• Antibiotics for bacterial vaginosis • Clindamycin also is used for desquamative inflammatory vaginitis		• Erythyma[1] • Vaginal moniliasis[2] • HPA-axis suppression[1]	• Hypersensitivity[1]	• Alcohol • Disulfirum[1] • Erythromycin[2]
• Amphotericin B: Amphotericin 50 mg suppository or cream Apply 50 mg vaginally every night for 14 nights	• Compound antifungal/anti-yeast				
• Flucytosine 17% Apply 5 grams every night at bedtime for 14 nights	• Compound antifungal/anti-yeast				

	Medication and Daily Dose Range	Medication Class	Therapeutic Effect	Side Effects	Contraindications	Main Drug Interactions
Vulvar/Vaginal Treatments for Atrophy, Inflammation or Infection (*continued*)	• Clotrimazole/ hydrocortisone 2% 50 mg 2% 100 mg Insert 1 suppository up to every 12 hours intravaginally Apply 1 gram every 12 hours intravaginally	• Compound antifungal/anti-yeast and topical steroid				
	• Vulvar steroid clobetasol (Temovate®), hydrocortisone cream and ointment Steroid used rarely inside the vagina, due to thinning of the tissue	• Topical steroid, usually applied *externally* • Check label re: vagina and perianal use	• Decreases inflammation	• Fissures • Skin changes	• Hypersensitivity[1] • Check with provider regarding use of steroid during infection	• Aldesleukin[1]

Continued

	Medication and Daily Dose Range	Medication Class	Therapeutic Effect	Side Effects	Contraindications	Main Drug Interactions
Vulvar/Vaginal Treatments for Spasm or Pain	• Diazepam (Valium®) vaginal suppositories or tabs: 5 or 10 mg suppository or tabs Insert 1 every 8 hours PRN intravaginally Cream/ointment: 5 mg/ml Apply 1–2 grams every 8 hours intravaginally Lidocaine 2% can be added Can be used rectally, but absorption might be as high as if taken orally	• Compound locally applied benzodiazepine	• *Sedative* and muscle relaxant	• Hypotension • Sedation • Diarrhea • Euphoria[2]	• High doses of other sedatives	• Flumazenil[2]
	• Baclofen (Lioresel®) Vaginal 5 or 10 mg suppository: Insert 1 suppository up to every 8 hours PRN pain Cream/ointment: 5 mg/ml Apply 1–2 grams up to every 8 hours PRN intravaginally Lidocaine 2% can be added	• Compound locally applied antispasmodic	• Muscle relaxant	• Hypotonia • Drowsiness • Confusion • Headache • Nausea • Vomiting	• Hypersensitivity[2]	• Azelastine • Paraldehyde • Thalidomide

	Medication and Daily Dose Range	Medication Class	Therapeutic Effect	Side Effects	Contraindications	Main Drug Interactions
Vulvar/Vaginal Treatments for Spasm or Pain (*continued*)	• Diazepam/baclofen/lidocaine combinations vaginally suppositories Most common doses below. Suppository: • 5 mg/5 mg/2% • 10 mg/10 mg/2% • Insert 1 suppository up to every 8 hours PRN intravaginally Cream/ointment: • 5 mg/5 mg/10 mg/ml • Apply 1–2 grams up to every 8 hours intravaginally • Lidocaine 2% can be added	• Compound locally-applied combination: sedative, antispasmodic, and topical anesthetic	• Muscle relaxant and pain reliever	• Hypotonia • Drowsiness • Confusion • Irritation at site or application • Headache • Nausea • Vomiting • Hypotension • Diarrhea • Euphoria[2]	• Hypersensitivity • Significant doses or other sedatives • Cardiac arrythmia	• Azelastine • Paraldehyde • Thalidomide • Flumazenil[2]
	• Gabapentin (Neurontin®) cream 2%–6% Apply 1 gram every 12 hours PRN pain intravaginally • Pregabalin (Lyrica®) 2%–5% Apply 1 gram every 12 hours PRN for pain intravaginally	• Compound locally-applied anticonvulsant	• Neuropathic pain relief	• Possible drug class side effects: dizziness, leg swelling, fatigue, weight gain, rash, constipation, nausea, or liver toxicity • Rarely, patients might experience a change in mood		

Continued

	Medication and Daily Dose Range	Medication Class	Therapeutic Effect	Side Effects	Contraindications	Main Drug Interactions
Vulvar/Vaginal Treatments for Spasm or Pain (*continued*)	• Amitriptyline (Elavil®) 2% cream ointment or suppository Apply 1 gram vaginally every 12 hours PRN per pain intravaginally	• Compound locally-applied tricyclic antidepressants	• Neuropathic pain relief	• Possible drug-class side effects: dry mouth, sedation, mood changes, blurred vision, weight gain, blood pressure changes, urinary retention, constipation, or abnormal heart rhythm		
	• Amitriptyline (Elavil®), Baclofen (Lioresel®), gabapentin (Neurontin®) 2%, 2%, 2% 2%, 2%, 6% Can be ointment or cream Apply 1 gram every 12 hours PRN per pain per vagina Most Common Combination: Amitriptyline/Baclofen/Gabapentin Commonly used topically in place of oral for pain in other areas	• Compound locally applied combination: tricyclic anti-depressant, antispasmodic, and anticonvulsant	• Muscle relaxant and neuropathic pain relief	• Possible drug-class side effects: dry mouth, sedation, mood changes, blurred vision, weight gain, blood pressure changes, urinary retention, constipation, or abnormal heart rhythm; side effects are less likely than with oral pill form of these medications because the medications are applied to the body surface rather than being ingested.		

Medication and Daily Dose Range	Medication Class	Therapeutic Effect	Side Effects	Contraindications	Main Drug Interactions
Vulvar/Vaginal Treatments for Spasm or Pain (*continued*)					
• Tacrolimus (Prograf®) 1–2 mg suppository Insert 1 suppository vaginally at night as directed					
• Naltrexone—low dose (Vivitrol®) 1.5–4.5 mg oral capsule every night Naltrexone 3 mg/ml vaginal cream Apply 1 ml at night intravaginally	• Opioid agonist	• Used with pain, inflammation, or autoimmune conditions			
Systemic Hormonal Medications					
Estrogen/progesterone, including: • Pills, including the birth control pill • Patches • Vaginal ring • Norethindrone (progestin-only pill) • Etonogestrel (Nexplanon®) progesterone implant	• Female hormones	• Suppresses menstrual cycle • Prevents ovulation	• Irritation at site or application • Headache • Pelvic pain[1] • Irregular bleeding • Mood changes • DVT • Loss of sexual desire	• Anaphylaxis • Hypersesitivity[1] • Personal hx of breast or uterine cancers • History of blood clots, stroke or heart disease • History of migraine with aura • Liver impairment • Unexplained vaginal bleeding	• Use of aromatase inhibitors • Anti-retrovirals

Continued

	Medication and Daily Dose Range	Medication Class	Therapeutic Effect	Side Effects	Contraindications	Main Drug Interactions
Systemic Hormonal Medications (*continued*)	• Medroxyprogesterone acetate (Depo-Provera®) injection	• Progestin-based female hormone shot given every 3 months	• Birth control: inhibits gonadotropin production which blocks follicular maturation and ovulation[2]	• Weight gain and bloating • Uterine bleeding • Clotting of blood • Injection site reaction	• Breast cancer • Use with caution if risk of blood clotting, stroke or heart disease	• Tranexamic acid • Carbamazepine • Isotretinon[2]
	• Goserelin (Zoladex®)	• Gonadotropin-releasing hormone analog	• Short-term relief of pain from pelvic venous disease	• Weight gain • Abdominal pain[2] • *Depression*	• History of severe depression • Osteoporosis • Personal history of breast cancer	
	• Elagolix (Orilissa®)	• *Gonadotropin releasing hormone antagonist*	• Short-term relief of pain from pelvic venous disease	• Hot flashes and bone loss		
			• Treats pain associated with endometriosis by reducing estrogen levels	• Hot flashes • Mood swings • Decreased bone density	• Liver impairment • Osteoporosis	• Griseofulvin[1] • Cytochrome P450 modifiers
	• Leuprolide acetate (Lupron Depot®)	• Gonadotropin releasing hormone agonist	• Potent reversible inhibition of gonadotropin secretion, through suppression of testicular and ovarian steroidogenesis[2]	• Edema • Acne • Flushing[2] • Osteoporosis (with long-term use) • Vaginal discomfort	• Hypersensitivity • Breastfeeding[2]	• Amisulphide[2]
	• Aromatase inhibitors: anastrozole (Arimidex®), letrozole (Femara®)	• Aromatase inhibitor	• Inhibits the conversion of androstenedione to estrone by aromatase[2]	• Vaginal atrophy with vulvar pain and UTI • Hypertension • Vasodilation • Peripheral edema[2]	• Hypersensitivity[2]	

	Medication and Daily Dose Range	Medication Class	Therapeutic Effect	Side Effects	Contraindications	Main Drug Interactions
Systemic Hormonal Medications (*continued*)	• *Testosterone* injections (Depot-Testosterone®) • Testosterone topical (Testim®, Androgel®) • Testosterone can also be compounded as 100 mg/ml or 200 mg/ml for ease of use (more common)	• Male hormone (*androgen*)	• Erectile dysfunction and other symptoms of male menopause • Low testosterone in women, some vulvar pain	• Injection-site bruising • Headache[2]	• Breast cancer in men[2] • Pregnancy[2]	• Warfarin[2]
Other Hormonal Medication	• Hormone-secreting intrauterine device (Mirena®, Liletta®, Skyla®)	• Progestin applied directly to lining of uterus	• Thins endometrial lining, inhibits inflammation, decreasing uterine pain and bleeding • Birth control	• Irregular bleeding • Acne • Breast tenderness	• Current pelvic infection or at risk for sexually transmitted illness • Abnormal uterine anatomy • Undiagnosed vaginal bleeding • Hormone-receptive cancer	
Immune and Anti-Inflammatory Medications	• Non-steroidal anti-inflammatory drugs (NSAIDs): See General Pain Medications • Mesalamine (Pentasa®, Asacol®, Apriso®, Delzicol®, Lialda®)	• Anti-inflammatory	• Relief of pain due to inflammation • Used for ulcerative colitis	• Chest pain, shortness of breath, blood in stool or vomit, or swelling	• Inform provider if you have myocarditis, liver or kidney disease, or, phenylketonuria, and if you are pregnant	• Aluminum hydroxide and magnesium hydroxide • Calcium carbonate • Aspirin • NSAIDs • Azathioprine

Continued

Medication and Daily Dose Range	Medication Class	Therapeutic Effect	Side Effects	Contraindications	Main Drug Interactions
Immune and Anti-Inflammatory medications (*continued*)					
• Corticosteroids: betamethasone (Celestone®), prednisone (Prednisone Intensol®), prednisolone (Orapred®, Prelone®), triamcinolone (Aristospan®, Kenalog®), methyl-prednisolone (Medrol®, Depo-Medrol®, Solu-Medrol®), dexamethasone (DexPak®)	• Steroids	• Control of inflammation, e.g., in vasculitis			
• Azathioprine (Azasan®, Imuran®), Remicade (Infliximab®), ustekinymba (Stelara®), and adalimumab (Humira®), vedolizumab (Entyvio®)	• *Immunosuppressants* • *Monoclonal antibodies*		• Immunosuppression	• Pregnancy, liver or kidney failure, bad infection, low platelets or white blood cells, pancreatitis, and lymphoma	• Febuxostat and cancer drugs such as cyclophosphamide, melphalan, rituximab, tofacitinib
• Immunomodulators • Interleukins (IL-1, IL-17) • Tumor necrosis factor alpha TNF-α		• Decreasing rheumatologic inflammation especially in ankylosing spondylarthritis (IL-17) and Schnitzler syndrome (IL-1)			
• IV immunoglobulin (IVIG)		• Useful for autoimmune disease causing small fiberpolyneuropathy			

Chapter 12: Which Medications Are Used to Manage Pain? 205

	Medication and Daily Dose Range	Medication Class	Therapeutic Effect	Side Effects	Contraindications	Main Drug Interactions
Blood Thinners	• Aspirin	• NSAID	• Used for pelvic ischemia, secondary prevention of acute coronary syndrome	• Gastrointestinal ulcer	• Hypersensitivity to NSAIDs	• Ketorolac • Dichlorphenamide
	• Clopidogrel (Plavix®)	• Antiplatelet	• Anticoagulation	• Hemorrhages	• Active bleeding	• Amlodipine, nifedipine, and diltiazem can increase risk of thrombotic events
	• Cilostazol (Pletal®)	• Antiplatelet	• Anticoagulation	• Headache, diarrhea	• Heart failure	
General Pain Medication	• Acetaminophen (Tylenol®) 325–500 mg tablets • For pain, dose is 1000 mg by mouth every 4 to 6 hours, not to exceed 4000 mg in 24 hours	• Analgesic	• Pain and fever relief	• Generally, well tolerated • Possible side effects: constipation, nausea, headache • In high doses, this medication can cause liver failure • No proven risk of harm to an unborn fetus if taken during pregnancy	• Liver failure	• Alcohol, Percocet®, and other opioid mixtures that contain acetaminophen
	• Ibuprofen (Advil®, Motrin®) 200–800 mg • For pain, dose is 400–800 mg every 8 hours as needed for pain, not to exceed 2400 mg/day Take with food	• NSAIDs	• Pain and fever relief	• Possible drug class side effects: gastrointestinal irritation or bleeding, increased risk of heart disease, kidney injury	• Kidney failure	• Other medications that impact bleeding

Continued

	Medication and Daily Dose Range	Medication Class	Therapeutic Effect	Side Effects	Contraindications	Main Drug Interactions
General Pain Medication (*continued*)	• Celecoxib (Celebrex®) 100–200 mg	• NSAIDs		• Less risk of gastrointestinal irritation than other NSAIDs, still carries increased risk of heart disease, kidney injury		
	• Diclofenac (Cambia®, Cataflam®, Voltaren-X®R, Zipsor®, Zorvolex®) • Indomethacin (Indocin®) • Naproxen (Aleve®, Anaprox®, Naprelan®, Naprosyn®) • Oxaprozin (Daypro®) • Piroxicam (Feldene®)	• NSAIDs	• Pain relief	• In addition to oral administration, diclofenac is formulated as a topical ointment or liquid • Topical application of NSAIDs might lead to local skin irritation, but generally causes fewer side effects		
	• Gabapentin (Neurontin®) Oral dosing: 300–3600 mg Topical dosing: 2%–6% cream • Pregabalin (Lyrica®) Oral dosing: 50–300 mg can go to 600 mg/day if patient tolerates Topical dosing: 2%–5% cream • Compounded versions, may have fewer systemic side effects	• Anticonvulsants	• Neuropathic pain relief	• Possible drug-class side effects: dizziness, leg swelling, fatigue, weight gain, rash, constipation, nausea, liver toxicity • Rarely, patients can experience a change in mood or behavior		

	Medication and Daily Dose Range	Medication Class	Therapeutic Effect	Side Effects	Contraindications	Main Drug Interactions
General Pain Medication (*continued*)	• Tegretol (Carbamazepine®) 200–1200 mg	• Anticonvulsant		• Dizziness • Drowsiness		• Abenaiclib • Apixaban
	• Topiramate (Topamax®)	• Anticonvulsant (carbonic anhydrase inhibitor)	• Fibromyalgia pain	• Fatigue	• Hypersensitivity	• Bromiperidol • Thalidomide • Azelastine[1]
	• Fluoxetine (Prozac®)	• *Selective serotonin re-uptake inhibitors (SSRIs)*		• Paresthesia • Drowsiness • Fatigue		• Nifedipine
	• Sertraline (Zoloft®) • Lamotrigine (Lamictal®) • Oxcarbazepine (Trileptal®) • Lacosamide (Vimpat®) • Venlafaxine (Effexor®) • *Duloxetine (Cymbalta®)* • Milnacipran (Savella®)	• Serotonin norepinephrine reuptake inhibitors (SNRIs)		• Insomnia • Headache • Anxiety[1] • Fatigue[1]	• Concomitant use of disulfram, MAOIs, pimozide • Discuss alcohol use or suicidal thoughts with provider prior to starting • Hypersensitivity[2]	• Mesoridazine[2]

Continued

	Medication and Daily Dose Range	Medication Class	Therapeutic Effect	Side Effects	Contraindications	Main Drug Interactions
General Pain Medication (*continued*)	• Amitriptyline (Elavil®) • Nortriptyline (Pamelor®) • Imipramine (Tofranil®) See Vulvar/Vaginal Treatments for Spasm or Pain for topical compounded version	• Tricyclic antidepressants		• Possible drug class side effects: dry mouth, sedation, mood changes, blurred vision, weight gain, blood pressure changes, urinary retention, constipation, or abnormal heart rhythm	• Concomitant use of MAOIs, • Hypersensitivity[2]	• Bromopride[1] • Monoamine oxidase inhibitors (MAOIs)[1]
	• Baclofen (Kemstro®, Lioresal®) • Oral dosing: 10–30 mg daily • Topical dosing: 2%–10% cream See Vulvar/Vaginal Treatments for Spasm or Pain for topical compounded version	• Muscle relaxant	• Spasticity	• Possible drug class side effects: Sedation, Dizziness, weakness, or reduced muscle tone • Changes in blood pressure, dry mouth, drowsiness, hypotonia, confusion, headache, nausea, and vomiting	• Hypersensitivity[2]	• Azelastine • Paraldehyde • Thalidomide
	• Cyclobenzaprine (Flexeril®, Amrix® and Fexmid®) • Oral dosing: 5–10 mg up to 3 times daily • Topical dosing: 0.5%–2% cream	• Muscle relaxant	• Skeletal muscle relaxant • Acts primarily at the brain stem within the central nervous system	• Peripheral anticholinergic actions • Sedative effect • Might increase heart rate	• Arrhythmias • Heart block • Hypersensitivity[2] • Hyperthyroidism • Congestive heart failure • Concomitant use with MAOI	• Monoamine oxidase inhibitors (MAOIs) • Saquinavir • Ziprasidone • Safinamid

	Medication and Daily Dose Range	Medication Class	Therapeutic Effect	Side Effects	Contraindications	Main Drug Interactions
Muscle Relaxant (*continued*)	• *Tizanidine* (Zanaflex®) 2–8 mg daily	• Alpha-adrenergic agonist	• Produces antihypertensive effects • Treatment of spasticity	• Hypotension • Drowsiness • Xerostomia	• Concomitant use of potent CYP1A2 inhibitors, such as fluvoxamine and ciprofloxacin	• Caution with drug interactions, such as fluvoxamine or ciprofloxacin
	• Benzodiazepines (Valium®, Xanax®, Ativan®) See Vulvar/Vaginal Treatments for Spasm or Pain for topical compounded version	• Benzodiazepine, with muscle relaxant effect, related to alcohol	• Muscle relaxant	• Drowsiness • Hypotension • Diarrhea • Euphoria[2] • In addition to typical side effects of muscle relaxants, diazepam can be habit-forming	• Acute angle glaucoma • Myasthenia gravis • Hepatic and respiratory insufficiency[2]	• Flumazenil[2] • Alcohol
Opioids	• Oxycodone (OxyContin®), hydrocodone (Vicodin®), Codeine • Meperidine (Demerol®) • Morphine (Roxanol®) • Methadone • Hydromorphone (Dilaudid®) • Tramadol (Ultram®) • Fentanyl (Duragesic®, Onsolis®, Fentora®)	• Opioids/synthetic opiates	• Short-term pain control	• Constipation • Affect on cognition • Habit-forming		• Tylenol® (as it is often mixed with opioids increasing the overall dose)

*Note: The side effects, contraindications, and drug interactions are not comprehensively listed. Please discuss these options with your prescriber and pharmacist, and read the information provided to you with your medication.

Key: All listed medications can be given orally unless specified. Select sources of information: [1]Lexicomp and [2]Micromedex Websites 2019. Doses listed above might vary, other side effects, contraindication, and drug interaction might exist. Please consult your prescriber or pharmacist, providing a full list of all your commercial, compound, and over-the-counter medications, as well as your medical history.

WHICH MINIMALLY INVASIVE INTERVENTIONS CAN TREAT NERVE PAIN?

Alexandra R. Adler, MD; Huy Truong, MD; Jianren Mao, MD, PhD; Julie G. Pilitsis, MD, PhD; and Antje M. Barreveld, MD

CHAPTER

In This Chapter

- Introduction
- What Is a Diagnostic Injection?
- What Is a Therapeutic Injection?
- What Are Peripheral Nerve Injections and How and Why Are They Used?
- What Risks Are Associated with Peripheral Injections?
- What Is Spinal Cord Stimulation?
- How Do Spinal Cord Stimulators Work?
- When Are Spinal Cord Stimulators Helpful?
- What Is a Spinal Cord Stimulator Trial?
- Will I Always Have to Feel Tingling with Spinal Cord Stimulators?
- What Is Needed Before Spinal Cord Stimulator Implantation Surgery?
- What Problems May Arise with Spinal Cord Stimulators?
- What Are Sacral Nerve Stimulators and Pudendal Nerve Stimulators?
- What Is an Intrathecal Pain Pump?
- What Should I Discuss with My Provider Regarding Minimally Invasive Interventions for Pain?

Introduction

The treatment of *pelvic pain* is *multi-modal*. It relies on a combination of approaches that include use of medications, injections, and procedures, behavioral medicine and psychology, alternative therapies, and surgery. *Minimally invasive* procedures and treatment are integral to the management of pelvic pain. Although some treatments are supported by rigorous scientific research, much of the treatment of pelvic pain draws on the experiences of patients and providers. This chapter discusses medications, injections, and other minimally invasive treatments (including *spinal cord stimulation* [SCS]).

What Is a Diagnostic Injection?

A *diagnostic injection* is an injection of *local anesthetic* (numbing medication) to localize your pain to a single structure. Diagnostic injections can be delivered into *muscles* (such as those in the back and the pelvic floor); joints (such as those in the hips); tendons, and around peripheral *nerves*, the *spine*, or *sympathetic plexus* nerves. A diagnostic nerve block aims to localize your pain to the territory of the nerve (Figure 13-1, 13-2, 13-3, and 13-4) involved by temporarily numbing the targeted nerve. Like the name implies, diagnostic injections can help your provider diagnose whether irritation of a specific nerve or muscle is causing your pain. The result of such an injection is positive if it temporarily relieves the pain (and therefore diagnoses the origin of the pain). This assessment leads to your pain-relief strategy. Your provider might ask you to complete a *pain diary* or perform movements that provoke your pain to assess your response. The effects of diagnostic injections generally last for the duration of action of the local anesthetic used (frequently, this is a matter of hours), but the effect of a diagnostic injection is variable and may last longer (weeks or even months). This surprising effect is attributed to the relief of *muscle spasms* or interrupting the pain cycle.

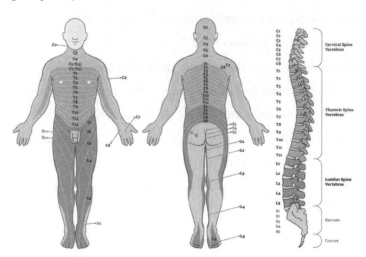

Figure 13-1: Dermatomes indicate which areas of the skin (*dermis*) are served by which nerves in the body.

What Is a Therapeutic Injection?

A therapeutic injection (Figure 13-2) is intended to provide longer-lasting relief than a diagnostic injection. A positive diagnostic injection does not ensure the success of a therapeutic injection, but it suggests that the targeted nerve is the primary generator of the pain. Therapeutic injections frequently include both a local anesthetic and a *steroid*. Steroids are a class of medications that reduce inflammation. Inflammation plays a significant role in the generation of pain, so if inflammation can be reduced, pain can also be diminished. Different therapeutic injections last for different amounts of time. In some cases, they can last for months or even years. It will be difficult for your provider to determine (before administering the injection) how long your injection will last. These injections can be repeated but might be limited in frequency because of concern for side effects of accumulated doses of steroids, which can affect nearly every organ system.

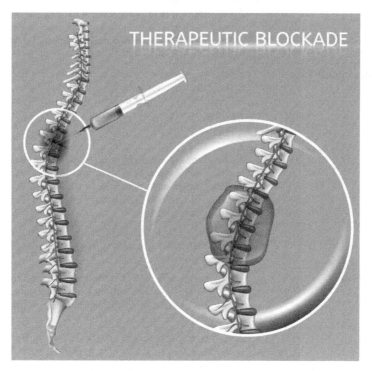

Figure 13-2: A *therapeutic injection* targets a nerve or group of nerves with medications to reduce pain or *inflammation*.

In addition to steroids, therapeutic injections might include other injectable medications or techniques at the discretion of your provider (Table 13-1) (Valovska, 2016; Mei-Dan, 2016). Procedures designed to heat tissue to 80° Celsius (*radiofrequency ablation/lesioning* [RFA/RFL]) or to freeze tissue *(cryoablation)* are sometimes used to prolong relief provided by an injection, but trauma to a nerve from the procedure can lead to painful regeneration of the nerve as well as *neuroma* (nerve tangle) formation. Therefore, these ablation procedures are generally limited to purely *sensory nerves*; in some cases, their use is avoided in non-cancer *chronic pelvic pain* (CPP).

Table 13-1: Substances Used in Therapeutic Injections

Procedure	Description
Botulinum Toxin	Botulinum toxin is a *neurotoxin* that can be injected into a muscle to decrease spasm. It has been Food and Drug Administration (FDA) approved for treatment of certain urinary symptoms and can be injected into the pelvic floor muscles (PFMs), abdominal wall, or iliopsoas muscle for treatment of spasms.
Platelet-rich plasma (PRP)	PRP is an injectable solution prepared with your blood. Specifically, cells from your blood called *platelets* are collected. They are then injected directly into your painful area. The platelets are believed to release *growth factors* that support regeneration, although more research is needed in this area.
Dextrose	*Prolotherapy* is a regenerative medicine injection technique in which small volumes of an irritant solution, such as dextrose, are injected to the site of painful muscles, tendon insertions, joints, and ligaments to promote the growth of normal cells and tissues.
Alcohol	A *neurolytic* injection is an injection of a substance such as alcohol that causes physical damage to a nerve to disrupt transmission of *pain signals*.
Local anesthetic	Local anesthetic is used in most diagnostic and therapeutic injections. These medications primarily numb a target, although some of them might have other beneficial effects (anti-inflammatory).
Steroid	A class of medications used to reduce inflammation. Sometimes, they might be used to prolong relief from injections, but their use is limited by possible side effects associated with frequent use (such as fluid retention, adrenal gland suppression, high blood sugar, muscle thinning, and increased infection risk). Also, steroids can cause a temporary flare-up of pain from nerve or muscle irritation.

What Are Peripheral Nerve Injections and How and Why Are They Used?

Peripheral nerve blocks or injections are used to relieve pain for a period of time. Unlike a surgical intervention, injections do not alter anatomy that might be contributing to chronic pain. Therefore, they are primarily meant to provide a diagnosis as well as pain relief and not to permanently resolve a condition. However, by recognizing that a peripheral nerve is contributing to pain, surgical revisions and therapeutic strategies to treat pain can be refined.

The innervation (sensory supply) of the pelvis is incredibly *complex*, but there are several nerves that are often identified as contributors to pelvic pain. These nerves serve as targets for injections. The most commonly targeted nerves are listed in Table 9-1 and below, along with their typical presentations that can occur when these nerves are irritated or damaged (Figures 13-3 and 13-4).

- *Pudendal nerve*: Pain stemming from the pudendal nerve can be described as knife-like pain or like a foreign-body sensation in the rectum, vagina, or perineum. This can make sitting painful. Pain might be relieved by lying down.

- *Ilioinguinal/genitofemoral nerve*: Pain in the groin can *radiate* (spread) into the vagina, *penis*, or scrotum. Also, the genitofemoral nerve can cause vaginal and penile pain as well as urethral or clitoral pain. These nerves are near each other and therefore, they are generally blocked together.

- Genitofemoral nerve: Pain of the upper *genitals* and pubic region, including the clitoris.

- *Obturator nerve*: Pain of the genitals or over the pubis, radiating to the inner thigh.

- *Posterior femoral cutaneous/inferior cluneal nerves*: Pain in the lower buttocks.

- *Lateral femoral cutaneous nerve*: Pain over the surface of your outer thigh.

- *Anterior abdominal cutaneous nerves*: When they are irritated, they can cause pain over the abdominal skin. The pain can be pinpoint or diffuse. There are many different abdominal cutaneous nerve branches.

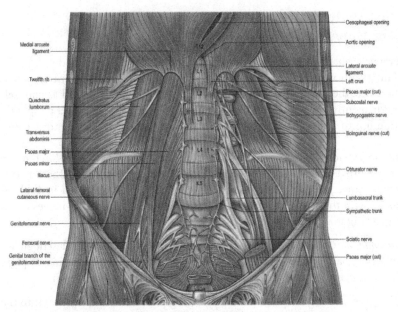

Figure 13-3: The lumbosacral plexus. These peripheral nerves (nerves that connect the spinal cord and brain to the limbs and organs) *innervate* many structures in the pelvis, even though some of them originate outside of the pelvis. (Reproduced with permission: Standring S, ed.: Figure 62.14. Muscles and nerves of the posterior abdominal wall. In: Gray's Atlas of Anatomy. *The Anatomical Basis of Clinical Practice*. 41st ed. Philadelphia, PA: Elsevier, Limited. 2016; 1083–1097.e2.)

What Risks Are Associated with Peripheral Injections?

Injecting adjacent to nerves and into muscles is generally well tolerated without complications. Risks can arise due to the needle itself (including bleeding, infection, nerve irritation, and rarely, nerve damage) or the substance injected (including allergic reaction). Imaging and/or *palpation* of landmarks, such as *bones* and blood vessels, is typically performed during your injection to minimize complications. The agents injected each carry their own set of risks. For example, a *neurolytic injection* with alcohol has the potential to cause damage if the alcohol spreads into tissue adjacent to the nerve.

Chapter 13: Which Minimally Invasive Interventions Can Treat Nerve Pain? 217

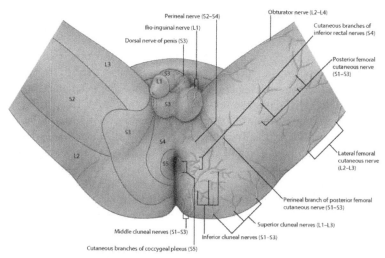

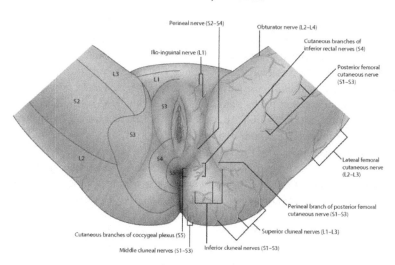

Figure 13-4: Sensory distribution (dermatome and cutaneous nerves) of select nerves of the pelvis. (Reproduced with permission: Drake RL, Vogl AW, Mitchell A, eds.: Dermatomes and cutaneous nerves of perineum in men. Dermatomes and cutaneous nerves of perineum in women. In: Gray's Atlas of Anatomy. Philadelphia, PA: Elsevier Limited. 2021; 213–292.)

What Is Spinal Cord Stimulation?

Spinal cord stimulation (SCS) uses small *electrodes* that can be placed near your *spinal cord* (Figure 13-5) to deliver an electrical current as a form of stimulation to interrupt sensory pain signals. There are two main types of spinal cord stimulators used to treat CPP, including one that is placed on the covering of the spinal cord (the *dura*) and one that is placed on the *dorsal root ganglia* (DRG, passageways from the spinal cord to the peripheral nerves). Traditionally, the electrodes for a SCS device are placed over the dura, the membrane that covers your spinal cord, usually in the lower-mid back. *Dorsal root ganglion stimulation* targets the group of *cell bodies* of the sensory nerves just before they return to the spinal cord. Both types of SCS are routed and connected to a battery-powered control unit hidden under the skin, called the *pulse generator*. The pulse generator will send an electrical signal to the electrodes to stimulate the *neural tissue*. Prior to placement of an SCS system, you will need to undergo evaluation by a physician as well as a trial procedure to see if this will help your pain.

How Do Spinal Cord Stimulators Work?

Some pelvic pain conditions may be caused by overactivity of your nerves, which deliver pain signals to your brain. Spinal cord stimulation uses an electrical current to mask or disrupt pain signals before they reach your brain, which is where pain is perceived. In addition, DRG stimulation is believed to change the function of our *autonomic nervous system*, which innervates the inner organs themselves. Over-activated nerves might be the cause of pain in some cases of pelvic pain. Neither SCS nor DRG stimulation is meant to cure your pain condition; the hope is that they will relieve at least 50% of your pain and improve your daily function and your quality of life.

SCS devices are approved by the *Food and Drug Administration* (FDA) for the treatment of pain in the trunk and extremities, such as with *post-laminectomy syndrome* (pain in the arms or legs in someone with a history of spine surgery); neuropathies (such as *diabetic peripheral neuropathy*); *complex regional pain syndrome* (CRPS), (severe nerve pain in an extremity such as the hand or leg); and *phantom limb pain*. DRG devices are approved for CRPS only. The use of SCS and DRG stimulation to treat CPP is considered *off-label* and might be helpful in patients who have suffered a nerve injury after a pelvic surgery, for instance, but more research is needed. Once implanted, many SCS systems are compatible with MRI imaging.

When Are Spinal Cord Stimulators Helpful?

SCSs can improve or relieve chronic *neuropathic pain*, which is a type of pain resulting from abnormal signals in the *sensory system*. It is not effective for pain from inflammation or muscle spasms. Because of the complicated natural progression of chronic pain, prolonged untreated pain can cause abnormal brain activity, which can be harder to treat. Therefore, use of a SCS should be considered once treatable causes are ruled out and reasonable attempts of medical treatment, organ-based therapy, and *physical therapy* have been tried.

Chapter 13: Which Minimally Invasive Interventions Can Treat Nerve Pain? 219

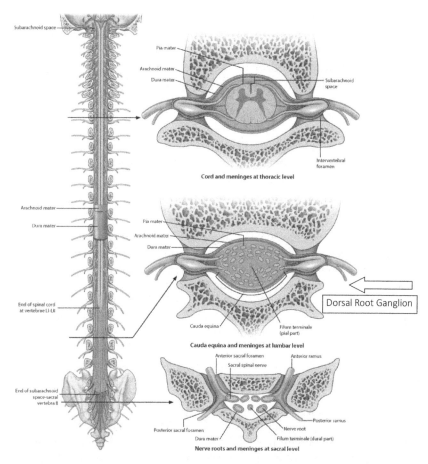

Figure 13-5: The spaces around the spinal cord and *cauda equina*, enveloped by the *meninges* or *thecal sac* (the *pia mater, arachnoid mater,* and *dura mater*). Spinal stimulators are either placed outside the dura mater or along the dorsal root ganglia. An intrathecal pain pump delivers medication directly to the fluid around your spinal cord, the cerebrospinal fluid. (Reproduced with permission: Drake RL, Vogl AW, Mitchell A, eds.: Meninges. In: Gray's Atlas of Anatomy. Philadelphia, PA: Elsevier Limited. 2021; 19–60.)

What Is a Spinal Cord Stimulator Trial?

SCSs do not work for everyone; you will have a "test-drive" trial of a SCS before permanent placement of the system. During the trial, electrodes are placed through your skin using specialized needles, and an *external* pulse generator is connected. You will use the trial system for five to ten days, as directed by your pain specialist and evaluate how the stimulation works for you. It might take two to three days to recover from the procedure itself, and ice can help to reduce the inflammation in the muscle after the leads are placed. You might need to try multiple programs to find which works best. A trial is considered successful when the SCS reduces your pain by at least 50% and/or improves your daily functioning. Permanent implantation of the SCS system underneath the skin surface might then be considered. For the permanent implantation, SCS leads are tunneled under the skin and attached to an *implantable pulse generator* (IPG) or "battery," which is also placed under the skin and attached to the implanted leads. The IPG is typically the size of a "Peppermint Pattie™" candy.

Will I Always Have to Feel Tingling with Spinal Cord Stimulators?

Many SCS devices will use *low-frequency pulses* to replace your pain with a buzzing, soothing, and massage-like sensation called a *paresthesia*. Other devices provide *higher-frequency pulses* to replace your pain without any sensation. Recently developed devices offer pulses that come in a variety of patterns that do not create any sensation. Some devices offer more than one kind of stimulation. You might try multiple settings during your *trial* and after the device has been permanently implanted to find the setting that works best for you. You will be trained on how to use a controller to adjust the stimulation.

What Is Needed Before Spinal Cord Stimulator Implantation Surgery?

Prior to surgery, you will need to undergo a regular health check-up and lab work to receive clearance for surgery. In addition, you will need to be *evaluated* by a *psychologist*. A *pain psychologist* is an important member of your care team, and prior to undergoing an SCS trial, you will be referred to a pain psychologist for an evaluation. The psychologist will assess your ability to tolerate the stress that comes with implanting a foreign object, discuss your support systems and expectations, and work with your physician to make sure you are prepared for the procedure. You can use this opportunity to ask the pain psychologist about the brain-based strategies for pain. You will need a *magnetic resonance image* (MRI) *scan* of your spine so that your *surgeon* can see the *anatomy* where she/he will be working to maximize the safety of your surgery. If you cannot have a MRI scan (for example, because of metal in your body), a *computerized tomographic* (CT) *myelogram* might be an alternative. With a *CT myelogram*, *contrast dye* is injected into the fluid space around your spinal cord.

What Problems May Arise with Spinal Cord Stimulators?

As with any surgery near the spine, there can be bleeding, infection, *cerebrospinal fluid* (CSF) leakage, sensory change or loss, muscle weakness, or dysfunction of your bowel, bladder, or sexual function. With an SCS procedure, there can be issues with movement of the device from its initial location, breakage, or malfunction of the system, which may require further surgery. The system might provide less benefit than expected over time or generate unwanted stimulation (such as burning, tingling, uncomfortable sensations, or muscle contraction). During the healing process and because of the interaction between your body and the device, you might develop minor changes in the stimulation necessitating reprogramming. Sometimes, these changes will require additional surgery and you will need to alert your health care providers to troubleshoot any of these issues. The SCS system might be surgically removed if indicated, but with increasing time from implantation, the leads may be more difficult to remove.

What Are Sacral Nerve Stimulators and Pudendal Nerve Stimulators?

Sacral nerve stimulators (SNS) and *pudendal nerve stimulators* target the peripheral nerves to the pelvis after they leave the spine. The SNS is approved by the FDA for urinary problems and *fecal incontinence*. The stimulators also produce a gentle vibration that acts like "white noise" that can theoretically lessen pain. These devices have not been approved by the FDA for the treatment of pain, but small studies (of 6 to 33 patients) have shown some benefit for people with CPP (Greene et al, 2010). Currently, these options are considered to be experimental.

What Is an Intrathecal Pain Pump?

An *intrathecal pain pump* is a pump system that consists of a *catheter* that carries pain medication from a pump/reservoir implanted between the muscle and skin of your abdomen to the fluid (CSF) around your spinal cord and nerves. It is called intrathecal because the catheter tip is inside the "thecal sac," which is the envelope around the spinal cord. This form of medication delivery bypasses the path that oral medication takes through your body, reducing the required dose of medication to about 1/300 what would be needed when taken by mouth. The intrathecal pain pump is used only when other therapies have failed, surgery is not likely to benefit you, when a test trial is successful, and if you have good psychological health to cope. This is a rare last step in treating CPP.

What Should I Discuss with My Provider Regarding Minimally Invasive Interventions for Pain?

Injections and stimulators are only used in a subset of individuals with CPP. If you believe that your pain matches the nerve patterns in the images included in this chapter or if you have consulted with a *gynecologist, urologist,* and *physical therapist* without relief of your pain, talk to your *primary care provider* (PCP) about the next step. You might also consider obtaining a second opinion within one of the specialties you have seen, versus a neurologic, orthopedic, rheumatologic, or minimally-invasive pain management referral. Referrals are often arranged concurrently, (seeing more than one specialty within an interval of time) including brain-based psychological aspects of pain management.

WHEN IS SURGERY CONSIDERED FOR THE MANAGEMENT OF PELVIC PAIN?

Miriam M. Shao, BS; Massarat Zutshi, MD; Elise J.B. De, MD; Carey York-Best, MD; Sijo J. Parekattil, MD; Julie G. Pilitsis, MD, PhD; Marilyn Heng, MD, MPH, FRCSC; Huy Truong, MD; Nucelio Lemos, MD, PhD; Peter Cole, MD; and Chun Hin Angus Lee, MD

CHAPTER 14

In This Chapter

- Introduction
- What Types of Problems Can Be Fixed with Surgery?
- What Should I Try Before Undergoing Surgery for Pain Relief?
- What Should I Learn About Having Surgery?
- Which Gynecological Conditions (Female Anatomy) Can Be Addressed with Surgery?
- How Can Gynecological Problems Be Addressed with Surgery?
- What Chronic Pain Problems Associated with Male Anatomy Can Be Treated Surgically?
- What Problems with the Bladder, Urethra, or Kidneys Can Be Addressed with Surgery?
- What Types of Anorectal Problems Can Be Fixed with Surgery?
- How Can Abdominal Hernias Be Fixed with Surgery?
- What Neurological Pelvic Pain Problems Can Be Corrected with Surgery?
- How Can Nerve Entrapment Be Fixed with Surgery?
- How Can a Herniated Disc Be Fixed with Surgery?

continued

- How Can Other Neurological Pain Problems Be Fixed with Surgery?
- What Musculoskeletal, Bone, and Ligament Problems Can Be Addressed with Surgery?
- What Vascular Problems Can Be Addressed with Surgery?
- Will I Remain on Medications for Pelvic Pain Around the Time of Surgery?
- Can Surgery Make My Problems Worse?

Introduction

Surgery is a treatment option for *pelvic pain* if an anatomic abnormality is strongly suspected as the cause of pain or if other therapeutic options, such as medications and injections, have been unsuccessful.

What Types of Problems Can Be Fixed with Surgery?

Surgery can often fix pain that arises from abnormalities in *anatomy* associated with reproductive functions, urination, digestion, joint function, vessel integrity, or nerve signaling. Some of the problems listed in Table 14-1 can be addressed with surgery.

Table 14-1: Problems That Can Be Addressed with Surgery

System	Problem
Gynecologic	Endometriosis, fibroids, ovarian cysts, hernia/prolapse of the female organs, pelvic adhesions, pelvic congestion syndrome
Urologic	Bladder outlet obstruction, urethral diverticulum, stones, neurogenic bladder, bladder pain, testes and prostate pain, hernias/prolapse of the female organs
Neurogenic	Entrapped peripheral *nerves*, herniated discs, tumors affecting the spinal cord, tethered spinal cord
Anorectal	Hemorrhoids, anal fissures, rectal prolapse
Orthopedic	Torn labrum, hip joint arthritis, widely displaced pubic diastasis, fractures
Vascular	Pelvic venous congestion

What Should I Try Before Undergoing Surgery for Pain Relief?

Depending on the diagnosis—and by this point, you have learned that there are many causes for pelvic pain—several options are available before surgery. These options include use of medications, *physical therapy*, *anesthetic* and *steroid injections*, stimulators, mindfulness, lifestyle changes, and *psychotherapy*. Sometimes, surgery is offered prematurely when more conservative options would have been effective. Sometimes, treatment requires surgery and no other strategy will work. Sometimes, surgery is performed as the last resort when more conservative interventions have been tried and failed. Sometimes, surgery fails to relieve pain. This can be frustrating, but it can be beneficial because it helps your providers direct their attention to other causes of the pain.

Chronic pelvic pain (CPP) often has more than one cause. Surgery might correct one component, but other etiologies can continue to create *symptoms*. As a result, CPP is often addressed with a multi-modal approach. For example, someone with pain from *hemorrhoids* might improve with:

- The use of mild pain medications, such as *acetaminophen* or *non-steroidal anti-inflammatory drugs* (NSAIDs)
- Avoiding narcotics (that are associated with addiction and constipation that might worsen the hemorrhoidal pain)
- Stool softeners
- *Pelvic floor muscle* (PFM) *physical therapy* (PT)

If surgery is still recommended, multi-modal therapies will support recovery and the overall success of the surgery in reducing pain over the long term.

What Should I Learn About Having Surgery?

Before undergoing surgery, you should talk to members of your health care team, including the specialists and your *primary care physician* (PCP), to confirm that surgery is your best option and review what you expect from surgery. Obtaining a second opinion can be useful. Your surgeon will discuss the risks, benefits, and alternatives before you provide written consent. You should write down your questions and make sure they are answered by your surgeon; try to be efficient but complete. Many procedures can be performed with a local anesthetic (numbing injection or gel), and some require deep sedation or *general anesthesia* to allow surgeons to operate without causing you discomfort. If you are scheduled to go home on the same day as the procedure, you will not be allowed to drive home after having received general or sedating anesthesia; you will need to have someone accompany you home. If it is likely you will be admitted to the hospital after your surgery, find out how long you are likely to stay and plan accordingly. Finally, you might have limitations placed upon you postoperatively (such as not lifting more than five pounds or restrictions on when you can return to work). When planning a procedure, make sure that you have someone to care for your pets, children, or work responsibilities in case you need to spend more time than expected while recovering.

Which Gynecological Conditions (Female Anatomy) Can Be Addressed with Surgery?

Gynecological abnormalities associated with CPP include *endometriosis, fibroids,* and *ovarian cysts* (Holloran-Schwartz, 2014; Senapati et al, 2016). The growth of endometriosis, fibroids, and ovarian cysts respond to *estrogen,* so *hormone therapy* is often prescribed before surgery.

Endometriosis refers to the process in which the tissue that lines the *uterus* is displaced and grows in other body parts, most commonly in the pelvic and abdominal cavity. The uterus is the hollow organ within the lower abdomen that serves as the womb during pregnancy. It is lined with *endometrium.* The displaced endometrial tissue grows and bleeds in the same way that the endometrium does every month for menstruation. CPP can arise if the displaced endometrial tissue is not expelled from the body as it grows and bleeds during the menstrual cycle; this leads to *inflammation* and *adhesions* (sticking together of the internal tissues). It isn't clear why endometriosis develops in certain women. However, two theories include: "retrograde menstruation," in which blood and endometrial tissue flows backward into the pelvic cavity via the fallopian tube and alterations in the *immune system* that decrease endometrial tissue expulsion during menstruation (Mehedintu et al, 2014).

Fibroids (Figure 14-1), also known as *leiomyomas* (non-cancerous growths of the uterus that are made up primarily of smooth muscle cells) and *ovarian cysts* (fluid-filled structures found in or on the surface of the *ovaries*) are also causes of pelvic pain that can be treated with surgery. They can cause pelvic pain when they grow big enough to put pressure on nearby organs and anatomical structures. However, they are common findings on imaging and do not always create symptoms.

The ovaries are the female reproductive organs that produce sex hormones, as well as harboring and releasing eggs for fertilization during *ovulation. Mittelschmerz* is mid-cycle pain that occurs during ovulation because of *corpus luteum cysts,* which are cysts that form in preparation for releasing an egg. Other ovarian cysts can occur independently of ovulation and menstruation.

How Can Gynecological Problems Be Addressed with Surgery?

Surgical treatment for endometriosis, fibroids, and ovarian cysts all center on removing the abnormal tissue with a *laparoscopy* or a *laparotomy.* Laparoscopies and laparotomies are incisions performed to allow visualization of and access to your reproductive organs. Laparoscopy is generally preferred over a laparotomy when technically feasible because it is less invasive and requires a smaller incision. During a laparoscopy, the surgeon will make a small incision near your navel and insert a viewing instrument called a *laparoscope.* Laparoscopies serve as a valuable diagnostic procedure to visualize lesions, but they are also used to remove *lesions.* Your surgeon can diagnose the extent of your disease and then treat it with a single procedure. Laparotomies require the surgeon to make a larger abdominal incision for direct visualization and manual access with hand-held instruments.

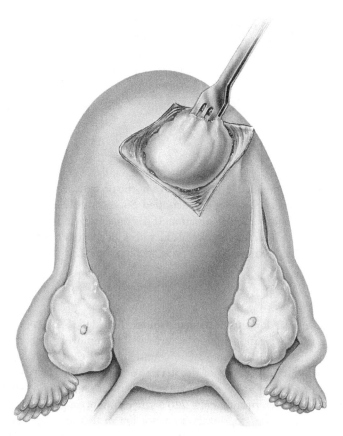

Figure 14-1: Uterine fibroids (leiomyomas) are non-cancerous growths of the uterus that are made up primarily of smooth muscle cells. They might require surgery.

Lesions are removed with *ablation* or *excision*. In an ablation, lesions are destroyed with beams of heat. With an excision, lesions are physically cut out and removed. More severe disease often requires complete excision of the affected organ with a *hysterectomy* (removal of the uterus), *oophorectomy* (removal of the ovary), or *salpingectomy* (removal of the fallopian tubes). A hysterectomy eliminates fertility and an oophorectomy limits it as well, depending on whether both ovaries are removed. A *myomectomy* (muscle removal) is a treatment for fibroids that removes only the fibroids while leaving the rest of the uterus intact; therefore, it is an option for individuals who have not yet completed childbearing.

Ovarian cystectomy is a treatment for ovarian cysts wherein the *cyst* is removed, and the rest of the ovary is preserved.

Pelvic congestion syndrome is a condition in which the veins that connect to the ovaries and/or the uterus become engorged—similar to varicose veins of the legs. These vessels might become painful with prolonged standing and might cause pain with sexual intercourse. It is thought that as many as one-third of women with CPP may also have pelvic congestion syndrome (Obrien and Gillespie, 2015). It can be complicated to decide whether to treat the veins: the symptoms, imaging characteristics, and results of other treatments and diagnostics help to determine if an intervention (typically, an *embolization* by an *interventional radiologist*, stenting, or formal surgery) is appropriate (see below).

What Chronic Pain Problems Associated with Male Anatomy Can Be Treated Surgically?

Prostate

Surgical therapy in men with *chronic*/relapsing bacterial inflammation *(microcolonies)* of the prostate might be recommended if a specific area of the prostate is suspected of harboring *bacteria*—especially if prostate stones are identified. Success rates range from 30%–70% in relieving symptoms in this particular situation. If the cause of pain is more consistent with *bladder outlet obstruction* (blockage by the bladder neck or prostate), especially if the *alpha blocker medications* helped somewhat, surgery to open up the inside of the prostate channel is likely to help.

Testis

Minimally-invasive procedures for testicular pain are discussed in Chapter 4. Rarely, after these treatments and medication trials, the testis will be removed. Pain can persist even after testis removal. For this reason, careful counseling and consideration of alternative options is required. Surgical cutting of the nerves to the testis can help. Rarely, men can have "intermittent *testicular torsion*" in which the testis turns on its blood supply, leading to lack of blood flow and then turning back into a safe position. Surgically tacking the testis into the correct position can stop intermittent torsion in this very rare cause of chronic pain. (Torsion is more often a sudden and urgent cause of pain that does not reverse itself.)

Vas Deferens

Sometimes, *vasectomy reversal* is used in men who experience pain after vasectomy.

Ejaculatory Ducts

Ejaculatory duct obstruction (blockage of the tubes allowing *semen* to pass into the urethra) is a rare cause of pain during or after ejaculation. Diagnosis is made by abnormal semen analysis with low ejaculate volumes and *transrectal ultrasound* showing dilation of the ejaculatory ducts. The surgical approach to the ejaculatory ducts is through the *urethra* (the tube through which you urinate) using a telescope. Small instruments can be used to undo the blockage in a procedure called *"transurethral resection of the ejaculatory duct."* Rare complications include rectal injury, *external* urethral sphincter injury (leading to difficulty holding back urine); bladder neck injury (with resulting flow of ejaculate back into the bladder during ejaculation (called *retrograde ejaculation*); and the possibility of urine *reflux* into the ejaculatory duct.

Penis

Pain in the *penis* from *Peyronie's disease* (a bend in the penis caused by scarring of the elastic sheath surrounding the erectile tissue) is only treated surgically when the bend makes sexual activity too painful for the man or his partner. Medications and injections are usually tried first. Surgery involves either shortening and folding (plicating) the side opposite the bend to straighten the penis or adding a graft material (an insert usually made of animal tissue) in the shortened scarred side (the grafting carries a risk of erection problems).

What Problems with the Bladder, Urethra, or Kidneys Can Be Addressed with Surgery?

Bladder

Surgical bladder problems fall into three categories: sensitivity/small capacity, blockage, and anatomic problems. Sensitivity or small capacity can occur because of *interstitial cystitis*, neurological problems with the bladder, or prior injury, such as from exposure to radiation. If medications are not successful in calming the bladder surface and relaxing the spherical bladder (detrusor) muscle, it is time to move on to the next step. Botulinum toxin can be injected into the wall of the bladder muscle *(detrusor muscle)*. A lower dose of 50–100 units often addresses sensation without relaxing the muscle contractions too much. Higher doses (100–300 units) can cause *urinary retention*, requiring you to place a catheter to empty the bladder several times each day (*clean intermittent catheterization* [CIC]). For those with serious urinary symptoms or neurologic problems, CIC can expand the treatment options, but it takes getting used to. If you are faced with this option and you have reasonable manual dexterity, keep an open mind and learn, hands-on, what it would be like before declining it. CIC is more comfortable when performed on oneself. Whereas botulinum toxin can be used in neurological and non-neurological bladder sensitivity problems, *sacral neuromodulation* is typically used for non-neurological problems. It is not *Food and Drug Administration* (FDA) approved for pain, but it can be of benefit in some cases. If bladder pain is caused by a small capacity bladder or a sensitive bladder caused by a neurological disease, the bladder can be expanded surgically using a segment of bowel; this is called *augmentation cystoplasty*. It is not as successful in non-neurological problems, such as interstitial cystitis.

Blockage of the bladder can cause pain from the turbulence of urine as it passes the blockage or from the high-pressure bladder contraction required to pass urine through or around the blockage. Bladder obstruction is diagnosed via *urodynamic testing*, a pressure test performed with a small catheter in the bladder during voiding. Sometimes, as in *bladder neck obstruction*, the blockage can be addressed by medication, injecting botulinum toxin into the circular muscle at that location, or a more permanent intervention at this location (a "bladder neck incision"). If the prostate is the source of the obstruction, several minimally invasive technologies exist for performing telescopic surgery to the prostate via the urethra (Figure 14-2). Without documented obstruction shown on urodynamic testing, these procedures have not been shown to help with male prostate pain. In women, a prior sling can cause blockage. If your bladder and pelvic pain started at the time of sling surgery, urodynamic testing can help identify if the sling is too tight. This is usually a straightforward surgical correction, but if a blockage has been present for a long time, you might continue to have changes in bladder function.

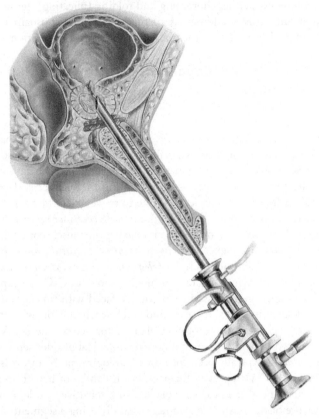

Figure 14-2: Many urologic surgeries are performed through *endoscopes*, which have both a camera and a working channel for tools. Pictured here is a *resectoscope* through which the prostate channel can be opened, relieving obstruction.

Anatomic issues that can benefit from surgical correction include *female cystocele/ anterior pelvic organ prolapse*. In an anterior prolapse, the bladder herniates into the vagina, causing a stretching or heavy feeling. This can lead to a blockage of the bladder through kinking of the urethra.

Stones in the bladder or a bladder diverticulum can cause bladder discomfort. If you have either of these diagnoses, they are usually caused by blockage or incomplete emptying; the cause needs to be addressed at the time of surgery.

Urethra

The urethra can have a *stricture* (a scarred segment) leading to blockage. This might be caused by a prior infection or injury (such as a *straddle* or *zipper injury*). The blockage or inflammation can cause pain. If you have this condition, unless you are in need of urgent intervention for urinary retention, be sure that the surgeon you see is an expert in urethral surgery. After one dilation of a short stricture, formal *urethroplasty* should be undertaken. For long strictures in men, urethroplasty is often recommended as the first step. A *urethral diverticulum* is most often seen in females; it is a pocket or out-pouching of the urethra that is thought to start as a blocked gland. The diverticulum causes pain that is primarily from *inflammation*. Surgical correction is performed vaginally by identifying and removing the *diverticulum*. Sometimes, a *Martius flap* (the fatty tissue from within the labia majora) is used to ensure good healing. Commonly, a *catheter* will remain in place for 1 to 4 weeks after these urethral surgeries.

Ureter

Happily, stones in the ureter are a straightforward condition to address. Once corrected, the pain usually resolves completely. Often, your surgeon will place a *ureteric stent*—a flexible tube between the kidney and the bladder—to dilate the ureter before the stone treatment to protect the ureter during healing. For many people with stones, having the stent is the most uncomfortable part of the procedure. This can be managed with medication (alpha blockers, *anticholinergics*, *ibuprofen*, and *phenazopyridine*). A small percentage of people with ureter stones have persistent pain after the stone has been treated and removed.

What Types of Anorectal Problems Can Be Fixed with Surgery?

Anorectal problems (such as hemorrhoids, *anal fissures*, and *rectal prolapse*) can be treated with surgery, depending on the disease severity. Surgical management for more *complex* anorectal issues (such as anorectal cancer and complications arising from *inflammatory bowel disease*) are beyond the scope of this chapter, but they are also treated surgically.

Anorectal surgery is usually performed by a *colorectal* or *general surgeon* in an ambulatory setting (day procedure). You might require a *bowel preparation* if you need to have a *colonoscopy* as part of the procedure. If not, a *fleet enema* on the day of surgery usually suffices. Most procedures require deep sedation or *general anesthesia* to allow the surgeon to fully examine the anorectal region without causing too much discomfort. *Local anesthesic injection* can be used during surgery to lessen the immediate postoperative pain.

Anal Fissures

An injection of botulinum toxin A under anesthesia can be used to treat anal fissures when medical management fails. Injection of the PFMs can be carried out during the examination under anesthesia for those diagnosed with *levator ani syndrome*.

Surgical Management of Hemorrhoids

Surgical management of hemorrhoids should be tailored to the severity and type (such as internal/external) of hemorrhoids (Table 14-2). Thrombosed hemorrhoids can be treated with removal of the clot *(enucleation)* or the hemorrhoid *(hemorrhoidectomy)* to relieve acute pain. For non-thrombosed hemorrhoids, mild to moderate internal hemorrhoids (grade II/III) can be treated initially with rubber band ligation, which can be readily performed through a *proctoscope* (a telescope that is placed in the rectum) in the outpatient clinic setting without use of anesthesia.

Table 14-2: Characteristics of Hemorrhoids

Grading of Hemorrhoids	Description
I	No hemorrhoidal prolapse
II	Hemorrhoidal prolapse, which spontaneously reduces
III	Hemorrhoidal prolapse, which requires manual reduction
IV	Irreducible hemorrhoidal prolapse

The inner lining of the rectum has a different sensory supply (visceral) compared to the skin (somatic), which means you might not feel any sharp pain. Minor bleeding can be expected but should not be severe. There is a small risk of re-bleeding, which typically happens if a band falls out a week or so after the procedure. You might require several treatment sessions if you have multiple hemorrhoids. Infrared coagulation (Marques et al, 2006; Poen et al, 2000) is another option for grade I/II symptomatic (such as painful or bleeding) internal hemorrhoids.

For the more severe hemorrhoids (such as grade IV) with external hemorrhoid components, *excisional hemorrhoidectomy* (removal by small surgical incision) is the traditional treatment. The significant downside is post-operative pain due to sensitive (somatic) nerves on the external skin. If the hemorrhoids involve a large area around the *anus* (i.e., circumferential), your surgeon may elect to perform a partial excision in one setting and wait for the wound to heal before embarking on the next section. This approach will minimize the risk of anal stenosis (such as scarring that would lead to a tight anus and difficulty defecating).

Another way to treat large circumferential hemorrhoids is called the hemorrhoidal artery ligation recto-anal repair (HAL-RAR). In this approach, ultrasound-guided (Doppler) ligation of the blood supply to hemorrhoidal tissues is performed further inside the anus. Your surgeon can place several *sutures* within the lower rectum to reduce prolapsing rectal mucosa (in other words, recto-anal repair), if needed.

Postoperatively, multi-modal pain control should be adopted, minimizing use of narcotics. Soluble fiber *supplements* are very important to prevent constipation. Sitz baths can help with inflammation and cleanliness around the area. You should try to relax the PFMs, rather than allowing the pain to lead to pelvic tension.

Rectal Prolapse

Rectal prolapse surgery is performed if the lining of the rectum or the rectum itself is slipping out through the anus. This should not be confused with a *rectocele* in which the rectum herniates forward into the vagina. Rectal prolapse surgery is more complex than the other anorectal surgeries, and you will remain in the hospital for at least 1 to 2 days. Surgery is carried out under general anesthesia; alternatively, *spinal anesthesia* can be used, based on your overall medical condition and the anesthesiologist's recommendations.

Two surgical approaches for rectal prolapse are recommended: the *transabdominal approach* (via an incision through the abdomen) and the *perineal approach* (via an incision through the anus). In the transabdominal approach, the rectum is mobilized from the surrounding structures and then fixed to the sacrum using sutures or mesh (*suture rectopexy* or *ventral mesh rectopexy*). This can be performed using a minimally-invasive (laparoscopic or robotic) approach. Sigmoid colon resection (removal of the part of the colon named the sigmoid colon) can also be carried out if there is underlying constipation and redundancy (extra looping) of this part of the colon. In the perineal approach, redundant rectal mucosa can be excised with the rectum being *plicated* (folded and sewn in a shorter position; *Delorme's procedure*). Redundant (extra) sigmoid colon and rectum can be removed (resected) through the same incision (the *Altemeier procedure*). Depending on the extent of the rectal prolapse and your particular situation, your surgeon will guide you as to which approach is likely to be more successful. Your co-existing medical problems and surgical history, such as previous colon and rectum resection, might preclude certain surgical procedures for rectal prolapse.

How Can Abdominal Hernias Be Fixed with Surgery?

Both femoral and inguinal hernias—out-pouching of the abdominal lining called the *peritoneum* and sometimes intra-abdominal contents (Figure 14-3)—are repaired by removing the extra herniated tissue and/or returning it to the abdomen. To provide strength to the abdominal wall, mesh is often sewn in place to prevent future hernias. Hernia repairs can be performed laparoscopically using surgical ports and cameras or via an open abdominal incision. You might hear the terms *transabdominal preperitoneal* (TAPP) or *totally extraperitoneal* (TEP) repair in reference to laparoscopic procedures for inguinal hernias. The two procedures differ in whether the *peritoneal cavity*, which is the space containing abdominal organs, is entered for placement of the mesh; the peritoneal cavity is entered for a TAPP but not for a TEP. The *Lichtenstein procedure* is an open-abdomen surgery that requires incisions to repair the inguinal hernias (Kockerling and Simons, 2018).

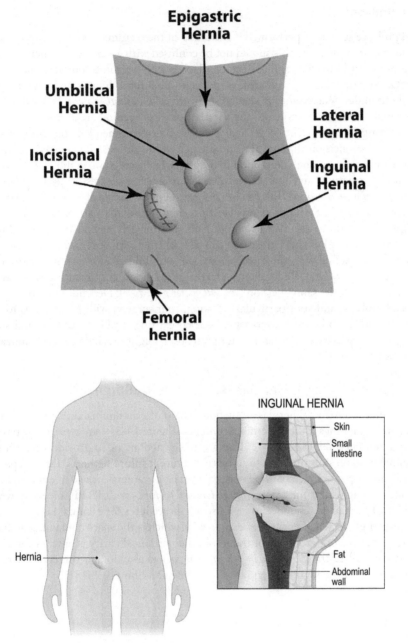

Figure 14-3: Schematic of hernia locations and the weakness in the abdominal wall that leads to the hernia (shown in red). The herniated contents will be returned to the abdomen prior to fixing the hernia.

What Neurological Pelvic Pain Problems Can Be Corrected with Surgery?

Pelvic pain that results from nervous system dysfunction, also known as *neurogenic pelvic pain*, can be treated with surgery. The innervation of the pelvis is extremely complex with the pudendal, ilioinguinal, genitofemoral, obturator, posterior femoral cutaneous, lateral femoral cutaneous, inferior cluneal, and anterior abdominal cutaneous nerves contributing to the sensory supply.

Pain produced by certain physical examination maneuvers (such as diagnostic nerve blocks and *electromyography* [EMG], which assess the functioning of *muscles* and the nerves that control them), and anatomy (identified by *magnetic resonance imaging* [MRI] *scans*), can be used to pinpoint the nerve(s) that cause pain (Elkins et al, 2017). After the nerve(s) are identified, surgery can be considered if other treatment options have failed or if imaging shows an anatomic abnormality causing nerve or spinal cord injury (such as a *herniated disc*, a *Tarlov cyst*, a *sacral tumor*, or a *tethered cord*).

How Can Nerve Entrapment Be Fixed with Surgery?

Nerves can be trapped, or compressed, between structures anywhere along the anatomic course, and imaging is useful for identifying the location. Common causes of entrapment include narrow tunnels through fibrous tissue, endometriosis, conflicts with dilated veins, sites where they run through muscle fibers, and scarring resulting from previous surgeries or tumors compressing on the nerves (Dong et al, 2012; Lemos and Possover, 2015; Elkin et al, 2017). The trickiest aspect of *nerve entrapment* is finding a clinician skilled in identifying the location. Generally, the best option for nerve entrapment pain is to widen the space where the nerve is traveling. This allows for the nerve to continue along its course and function to hopefully improve over time.

How Can a Herniated Disc Be Fixed with Surgery?

A herniated disc (Figure 14-4) within the spinal column in your lower back can pinch a nerve contributing to pelvic sensory input, which can cause pelvic pain that can be treated with surgery. Understanding what a herniated disc is and how it might contribute to pelvic pain requires some knowledge on the anatomy of your *spine* and spinal cord. The *bones* that make up the spine are known as *vertebrae*, and under normal conditions, they stack up perfectly aligned on top of each other. The spinal cord sits in the *spinal canal* and has *spinal nerves* originating from it on both sides. Within the spinal canal, the spinal cord and its nerves are surrounded by the vertebrae. Stacked between the vertebral bodies are *intervertebral discs*, which serve as cushions between the vertebral bodies. They are composed of a softer interior called the *nucleus pulposus* and a harder exterior called the *annulus fibrosus*.

In the setting of a herniated disc, the nucleus pulposus squeezes out between the vertebrae and compresses and irritates the spinal nerves that sit immediately posterior to it. Classically, pelvic pain from a herniated disc occurs if the herniated disc occurs at the lower-back portion of the spinal cord, also known as the *lumbar spine*. Signs that your pelvic pain might be the result of a herniated disc include left- or right-sided pain that *radiates* down your legs and pain that affects only one side of your body. Additional symptoms of bladder dysfunction, bowel incontinence, sexual dysfunction, and *saddle anesthesia* (in which sensation is lost in the buttock and groin region) indicate *cauda equina syndrome* (which is most commonly caused by a herniated disc at the lower level of the spinal cord that looks like a "horse's tail"). Cauda equina syndrome is an emergency because nerve compression of these smaller unprotected nerves for too long can cause permanent damage.

If a herniated disc is diagnosed based on the history and physical exam and is confirmed by an MRI scan, then a surgery known as *discectomy* can be performed. In a discectomy, the damaged portion of the herniated disc is removed so that it can no longer compress the nerve. To access the damaged disc, a piece of the bony *vertebral arch*, known as the *lamina*, surrounding the spinal cord will need to be removed.

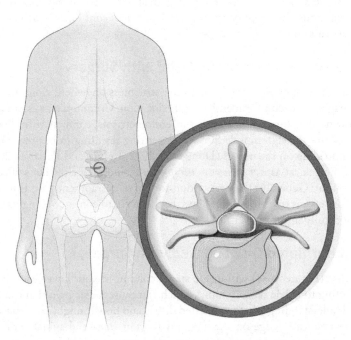

Figure 14-4: Schematic of a herniated disc. Under normal conditions, the spinal cord is protected between the vertebral bodies and arches. Stacked between vertebral bodies are intervertebral discs. Intervertebral discs are composed of a soft nucleus pulposus in the center and hard annulus fibrous in the periphery. With a herniated disc, the nucleus pulposus can bulge out through the annulus fibrous and pinch a nerve originating from the spinal cord, or the cord itself. A discectomy can treat a herniated disc. A piece of the bony vertebral arch known as the lamina is removed to gain access to the damaged disc. This procedure is called a *laminectomy*. Once access is gained, the damaged portion of the herniated disc is removed so that it no longer pinches the nerve.

How Can Other Neurological Pain Problems Be Fixed with Surgery?

Tarlov cysts, sacral tumors, and tethered cord syndrome (TCS) are other causes of pelvic pain. Tarlov cysts and sacral tumors are space-occupying lesions that cause pain by compressing nearby nerves and structures. Tarlov cysts are filled with *cerebrospinal fluid* (CSF) and occur at the level of the *sacral* vertebral bodies in the pelvis. These are most often associated with sensory symptoms because they are commonly found near the *dorsal root ganglion* (DRG), which contain the *cell bodies* of sensory nerves (Elkins et al, 2017). Surgical treatments for sacral tumors include a laminectomy to open the lamina and gain access to the mass for excision, often with reconstruction. Tarlov cysts are generally not operated on; the CSF builds up after they are drained, since they are connected with nerves they cannot often be completely resected. In cases where there is clearly neuropathic pain but no definitive surgery to offer, neuromodulation, including *spinal cord stimulation* (SCS) or *dorsal root ganglion stimulation* (DRGS) can be employed.

In tethered cord syndrome (TCS), the spinal cord is abnormally attached to surrounding tissue and is thereby limited in its movement. TCS is most commonly *congenital* (in other words, present at birth). TCS can be acquired due to scarring from trauma, tumors, or infections. In congenital cases, TCS is often associated with a *myelomeningocele* in which the spinal cord is not completely encased within the protective bony spine during development (Safavi-Abbasi et al, 2016). This leaves the spinal cord exposed and more likely to tether onto nearby structures. Complications result as the spinal cord is pulled and stretched because of its immobile attachments. Children and adolescents are especially affected because they experience higher degrees of spinal cord stretching during periods of growth. During surgical intervention, a laminectomy is performed to access the spinal cord and detach it from the structure to which it is tethered.

What Musculoskeletal, Bone, and Ligament Problems Can Be Addressed with Surgery?

Surgery for the bones and ligaments is complicated, and dependent on the diagnosis as well as response to physical therapy. Surgery will be recommended for certain types of pelvic bone fractures (breaks), especially when they are unstable (the bones may further separate if not stabilized), or displaced (lined up poorly). Surgery for a labrum tear (tear of the cartilage within the hip joint) is sometimes recommended based on severity and response to physical therapy and whether the torn labrum is causing a mechanical block to the hip joint motion. Tumors (cancer and benign masses) of the bones are rare, but they are sometimes treated with surgery. The ligaments (bone to bone attachments) and tendons (muscle to bone attachments) can also need surgery. One example is *pubic symphysis diastasis*, which is when the bones of the front part of the pelvis and the pubic bone separate (for example, rarely, after childbirth). Surgery might be a consideration for a very widely displaced pubic symphysis but smaller degrees of widening are often tolerated. Tendon tears or avulsions (complete separations) might heal with rest or might need surgery, depending on how severe they are.

What Vascular Problems Can Be Addressed with Surgery?

Pelvic venous disorders include:

- Pelvic congestion syndrome, which is the general word for dilated pelvic veins causing pain and can be caused simply by poor function of the valves in the vein
- *Nutcracker syndrome* (blockage and/or stretching of the *left renal vein* by anatomic compression of the superior mesenteric artery against the aorta, the largest artery in the body)
- *May-Thurner Syndrome*, which is the external compression of the pelvic (iliac) veins between the pelvic (iliac) *arteries* and bones (the bony pelvis or lumbar-sacral bones)

Pelvic venous disorders are usually associated with vague or complex symptoms and signs from the swollen vessels (Figure 14-5). Surgical intervention involves undoing blockage and improving flow **out of** dilated veins or sealing the veins and preventing flow **into** dilated veins, and is discussed in more detail in Chapter 10.

Will I Remain on Medications for Pelvic Pain Around the Time of Surgery?

To prevent bleeding, NSAIDs should not be taken peri-operatively due to their blood-thinning properties. In addition to being analgesics, NSAIDs are *antiplatelet medications* that prevent *platelets* in the blood from adhering to each other to stop bleeding. Also, *anticoagulants* are blood thinners and should be avoided ahead of the surgery. *Heparin, warfarin (Coumadin®), enoxaparin sodium (Lovenox®)*, and *apixaban (Eliquis®)* are commonly used anticoagulants.

Estrogen and progesterone pills that you might be taking for menstruation-related pelvic pain such as oral contraceptives have properties that increase the chances of forming blood clots after surgery. These risks are generally small. Your doctor will make a decision as to whether you should stop or continue your medications before surgery.

Monoamine oxidase inhibitors (MAOIs) also should be stopped before surgery. MAOIs belong to a class of medications that you might be taking for your pelvic pain. Examples include *tranylcypromine (Parnate®), phenelzine (Nardil®)*, and *Marplan®*. They should not be taken around the time of surgery because they can interfere with many of the drugs used for anesthesia during surgery. Talk to your physician and the pre-operative anesthesiology clinic for a list of medications to avoid and a timetable of when to stop them relative to your surgery.

Can Surgery Make My Problems Worse?

Surgery can fix anatomic abnormalities that cause pelvic pain, but it can also lead to more pain in the future. Surgical procedures done in the abdominal and pelvic areas, such as those performed for gynecological conditions and hernias, commonly result in adhesions (scar tissue that forms between organs and tissues and causes them to stick together). Complications from adhesions include chronic pain, bowel obstruction, infertility, and need for subsequent operations. The mechanism behind adhesion development likely involves excessive scar tissue formation on the peritoneum (the membrane lining the abdominal cavity and covering the abdominal organs). To decrease peritoneal trauma and potentially reduce the risk of adhesion formation, laparoscopic procedures should be considered over laparotomies where feasible (Kavic and Kavic, 2002).

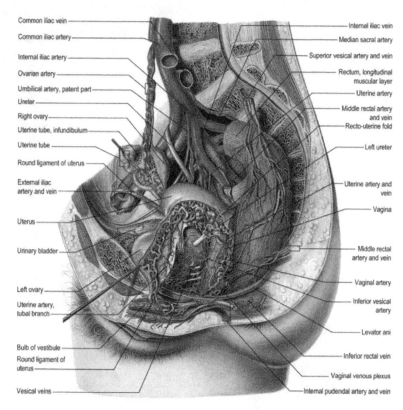

Figure 14-5: Demonstration of the complex veins within the pelvis, including the ovarian vein, which follows the course of the ovarian artery. One can visualize that poor drainage of this vein could lead to congestion in the pelvis. (Reproduced with Permission: Standring S, ed.: Figure 77.3 A. The vessels of the female pelvis: Sagittal view. In: Gray's Atlas of Anatomy. *The Anatomical Basis of Clinical Practice*. 41st ed. Philadelphia, PA: Elsevier, Limited. 2016; 1288-1313.e1.)

You can work with your physicians and surgeons to optimize your surgical outcomes and reduce your risk of complications. Prior to surgery, have a discussion with your health care team about what results you expect from surgery. Keep in mind that surgery seldom serves as a panacea that can completely eliminate your pain, but it has the potential to greatly reduce it and improve your quality of life.

HOW IS PELVIC PAIN DIFFERENT IN CHILDREN AND ADOLESCENTS?

Susan L. Sager, MD, FAAP and Sarah Nelson, PhD

CHAPTER

In This Chapter

- What Causes Pelvic Pain in Children and Adolescents?
- What Will Be Involved in My Child's Initial Evaluation?
- Is Pelvic Pain Different in Boys and Girls?
- Isn't Menstrual Pain a Normal Part of Life, and Don't Most Teenage Girls Have Irregular Periods?
- Will My Daughter Need an Internal Vaginal Exam?
- Is Endometriosis Different in Adolescents Than in Adults?
- What Else Can Cause Pelvic Pain in Adolescents?
- Can Nerve Blocks Help Alleviate My Child's Pain?
- How Can a Pelvic Floor Physical Therapist Help an Adolescent with Pelvic Pain?
- Although My Doctor Assures Me That My Child's Condition Is Under Control, Why Does He Still Have Pain?
- Why Is It Good to Be Young, and What Is Neuroplasticity?
- What Should I Do If My Child Has Developmental Delay and Pelvic Pain?
- How Can I Best Support My Child?

continued

- Should I Worry If Health Care Providers Ask Questions About Sexual Abuse?
- What Is a Multidisciplinary Approach to Pain Management for Adolescents?
- How Can a Psychologist Help to Alleviate My Child's Pain?
- Conclusion

What Causes Pelvic Pain in Children and Adolescents?

Many of the chapters in this book are relevant to children with *pelvic pain*, so if you are starting with this chapter, we encourage you to read other chapters as well. Most children and adolescents describe their pelvic pain as a "stomach ache," even when the pain comes from the hips, *muscles* of the abdominal wall and pelvic floor, or from the bladder, *gastrointestinal* (GI) tract, or reproductive organs. *Nerves* in the pelvis *innervate* more than one organ, and nerve "cross talk" can make localization of the source of the pain difficult. A careful history, including a menstrual history, bowel function, athletic injuries, and falls (such as a fall on the *coccyx*) can guide the evaluation.

What Will Be Involved in My Child's Initial Evaluation?

This chapter discusses some common diagnoses (Table 15-1) and concepts. You can help your *pediatrician* by bringing a list of questions to your appointment, providing a concise description of the pain and any related *symptoms* or tests you have had, and asking for a complete exam. Related symptoms, such as bowel and *bladder incontinence*, are helpful to communicate; they might raise suspicion for a neurological diagnosis. The interview should include questions about bladder, bowel, sexual symptoms and exposures (if relevant), menstrual history, athletic injuries, straddle or coccyx falls, and inappropriate touching or other non-consensual sexual exposures. In older children, it is most thorough to conduct part of the interview without a parent being present. A thorough history will help determine the need for further investigation. Some questions are off-putting for parents; it is simply the pediatrician's professional obligation to screen for abuse, and it does not imply anything about the parent or the child. If the parent has an angry or embarrassed reaction, the child might become stressed, or it might prevent him or her from identifying difficult memories or revealing current unsafe situations. When indicated, the neurological exam might include observation of the gait (for example, walking on the toes and heels) and reflexes (including those of the kneecap, heel, and *anus* (peri-anal sensation and anal wink). The exam of the peri-anal tissues can help identify *tethered spinal cord* and *spina bifida occulta*. If the child has multiple pain syndromes (for example, migraine, heartburn, and pelvic pain), a systemic *inflammatory* problem leading to *small fiber polyneuropathy* might explain the combination. Labs and imaging can be ordered based on the history and exam, and a *urinalysis* should be performed at least once.

Table 15-1: Causes of Pelvic Pain in Children

Category	Diagnoses
Gastrointestinal	- Constipation - *Inflammatory bowel disease* - Adhesions - Bowel obstruction - Appendicitis
Reproductive system	- Dysmenorrhea - Endometriosis - Ovarian cysts - Tumors - Prostatitis - Ovarian or testicular torsion - Tubal pregnancy
Orthopedic	- Congenital hip dysplasia - Vertebral anomalies in the lumbar and sacral *spine* - Occult fractures of the tailbone, hips, or pubis - Gait disturbance and pelvic malalignment - *Muscle spasm* and trigger points - Psoas tendonitis - Hamstring tears - *Nerve entrapment* - Osteitis pubis due to athletic stress
Neurological	- Tethered spinal cord - Neuropathy - Abdominal migraine - Small fiber polyneuropathy
Congenital anomalies	- Abnormalities of the reproductive, urinary, and gastrointestinal organs - Venous malformations
Injuries	- Of the tailbone, low back, hips, and perineum
Infections	- Lyme disease - *Pelvic inflammatory disease* - Sexually transmitted infection (gonorrhea, chlamydia, and herpes)

Is Pelvic Pain Different in Boys and Girls?

Painful periods and constipation are the most common causes of pelvic pain in adolescent females. Constipation often co-exists with painful periods, and those with *dysmenorrhea* might report a preponderance of gastrointestinal (GI) symptoms, such as bloating, nausea, and heartburn. Painful or irregular periods might be a sign of pelvic disease, even in early adolescence. In children, congenital anomalies of the reproductive tract should be considered, but 70% of adolescent girls with *chronic pelvic pain* (CPP) who are *evaluated* by a *gynecologist* are diagnosed with *endometriosis* (Janssen et al, 2013).

Boys rarely have pelvic pain until after puberty, and pain is most commonly from urologic disorders that affect the bladder and prostate or injuries to the tailbone, *genitals*, or hips that lead to spasm of the *pelvic floor muscles* (PFMs) or nerve compression.

Isn't Menstrual Pain a Normal Part of Life, and Don't Most Teenage Girls Have Irregular Periods?

Menstrual pain is the most common cause of CPP in adolescent girls and is the leading reason for missed school and work (Schroeder et al, 1999). Yet, many adolescents do not seek treatment, even when symptoms are severe and school days are missed (Klein and Litt, 1981; Suvitie et al, 2016). Why youngsters do not speak up about menstrual pain or irregular periods is unclear, but many girls (and adults) believe painful periods and irregular cycles are normal in adolescence. Severe menstrual pain or pain that prevents participating in daily activities, such as school or sports, should be a cause for concern. Irregular periods are common in early adolescence, but missing a period for three months in a row, periods that occur fewer than three weeks apart, or frequent bleeding between periods should be evaluated by a doctor, even during the first or second year after the start of menses (Seidman et al, 2018; American College of Obstetrics and Gynecology Committee Opinion, 2015).

Will My Daughter Need an Internal Vaginal Exam?

Many teens are reluctant to see a doctor for painful periods because they are fearful of undergoing an internal pelvic exam. Gynecologists who specialize in treating children and adolescents with pelvic disorders are mindful of the physical, developmental, and psychological concerns unique to younger individuals. When evaluating pelvic pain, an internal exam of the vagina is usually not necessary for children or for adolescents who are not sexually active. When an internal exam of the vagina is indicated, it can be done by having the patient lie on her side in a knee-chest position, if preferred. A cotton swab may be inserted into the vagina to determine if the there is an obstruction or to check for infection. When further information is needed, a pelvic ultrasound might be ordered to rule out a *congenital malformation* or a tumor of the reproductive system. In children and adolescents, the *ultrasound* exam can be done with the probe over the lower abdomen and not inside the vagina or rectum, as is frequently done in adults. Exams are always the decision of the child/adolescent and her guardian.

Is Endometriosis Different in Adolescents Than in Adults?

Endometriosis has been thought of as an adult disorder, but most women who are diagnosed with endometriosis say that they have had pelvic pain and other symptoms of endometriosis since adolescence (Ballweg, 2004). The diagnosis of endometriosis is typically delayed for years in adults and even longer when symptoms were present during the early teens. In addition, adolescent endometriosis can be missed when surgery is performed by someone who is unfamiliar with endometriosis in youngsters. The appearance of endometriosis might not be as striking in younger individuals as it is in adults. Adolescent endometriosis can appear smaller and lighter in color than adult endometriosis, and it might be difficult to see if special light-refraction techniques are not used at the time of surgery (Laufer et al, 2003). Therefore, you should make sure that your doctor knows what endometriosis can look like in adolescents. Fortunately, adolescent endometriosis does not progress when treated and most affected people are diagnosed with the lower Stages (I or II). As a result, complications of endometriosis are rare in adolescents who are treated early.

What Else Can Cause Pelvic Pain in Adolescents?

Most adolescents with CPP—both male and female—have *myofascial pain* (such as *levator muscle* pain, which is discussed in Chapters 7 and 11) that co-exists with a known pelvic disorder or as a primary source of pain from sports or injuries. Muscles surrounding the pelvis can develop spasm and *trigger points*, much the same as other muscles. Muscles of the pelvic floor surround the vagina, *penis*, urethra, and rectum and can become tender to touch and with contraction. Pelvic floor dysfunction can cause shooting pain with urination or painful bowel movements. Other pelvic muscles include the muscles of the lower abdominal wall, the upper thighs (*ileopsoas* and *rectus femoris*), and low back. Pelvic muscles with *chronic* tension have less blood coming to the tissues and nerves, and can become tender and hypersensitive to light touch or movement of those muscles. Similar to a tight shoulder muscle or a leg cramp, the muscles of the pelvis respond to massage, stretching, trigger point release, and strengthening. Almost 95% of adolescents with myofascial pelvic pain improve with *physical therapy* (PT) (Shroeder et al, 2000). In adolescents, myofascial pain is less commonly associated with nerve entrapment or localized nerve irritation. A diagnostic *nerve block* can help distinguish myofascial pain caused by the abdominal wall, spine, and pelvic muscles from pain sources within the abdominal cavity.

Can Nerve Blocks Help Alleviate My Child's Pain?

A nerve block might be indicated if an injury to a nerve is suspected, or it might be conducted as a diagnostic aid to identify a source of the pain. Nerves can become entrapped within the abdominal wall or within scar tissue. In these instances, an injection with a *steroid* and a *local anesthetic* can reduce *inflammation*, swelling, and pain. While adults might benefit from nerve blocks for pain caused by pregnancy-related injuries to the vulva, rectum, and pelvic floor muscles (PFMs), adolescents rarely have similar causes for their pelvic pain. Most instances of nerve pain in adolescents can be expected to improve over the course of several months with PT. A nerve block might be done to help you participate in PT more effectively. Most nerve blocks wear off after days or weeks. In adults, nerve blocks that have been helpful in reducing pain are often followed by more permanent nerve *ablation* procedures. Because of their greater ability to heal and because of the concept of *neuroplasticity* (the ability of the nerves to make new connections and adapt), adolescents rarely need permanent nerve-modifying procedures. It is unusual for a healthy child or adolescent to require a *spinal cord stimulator* or nerve ablation procedure.

How Can a Pelvic Floor Physical Therapist Help an Adolescent with Pelvic Pain?

Pelvic floor PT focuses on relieving spasm, trigger points, weakness, and pain in the muscles of the pelvis. In adults, the deeper PFMs are often reached through the vaginal wall. However, this internal approach can be frightening and uncomfortable for the young adolescent. Fortunately, physical therapists can also address pelvic floor pain by working indirectly with *external* abdominal, hip, thigh, and low back muscles. *Biofeedback* sticky-patch sensors can be placed by the patient on the perineum and surrounding soft tissues and the patient can remain covered. Adolescents of all ages can engage in pelvic floor PT as long as the patient and therapist are comfortable and have established rapport, usually over a few sessions.

PT improves circulation, decreases the body's response to stimulation, and desensitizes painful tissues.

Although My Doctor Assures Me That My Child's Condition Is Under Control, Why Does He Still Have Pain?

When pain symptoms are not improved after all active pain triggers are treated, it is important to consider that the nervous system has changed the way it processes *pain signals*. Chronic pain changes the brain and distorts pain perception, often amplifying the pain signal. When painful events occur repeatedly or over a long period, the brain adapts and creates new connections among nerves in the brain, an over-reactive form of learning. The result is a more widespread pain network and an exaggerated or amplified response to pain. To the person with chronic pain, sensations that are normally mild (such as digestion or a full bladder) are felt as painful, and painful sensations (such as menstrual cramps and spasms) are perceived as disproportionately severe. In fact, other physiologic functions regulated by the brain (such as blood pressure, heart rate, sleep, and mood), can also be distorted. Hypersensitivity, dizziness, fatigue, *depression*, and difficulty concentrating are byproducts of the "pain brain." These changes can be thought of as *central nervous system* (CNS) sensitization of pain pathways. *Central sensitization* can occur as the brain's response to chronic pain and/or peripheral nerve fibers can demonstrate peripheral sensitization in response to injury. More widespread *systemic diseases* (such as *diabetes* or *small fiber polyneuropathy* [SFPN]) may alter pain processing.

Why Is It Good to Be Young, and What Is Neuroplasticity?

Treating chronic pain involves not only identifying and treating pain triggers but also returning the brain back to its resting state and lowering the level of arousal in the nervous system.

When it comes to treating chronic pain, younger people have an advantage over adults because their brains are still developing and growing. Young brains make new neural connections faster than older brains, which is why it's easier to learn when you're young. The ability of the brain to make new connections and continually adapt to new information is called neuroplasticity. Neuroplasticity is much greater in the developing brain than in the adult brain. While many adults report a lifetime of pain, most adolescents can reverse these maladaptive changes in the brain.

What Should I Do If My Child Has Developmental Delay and Pelvic Pain?

Children and adolescents with developmental delay often require additional support and assistance for the appropriate diagnosis and treatment of pelvic pain. Alerting health care providers to the extent to which a child/adolescent is developmentally delayed is often a good first step and will allow providers to alter their exams and interactions to your child's developmental level. For example, there might be mild delays in language or memory processing speed, other aspects of cognitive functioning might be more difficult, or delays might be more global and severe. Depending on the severity of delays, parents might also want to consider having an aide or advocate accompany them to appointments to facilitate developmentally appropriate communication during exams or discussions. Consistent with typically developing children, parents should come to appointments with accounts of symptoms, including detailed observations. If the child is non-verbal, parents should provide indications or descriptions of how the child shows they are in pain (for example, grabs stomach or cries). Following diagnosis, treatment options exist for each developmental level. If the child has milder developmental delays, engaging in regular *cognitive-behavioral therapy* (CBT) or *relaxation training* as adjunctive therapy to hormonal or other medical treatment is often recommended and should be feasible. Children with more severe or global developmental delays might benefit from learning strategies (to distract or relax from pain); these should be explored in collaboration with a developmentally trained psychotherapist or clinician.

How Can I Best Support My Child?

Parenting a child with pelvic pain can often be difficult and stressful. Successful treatment requires striking a balance among listening, communicating understanding, supporting, and establishing boundaries. Many children (even young ones) are concerned about overburdening or putting more stress on their parents, which can lead to hiding or internalizing their own stress and worry. Parents can help alleviate this by keeping open lines of communication; validating fears and worries (for example, "I can see you are upset." or "It is understandable that you are worried"); and providing strong messages of confidence and hope (for example, "I know we are going to figure this out"). Children frequently struggle with managing pelvic pain in their daily lives, which might require some "tough love" from parents. For example, if your child is fearful of having pelvic pain at school, you can help alleviate acute distress by engaging in active problem solving with them to increase confidence and address their fear instead of letting them stay home from school. For example, parents can work with schools to develop special accommodations (for example, a 504 plan) to allow children to address their needs surrounding pelvic pain (such as taking a break or going to the nurse) without fear of penalty in grades or being marked absent. Steps such as these create long-term solutions to a health care problem that can be difficult to manage. Finally, if cognitive-behavioral therapy (CBT) is recommended by health care providers, or if as a parent, you believe that it is a good adjunct to try, assure your child that this is an *evidence-based therapy* that will help reduce pain along with other medical treatments and it is not because your child's pain is not real. Parent "buy-in" to *non-pharmacological treatments* will increase motivation and engagement in children, which will improve the chance of a positive outcome.

Should I Worry If Health Care Providers Ask Questions About Sexual Abuse?

Sexual abuse and pelvic pain can co-occur in children. If providers are asking about this, it is because they are trained to screen every child for the possibility of abuse and to carry out a thorough and developmentally appropriate exam on every child. All health care providers are *mandatory reporters*, which means that if abuse is suspected, their number one priority is to ensure the safety of your child, and they are mandated by law to report any suspected abuse to the proper authorities. If you do not have knowledge that your child has been abused and you have no reason to suspect this, the doctor's assessment for the presence of sexual abuse should be minimal and routine, and your child's exam should proceed as expected.

If you, as a parent, have concern or knowledge that your child has been sexually abused, this should be disclosed to your health care provider immediately. Depending on whether this has been disclosed prior to your appointment, health care providers might involve a child protection team specialist who can document details of the abuse. This might then get reported to state protective agencies who can follow-up with you further on the process and provide more details to help you understand what might need to happen to help your child.

If your child has a known history of sexual abuse and this has been reported/investigated, alerting the child's health care provider of this history will establish open communication and also facilitate a sensitive exam that will take into account the child's history, and avoid or minimize the risk of re-traumatization (in other words, feeling like they are being abused again). For example, this might include a less-invasive exam or the presence of a support person (you, as the parent, or another advocate) to ensure that your child feels safe at all times. Whereas it is important to be open to the possibility that abuse can occur in all families, you do not need to worry that you are overlooking a history of abuse just because your child has pelvic pain. Your child's comfortable experience with an open conversation will facilitate future disclosures if something was missed.

What Is a Multidisciplinary Approach to Pain Management for Adolescents?

Chronic pain in adolescents is approached with the goal of rehabilitating the nervous system. A multidisciplinary approach to pain treatment focuses on all aspects of nervous system regulation. *Aerobic activity*, desensitization, stretching and strengthening, restorative sleep, and brain-based interventions to reduce stress provide new sensory information for the brain to learn and signal the brain to reduce hyperarousal and decrease pain. In one study, pain and functioning improved after an intensive program of daily PT, *occupational therapy* (OT), and CBT; more than 95% of adolescents returned to school, extracurricular activities, sports, and social activities, and pain improved in the majority (Randall et al, 2018). While returning to activities with pain might seem counterintuitive, movement is needed to induce change. Pain improves after the brain changes its processing. Parenting a child with chronic pain is challenging, and the assistance of a treatment team is often needed to get back on track (Coakley, 2016). A typical multidisciplinary team might include providers who specialize in treating children and adolescents (such as pediatricians, *adolescent gynecologists*, *urologists*, *gastroenterologists*, *pediatric pain physicians*, *physical* and *occupational therapists*, and *child and adolescent psychologists*).

How Can a Psychologist Help to Alleviate My Child's Pain?

Psychological support and treatment of depression or anxiety reduce the level of arousal in the brain. Stress causes your blood pressure to rise, your heart to beat faster, and your body to become hot and flushed. These *physiologic changes* also occur when we feel pain. Both stress and pain alert the nervous system and can maintain a high state of arousal, defeating attempts to reduce the pain response. Many young patients report that their pain is worse when they are stressed, and their pain is better when they are distracted or relaxed. Cognitive-behavioral therapy (CBT) is a type of psychotherapy that focuses on thoughts and behaviors. Similar to therapy in adults, CBT and other brain-based strategies include biofeedback, *meditation*, *yoga*, *deep breathing*, *progressive muscle relaxation*, and *guided visualization*—all techniques that help the nervous system reduce pain signaling. By reducing the stress response, the brain can "reset" and respond to sensations in a less amplified way.

Conclusion

Pelvic pain in children and adolescents can be difficult to diagnose because of the nature of interviewing and examining children and teens, the different causes of pain, and the access to pediatric subspecialists. On the other hand, children have a greater capacity to heal and resolve their pain than do adults. You will benefit from keeping an organized account of the symptoms, records, and images, what has been tried so far, and from continuing to read as you consult with your providers.

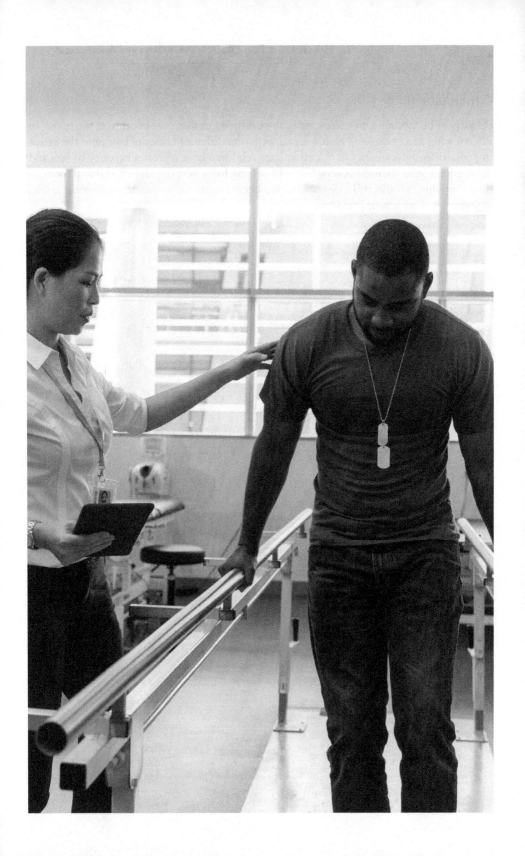

HOW CAN PELVIC PAIN BE AFFECTED BY PHYSICAL DISABILITY?

Chloe Slocum, MD, MPH and Andrew Dubin, MD, MS

CHAPTER

In This Chapter

- Introduction
- How Does Mobility Impact Pelvic Pain and Treatment?
- How Do Neurologic Diseases Affect My Pain and Treatment?
- What Treatments Are Available for Pain Related to Rheumatologic Diseases?
- What Treatments Are Available for Neuropathies?
- Is My Condition Reversible?

Introduction

Pelvic pain can result from multiple causes. Treatment is guided by an understanding of the relationships among *pelvic floor muscles* (PFMs), posture, and onset of pelvic pain. Significant neurologic and arthritic problems can affect *muscles* and cause pain.

How Does Mobility Impact Pelvic Pain and Treatment?

Seemingly innocuous *gait deviations* or asymmetries can initiate a cascade of muscle overuse, strain, and *biomechanical compensation*, and lead to pelvic pain. For example, weakness of *hip abductors* (the muscles that open your hips) can be caused by:

- A *radiculopathy*, which is radiating pain that originates within the spinal cord (Figure 16-1)
- A focal compression of a *peripheral nerve*
- A muscle deficit *(myopathy)*
- An *orthopedic* issue (such as a hip or knee replacement)
- Neurologic conditions (such as *cerebral palsy*, a *stroke/cerebrovascular accident*, or an acquired brain condition)

Spastic diplegia, a term that describes tightness of the closing muscles of the hips on both sides called the *adductors* (Figure 16-2), and *spastic hemiplegia* (with tightness on just one side) can:

- Affect the function of the large *gluteus medius* (buttock) muscle (Figure 16-3)
- Cause pain (for example, from *trochanteric bursitis* or irritation of the cushion of the hip joint)
- Lead to overactive hip adductors (closing muscles) that cause weakness of the hip abductors (hip opening muscles), such as seen in people with cerebral palsy

These and related examples can cause deep aching pain in the pelvic region.

Typically, first-line interventions for gait deviations include strengthening exercises that aim to re-balance muscular asymmetries. This can be especially helpful after hip replacement surgery and can also be part of the treatment for trochanteric bursitis. Strengthening and *range-of-motion exercises* are critical components in the management of symptoms of cerebral palsy or stroke in which there are painful spastic hips (spastic diplegia or hemiplegia). After steps are taken to relax the spastic hip adductors, strengthening of the other muscles can reduce the muscular stresses that cause pelvic pain.

Chapter 16: How Can Pelvic Pain Be Affected by Physical Disability?   255

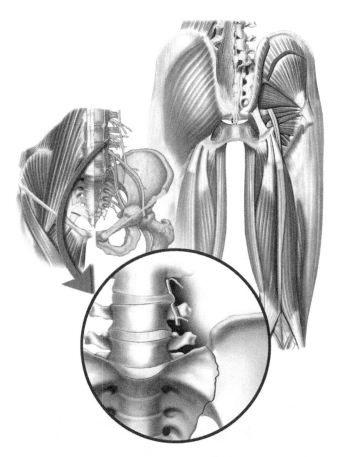

Figure 16-1: A "radiculopathy" of the sciatic nerve can lead to hip muscle weakness and gait problems.

The overactive hip adductor (closing) *complex* is the underlying issue in patients with spastic diplegia or spastic hemiplegia with a painful hip. The powerful combined inward pull of the *adductor longus* and *adductor magnus muscles* serves to place the hip in an overly inward and flexed position. This results in abnormal weight-loading mechanics and alterations in multiple aspects of the standing phase during the gait cycle. Excessive stress is placed on the gluteus medius (the inner buttock) to stabilize the pelvis during *single leg stance* (the phase of walking in which the weight is on one leg). The result is deep pain in the pelvic side region that is secondary to fatigue and overuse.

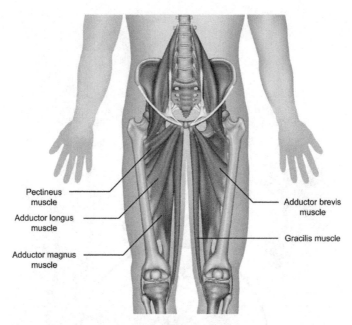

Figure 16-2: The adductors—the muscles that pull the hips and legs inward.

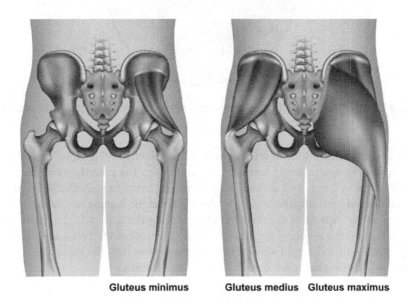

Figure 16-3: The gluteus muscles.

Botulinum toxin (such as onabotulinum toxin A [Botox®], rimabotulinumtoxinB [Myobloc®], and abobotulinumtoxinA [Dysport®]) *injections* can relax the overactive hip adductors and help to re-balance the dynamic forces between adduction and abduction (closing and opening) at the hip. When the spastic hip adductors are relaxed in this manner, the abnormal hip flexion posture issues will decrease as well. If injection to the adductors is only partially successful, botulinum toxin injection to the *iliopsoas muscle* (a powerful hip flexor that runs on both sides along the inner trunk to the legs), can address spastic hip flexors and associated pelvic pain. The iliopsoas muscle is both a major pelvic floor muscle as well as a major postural muscle, and it is responsible for dynamic stabilization of the *lumbar spine* over the pelvis. Therefore, it can be critical to address as one of the more common causes of pelvic pain. Beyond botulinum toxin injections to the iliopsoas muscle, a therapeutic exercise program that focuses on stretching of the *hip flexors* in combination with strengthening of *hip extensors* and hip abductors will be key to improving the outcome for this type of muscular pelvic pain.

How Do Neurologic Diseases Affect My Pain and Treatment?

Myopathy and Stroke

When muscle weakness becomes permanent because of a neurologic disease, *adaptive equipment* in the form of a cane or walker can be useful to prevent strain from gait problems. These situations can include stable (unchanging) weakness of *proximal* (close to the trunk) hip girdle musculature or *progressive neuromuscular disorders* (such as *myopathies*, like *muscular dystrophy*) that result in progressive (worsening) proximal muscle weakness. Stabilizing the pelvis during the gait cycle will allow the weak musculature to avoid overexertion and the associated pain of muscular fatigue.

Different adaptive equipment is needed for different situations. For those with focal unilateral gluteus medius weakness, a cane is typically the device of choice. Canes or *hemi-walkers* can be useful for those with more weakness, such as a post-stroke spastic *hemiplegia*. Judicious use of botulinum toxin injections to the hip adductor muscles might be beneficial in this population. Even more support with a walker can be of use for those with myopathies, as they have symmetric proximal muscle weakness and require two-sided support at all times when walking.

Spinal Cord Injury

People with *spinal cord injury* (SCI) can have pelvic pain related to mechanical causes from gait impairment, *neuropathic pain* at or below their neurologic level of injury, or from conditions that affect the pelvic floor (pelvic muscle or bony anatomical structures). For people with *incomplete SCI* (in which some of the nerve function is still present), muscle spasticity might contribute to gait impairment and is addressed much the same way as in other neurological conditions. This can be addressed with adaptive equipment for mobility (such as canes, crutches, and/or walkers, as well as bracing). If needed, targeted botulinum toxin injections for overactive *(hypertonic)* muscles can be used. For neuropathic pain, *gabapentinoid medications* such as *gabapentin* or *pregabalin* might be especially helpful, although their dosing might be limited by their side effect profiles. Additionally, *intrathecal baclofen therapy* (baclofen pump) is another option that can be used to help modulate pelvic pain from muscle spasticity and/or neuropathic pain. Conditions that affect the pelvic floor in individuals with SCI can include *hemorrhoids, anal fissure,* and less common issues, such as inflamed internal organ fistula *(vesicovaginal, rectovaginal,* or *perirectal).* For such cases, radiologic imaging and consultation with a surgical specialist to address the underlying cause should be obtained in addition to use of symptomatic measures to treat pelvic pain.

What Treatments Are Available for Pain Related to Rheumatologic Diseases?

Rheumatologic disorders present unique challenges. Many disorders—which in the past, resulted in significant secondary joint deformities—are now well managed with *disease-modifying anti-rheumatic drugs* (DMARDs) and the ever-expanding family of *biologically-based medications,* such as *monoclonal antibody therapy.* Some people with *rheumatoid arthritis* (RA) or *inflammatory vasculitis*-type syndromes might receive *steroids* for extended periods. This can result in a *steroid-induced myopathy* (muscle weakness) and associated *hip girdle weakness.* The consequences of hip/pelvic girdle muscle weakness include a waddling-type gait that is secondary to gluteus medius weakness and an over-extended sway back posture abnormality *(hyperlordosis)* to compensate for hip extensor weakness. This constellation of posture and gait deviations can lead to pelvic pain from compensatory overactivity of the iliopsoas in an effort to stabilize the trunk (proximal) structures. Worsening the issue is that in steroid myopathies, as with many myopathies, the hip flexors are weak as well. In this scenario, a slow taper of steroids should be attempted under the care of the *rheumatologist.* At the same time, strengthening exercises can be added. While your steroids are being slowly tapered, gains in strength occur, albeit at a slower rate.

Ankylosing spondylitis presents challenges. To date, there are no specific agents that stop the disease. *Non-steroidal anti-inflammatory drugs* (NSAIDs) can be useful, but their benefits might be limited by their *side effect profile.* The involvement of the *sacroiliac joints* (SIJs), hip joints, and spine all affect mobility, posture, and gait, as well as pain. People with ankylosing spondylitis benefit from exercise designed to maintain thoracolumbar and hip range-of-motion, as well as pelvic girdle muscle strength. *Yoga* and *Tai Chi* can be of benefit, both for range-of-motion and pain modulation.

What Treatments Are Available for Neuropathies?

Neuropathies are an uncommon source of pelvic pain. The classic *length-dependent polyneuropathy* (such as *diabetic neuropathy*) must be very advanced before it will affect pelvic *nerves. Focal neuropathies* from pelvic trauma, such as isolated *pudendal neuropathy* from pelvic fracture or *post-partum,* can occur. *Small fiber polyneuropathy* is a different type of neuropathy of the small nerves. In general, the first-line treatment in these situations is the use of *neuromodulators*, including gabapentin and related compounds, as well as *serotonin norepinephrine re-uptake inhibitors* (SNRIs). *Pelvic floor physical therapy* should be tried in most of these seemingly different cases.

In general, physical activity, improvement in overall mobility, and strengthening that targets postural muscle activation and function can be beneficial in the management of pelvic pain. Release of *endogenous* (naturally made by the body) *neurotransmitters* with physical activity can have a pain-modulating effect, and the overall sense of wellbeing associated with activity can be efficacious.

Is My Condition Reversible?

Neurological and rheumatologic conditions that contribute to pelvic pain might be acquired at birth or later in life, and they might be reversible. Addressing the underlying mechanisms that contribute to pain can offer some degree of relief. It is usually possible to manage and even reverse pelvic pain caused by rheumatologic and/or neurologic conditions with *non-pharmacologic approaches*, such as bracing, use of adaptive equipment, and *physical therapy*. Medications and interventional treatments, such as botulinum toxin injections and/or intrathecal baclofen therapy, can improve pain where the physical interventions leave off. Finally, it is important to consider behavioral and mental health support for anyone experiencing severe or *chronic pelvic pain* (CPP); supportive therapy by a specialist in pain psychology, *cognitive-behavioral therapy* (CBT), or *mindfulness* can be indispensable as an adjunct treatment.

HOW CAN I BETTER COPE WITH PELVIC PAIN?

Amelia M. Stanton, PhD; C. Andres Bedoya, PhD; and Christina Psaros, PhD

CHAPTER

In This Chapter

- Introduction
- What Feelings or Thoughts Arise with Pelvic Pain?
- Which Psychological Factors Are Associated with Pelvic Pain?
- How Might Pelvic Pain Affect My Relationships?
- Do Past Experiences Contribute to My Pelvic Pain?
- Can Psychological Interventions Improve My Ability to Cope with Pelvic Pain?
- Can Mindfulness Diminish Pelvic Pain?
- What Happens When You Integrate Evidence-Based Treatments for Pelvic Pain?
- Conclusion

Introduction

Pelvic pain that occurs independently of or during sexual activity can be incredibly distressing. People who have pelvic pain often feel confused, angry, or frustrated by persistent *symptoms* and/or guilt and think the pain affects their partners and their relationships. People with pelvic pain wonder where the pain is coming from, wonder if the pain is in their head, and wonder if sex will always be painful. Although pelvic pain can be the consequence of physical (*physiological* or biomedical) factors that can be addressed via different medical treatments, psychological or sexual factors also contribute to the *etiology* and maintenance of pelvic pain. Indeed, a *biopsychosocial* (physical and psychological) combination model might be the best framework for understanding pelvic pain and its associated impairments (Bergeron et al, 2014).

Pelvic pain occurs in both men and women; however, much of the research that focuses on psychological contributors to pain and its treatment has been conducted on women. Some evidence indicates that patterns of pain sensitivity and *pelvic floor muscle* (PFM) function among men who report pelvic pain are similar to those of women (Davis et al, 2011), so it is possible that some of the conclusions we make about women will also apply to men with pelvic pain. However, given the lack of published data on psychological treatments for men with pelvic pain, this chapter focuses on women.

What Feelings or Thoughts Arise with Pelvic Pain?

Women with sexual pain tend to be more *hypervigilant* (have increased sensitivity and reactivity) to their bodies compared to women without pain (Payne et al, 2005). In other words, women in pain are sensitive and highly attentive to physiological changes, and they feel that a new or unexplainable bodily sensation might be a cause for alarm. Indeed, people who are hypervigilant are constantly on alert and perpetually concerned that danger is near; therefore, they might scan their bodies to detect changes in the quality, location, and intensity of their pain. Higher pain hypervigilance has been linked to *depression* and disability (McCracken, 1997). Waiting for signs of pain on a daily basis often leads to increased frustration and anger, as well as sadness and fear.

Pelvic pain is also associated with a fear of pain and lower feelings of *self-efficacy* (Desrochers et al, 2009). The *fear-avoidance model* of pain posits that when a person responds to pain with catastrophic interpretations about its causes and consequences, pain-related fear is likely to develop (Vlaeyen and Linton, 2000). This means the way you think about your pain affects your relationship with and your experience of the pain. For example, if you focus on the negative rather than acknowledging the good **and** the bad (for example, not all days are good, but that does not mean that every day will be painful), you might assume that there are no pain-free days in your future. This approach could lead to hopelessness and, in turn, to greater pain. Also, "should" statements (such as, "I am doing everything the doctor told me to do, so I should have no pain," or "I am so young, this really shouldn't be happening to me") might also set you up for more distress. Generally, self-efficacy refers to an individual's confidence in her ability to exert control over her motivation, behavior, and environment. Women with pelvic pain can feel unable to cope with the pain or perform certain tasks. Thoughts like, "I can't do this," or "I'll never be able to manage my pain," will likely lead to choosing less-effective coping strategies, such as avoidance.

You might be changing your lifestyle to avoid or accommodate to the pain if you are constantly on guard or thinking about your pain non-stop or if you have the belief that your pain will continue to interfere with your life. For example, you might be cutting back on work, reducing the amount of time that you spend with friends and family, and decreasing the frequency of your physical and sexual activity (or stopping it altogether). Pain avoidance will likely perpetuate these problematic thoughts and beliefs, increase your anxiety, and reduce your engagement with activities that you enjoy, potentially leading to depression. Your thoughts are important! Changing your thoughts can have a huge effect on your pain. Indeed, positive—but still realistic—thoughts can reduce avoidance, shift attention away from pain, and encourage a more approach-oriented way of coping, which ultimately can reduce your pain and impairment (Rosen et al, 2012). Many of the *psychosocial* interventions that we highlight in the next section target these feelings, thoughts, and beliefs, while also focusing on pain intensity.

Pain has been described as an emotional experience (Merskey and Bogduk, 1994). If you are in pain, it might be difficult for you to manage your emotional state and the ways in which you experience and express your emotions. This concept is called *emotion regulation*. Though no studies have directly linked poor emotional regulation to pelvic pain, there is some evidence suggesting an association among *response-focused emotion regulation*, *chronic* pain, pain-related disability, and depressive symptoms (Koechlin et al, 2018). Response-focused emotion regulation occurs during an emotional experience; this could mean intensifying, diminishing, or prolonging an emotional response (Gross, 1998). Instead of regulating emotions in the moment, it will likely be more beneficial to change the situation, the focus of your attention, or your thoughts in anticipation of an emotional experience (also known as *antecedent-focused emotion regulation* in which you prepare for the feelings). This type of emotion regulation can reduce pain intensity and improve other pain-related issues.

Which Psychological Factors Are Associated with Pelvic Pain?

If you are feeling anxious or depressed about your pain, you are not alone. Both anxiety and depression are common among women with pelvic pain. A recent study of women seeking treatment for pelvic pain (Bryant et al, 2016) found that the majority of these women had pain for at least two years and suffered moderate or severe anxiety. In general, high anxiety levels and *pain catastrophizing* are common in those with chronic pain, and women with sexual pain often have exaggerated and pessimistic thoughts around their pain (Payne et al, 2007; Pukall et al, 2002). Pain catastrophizing refers to a set of negative thoughts or emotions during an actual or anticipated painful experience (Quartana et al, 2009). People who have high levels of pain catastrophizing tend to ruminate (think over and over) about the pain and feel helpless when attempting to cope with their pain. For example, when you experience pain, you might think that the pain will never go away or that there is nothing that you can do to alter your experience of the pain. You might continue to think about the pain for hours and hours without reprieve, which could affect your ability to work and make it difficult for you to engage in activities.

In one study, just over one-fourth of women seeking treatment for pelvic pain reported moderate to severe depression (Bryant et al, 2016), but findings on the relationship between pain and depression are inconsistent; we cannot predict who will be depressed, and it is unclear whether pain causes the depression or whether the depression increases the pain. Depressive symptoms and pelvic pain can be linked because living with persistent pain leads to low mood (Bair et al, 2003). It is also possible that depression and pain share similar biological pathways and neurotransmitters, which leads to a strong connection between the two (Leitl et al, 2014). If you experience constant pelvic pain or pelvic pain before, during, and after sexual activity, you might feel down and uninterested in doing things that you once enjoyed. For instance, you might stop hanging out with friends or going to the gym if you are in pain. By avoiding these activities and places, you miss opportunities to experience positive emotions. The avoidance can lead to negative thoughts such as:

- "Life isn't really worth living like this."
- "The pain will never go away."
- "What's the point of doing anything if I'm going to be in pain?"

If these thoughts persist, they will likely reinforce the avoidance of positive activities, making it difficult to interrupt the depressive cycle.

How Might Pelvic Pain Affect My Relationships?

Women experiencing pelvic pain might fear that their pain will make it difficult to start new relationships, ruin existing relationships, decrease their satisfaction, and compromise their sense of intimacy with their partners. They might also be concerned that pelvic pain will make them less desirable or attractive to partners because they might be less interested in sexual activity than they once were (because of anticipatory anxiety and/or fear of pain). Indeed, women with pain report poorer body image and lower sexual self-esteem compared to those who are pain-free (Desrochers et al, 2008; Maillé et al, 2015), and both body image and sexual self-esteem are known to affect relationship dynamics. Most couples affected by pelvic or sexual pain remain satisfied with their relationships (Smith and Pukall, 2011), but some studies have reported decreased satisfaction among women in pain compared to women without pain (Hallam-Jones et al, 2001; Masheb et al, 2002). Couples in both same-sex and mixed-sex relationships have indicated that pain affects their intimacy and their ability to show affection toward their partners, which puts strain on their relationships (Blair et al, 2015). Unfortunately, the relationship stressors that result from pelvic pain can ultimately maintain the pain and its associated consequences.

It might be surprising to learn that partners' reactions to pain affect pain intensity. If pain interrupts a sexual experience, partners' reactions can be negative or hostile, solicitous (such as expressing sympathy or concern about the pain), or facilitative (such as expressing encouragement or praising efforts to cope with the pain). Highly solicitous partner responses have been associated with greater pain during intercourse, whereas facilitative partner responses have been associated with less pain (Rosen et al, 2012). Facilitative responses are also linked with greater relationship and sexual satisfaction (Rosen et al, 2012; Rosen et al, 2015). Why are partner responses to pain so important? Facilitative responses can promote healthy, shared coping and emotion regulation, whereas negative or solicitous responses can reinforce pain avoidance, ultimately making it more challenging to manage the pain (Bergeron et al, 2015).

But, what about sex? Does pelvic pain affect your sexual function and sexual activity, too? In addition to bringing some relationship challenges, pelvic pain also disrupts different aspects of sexual function. In women, sexual function encompasses multiple domains, including sexual arousal, sexual desire, *orgasm*, lubrication, satisfaction, and pain. Women with pelvic and sexual pain report low desire, arousal and satisfaction, as well as decreased frequency of intercourse and orgasm (Brauer et al, 2008; Cherner and Reissing, 2013; Farmer and Meston, 2007; Meana et al, 1997; Sutton et al, 2009). If your pelvic pain increases with sexual activity, you might perceive sexual cues (internal, *external*, or from a partner) as negative, and you might have lower sexual self-esteem compared to women who do not have pelvic pain (Cherner and Reissing, 2013; Gates and Galask, 2001; Meana et al, 1997; Pazmany et al, 2014).

Do Past Experiences Contribute to My Pelvic Pain?

Yes, past experiences can contribute to pelvic pain, especially if you have a history of *sexual abuse* and/or other negative or non-consensual sexual experiences. Approximately one-fourth of women who are newly diagnosed with pelvic pain report a sexual abuse history (Spiegel et al, 2016). In a large study that compared adolescent girls with sexual and pelvic pain to those who did not report pain, adolescents with pain were more likely to report previous sexual abuse and a fear of physical abuse (Landry and Bergeron, 2011). In fact, young women who reported a history of sexual abuse were almost twice as likely to report pain compared to women who had not experienced trauma. In a separate study, women with *vulvodynia* (pain that is specifically located in the external genital area), were more likely than women without pain to have had severe sexual and/or physical abuse or to have lived in fear of such abuse as a child (Khandker et al, 2014).

Although there is a long-standing association between chronic pelvic pain (CPP) and childhood sexual abuse, some research does not support this link. One study failed to find an association between a history of childhood abuse (either physical or sexual) and pain severity in women with CPP (As-Sanie et al, 2014). However, more recent abuse (abuse in adulthood) was predictive of pain-related disability among women. Pain-related disability involves more days spent in bed, decreased productivity at work, and more time seeking medical care and undergoing medical procedures. It can be particularly delayed to reach out to and find an appropriate health care provider because these people might feel fearful, discouraged, ashamed, or uncomfortable. Notably, adult sexual abuse has been associated with more severe depressive symptoms, which suggests that pelvic pain, traumatic experiences, and depression might be interrelated. Regardless of the timing of the abuse, it is clear that these negative experiences can affect the intensity and management of pain, and in turn, these negative experiences may make it more challenging for patients to discuss their pelvic pain with their providers.

Can Psychological Interventions Improve My Ability to Cope with Pelvic Pain?

Yes, tools are available to help you cope with pelvic pain! In general, people with pelvic pain benefit from medical and behavioral treatments. Several psychological interventions have improved coping and decreased pain intensity. Both cognitive-behavioral therapy (CBT) (which focuses on challenging unhelpful thoughts and behaviors) and mindfulness-based therapy (which builds non-judgmental awareness of thoughts and feelings) show promise in the treatment of pelvic pain.

CBT for pelvic pain typically lasts for three months and focuses on reducing catastrophic fear of pain, while re-establishing satisfying sexual activity. Women learn how to reduce and/or manage pain in the moment. These interventions are often group-based, which can help normalize what might otherwise be an embarrassing or shameful experience. Typically, the treatment starts with some education and information about pelvic pain and its effects on sexual function; a description of the multiple factors that lead to and help maintain pelvic pain; and some additional information on sexual anatomy and physiology (ter Kuile et al, 2010). During the sessions that follow, therapists teach patients a range of coping skills, including progressive muscle relaxation, *abdominal breathing*, Kegel exercises, *vaginal dilation*, distraction techniques that focus on sexual imagery, coping self-statements, communication skills, and thought challenging (ter Kuile et al, 2010). Patients can return for booster sessions if they need extra help after treatment has ended.

In one of the first studies that tested a psychological treatment for women with dyspareunia (persistent or recurrent genital pain that occurs before, during, or after sexual activity) resulting from vulvar vestibulitis (pain at the vaginal entrance), women received group CBT, surface electromyographic feedback, or *vestibulectomy* (a surgical removal of the painful tissues at the vaginal entrance) (Bergeron et al, 2001). In the CBT group, women were offered information about vulvar vestibulitis and dyspareunia, and they were educated on sexual anatomy, desire, and arousal. Also, they were taught how to engage in specific behaviors or activities to reduce pain intensity and improve coping, such as progressive muscle relaxation, abdominal breathing, Kegal exercises, vaginal dilation, and distraction techniques that focused on sexual imagery. Some of the more thought-based cognitive tools included writing coping self-statements, learning communication skills, and challenging unhealthy thoughts. Coping self-statements can be particularly useful for those with pelvic pain. Some examples include:

- "This will pass."
- "This won't last forever."
- "This is difficult and uncomfortable, but it is only temporary."

Women in all three groups (CBT, surface electromyographic feedback, and vestibulectomy) showed significant improvements in pain at their six-month follow up visits, and they also experienced similar increases in psychological adjustment and sexual function. Participants in the CBT group were more likely to complete the treatment and expressed greater satisfaction with the intervention than did participants in the other two groups.

Subsequent studies have tested CBT interventions for different types of pelvic and sexual pain, both individually and for couples. Engman and colleagues (Engman et al, 2010) examined the long-term sexual behavior among women who were treated for vaginismus and surface-level sexual pain with exposure-based CBT. Weekly sessions used a form of *systematic desensitization* in which women first learned to consciously contract and completely relax their PFMs and to then work their way up a hierarchy of reflex-provoking or painful situations. These situations included touching the vaginal opening, followed by the insertion of one or two of the woman's fingers into her vaginal opening, followed by the partner's fingers, and finally, the partner's *penis*. (The study was done on heterosexual women.) Women also completed daily homework assignments. Not only were the majority of women able to engage in intercourse after treatment, some women were even able to do so without pain, and participants reported a greater sense of self-worth at the end of the intervention. In a similar study that tested the efficacy of therapist-aided exposure therapy to treat pelvic pain, close to 90% of women were able to achieve vaginal intercourse at the end of treatment (ter Kuile et al, 2013). A small pilot study of couples-based CBT also demonstrated that this approach reduced pain intensity for women with provoked *vestibulodynia*, which is recurrent, localized vulvovaginal pain (Corsini-Munt et al, 2014). Women and their partners completed 12 CBT sessions, with both members of the couple reporting improvements in pain-related thoughts, anxiety symptoms, and depression symptoms. Given the relationship factors that contribute to and are associated with pelvic pain, it makes sense to include partners in treatment.

Can Mindfulness Diminish Pelvic Pain?

Typically, mindfulness interventions aim to foster greater attention to and awareness of the present moment, without judgment of sensations or experiences. You might have heard that mindfulness practices are now being used in a variety of settings to improve different aspects of physical and psychological health. Indeed, an increasingly large body of work has demonstrated that mindfulness interventions improve outcomes for chronic pain, depression relapse, and substance use (Creswell, 2017). After participating in a group-based, four-session mindfulness intervention, women with provoked vestibulodynia experienced significant improvements in pain self-efficacy, pain catastrophizing, genital pain induced by a cotton swab exam, pain hypervigilance, and pain-related distress. The intervention included psychoeducation on the etiology of the pain, mindfulness skills (such as mindful eating meditation, body scanning, and progressive muscle relaxation), and some CBT elements, such as thought records and discussions about the relationship between thoughts and pelvic pain. However, despite these benefits, it is worth noting that pain during intercourse did not decrease as a result of the intervention. A recent study compared mindfulness-based cognitive therapy to CBT for the treatment of provoked vestibulodynia in a hospital clinic (Brotto et al, 2019). The mindfulness-based intervention led to greater decreases in pain intensity during intercourse than the CBT intervention; however, the CBT intervention and the mindfulness intervention were equally as effective for all other outcomes, including sexual distress, sexual functioning, pain catastrophizing, pain vigilance, and chronic pain acceptance.

What Happens When You Integrate Evidence-Based Treatments for Pelvic Pain?

You likely have read about the various medical approaches to pelvic pain treatment in other chapters. Given the multi-faceted nature of pelvic pain, it might be best to integrate medical, physical, and psychological therapies to increase the likelihood of a successful outcome. Beckman and colleagues (Beckman et al, 2008) combined sex therapy, which focused on sexual functioning, psychosocial adjustment, and stress elimination with pelvic floor physiotherapy; the goal was to decrease mucosal (vaginal surface) sensitization and re-establish pelvic floor function. Women who completed the program reported less pain and a higher frequency of sexual activity, as well as improvements in sexual functioning and the adoption of helpful coping strategies. Similarly, a 10–12 week combined treatment that included educational seminars, medical management, group psychological skills training, and pelvic floor physiotherapy led to reductions in both pain and distress as well as improvements in sexual function and satisfaction (Brotto et al, 2015). These results are very promising.

Conclusion

When seeking to decrease your pelvic pain, do not lose hope; multiple effective strategies exist that can be combined to bring you relief. If your provider recommends psychological therapies for your pain, you should embrace this aspect of treatment. Mind-based therapies are effective in managing pain, and employing them—either on their own or in combination with physically directed medical therapies—might be the best way to reduce your pain.

HOW DOES SEXUAL ACTIVITY AFFECT PELVIC PAIN?

Rachel S. Rubin, MD and Talli Y. Rosenbaum, MSc

CHAPTER

In This Chapter

- How Is Pain During Sexual Activity Different for Men and Women?
- Is Sexual Pain Different Based on My Sexual Orientation or Gender Identity?
- How Can I Decrease Pain During Sexual Acts, Physically and Mentally?
- What Alternative Strategies Can I Use to Have an Active Sex Life Despite My Pain?
- Does Persistent Pelvic Pain Mean an End to Intimacy and Sex?
- How Can Pelvic Pain Affect Sexual Function?
- How Might I Feel If I Have Pain with Sex?
- What Can I Do to Manage Living with Sexual Pain?

How Is Pain During Sexual Activity Different for Men and Women?

Sexual dysfunction is common in both men and women, but when sex causes distress or pain, it should be *evaluated* by a medical professional. People can experience pain with penetrative sex, pain with arousal, pain with deep penetration, or pain with *orgasm*. Pain should not routinely be a part of a sexually intimate experience. Any part of sex or intimacy that is painful should lead you to seek an evaluation by a specialist.

Is Sexual Pain Different Based on My Sexual Orientation or Gender Identity?

Sexual pain can take many different forms and depends on your anatomy and the type of sexual activity that is causing your pain. The genitals are hormonally sensitive organs, and changes in *hormones* from *menopause* in women or from a *gender-affirmation,* hormones and surgery in people with *gender dysphoria* can cause tissue changes that can lead to sexual pain. You should talk with your doctor about the type of sexual activity that is causing pain so that your doctor can better understand the underlying cause and offer helpful treatment strategies.

How Can I Decrease Pain During Sexual Acts, Physically and Mentally?

If you are experiencing pain with sexual activity, it can usually help to obtain a diagnosis and treatment plan. Treatments might consist of medications, *physical therapy* (PT), *sex therapy*, or a combination of all three. No matter what type of sex you are having or want to have, communication is the key to making it better, more intimate, and more fun. Remember, most people have their quirks talking about sex, and many doctors don't routinely ask about sexual activity. You should bring up problems you are having, and if your provider does not seem knowledgeable, politely ask your doctor to help you find a more informed provider. Many doctors will give you feedback on research you have done on your own before the visit if you ask about the information in a concise manner. For example, "This urologist advertises treatment of *Peyronie's disease*. Would you recommend him, or is this something you have treated before? Is there someone you prefer for this diagnosis?"

Many people benefit from sex therapy and *couples therapy* to improve how they communicate and navigate sexual problems. Sometimes, that means scheduling sex after preparatory work (such as a warm bath); sometimes, it means changing positions or the goals of sex; and sometimes, it means learning how to tell your partner what you like and what is painful. Peoples' experiences can profoundly affect sex. Sex therapists can work on these issues and release you from some of the obstacles posed by these experiences. Some sex therapists market their teachings directly (online) to the public, but it is often useful to work one-on-one, in person, with a talking therapist. Many sexual aid devices you may find on your own or your providers may recommend can make sex more comfortable and pleasurable. You deserve pleasure and intimacy in your life!

You know yourself and your body better than anyone, and you should keep sight of what proportion of your symptoms are physical and what portion of your symptoms are related to your brain's contribution (fear, anxiety, and attitudes toward sex). Both usually play a role in sexual pain and providers who focus only on the physical or only on the psychological may not be able to provide you with the best outcome.

What Alternative Strategies Can I Use to Have an Active Sex Life Despite My Pain?

The goal of sex should be pleasure and intimacy. That does not obligate you to a partner, penetration, erection, orgasm, gender, or orientation. Pleasure and intimacy are defined differently by every person and every couple. When you have pain, it's even more important to find out what gives you pleasure and makes you feel good. Many couples with pain or neurological alterations of the sexual organs find pleasure in alternate erogenous zones, such as the neck, ears, axillae (armpits), chest, or inner thighs. Improving intimacy and pleasure is the key to maintaining a happy sex life while navigating *pelvic pain*.

Does Persistent Pelvic Pain Mean an End to Intimacy and Sex?

Absolutely not. Working with specialists who understand your specific issues can help you navigate treatment strategies and should give you hope that intimacy and sex are not over. Pelvic pain can mean the strategies might change, but you don't have to stop enjoying this aspect of life as long as you have a desire for it.

How Can Pelvic Pain Affect Sexual Function?

The experience of *chronic* pain anywhere in your body affects your mental and emotional health as well as sexuality. Pain is associated with feelings of loss, grief, anxiety, and *depression*, all of which are likely to affect your mood and the backdrop for sexual relations. Also, chronic pain is fatiguing, and medications used for pain relief can contribute to drowsiness and a lack of vitality. However, when pain involves the pelvis and the genital areas, it can be devastating for your sexual health and your intimate relationships. Pelvic and/or genital pain affect sexuality and sexual functioning because experiencing pain in general reduces the desire to engage in sex and because the pain is located in a part of your body most closely associated with sexuality and with sexual pleasure.

Pelvic pain has biological, psychological, and social implications. This does not mean that the pain is either physical or psychological; instead, these factors combine to contribute to your pain and to perpetuate it. Moreover, the physical, psychological, and social aspects of one's life are all affected. Pain is both physical and emotional. Pelvic pain is located in an intimate area and its accompanying physical disability often goes unrecognized. Many people with pelvic pain visit multiple practitioners before receiving an adequate diagnosis, so they might even have already begun to question their own sanity. These are factors that contribute to psychological distress. Distress about the condition, feeling "broken" as a person, and having a condition that is difficult to discuss publicly, all affect one's sense of self and one's sexual sense of self.

During sexual activity, pain or discomfort can coincide with arousal, touch, penetration, and orgasm. This experience is likely to affect the desire to engage in sexual activity, the ability to become or remain aroused, and the ability to consciously relax the pelvic floor sufficiently to allow for comfortable penetration or orgasm. In a cyclic manner, these factors further contribute to increased friction and tissue trauma, decreased *genital* arousal responses, increased pain, and personal and relationship distress.

How Might I Feel If I Have Pain with Sex?

For the person who experiences pain, not desiring sex and not enjoying sex are difficult losses, especially if past sexual experiences have been positive. If the person has never been able to enjoy sex because of pain, then he or she might carry additional feelings of frustration and loss. In either case, it is not unusual for people with pelvic pain to continue to engage in sex, despite the pain, for a variety of reasons. This can include wanting to feel normal, wanting to please or not wanting to lose their partner, or not feeling that abstaining from intercourse is a viable option.

Societal messages perpetuate the belief that heterosexual women must allow vaginal penetration to please or fulfill her partner's sexual needs. In any partnered relationship, decreased desire and willingness can lead to feelings of guilt and responsibility for not having sex. A woman can engage in sexual penetration when she is neither aroused nor interested, which contributes to a lack of autonomy and control of her body. This has the potential to turn sex into a chore and to further affect desire. In the worst case, continuing to engage in sex, despite the pain and out of obligation, can result in aversive and traumatic responses regarding sex.

Furthermore, these feelings might compel a woman to undergo treatments and procedures that are painful and exposing, which can lead to dissociation from emotions to get through the painful experience. People with pain should consider whether they are undergoing uncomfortable or painful treatments solely to please a sexual partner, and these procedures should be discussed with a mental health professional as well as with their medical providers. Also, it is important to note that while sexual relations are difficult for those with pelvic pain, the medical and physical therapy procedures that they undergo to treat the pain can also create distress. Many people with pelvic pain have trouble with the physical examination and treatments required to restore sexual function. Fear, aversion to touch, and pain avoidance are characteristic of the response to physical examination and treatment.

Men with pelvic pain can face a separate set of issues. The societal expectation is that men always desire sexual relations and are consistently able to reach climax. Men feel pressure to have and maintain an erection to function. In addition to feeling the loss of prior enjoyment and grief for the pain, they might also feel less masculine or normal, which is a feeling that can be difficult to discuss.

In both genders, anger, frustration, or emotional withdrawal can be easier to express than discussing sexual pain and finding solutions for intimacy.

What Can I Do to Manage Living with Sexual Pain?

Mindfulness-based treatment for pelvic pain (Rosenbaum, 2013) provides a way to address pain, improve sexual function, and promote feelings of safety. Mindfulness aims to encourage people to suspend self-judgment, stay connected and present during treatment, and experience personal autonomy (the ability to make decisions for oneself) such that they might find meaning in the sexual connection. Look for practitioners—whether they are physical therapists or sex therapists—who are aware of mindfulness-based forms of therapy, rather than goal-oriented forms of therapy.

If you are living with pelvic and/or genital pain, it is imperative for the lines of communication about sexuality to stay open with your partner. Partners might fear that any loving or connecting behaviors will "lead to sex" and might avoid emotional intimacy, affectionate hugs, or cuddling. This can lead to greater feelings of loneliness and abandonment for both partners.

You and your partner can learn and re-learn to enjoy intimacy and sexual activities that are based on pleasure and connection.

These strategies can lead to a reliable and consistent intimate life, which supports the other positive aspects of your relationship and your life. Lastly, many of the above strategies can be employed without a partner to allow enjoyment of one's own body.

Ideally you will be able to find treatment for your pain and the treatments aimed at improving your life and relationships. Whether the approach decreases the pain or helps you find ways to cope, to restore intimacy and regain a sense of control, these treatments can improve your quality of life.

WHY DOES PAIN PERSIST AND BECOME CHRONIC?

Elise J.B. De, MD and Serge Marchand, PhD

CHAPTER

In This Chapter

- Introduction
- Am I Predisposed to Pain?
- How Does Communication Occur Between the Peripheral Nerves and the Brain?
- What Happens When Messages Enter the Spinal Cord?
- What Is Visceral Pain?
- How Do the Brain and Emotions Affect Your Gut?
- How Do the Spinal Cord and Brain Communicate?
- How Does the Brain Compile and Integrate Pain Messaging?
- What Is Central Sensitization?
- How Does Central Sensitization Relate to Small-Fiber Neuropathy?
- Can My Brain Control My Pain?
- Conclusion

Introduction

Pelvic pain can originate from several structures in the pelvis, such as *bones*, *muscles*, viscera, *nerves*, and connective tissue. Adding to the complexity, pain can be perceived in a location distant from the originating organ, especially when there is *visceral* pain (internal organ pain). A comprehensive clinical evaluation helps to identify the source of pain. However, as with several *chronic* pain conditions, pain can appear or persist even when there is no longer an active injury or a source of irritation.

This chapter introduces the *neurological (neurophysiological)* mechanisms that explain how pain sensitization contributes to some types of *chronic pelvic pain* (CPP) and what *nociception* and *pain* encompass. Nociception refers to the processing of information about your environment, starting from peripheral nerves and moving to the spinal cord and then to the brain. These pathways explain why you jerk your hand away from a hot stove before you even know that it hurts. Pain involves higher brain centers in which the pain is experienced, and it is altered by emotions such as fear and anxiety. Nociception can be thought of as **sensing**, and pain can be thought of as **experiencing** a harmful stimulus.

Persistent pain can involve different mechanisms.

- Chronic pain can be derived from an abnormal increase in activity in the peripheral nerves that are responsible for nociception, or pain can come from nerve cells in the *central nervous system* (CNS)—in other words, in the *spine* and brain.

- Chronic pain can result from a decrease of natural internal *(endogenous)* pain-reduction mechanisms; these normally reduce pain perception by partially blocking nociceptive activity or by reducing pain perception.

Pain is a dynamic process. The association between nociceptive activity and pain perception depends on internal and *external* influences. From the same nociceptive stimulus, pain perception and brain activity differ among people. Those who have more knowledge about pain neurophysiology tend have less fear avoidance and lower perceived disability from pain (Fletcher et al, 2016).

Am I Predisposed to Pain?

The importance of endogenous factors, including our genetics, influences our sensitivity to pain (Williams et al, 2012). In one study of identical twins with identical *deoxyribonucleic acid* (DNA, our genetic code) and fraternal twins with DNA shared similar to any brother or sister, 60% of the variation in pain induced by cold-pressor tests (involving immersion of the hand in very cold water) and one-fourth of the variance in heat-induced pain was genetically mediated (Nielsen et al, 2008). This suggests that environmental and genetic factors both play roles in pain. Also, the effect of the environment on epigenetics (lasting changes in *gene expression* without alteration of the DNA sequence) is crucial (Buchheit et al, 2012). Nerve injuries or psychological factors can impact the central nervous system (CNS) by affecting DNA expression (via *methylation*) and produce a *genomic memory* of pain (Descalzi et al, 2015). It could even explain the relationship between *depression* and pain (Swiergiel et al, 2015; Turk et al, 2002). Pelvic pain has a genomic component with some people being more prone to developing CPP (Nickel and Tripp, 2015; Reichard et al, 2015; Shoskes et al, 2016; Vassilopoulou et al, 2019).

Pain perception is the result of inherited physical and psychological factors that are influenced by our environment. Together these factors frame our reaction to painful situations, and our predisposition to chronic pain.

Fortunately, external factors also modulate pain in favorable ways. Exercise, *meditation*, or yoga can produce brain activity changes that reduce chronic pain (Bushnell et al, 2015).

How Does Communication Occur Between the Peripheral Nerves and the Brain?

There is no direct relationship between nociceptive activity and pain perception. (Sherrington, 1906). Messages about potentially painful stimuli (for example, soap in the eye) are described as nociceptive. Frequently, a nociceptive stimulus will be converted into pain. Several factors change the perception of pain when that information reaches consciousness (Wiech et al, 2010). Normally, pain is protective. However, in an emergency, the importance of pain may be felt with a lower intensity. For example, if you scrape your shin while falling out of a row boat, you might not notice the pain until you are safely back on the dock.

What Happens When Messages Enter the Spinal Cord?

For nociceptive fibers that affect pelvic pain, the signal is transported through peripheral nerves to a part of the spinal cord called the *dorsal horn* (Figure 19-1), where the *cell bodies* (control centers) of the sensory nerves connect (in *synapses*) with other neurons (projection neurons) at the entrance to the dorsal horn. This same secondary neuron of the spinal cord will then travel to the brain and can also receive messages from the skin, muscles, and visceral organs (Bars, 2002). Two completely different types of sensory nervous systems are involved here! The *somatic nervous system* involves mainly external perceptions (from the ear and nose, skin, and muscles). The *autonomic* or *visceral nervous system* (Figure 19-2), which includes the *sympathetic* and *parasympathetic nerves* mainly in the internal organs, senses internal conditions (such as pressure in the blood vessels, airways, bladder, or digestive tract). The *enteric nervous system* serves the *gastrointestinal* (GI) tract and is one of the main divisions of the autonomic nervous system. It is capable of acting independently of the sympathetic and parasympathetic nervous systems, although it is influenced by those systems. Muscle pain (such as pain in the levator muscles) could be exacerbated by visceral organ pain (such as pain from the bladder) and vice versa due to the cross talk among different nerve types. Nerves from the skin, muscles, and visceral organs could interact and produce increased pain. Therefore, skin-surface stimulation techniques, such as *transcutaneous electrical nerve stimulation* (TENS), can reduce visceral pain (Tugay, 2007) or chest pain (Sanderson, 1991) even if the electric current is only on the skin's surface and will not directly affect the organ. This helps explain improvement in bladder symptoms with pelvic floor physical therapy, which relaxes the levator muscles.

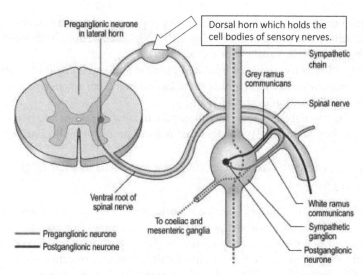

Figure 19-1: Lateral horn of the spinal cord. The green shows the messages leaving the spinal cord in the sympathetic nervous system. Arrow shows the dorsal horn, which holds the cell bodies of the sensory nerves. (Reproduced with permission: Standring S, ed.: Figure 16.13. Outflow from preganglionic sympathetic neurones in the lateral horn of the spinal cord. In: Gray's Atlas of Anatomy. *The Anatomical Basis of Clinical Practice*. 41st Edition. Philadelphia, PA: Elsevier Limited. 2016; 225–237.e3.)

The interactions of the nociceptive neurons through the spinal cord are also important for processing nociceptive information. The spinal cord's *complex* network of neurons, which includes primary nociceptive neuron endings, secondary neurons, *interneurons*, and neurons of the descending tracts, contains different *neurotransmitters* and types of *receptors*. These process the nociceptive messages before they are transmitted to the higher brain centers to create a sensation of pain.

Direct and indirect interactions between the *visceral* and *somatosensory* systems are meaningful for pelvic pain (Sato, 1995; Beal, 1985). For example, the treatment of pain associated with *irritable bowel syndrome* (IBS) reduces both the visceral pain and seemingly unrelated back or leg pain (Verne et al, 2003). The reverse effect, reducing visceral pain by a somatic treatment, also is evident. Menstrual pain *(dysmenorrhea)* or esophageal pain can be treated by the use of TENS, suggesting a somatovisceral reflex effect of the skin stimulation on visceral pain (Chang et al, 1996; Lundeberg et al, 1985).

Chapter 19: Why Does Pain Persist and Become Chronic? 281

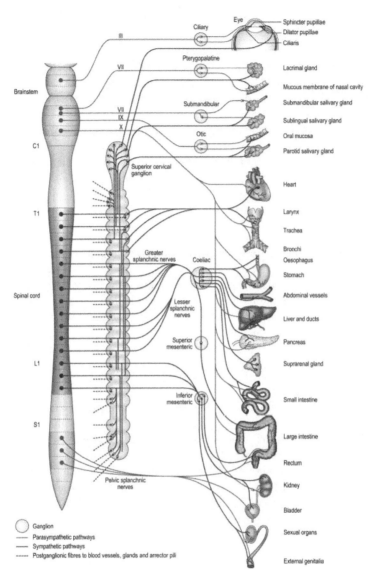

Figure 19-2: The autonomic or visceral nervous system (sympathetic and parasympathetic nerves), mainly of the internal organs, senses internal conditions, such as pressure in the blood vessels, airways, bladder, or digestive tract. (Reproduced with permission: Standring S, ed.: Figure 16.11. Efferent pathways of the autonomic nervous system In: Gray's Anatomy. *The Anatomical Basis of Clinical Practice*. 41st Edition. Philadelphia, PA: Elsevier Limited. 2016; 225–237.e3.)

What Is Visceral Pain?

Described above, the visceral nervous system (including the brain-gut axis) includes a very sophisticated *sensory system* (Knowles and Azizn, 2009) that operates independently but in relation to the rest of the CNS. Several visceral pain syndromes, such as IBS, present without a clear injury to the intestines or its nerves (Jones et al, 2006). Also, emerging data stress the importance of the *microbiome* (the natural mix of *bacteria* that co-exists with our bodies) (Borre, 2014). Alteration in the gut microbial composition is associated with marked changes in mood, pain, and thought processes, that are related to communication between the brain and the gut microbiota (Tillisch, 2014). Understanding these interactions might lead to treatments that act on the microbiota and affect brain functions.

How Do the Brain and Emotions Affect Your Gut?

Chronic visceral pain is related to both *peripheral* and *central sensitization*. Connections from the brain increase and decrease nerve activity of the visceral nervous system. In addition, the autonomic nervous system influences visceral sensitivity and helps explain the role of emotional modulation of visceral pain (Knowles and Aziz, 2009; Craig, 2002; Damasio and Carvalho, 2013). (The autonomic nervous system includes the sympathetic nervous system, which is thought of as the fight-or-flight, or stress response system, and the parasympathetic nervous system, which is thought of as the calming and digesting system.)

How Do the Spinal Cord and Brain Communicate?

Before impulses reach the brain, secondary neurons in the spinal cord travel in pathways to a brain structure called the thalamus (Figure 19-3). The thalamus is the hub that receives all the incoming information from the body, including nociceptive signals, before relaying them to different brain structures that form our perceptions. For instance, the primary and secondary somatosensory cortex gives us information about the location, nature, and intensity of a painful stimulus *(sensory-discriminative component of pain)* and sorts the physical quality of the nociceptive activity. Different structures in the brain, such as the *frontal lobe* and the *limbic system* (Hodge and Apkarian, 1990), form the emotional *(affective)* components of pain; the affective components are associated with unpleasant sensations and the desire to escape from the suffering. Thus, perceptions and emotions should be considered when treating chronic pain.

How Does the Brain Compile and Integrate Pain Messaging?

It is easier than ever to accept the importance of the mutual influence between emotions and sensations in the pain experience without implying that pain is "all in one's head." Certain higher brain centers specialize in the sensory-discriminative component of pain to give precise information on the location, intensity, and all the other characteristics of the nociceptive stimulation. Other centers focus on the emotional appreciation of pain. The affective component is not only associated with the intensity of the stimulation, but it also refers to other emotions, such as anticipation or fear (Price, 2000; Singer et al, 2004).

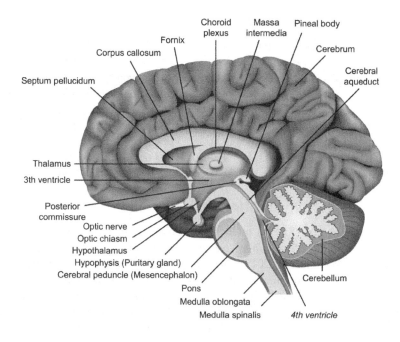
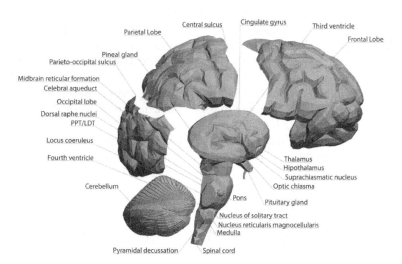

Figure 19-3: Anatomy of the brain, from central (midline) view and external view.

What Is Central Sensitization?

Central sensitization relates to pain that is maintained by the CNS with or without a signal from the periphery. It can be described as a *plasticity* of the CNS that reduces the threshold to produce a painful sensation to the point that even a non-painful stimulus will be perceived as painful *(allodynia)* or more painful than usual, which is known as *hyperalgesia* (Woolf, 2011; Bliss and Collingridge, 1993; Ji et al, 2003; Sandkuhler, 2007). A good example is postsurgical pain. After surgery, it is normal to experience pain at the site of the surgery until the wound is completely healed. However, pain can persist even after the healing from the operation is complete. Pain that was originally from the wound can be imprinted on the CNS to result in pain that now comes directly from the CNS.

How Does Central Sensitization Relate to Small-Fiber Neuropathy?

Small-fiber polyneuropathy (SFPN) refers to preferential damage to the small-diameter somatic and autonomic fibers (*unmyelinated C-fibers* and/or thinly-*myelinated A-delta fibers*) (Oaklander and Nolano, 2019). It is common in a variety of conditions, including *diabetes, fibromyalgia,* autoimmune disease, and some *metabolic syndromes* (Chen et al, 2019). The diagnosis can be made through the documentation of decreased *intraepidermal* small-fiber nerve density, as demonstrated on *multi-molecular immunofluorescence analyses* (a simple skin biopsy that identifies the changes in the peripheral nerve fibers), as well as other factors.

The link between central sensitization and SFPN can be explained by at least three mechanisms that are not mutually exclusive. First, the changes in SFPN that are characterized by peripheral skin biopsy could also be present in the CNS and be responsible for more widespread symptoms, such as fatigue or concentration deficits (Oaklander and Nolano, 2019).

Second, certain brain regions or connectivity among brain regions (such as cingulate, insular, and prefrontal cortices) related to pain modulation are shown to be dysfunctional in chronic pain conditions, such as fibromyalgia, chronic back pain, and headache (Absinta et al, 2012; Ivo et al, 2013; Jensen et al, 2012; Kuchinad et al, 2007; Seminowicz et al, 2011).

Third, pain induced by SFPN can trigger central sensitization and increase pain by having a direct "pain memory" effect in the supraspinal CNS.

Can My Brain Control My Pain?

Yes! Remember, the brain tells the body what nerve input means. The brain-based treatments have to do with re-interpreting the messages from the nerves. This relationship between pain and memory (Price and Inyang, 2015) supports the role of interventions that erase or alter pain memories and the fear of pain (Sandkuhler and Lee, 2013). Non-pharmacological approaches such as *mirror therapy* can also change the re-organization of the cortex following *phantom pain* or *complex regional pain syndrome* (CRPS) (Moseley et al, 2008). When successful, the results are astonishing.

Specific steps to try at home include the following:

- Use a massage or TENS unit over the painful regions.
- Understand that when you are feeling pain in multiple locations, reducing the pain at one location will have a positive effect on the other locations.
- Use meditation, relaxation, or cognitive-behavioral therapy (CBT) to trigger pain reduction mechanisms in the CNS.
- Exercise to enhance the efficacy of your natural pain reduction mechanisms.

Professional and medical therapies include the following:

- Continue with medical approaches to pain.
- Work with a psychologist.
- Engage in alternative therapies, such as mind-body medicine.

Conclusion

Pelvic pain can be the end result of several factors. Malfunction of pelvic organs (including skin, muscle, viscera, and bones) can produce pain that will be enhanced by movement or certain positions. However, central sensitization exists when persistent pain that comes directly from the CNS has been sensitized by previous painful situations. Peripheral fibers, such as occurs in SFPN, produce nociceptive stimuli that activate a "central memory" or central sensitization. In every chronic pain situation, psychological factors increase or decrease the pain experience. The treatment of pelvic pain needs to account for contributing factors for a better result.

Pain is influenced by *biopsychosocial factors* that should be addressed through appropriate medical and rehabilitative management. This is especially true for pelvic pain in which multiple organs are implicated in an interaction of the peripheral nervous system and CNS.

The sensory aspect of pain is noteworthy, but the affective component is responsible for many of the pain-processing mechanisms.

Understanding the neurological mechanisms of the pain process allows us to put them to use for the treatment of pain. This helps maximize the efficacy of drug therapies and opens a variety of non-pharmacological interventions.

Better understanding of pain complexity will explain the variability of pain responses in those who have comparable disease but who respond differently to the same treatments.

Understanding the mechanisms of pain allows health care providers and the person with pain to maximize the efficacy of drug therapies and use a variety of non-pharmacological interventions.

HOW DO FAMILY MEMBERS TYPICALLY RESPOND TO PELVIC PAIN?

Gretchen H. Wilber, PsyD

CHAPTER

In This Chapter

- Introduction
- Who in My Family and Circle of Friends Is at Risk for Becoming Stressed?
- What Are Some Indicators That a Family Member Is Not Coping Well?
- Should I Talk to Family and Friends About the Changes My Body Is Experiencing?
- How Can I Prevent My Pain from Being a Burden on Those Who Are Important to Me?

Introduction

This chapter explores how your *pelvic pain* can influence others, such as your supporters, loved ones, and those who count on you for the things they need. Most likely, those around you wish you well, empathize with your pain, and want to help. Everyone experiences the supportive role differently. Your family and friends might not fully realize what you are experiencing because they are not in pain themselves. They might even forget you are in pain, or they might worry more than is needed. Some will feel angry or frustrated that you cannot do more and believe they might be adding to your stress. Some will feel guilty or responsible for your experience. No matter how one looks at the situation, the reaction of those around you has the potential to help or worsen your experience.

Who in My Family and Circle of Friends Is at Risk for Becoming Stressed?

Depending on the severity of your pelvic pain, it is possible that your spouse, partner, children, closest friend(s), or family members might experience stress or *caregiver burnout*, a term that refers to a state of fatigue that occurs when a person provides emotional or physical support for a loved one over an extended period (Cleveland Clinic, 2019). Sometimes, the caregiver is so consumed with meeting your needs that they neglect to take care of their own health and needs. Over time, this can lead to hopelessness, irritability, *depression*, and/or anxiety. Resources are available (see below) to assist your caregiver if he or she is having a difficult time managing the stress that can accompany helping you with your *chronic pelvic pain* (CPP). It might also be helpful for you to enlist the support of others if caregiver burnout is a concern for your loved one.

If pelvic pain prohibits you from engaging in sexual activities or intercourse, it might be helpful for your romantic partner or spouse to obtain support from their *primary care provider* (PCP), a mental health professional, or a support group. Often, well-intentioned loved ones don't want to discuss their frustration, exhaustion, or lack of empathy with the person who is in pain. It might be helpful for your partner to accompany you to some medical appointments because he or she can benefit from learning more about your condition. Your partner might have questions for your medical providers that can promote a more collaborative approach to your treatment. If your partner discusses his or her fatigue, depression, or anxiety with a mental health professional, your partner might be able to receive guidance. This could be helpful to everyone involved because it can improve communication and decrease pressure on both of you.

What Are Some Indicators That a Family Member Is Not Coping Well?

Common signs of poor coping or caregiver burnout include the following:

- The caregiver's mood or pattern of communication changes from warm and supportive to cold, dismissive, or angry.
- The caregiver has trouble meeting his or her own needs.

- You might notice a decline in your caregiver's ability to care for him or herself or family members or to attend work.

- You might find that your family member changes his or her eating habits (such as eating too much or not enough) or he or she no longer makes healthy choices about food, sleep, or exercise.

- You might also notice that your caregiver is not making or keeping routine health appointments or attending his or her recreational activities.

- Your caregiver might withdraw from other friends and family.

It can be helpful to initiate a discussion around some of these areas if they have not already been directly addressed.

Other signs that your family member or friend is not coping well include an increase in fearful or worried thoughts, worsening of *chronic* health conditions (such as high blood pressure or heart disease) and insomnia. Sometimes, the nervous system reacts as if there were a life-or-death threat when there is an ongoing, unresolved stressor. When this occurs, the body senses danger and initiates a stress response involving *hormones* and other physical reactions to assist with the body's reaction to the threat. This would be an adaptive response if the stressor were a threat to survival. However, when this response occurs over a prolonged period, it can contribute to negative health consequences.

Common symptoms of an increased stress response include irritability; feeling overwhelmed and anxious; sadness; depression; panic attacks; impaired concentration ability or decision-making; increased consumption of alcohol or drugs; allergic reactions (such as hives, skin conditions); headaches; and chest pain. If you believe that your loved one is struggling with these symptoms, he or she might benefit from *cognitive-behavioral therapy* (CBT). This therapy can teach him or her how to cope with negative thoughts and behaviors that could contribute to increased anxiety and depression. Also, your caregiver might benefit from working with a mental health professional to receive validation and strategies for healthy coping. They can also learn *progressive muscle relaxation training*, *meditation*, and *deep breathing* to cope with the increased stress.

Should I Talk to Family and Friends About the Changes My Body Is Experiencing?

Given the complexities of pelvic pain, it can be daunting to discuss your health concerns with family and friends. However, having the courage to discuss your vulnerability can lead to close, meaningful engagement in life and relationships (Brown, 2010). It can be helpful to plan a time and place where you can have a private conversation with your loved ones. If you have not previously discussed your concerns about pelvic pain, you might benefit from forewarning your support system that you have something sensitive or stressful that you would like to discuss and that you will be asking for their undivided attention and support. That allows you to decrease the likelihood that you will receive an unsympathetic or hurried response.

Too often, people are ashamed of their pelvic pain and instead of reaching out for support, they remain silent and/or secretive. Shame can decrease dramatically when you discuss your sources of shame with someone whom you trust and if that person's response is empathic.

"Owning our story can be hard but not nearly as difficult as spending our lives running from it. Embracing our vulnerabilities is risky but not nearly as dangerous as giving up on love and belonging and joy—the experiences that make us the most vulnerable. Only when we are brave enough to explore the darkness will we discover the infinite power of our light" (Brown, 2010).

Even if your friend or family member cannot relate to your physical symptoms, it is likely that they have experienced something in their life that generated shame and/or vulnerability. While the discussion might be difficult to begin, it can increase the emotional closeness in your relationship, and perhaps explain confusing patterns that have resulted from your pain, for example canceling plans.

It can help your friend or family member to be informed about the changes in your body and/or treatment, especially if he or she will be involved in your care or daily routines. For example, if you know that you will need to attend treatment on a regular basis and might need help fulfilling ongoing responsibilities, your friend or family member might be able to help. It is common for people with pelvic pain to be anxious or apprehensive when they experience new symptoms or start new treatments. If you are experiencing a sense of isolation, depression, or anxiety that is secondary to your pelvic pain, your loved one might benefit from a better understanding of your overall health condition and concerns. Carrying the burden of pelvic pain alone can magnify the problem; sharing the burden with an actively involved and educated significant other can lighten the load and perhaps deepen the relationship.

How Can I Prevent My Pain from Being a Burden on Those Who Are Important to Me?

Most likely, your symptoms are a greater burden on you than on anyone around you, and your symptoms are less of a problem for your caregiver than you think. Following are some simple suggestions:

- Communicate when the pain is bad so your actions can be interpreted appropriately.
- Express appreciation for your caregiver's efforts.
- Demonstrate a commitment to your health and relationships by seeking out and following medical advice; these actions will provide your caregiver with the security that other people can help you and there might be answers for your pain on the horizon.
- Avoid angry outbursts. Words uttered when angry can erase the satisfaction your caregiver derives from doing nice things for you.

- Set boundaries and encourage your loved one to attend to his or her own hobbies and needs even when you might not be able to participate. If your loved one is a romantic partner, if you desire sexual activity and your pain prohibits it, work together or with a sex therapist to find alternate erogenous zones and alternate means of having physical intimacy.
- Set boundaries on the relationship with your caregiver where interventions have become negative. If your caregiver has developed poor coping strategies (such as anger, criticism, or avoidance), setting boundaries—often with the help of a third person, such as another family member or health professional—can help with healing (or exiting) that relationship.
- Seek broad support from other family members and friends.
- Be fair to yourself without being overly critical of the roles you think you should be playing, and give back in the ways that you are able.

You should feel good about taking the time to read this chapter for the sake of your supporters, and for reading this book, to help you manage your pelvic pain. These positive steps will be noticed by your loved one.

HOW CAN I LEARN MORE ABOUT PELVIC PAIN?

Jill H. Osborne, MA

CHAPTER

In This Chapter

- Where Can I Turn for More Information About Pelvic Pain?
- Should I Seek a Second Opinion?
- Should I Seek Care at a Specialized Center for My Pelvic Pain?
- How Can My Local Library or the Internet Be of Assistance to Me?
- What Are the Most Reliable Internet Resources for Me to Use for Information?
- What Should I Be Concerned About When Using the Internet?
- What Local, Regional, or National Organizations Provide Information About Pelvic Pain?
- What Articles or Videos Offer Sound Advice or Information?
- Would It Be Helpful for Me to Speak with Someone Who Has a Similar Condition?
- What Is the Role of Social Media in Learning About Pelvic Pain?

Where Can I Turn for More Information About Pelvic Pain?

If you were diagnosed with *pelvic pain* 20 years ago, you might have been prescribed antibiotics for months or years at a time under the mistaken assumption that you had a *chronic* infection (Fleming-Dutra, 2016; Pew Charitable Trust, 2018). You might have agreed to a *hysterectomy* only to discover later that your symptoms were coming from your bladder (Lee et al, 2016). You might have been told that your pain was "all in your head."

Today, you can carry hope in your heart. A revolution is occurring in the treatment of pelvic pain. *Urologists, gynecologists, physical therapists, physical medicine specialists, neurologists*, and others are working together more to provide comprehensive diagnostic and *multi-modal treatment* services. Dedicated networks of medical professionals are conducting vital research studies. Medical and patient (consumer) organizations are providing essential support services. You are not alone.

People with pelvic pain are now vocal, assertive, and empowered. You can walk into a medical office without shame or blame. You can communicate clearly about your symptoms and concerns. You can share your history. Most importantly, you can educate yourself and engage in thoughtful discussions about tests and treatments. You are an active participant in your medical care.

Thankfully, there are many resources that can help. A web search will yield thousands of links about any medical conditions or symptoms. YouTube offers videos from both medical professionals and people who have experienced pelvic pain. Websites and *social networking* sites host support groups that you can participate in from the comfort of your home. New articles and books are released regularly by experts in pelvic pain.

As you've learned from other chapters in this book, pelvic pain can be triggered in the *urinary tract*, the bowel, the *pelvic floor muscles* (PFMs), the reproductive organs, and even from skeletal dysfunction (your *bones*). You and your providers will need to work together to discover the cause of your pain—and this begins with the information that you give to them. Don't just say, "I hurt down there." Be willing to talk about it. Where is your pain located? Is it inside your body or on your skin? Is it high, low, to the left or to the right in your pelvis? Is it constant, or does it come and go? Is it sharp or dull? What makes it better or worse? If you don't know where your urethra is compared to your rectum, then it's time to turn on your computer or visit your local library and learn.

If you're having *urinary frequency*, urgency, pressure or pain, take a few moments and read about the urinary tract before your appointment. Can you sleep through the night? Do you struggle with *incontinence*? Do you have to strain to empty your bladder? Is there occasionally blood in your urine? Does the pain improve after you empty your bladder? Does it get worse? You should know the basic structures of the urinary tract, including: the kidneys, *ureters*, bladder, prostate and *urethra*.

If your symptoms appear to be related to your reproductive tract, refresh your knowledge of those organs. In women, pelvic pain can originate from the vagina, uterus, *fallopian tubes*, or *ovaries*. Tell your doctor if you have painful, heavy periods or a family history of *endometriosis, fibroids,* or *ovarian cysts*. Men with pelvic pain might report pain at the tip of their *penis*, in their *testicles,* or *prostate*. If your pain is *external,* such as burning on your skin when you urinate, take a moment to look "down there." For women, squat over a mirror and look at your *vulva, labia, perineum,* and *rectum*. Are they bright red or a normal healthy pink color? Is there any discharge? Are there any tender spots? The more specific you can be, the better.

Do you struggle with constipation or diarrhea? Do you have painful bowel movements or have to strain to empty your bowels? Do you struggle with hard or loose stool? Do you experience painful cramping after eating? Even *hemorrhoids* can trigger intense pelvic pain. Take a moment to read about how the bowel functions, as well as the role of diet, fiber, and *probiotics*.

People with pelvic floor muscle (PFM) problems are often the most surprised by their diagnosis. Tight, dysfunctional PFMs can trigger *chronic pelvic pain* (CPP), as well as urinary and bowel discomfort. You might find it difficult to start your urine stream, experience tightness and pain with intimacy, or strain to empty your bladder and bowels. Sitting for long periods of time and driving in a car might be uncomfortable. Is your pain worse after your commute? Did your symptoms start after a trauma? Had you fallen, had surgery, delivered a baby, been in a car accident, suffered *sexual abuse*, sustained an athletic injury, or had an accident in childhood that could lay the foundation for chronic muscle dysfunction and pelvic pain as an adult? This is vital information to share with your doctor and/or physical therapist.

Do any relatives have a history of pelvic pain, bladder or bowel issues, painful periods, or extreme sensitivity of their skin? Some conditions, such as *irritable bowel syndrome* (IBS), *interstitial cystitis* (IC), *polycystic ovarian syndrome* (PCOS), *fibroid tumors,* endometriosis, *small fiber polyneuropathy* (SFPN), and *central sensitization* can run in families.

Your pelvic pain is an anatomical or systems-based mystery to be solved. When you share your symptoms and history with your physicians, you're giving them vital diagnostic clues.

Should I Seek a Second Opinion?

If you are not responding to treatment, your pain is worsening, and/or you aren't sure if your doctor has made a correct diagnosis, it's worth pursuing a second, third, or fourth opinion. It's not unusual for people with pelvic pain to see several doctors before they receive a correct diagnosis. *Primary care providers* (PCPs) handle basic medical issues, such as simple *urinary tract infections* (UTIs). However, they usually refer more *complex* cases to specialists. A *urologist* will focus on the urinary tract (kidneys, ureters, bladder, prostate, and urethra). A *gynecologist* will focus on the reproductive system (uterus, ovaries, vagina, and vulva). A *gastroenterologist* will focus on the bowels. A physical medicine specialist and an *orthopedist* usually focus on your skeleton, bones, and *nerves*. A physical therapist works with *muscles*. A neurologist and a *neurosurgeon* focus on nerves.

Every doctor brings certain skills, training, and personal beliefs into the examination room. Some might be knowledgeable, while others shrug and say, "I don't know." If that happens, it is worth seeking a second opinion from a pelvic pain specialist. Your physician and/or health insurance company should provide a referral and travel may be required. These doctors have more interest and experience in the treatment of pelvic pain.

Your case could be so complex that you would benefit from seeing a national specialist who has seen thousands of patients over the course of his or her career. They have exceptional diagnostic skills and are often involved in cutting-edge research studies and clinical trials. You might learn more in one appointment with a national specialist than you have learned in years with local physicians. The local physicians who have supported you through the early evaluations will most likely welcome the input and might be able to partner with the specialist in your care.

How does one find experts in pelvic pain? Your doctor might make a referral, or you can reach out to medical or client organizations, such as:

- American Urogynecological Society (AUGS): www.voicesforpfd.org
- American College of Ob-Gyn: www.acog.org
- American Physical Therapy Association: www.apta.org
- Herman Wallace Institute: www.pelvicrehab.com
- Global Pelvic Health Alliance: www.pelvicguru.com
- Endometriosis Association: www.endometriosisassn.org
- International Foundation for Functional Gastrointestinal Disorders: www.iffgd.org
- Interstitial Cystitis Network: www.icnetwork.org
- Interstitial Cystitis Association: www.ichelp.org
- International Pelvic Pain Society: www.pelvicpain.org
- Vulvodynia Association: www.nva.org
- Vulvar Pain Foundation: www.thevpfoundation.org
- Pudendal Neuralgia Association: www.pudendalassociation.org

Should I Seek Care at a Specialized Center for My Pelvic Pain?

If your initial evaluation with local doctors is not helpful, you should consider contacting a pelvic pain specialty center. It's not unusual for people with pain to travel across states or the nation to visit experts in pelvic pain, or for insurance companies to pay when local specialists are not available. Pelvic pain specialists have cross-disciplinary training regarding the structures and organs of the pelvis, and they understand their complex inter-relationships. They will consider the bladder, bowel, reproductive tract, muscles, and nerves as they try to determine what could be triggering your pain. You can gain valuable insight and guidance from these appointments that can then be shared with your local medical providers.

How Can My Local Library or the Internet Be of Assistance to Me?

Congratulations on reading this book! The most successful health care consumers take the time to learn more about their diagnoses. At this point, the more you know about the structures (organs, muscles, and nerves) and where they are located, the better you will be able to understand how a diagnosis is made and how treatment works.

Your local library should have basic health education books and videos to help you build your knowledge about how the bladder, bowel, reproductive tract and muscles work. Then look for resources on your suspected medical condition (e.g., endometriosis, irritable bowel syndrome, interstitial cystitis). If the library books are more than five or ten years old, ask the librarian if they can order more recent books. Here are some excellent books and/or videos:

- Breaking Through Chronic Pelvic Pain: A Holistic Approach For Relief: Jerome Weiss
- Pelvic Pain Explained: Stephanie Prendergast & Elizabeth Akincilar
- Interstitial Cystitis Solution: Nicole Cozean
- Heal Pelvic Pain: Amy Stein
- Healing Pelvic & Abdominal Pain: Amy Stein
- Ending Female Pelvic Pain: Isa Herrera
- Ending Male Pelvic Pain: Isa Herrera
- Ending Pain in Pregnancy: Isa Herrera
- When It Hurts Down There: Angie Stoehr
- Secret Suffering: Susan Bilheimer & Robert Echenberg
- A Headache in The Pelvis: David Wise & Rodney Anderson
- Healing Painful Sex: A Woman's Guide to Confronting, Diagnosing, and Treating Sexual Pain: Dr. Deborah Coady & Nancy Fish

Local libraries usually provide free access to the internet and reference librarians who can help with your search.

What Are the Most Reliable Internet Resources for Me to Use for Information?

If you search for "pelvic pain" on the internet, you will find thousands of links to websites, *blogs*, news stories, videos, and shops. Search engines try to help by preferentially listing websites that are actively updated and have good content authority. That said, you'll want to review several websites to get a fair and balanced look at any medical issue or concern. Don't just settle on the first search results. You'll find some gems on page two and deeper into the search engine results. Beware of the advertisements you will encounter, and discuss any purchases you would like to make during your next doctor's appointment before you make them.

Websites

The United States *National Institutes of Health* and MedlinePlus provide excellent overviews of various pelvic pain conditions, and the information provided has been carefully screened for accuracy. Many major hospitals also provide in-depth articles that describe medical conditions, tests, and treatments available in their facility.

- National Institutes of Health: www.nichd.nih.gov/health/topics/pelvicpain
- MedlinePlus: www.medlineplus.gov/pelvicpain.html
- Harvard Medical School Patient Education Center: www.health.harvard.edu
- UCLA Health: Pelvic Pain: www.healthinfo.uclahealth.org/Search/85,P01550
- Mayo Clinic Health Information: www.mayoclinic.org/symptoms/pelvic-pain/basics/definition/sym-20050898

Wikipedia is an online encyclopedia featured near the top of most search engine results. It relies on a strong community of volunteers to review their content. For basic information (such as definitions of medical terms), it's very reliable, though longer articles may not be precise. One researcher of Wikipedia content wrote: "The findings indicate that overall articles are objective, clearly presented, reasonably accurate and complete although some are poorly written, contain unsubstantiated information and/or provide shallow coverage of a topic." (West and Williamson, 2009).

Your next stop should be the websites of national support groups and organizations. In addition to information on diagnostic tests and treatments, they will share day-to-day self-help tips, such as how to manage painful flares, how to work with doctors, how to travel, how to be intimate, how to prepare for medical appointments, how to handle holidays, and more. Most also have print magazines and fact sheets for members without internet access. Here are some consumer groups that might help:

- Endometriosis Association: www.endometriosisassn.org
- International Foundation for Functional Gastrointestinal Disorders: www.iffgd.org
- Interstitial Cystitis Network: www.icnetwork.org
- Interstitial Cystitis Association: www.ichelp.org
- International Pelvic Pain Society: www.pelvicpain.org
- Vulvodynia Association: www.nva.org

- Vulvar Pain Foundation: www.thevpfoundation.org
- Pudendal Neuralgia Association: www.pudendalassociation.org
- Men's Health Network: www.menshealthnetwork.org
- World Federation for Incontinence and Pelvic Problems: www.wfip.org

Blogs

Many professionals publish articles (blogs) for people with pain and/or their peers through their websites.

- Pelvic Health and Rehabilitation Center: www.pelvicpainrehab.com/blog/
- Beyond Basics Physical Therapy: www.beyondbasicsphysicaltherapy.com
- Sarton Physical Therapy: www.pelvichealing.com/blog
- Pelvic Sanity: www.pelvicsanity.com/blog
- Urology Care Foundation: www.urologyhealth.org/careblog
- Herman Wallace Pelvic Rehab: www.pelvicrehab.com/blog/
- Interstitial Cystitis Network: www.icnetwork.org/category/blog/

Videos

YouTube offers a variety of videos created by a diverse community of health experts, authors, and people with pain. Some provide excellent information on diagnosis, testing methods, treatments, and physical therapy (PT), while others share controversial theories and approaches. Be cautious of videos that promise quick and unsubstantiated cures. New videos are added daily.

- Pelvic Pain Explained Webinar (2019): www.youtube.com/user/PelvicPainRehab/videos
- Pelvic Health Summit (2018): www.youtube.com/watch?v=l1W47ycsx_I
- Robert Echenberg on Chronic Pelvic, Genital and Sexual Pain: www.youtube.com/watch?v=hb92JZu8U9s
- Mayo Clinic Pelvic Pain: www.youtube.com/watch?v=yxtMCjK7MWg
- Stanford Health Care Pelvic Pain Causes and Treatment: www.youtube.com/watch?v=xnJc-3M9NRQ
- American Urologic Association Hunner's Ulcer Video: www.youtube.com/watch?v=gDtybIafNW8

- Living With IC Video Series: www.icnetwork.org/videos
- Pelvic Floor Relaxation Exercises For Pelvic Pain: www.youtube.com/watch?v=Auca88tmUu8

Streams and Podcasts

The newest trends online are live-streams (video) or podcasts (audio) broadcast via the internet into your home or office. From free (or paid) seminars to support group meetings, you can ask questions and interact with experts. If you can't attend during the actual meeting, there may be a video that you can watch after the fact. Family members and friends are welcome.

- IC Network streamed support group meetings: www.icnetwork.org/support/
- Pelvic Messenger podcasts: www.blogtalkradio.com/pelvicmessenger/

What Should I Be Concerned About When Using the Internet?

When you search the web and social networking sites for information, you will be bombarded by advertisements promising that they can treat or cure your medical condition. Be cautious of them. Newly diagnosed and/or desperate people with pain often fall victim to these online scams.

You can also find yourself confused and conflicted by people or groups with different opinions about the cause of or treatments for pelvic pain, leaving you to wonder who you should believe. To find the right treatments for you, you must work with your medical team. No one online can do this for you.

Be cautious of anyone who offers to treat you by phone. Working "face to face" with medical care providers is important.

What Local, Regional, or National Organizations Provide Information About Pelvic Pain?

If you are seeking a medical care provider, you'll want to turn to medical organizations that maintain lists on their websites:

- International Pelvic Pain Society: www.pelvicpain.org
- American Urologic Association: www.auanet.org
- American Urogynecological Society (AUGS): www.voicesforpfd.org
- American College of Ob-Gyn: www.acog.org
- American Physical Therapy Association: www.apta.org
- Herman Wallace Institute: www.pelvicrehab.com
- Global Pelvic Health Alliance: www.pelvicguru.com

Turn to the national patient organizations if you are looking for educational materials and personal support. In addition to providing extensive information on the diagnosis and treatment of pelvic pain, they may also facilitate support groups (on-line or in your community). Annual awareness month campaigns can also be quite informative. Your local physician, hospital information desks, and library should also have lists of local resources and groups.

- Endometriosis Association: www.endometriosisassn.org
- International Foundation for Functional Gastrointestinal Disorders: www.iffgd.org
- Interstitial Cystitis Network: www.icnetwork.org
- Interstitial Cystitis Association: www.ichelp.org
- Interstitial Cystitis Awareness Month: www.icawareness.org
- Interstitial Cystitis Diet Project: www.icdietproject.com
- International Pelvic Pain Society: www.pelvicpain.org
- Vulvodynia Association: www.nva.org
- Vulvar Pain Foundation: www.thevpfoundation.org
- Pudendal Neuralgia Association: www.pudendalassociation.org
- Men's Health Network: www.menshealthnetwork.org

What Articles or Videos Offer Sound Advice or Information?

You will find many good articles and videos online, usually from medical organizations, consumer groups, and experts. While they might have been accurate when written, new advances and discoveries occur throughout the year. Here are some articles to get you started:

Articles

- 12 Possible Causes of Chronic Pelvic Pain: www.webmd.com/women/guide/causes-symptoms-chronic-pelvic-pain#1
- Pelvic Floor 301 – Pelvic Floor Dysfunction: www.pelvicsanity.com/single-post/2018/02/23/Pelvic-Floor-301-Pelvic-Floor-Dysfunction
- Pelvic Floor 201 – What Does The Pelvic Floor Do: www.pelvicsanity.com/single-post/2018/02/23/Pelvic-Floor-201-What-Does-the-Pelvic-Floor-Do
- What Is a Good Pelvic PT Session Like?: www.pelvicpainrehab.com/pelvic-health/5974/part-1-of-2-what-is-a-good-pelvic-pt-session-like/

- Don't Let Fear of Physical Therapy Stop You: www.icnetwork.org/self-help-tip-dont-let-fear-of-physical-therapy-stop-you/
- Get to Know Your Vulva with a Good Self-exam: www.pelvicpainrehab.com/female-pelvic-pain/2809/get-to-know-your-vulva-a-guide-to-self-examination/
- PT—Don't Let the Penis Come Between Us: www.pelvicpainrehab.com/male-pelvic-pain/3805/physical-therapy-male-pelvic-pain-dont-let-penis-come-us/
- Male Pelvic Pain: It's Time to Treat Men Right: www.pelvicpainrehab.com/male-pelvic-pain/4342/male-pelvic-pain-its-time-to-treat-men-right-2/
- Pelvic Floor Physical Therapy Helps Men After Prostatectomy: www.pelvicpainrehab.com/male-pelvic-pain/4630/what-does-physical-therapy-do-for-men-following-prostatectomy/
- Vulvodynia, Vestibulodynia and Vaginismus: What's the Difference and Why Does It Matter?: www.pelvicpainrehab.com/female-pelvic-pain/vulvodynia-female-pelvic-pain/5458/ten-things-you-need-to-know-about-vulvodynia-vestibulodynia-and-vaginismus/
- IC Subtypes and Phenotypes: www.icnetwork.org/interstitial-cystitis-subtypes-phenotypes/
- Beating Interstitial Cystitis: pelvicpainrehab.com/female-pelvic-pain/female-interstitial-cystitis-painful-bladder-syndrome/4998/beating-interstitial-cystitis/
- The Most Proven IC Treatment: Pelvic Floor Physical Therapy: www.pelvicpainrehab.com/female-pelvic-pain/female-interstitial-cystitis-painful-bladder-syndrome/5291/the-most-proven-ic-treatment-pelvic-floor-physical-therapy/
- How to Stop Worrying about Pelvic Pain Symptoms: www.pelvicpainrehab.com/female-pelvic-pain/4900/how-to-stop-worrying-and-obsessing-about-pelvic-pain-symptoms/

Podcasts and CDs

- The Pelvic Messenger: www.blogtalkradio.com/pelvicmessenger/
- Hard Conversations—Pelvic Pain and No Hope?: www.hardconversations.libsyn.com/ep-14-pelvic-pain-and-no-hope-you-need-to-know-this-expert-0
- Intelligent Medicine: Proper Diagnosis and Treatment of Pelvic Pain: www.drhoffman.com/podcast/proper-diagnosis-and-treatment-of-pelvic-pain-part-1/
- Women's Pelvic Health Podcast: www.soundcloud.com/womenspelvichealthpodcast/episode-19-dr-cristina-palmer-urologist-cedars-sinai-medical-center
- Beaumont Health Guided Imagery For Men & Women With Pelvic Pain: www.beaumont.org/services/urology/guided-imagery

Videos/DVDs

- Pelvic Pain Explained Webinar (2019): www.youtube.com/user/PelvicPainRehab/videos
- Pelvic Health Summit (2018): www.youtube.com/watch?v=l1W47ycsx_I
- Living With IC Video Series: www.icnetwork.org/videos/
- Healing Pelvic and Abdominal Pain: www.healpelvicpain.com/about-video
- New Dawn Pilates For Pelvic Pain: (available at www.Amazon.com)
- Your Pace Yoga: Relieving Pelvic Pain: (available at www.Amazon.com)

Would It Be Helpful for Me to Speak with Someone Who Has a Similar Condition?

Yes! There is wisdom to be gained from others who share your journey. You don't have to re-invent the wheel. Thousands of people with pain have already walked in your shoes, learned painful lessons, and have hard-earned wisdom to share. When you walk into a support group meeting for the first time, you will quickly realize that you aren't abnormal, and that illness or injury can strike anyone at anytime. Support groups educate, empower, and provide comfort to those living with pain and their family members. Try to develop a circle of friends you can call when you need support or are having a flare.

Finding a group can be challenging. There are few "pelvic pain" support groups in the United States, but you should be able to find groups dedicated to specific conditions, such as interstitial cystitis, irritable bowel syndrome, vulvar pain, and *prostatitis*. Many national organizations list groups on their websites and others offer phone support.

You can also participate in online support groups from the comfort of your home. The *Interstitial Cystitis Network* provides live support group meetings through YouTube and/or Facebook most Sunday afternoons for anyone with bladder and pelvic pain.

What Is the Role of Social Media in Learning About Pelvic Pain?

Did you first turn to Facebook for information about your medical condition? People often congregate on social networking sites because it's comforting to find others who share your symptoms and understand your frustrations. You can participate in hundreds of health-related support groups on Facebook. Non-profit organizations frequently conduct awareness and educational campaigns. You might attend live events and support group meetings. The best part of social networking (and online gaming) is that it can break the isolation you might be feeling. The opportunity to interact, laugh, cry, share, give, and receive support can bring some normalcy back into your life. It can also be a great distraction from the pain.

Social networking sites also have some alarming concerns. There are no professional fact checkers who review discussions and/or consumer postings to determine if they are correct or safe. Research studies routinely find inaccurate, misleading, and potentially harmful information distributed through social networks (Zhao and Zhang, 2017).

Your privacy may be at risk. Not only are your posts potentially shared with family members, friends, and other group members, but advertisers may be collecting your personal and health information for their own purposes. A complaint filed with the *Federal Trade Commission* (FTC) alleged that confidential information posted in private Facebook health groups was distributed to advertisers and/or used to generate advertising (HIPAA Journal Post, 2019; Landi, 2019). If you use mobile health applications, your personal data might also be seen by multiple outside companies. A study found that 19 out of 24 apps (79%) shared user data outside of the app, where it was received by multiple parties, including developers, parent companies, and service providers (Grundy et al, 2019).

Facebook, Twitter, and other social networks are not ideal platforms for sensitive health discussions. Personal attacks are common, even in protected support groups. You might find yourself in the middle of a "*flame war*" or be banned from a group if you disagree with a leader's opinion. Don't take it personally. Join a few groups until you find one that feels right for you.

You might feel more depressed and lonely after spending a few hours on Facebook (Hunt et al, 2018). Online support groups can be filled with negative and discouraging pain stories. It can be frustrating to watch videos or read stories from family members and friends who are living their lives while you are struggling. Don't let social networks consume you. Check in for a brief period every day or so if you find it fun, but don't feel you must. Experts suggest limiting *social media* use to 30 minutes per day.

Your personal safety matters. Never give your personal contact information (phone, address, or email) to people you have just met online. Maintain your distance until you have spent significant time getting to know someone via social networking sites.

Do not send money or donate to "friends" or other "patients" online who claim that they are struggling financially. They could be scamming you. Fake patient stories in which the recipient falsely claims to have cancer or another disease are common (GoFraudMe, 2017). The pelvic pain community has been victimized by people claiming to raise money for research only to discover, after the fact, that they kept the money (Lake, 2019; Federal Trade Commission, 2019). Funds should be donated directly to organizations or people you know personally.

Name:_____ MGH #_____ Date of Birth: __/__/__ Date: __/__/__

**Facing Pelvic Pain
TREATMENT MAP**

This tool will allow you to communicate and map treatment over time. Your health care providers can use this information to understand your diagnosis and to plan future treatments. This document is based on official guidelines as well as multidisciplinary provider experience.

My primary symptoms are:

Special considerations I wish to communicate (exam anxiety, gender, requests):

Timeline and story of symptoms:

I Have the Following Conditions	Yes	Suspected	No
Pelvic Conditions:			
Pelvic/lower abdominal pain			
Urethra and bladder pain:			
☐ Pain as my bladder fills with urine that is relieved by urination			
☐ Pain during urination			
☐ Pain that worsens after urination			
☐ Pain on the skin/vulva/tip during urination			
Perineum (bicycle seat) pain			
Vulvar/vaginal pain			
Clitoral pain or unwanted arousal			
Testicular/penile pain			
Anal/rectal pain (incl. pain with bowel movement)			
Pain with sitting relieved by standing			
Lubrication or erection trouble			
Sexual pain			
Endometriosis			
Irritable bowel syndrome			
Pelvic floor muscle dysfunction			
Recurrent urinary tract infections			
History of sexually transmitted infection			
Pelvic cancer			
Urinary incontinence			
Bowel incontinence			
Constipation			
Blood in the stool			

©Elise De MD et al for the MGH Facing Series

Name:_____ MGH #_____Date of Birth: __/__/ Date: __/__/

Pelvic organ (bladder, rectum, uterus) prolapse			
Prostate problems			
Difficulty starting urine stream			
Urinary urgency, frequency, nighttime urination			
Blood in the urine			
Neurogenic bladder or bowel			
Balance problems or leg or arm weakness			
Varicose veins on ☐legs ☐buttocks ☐privates			
Other pelvic conditions:			
Conditions Affecting Other Areas of the Body	**Yes**	**Suspected**	**No**
GERD (heartburn)			
Migraines			
Fibromyalgia			
TMJ (jaw pain)			
Nerve pain – spine or back, or sciatica			
Nerve pain – peripheral e.g. sensitive feet			
Loss of hair on extremities			
Palpitations (rapid heat beat)			
Ringing in the ears			
Asthma or respiratory problems			
Nausea			
Dizziness			
All over body pain or joint pains (where?)			
Vision Changes			
Depression or anxiety			
History of sexual abuse or other trauma			
Dependence on medication alcohol or drugs			
Other Medical Problems or Surgical History	**Year of Diagnosis**	**Doctor**	**Comments**

©Elise De MD et al for the MGH Facing Series

308 Facing Pelvic Pain: A Guide for Patients and Their Families

Name:_____ MGH #_____ Date of Birth: __/__/ Date: __/__/

Please mark ALL areas on the body maps (not just the pelvis) where you have had pain in the last week.

Area # or letters	Left Right or Center	No Pain 0	1	2	3	4	5	6	7	8	9	Pain as bad as you can imagine 10

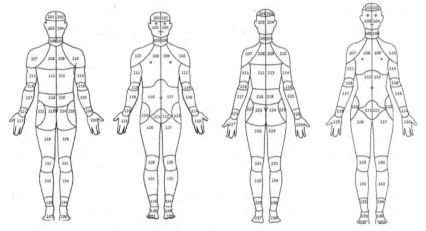

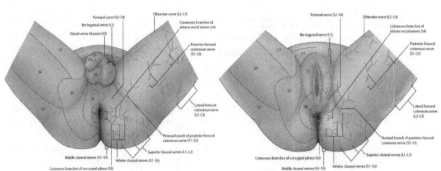

©Elise De MD et al for the MGH Facing Series

MAPPII Interactive CHOIR Body Map https://choir.stanford.edu
Reproduced with permission: Drake RL, Vogl AW, Mitchell A, eds.: Dermatomes and cutaneous nerves of perineum in men. Dermatomes and cutaneous nerves of perineum in women. In: Gray's Atlas of Anatomy. Philadelphia, PA: Elsevier Limited. 2021; 213–292.

Name:_____ MGH #_____ Date of Birth: __/__/ Date: __/__/

Prior Medications Tried			
Bladder Relaxing Medications	**Tried?**	**Relief?**	**Still Using?**
Oxybutynin (Ditropan®)			
Oxybutynin Gel (Gelnique®) transdermal sachet daily			
Oxybutynin Transdermal Patch (Oxytrol®)			
Tolterodine (Detrol®)			
Fesoterodine (Toviaz®)			
Trospium (Sanctura®)			
Darifenacin (Enablex®)			
Solifenacin (Vesicare®)			
Mirabegron (Myrbetriq®)			
Hyoscyamine (Levsin®)			
Medications to Open Bladder Outlet			
Terazosin (Hytrin®)			
Tamsulosin (Flomax®)			
Doxazosin (Cardura®)			
Alfuzosin (Uroxatral®)			
Silodosin (Rapaflo®)			
Bladder Therapeutics and Pain Medications			
Pentosan Polysulfate Sodium (Elmiron®)			
Phenazopyridine (Pyridium®)			
Amitriptyline (Elavil®), Nortriptyline (Pamelor®)			
Uribel® (methenamine, sodium phosphate monobasic, phenyl salicylate, methylene blue, and hyoscyamine sulfate)			
Allergy Medications: Hydroxyzine (Atarax®) Diphenhydramine (Benadryl® Genahist®, Sominex®, Unisom®), Cimetidine® (Tagamet®), Cetirizine hydrochloride (Zyrtec®), Fexofenadine (Allegra®), Loratidine (Claritin®)			
Bladder instillations (heparin, lidocaine, sodium bicarbonate, antibiotic)			
Bladder instillations Dimethyl sulfoxide, DMSO (Rimso-50®)			
Cyclosporine A (Gengraf®, Neoral®, Sandimmune®)			
Infection Management	**Tried?**	**Relief?**	**Still Using?**
Oral or IV Antibiotics (doses and # days)			
Proanthocyanidins (Ellura®, PRVNT®, Theracran®) or other cranberry extract			
D-Mannose			
Methenamine (Hiprex®, Mandelamine®, Urex®)			
Probiotics			
Antibiotic Instillation in the Bladder			
Other			

©Elise De MD et al for the MGH Facing Series

Name:_____ MGH #_____ Date of Birth: __/__/__ Date: __/__/__

Vulvar/Vaginal Treatments	Tried?	Relief?	Still Using?
Avoidance of Irritants (select toilet paper, soap)			
Vaginal creams, ointments, etc.:			
☐ Barrier cream/ointment (type): zinc oxide, dimethicone, petroleum			
☐ Estrogens (commercial or compounded)			
☐ Anti-yeast/antifungal agents			
☐ Antibacterial agents for bacterial vaginosis			
☐ Steroid (clobetasol, hydrocortisone)			
☐ Diazepam (Valium®) vaginal suppositories			
☐ Baclofen (Lioresel®)			
☐ Lidocaine			
☐ Gabapentin (Neurontin®)			
☐ Amitriptyline (Elavil®)			
☐ Tacrolimus (Prograf®)			
☐ Naltrexone - low dose (Vivitrol®)			
☐ Douches			
☐ Other Inserts			
☐ Wipes			
Hormonal Medications	**Tried?**	**Relief?**	**Still Using?**
Vaginal estrogen cream, tablet or ring			
Estrogen/progesterone pills or patches			
Hormone-secreting intrauterine device (Mirena®, Liletta®, Skyla®)			
Medroxyprogesterone acetate (Depo-Provera®) injection			
Etonogestrel (Nexplanon®) progesterone implant			
Norethindrone (Norlutate®, Aygestin®)			
Elagolix (Orilissa®)			
Leuprolide Acetate (Lupron Depot®)			
Aromatase inhibitors: -Anastrozole (Arimidex®) -Letrozole (Femara®)			
Testosterone injections or implants			
Testosterone applied to skin (Testim®, Androgel®)			
Specific Penile/Testicular Pain Medications	**Tried?**	**Relief?**	**Still Using?**
Penile injection medications for pain - Collagenase clostridium histolyticum (Xiaflex®)			
Other			
Anorectal Pain Medications	**Tried?**	**Relief?**	**Still Using?**
Sitz bath			
Barrier cream/ointment: e.g. zinc oxide, corn starch, dimethicone, petroleum			
Wipes			

©Elise De MD et al for the MGH Facing Series

Name: _____ MGH # _____ Date of Birth: __/__/__ Date: __/__/__

Loperamide (Imodium®)			
Sphincter relaxing ointments: nifedipine or diltiazem (calcium channel blockers) and glyceryl nitrate (GTN)			
Lidocaine numbing gel or cream			
Anti yeast creams, ointments or oral medications			
Agents to soften stool: Docusate sodium (Colace®), Psyllium (Metamucil®) or other fiber			
Agents to bulk stool: Psyllium (Metamucil®) or other Fiber			
Immune and Anti-Inflammatory Medications	**Tried?**	**Relief?**	**Still Using?**
NSAIDs: Ibuprofen, Celecoxib, Diclofenac, Indomethacin, Naproxen, Oxaprozin, Piroxicam			
Mesalamine (Pentasa®, Asacol®, Apriso®, Delzicol®, Lialda®)			
Steroids			
Immunosuppressants: Azathioprine (Azasan®, Imuran®), Remicade (Infliximab®), Ustekinymba (Stelara®), and Monoclonal antibodies: Humira (Adalimumab®),Vedolizumab (Entyvio®)			
Immunomodulators Interleukins (IL-1, IL-17) Tumor necrosis factor alpha TNF-α			
IV immunoglobulin (IVIG)			
General Pain Medications	**Tried?**	**Relief?**	**Still Using?**
Acetaminophen (Tylenol®)			
Tegretol (Carbamazepine®)			
Neurontin (Gabapentin®)			
Lyrica (Pregabalin®)			
Topiramate (Topamax®)			
Fluoxetine (Prozac®)			
Duloxetine (Cymbalta®), Lamotrigine (Lamictal®), Oxcarbazepine (Trileptal®), Lacosamide (Vimpat®), Venlafaxine (Effexor®), Milnacipran (Savella®), Sertraline (Zoloft®)			
Amitriptyline (Elavil®)			
Nortriptyline (Pamelor®)			
Imipramine (Tofranil®)			
Opioids: Oxycodone (OxyContin®), Hydrocodone (Vicodin®), Codeine, Meperidine (Demerol®), Morphine (Roxanol®), Methadone, Hydromorphone (Dilaudid®), Tramadol (Ultram®), Fentanyl (Duragesic®, Onsolis®, Fentora®)			
Oral Muscle Relaxants			
Baclofen (Kemstro®, Lioresal ®)			
Tizanidine (Zanaflex®)			
Cyclobenzaprine (Flexeril®, Amrix®, Fexmid®)			
Benzodiazepines (Valium®, Xanax®, Ativan®)			

©Elise De MD et al for the MGH Facing Series

Name:_____ MGH #_____ Date of Birth: __/__/ Date: __/__/

Blood Thinners			
Aspirin			
Clopidogrel (Plavix®)			
Cilostazol (Pletal®)			
Other Medications (list):	Tried?	Relief?	Still Using?
Surgery (Cite Hospital and Surgeon, Obtain OP Note)	Year:	Relief?	Details
Laparoscopy, fulgaration, or excision of endometriosis			
Hysterectomy (removal of uterus)			
Myomectomy (uterine fibroid removal)			
Ovarian cyst removal			
Ovary removal			
Caesarian section			
Prolapse surgery, vaginal or rectal (details):			
Urinary incontinence surgery			
Urinary incontinence injection (e.g. Collagen, Macroplastique®, Coaptite®)			
Urethral diverticulum or fistula surgery			
Cystoscopy (may include biopsy)			
Urethral dilation			
Bladder hydrodistension			
Kidney stone surgery (shock wave or telescopic)			
Prostate surgery			
Testis surgery (including vasectomy)			
Ejaculatory duct surgery			
Bowel or rectal surgery			
Anal surgery			
Lysis of Adhesions			
Sacral nerve stimulation (Interstim®)			
Spinal stimulator (type and level if known)			
Medication pump (e.g. baclofen or pain medication)			
Release of nerve entrapment			
Surgical denervation (cutting of nerves)			
Back surgery			
Hip, knee or foot surgery			
Pelvic bone surgery			
Blood vessel surgery			
Botulinum toxin: OnabotulinumtoxinA (Botox®), RimabotulinumtoxinB (Myobloc®), AbobotulinumtoxinA (Dysport®) to: ☐ Bladder detrusor muscle			

©Elise De MD et al for the MGH Facing Series

Name:_____ MGH #_____ Date of Birth: __/__/ Date: __/__/

☐ Bladder exit (neck or external sphincter)			
☐ Pelvic floor muscles (trigger point)			
☐ Skin surface (e.g. vulva, scrotum)			
☐ Spermatic cord (nerves to testis)			
☐ Anal sphincter			
☐ Hip/leg muscle			
☐ Iliopsoas muscle			
Other surgery:			
Procedures and Treatments	**Tried?**	**Relief?**	**Details**
Acupuncture			
Massage			
Nerve blocks or injections (name nerves and what medication was used if known):			
Pessary			
PTNS			
TENS Unit			
Radiofrequency Ablation			
Cryoablation (freezing) e.g. nerves of Spermatic Cord			
Vaginal Laser Therapy			
Blood vessel embolization or stenting			
Emsella® Chair			
Other Treatments			
Bladder Management	**Tried?**	**Relief?**	**Details**
☐ Bladder empties naturally			
☐ Timed voids by the clock			
☐ Intermittent catheterization ____ times per day			
☐ Indwelling tube changed every ____ weeks			
☐ Supply information:			
Pelvic Floor Physical Therapy	**Tried?**	**Relief?**	**Details**
☐ Pelvic Floor Physical Therapy in general (any type)			
☐ Hands on work/joint and tissues mobilization			
☐ Stretching or yoga exercises			
☐ Aerobic exercises			
☐ Strength exercises: abdominal, legs			
☐ Biofeedback			
☐ Body mechanics and posture training			
☐ Physical Therapy focused on pain management			
☐ Physical therapy for back, knees, hips, etc.			
Lifestyle and Behavior Changes			
Diet alteration to avoid irritants			

©Elise De MD et al for the MGH Facing Series

Name:_____ MGH #_____ Date of Birth: __/__/ Date: __/__/

Avoidance of Caffeine, Sweeteners, Tea			
Fluid alteration to target 1500-2500 cc per 24 hours			
Attention to seat surface and ergonomics at work, commute, home			
Avoidance of vulvar or scrotal irritants			
Counseling and Psychological Therapies	**Tried?**	**Relief?**	**Details**
Meditation, Relaxation Strategies			
Any psychotherapy			
Individual therapy			
Cognitive behavioral therapy			
Mindfulness-based therapy			
Group therapy			
Couples therapy			
Formal Sex Therapy			
Other			
Testing Completed	**Approx Date**	**Location/ Institution**	**Results**
Urinalysis and Culture			
Urine cytology			
Urine Ureaplasma and Mycoplasma			
Testing for genital infections			
Pregnancy test			
Blood tests			
Stool Test			
Completion of a Voiding Diary			
Measurement of post void residual (PVR) urine volume (the amount left after urinating)			
CT Scan of:			
☐ Spine			
☐ Head			
☐ Abdomen			
☐ Pelvis			
Ultrasound of:			
☐ Abdomen			
☐ Kidneys			
☐ Pelvis			
☐ Scrotum/Vagina			
☐ Veins			
MRI of:			
☐ Spine/sacrum			
☐ Head			
☐ Abdomen			
☐ Pelvis			

©Elise De MD et al for the MGH Facing Series

Name:_____ MGH #_____ Date of Birth: __/__/__ Date: __/__/__

Spine Xray (type)			
Pelvis Xray			
Defacography (bowel movement under X-ray with dye)			
Anal manometry (bowel movement with measurement of pressure in rectum)			
Upper GI Study (X-ray after swallowing dye)			
Cystogram, voiding cystourethrogram (VCUG), urethrogram (X-ray with dye in bladder or urethra)			
Angiogram (X-ray with dye in artery)			
Cystoscopy (small camera passed into bladder)			
Ureteroscopy (small camera passed into ureter)			
Urodynamic testing (pressure measurement during void)			
Endoscopy (small camera passed into throat)			
Colonoscopy/Proctoscopy/Sigmoidoscopy (small camera passed via anus)			
Sitzmark Study (X-ray or beads passing through GI tract)			
Laparoscopy (small camera passed into abdominal wall)			
EMG (test of nerve response to stimulation)			
Autonomic testing (tilt table testing)			
Nerve biopsy (for small fiber polyneuropathy)			
Other:			
Types of Health Care Providers Seen	**Name**	**Location**	**Current provider?**
☐ Allergy			
☐ Cancer Medicine			
☐ Cardiology			
☐ Colorectal Surgery			
☐ Gastrointestinal Medicine			
☐ Gynecology			
☐ Infectious Disease			
☐ Neurology			
☐ Ophthalmology			
☐ Orthopedics			
☐ Pain Management			
☐ Physical Therapy			
☐ Primary Care			
☐ Psychology/Psychiatry			
☐ Pulmonology			
☐ Rehabilitation Medicine (Physiatrist)			
☐ Rheumatology			
☐ Urology			
☐ Other			

©Elise De MD et al for the MGH Facing Series

Name:_____ MGH #_____ Date of Birth: __/__/ Date: __/__/

Current Working Diagnoses (check all that apply)	Details
☐ Unsure of diagnosis	
☐ Bladder obstruction	
☐ Overactive bladder	
☐ Underactive bladder	
☐ Neurogenic bladder	
☐ Interstitial cystitis	
☐ Incontinence of urine	
☐ Recurrent urinary tract infections (UTIs)	
☐ Vulvar atrophy	
☐ Vulvodynia or chronic vaginitis	
☐ Endometriosis	
☐ Erectile dysfunction	
☐ Peyronie's disease	
☐ Prostatitis	
☐ Pelvic floor muscle dysfunction	
☐ Prolapse	
☐ Constipation, diarrhea, IBD or IBS	
☐ Anal fissures or hemorrhoids	
☐ Incontinence of bowel	
☐ Neurogenic bowel	
☐ Nerve pain - spine	
☐ Nerve pain - peripheral nerves	
☐ Systemic pain syndrome	
☐ Autoimmune disease	
☐ Rheumatologic disease	
☐ Other:	

Next Steps

☐

☐

☐

☐

☐

☐

☐

☐

☐

©Elise De MD et al for the MGH Facing Series

GLOSSARY

Abdominal breathing: A mode of breathing using the diaphragm or belly, rather than the chest-cage muscles to move air in and out of the lungs.

Ablation: Method of removing or destroying tissue, such as with radiofrequency, heat, and/or surgery.

Abscess: A walled-off collection of pus (inflammatory cells) in tissues, organs, or confined spaces of the body, which is typically caused by infection.

Acetabular fracture: Fracture (break) of the acetabulum, the socket of the hip joint.

Acetabulum: The hip joint socket.

Acetaminophen (paracetamol, Liquiprin®, Panadol®, Tylenol®): Over-the-counter pain medication that does not interfere with blood-clotting ability. It also helps lower body temperature. Metabolized primarily in the liver.

Achilles heel reflex: A stretch reflex activated by tapping the Achilles tendon (on the back of the ankle) with a reflex hammer. It tests the S1 and S2 nerve roots and the spinal reflex arc at that level, as well as the health of the upper spinal nerves that dampen the reflex.

Acne: A condition with inflamed sebaceous glands (pimples) on the skin.

Active ingredient: The ingredient in a drug that is biologically active.

Activities of daily living (ADLs): The fundamental activities or skills people need to perform for independent living, such as eating, bathing, getting dressed, toileting, moving around, and maintaining continence (dryness) of bowel and bladder.

Acupuncture: An ancient Chinese medical practice that is still widely used. It involves inserting fine needles at anatomical points called acupoints and can be used to treat pain.

Acupuncturist: A practitioner of acupuncture.

Acute: A relatively sudden event. With pain, it refers to pain that has started recently.

Acute abdomen: A surgical emergency that requires emergent intervention (such as bleeding, torsion/twisting of an ovary or tube, severe infection, or intestinal blockage).

Acute ischemia: A state in which organs are deprived of their blood supply and are in jeopardy of irreparable harm.

Acute pain: Pain that is more sudden or of shorter duration, such as a sprained ankle or an abdominal surgical emergency. This pain improves as the injured tissues heal.

Acute pelvic pain: Pelvic pain that has been present for under 3 to 6 months, often only for a few hours, as in the case of an ovarian torsion.

Acute prostatitis: Bacterial infection in the prostate that is active enough to cause pain, difficulty urinating, and if severe, fever and vomiting. It can quickly turn into a medical emergency.

Adalimumab (Humira®): An immunosuppressive medication known as a TNF inhibitor, which is used to treat rheumatoid arthritis, psoriatic arthritis, ankylosing spondylitis, Crohn's disease, ulcerative colitis, psoriasis, hidradenitis suppurativa, uveitis, and juvenile idiopathic arthritis.

Adaptive equipment: Equipment and devices (such as a shower chair, lift, or tools that improve ease of grip) that assist with daily living activities.

Adductor: A muscle whose direction of contraction moves the limb or other part of the body toward the center of the body (midline).

Adductor longus muscle: A muscle that adducts the thigh, bringing it inward.

Adductor magnus muscle: A two-part muscle that adducts the thigh, pulling it inward.

Adenoma: A benign tumor of a glandular structure or of glandular origin.

Adenomyosis: A condition in which cells that typically line the cavity of the uterus grow into the muscular walls of the uterus.

Adhesion: Scar tissue that forms between organs and tissues that causes them to stick together.

Adolescent gynecologist: A physician who specializes in the care of adolescents with gynecological issues.

Adrenal gland: A pair of glands that sits above the kidneys that produce hormones, including steroids and adrenaline (the "fight or flight" hormone).

Adrenaline: Also known as epinephrine, adrenaline is the "fight or flight" hormone. It is secreted by the adrenal glands, especially when you are under stress, increasing blood circulation, breathing, and carbohydrate metabolism and preparing muscles for exertion.

Aerobic activity/exercise: Exercise (such as walking, running, or cycling) that uses oxygen as an energy supply, as opposed to anaerobic exercise (such as weightlifting), which uses energy stored in muscles.

Affective: Relating to expressed emotion.

Agenesis: Absence or failure of development of an organ or body part while the fetus is forming in utero.

Allergy medications: Medications designed to relieve symptoms of allergies, (e.g. seasonal allergies). These include over-the-counter antihistamines, nasal steroids, pseudoephedrine, decongestants, and additional prescription medications.

Allodynia: Pain that occurs with a normally non-painful sensation (such as touching).

Alpha blocker medication: Commonly prescribed medication that relaxes the internal muscles of the prostate, ureter, and bladder neck by blocking alpha receptors, allowing urine to flow more easily.

Alpha receptors: A receptor on the cell surface of some areas of the body, for example the smooth muscle of the bladder neck and blood vessels, which are innervated by the sympathetic nervous system. When activated (bound) by sympathetic adrenergic neurotransmitters, this smooth muscle contracts—alpha blocker medications prevent that contraction.

Altemeier's procedure: A surgical procedure in which a surgeon pulls the rectum through the anus, removes a portion of the rectum and sigmoid colon, and attaches the remaining rectum to the large intestine.

American College of Obstetrics and Gynecology (ACOG): A professional organization of physicians specializing in obstetrics and gynecology in the United States.

American Urological Association (AUA): Urological professional society in the United States, with more than 20,000 members worldwide. The AUA's mission is to promote the highest standards of urological clinical care through education, research, and the formulation of health care policy.

Amitryptyline (Elavil®, Amitid®, Amitril®, Endep®): A tricyclic anti-depressant (TCA) medication used in low doses to treat pain. It blocks reuptake of the neurotransmitters serotonin and norepinephrine, making them more available to the nervous system. It should not be combined with certain medications, such as monoamine oxidase inhibitors.

Amyloidosis: The deposition of abnormally formed proteins throughout the body.

Anal cancer: Malignant growths (cancers) in the tissues of the anus—usually related to past infection with human papillomavirus.

Anal fissure: A split in the skin and muscle that line the anus.

Anal fistula: A tunnel that runs from inside the anus to a connection on the skin around it.

Anal sphincter: A structure with two sphincters, the voluntary outer external sphincter, which is made up of striated muscle, and the internal smooth-muscle sphincter. They both control the closing of the anus.

Anal sphincter complex: Overlapping internal anal sphincter, external anal sphincter, and puborectalis muscle.

Anastomosis: A connection created surgically between two channels, such as reconnecting the bowel or blood vessels to themselves, or the bladder to the urethra or ureter.

Anatomic/anatomical: Of or relating to anatomy, which is the science of the bodily structure of organisms (body parts).

Anatomical obstruction: Obstruction or blockage, for example of the bladder, that is related to an anatomic cause (e.g., a tight prostate) rather than a neurological reason (e.g., a spastic sphincter muscle).

Anatomy: Bodily structures.

Androgens: A hormone or group of hormones (testosterone and androstenedione) that plays a role in male traits and reproduction. Androgens are present in females in lower concentrations.

Anesthesia: Loss of sensation to touch or pain. In medicine, this is usually intentional, with the help of medication provided by an anesthesiologist, but the word can also refer to loss of feeling caused by nerve injury or disease. Anesthesia can be performed using local injection, inhaled gas and intravenous sedation with the help of a spinal or epidural injection, face mask, laryngeal mask, or endotracheal tube (a breathing tube).

Anesthetic: Synonym for anesthesia.

Anesthetic block: A short-term nerve block involving the injection of local anesthetic as close to the nerve as possible for pain relief.

Angioplasty: A procedure performed from within a vessel to dilate it, often leaving a small wire mesh cylinder to keep it open.

Ankle-brachial index: A calculation comparing the non-invasive blood pressure of the ankle to the blood pressure in the arm.

Ankylosing spondylitis: A disorder characterized by arthritis involving the inflammation of the connective tissue of the spine.

Annulus fibrosus: Peripheral portion of the intervertebral disc that surrounds the nucleus pulposus.

Anorectal manometry: A diagnostic test that examines pelvic floor function in relation to bowel movement.

Anoscope/anoscopy: An examination performed by passing a small lubricated telescope into the anus for visual inspection within.

Antecedent-focused emotion regulation: A form of emotion regulation where one changes the situation, focus of attention, or thoughts in anticipation of an emotional experience.

Anterior: Situated toward the front of the body.

Anterior abdominal cutaneous nerve: Skin branches of the sensory nerves of the abdominal wall, which arise from thoracic spinal levels T7 through T12. They traverse channels within the abdominal fascia, which makes them vulnerable to injury.

Anterior pelvic organ prolapse: *See* cystocele.

Antibiotic: Medication that inhibits growth or destroys bacterial microorganisms.

Antibodies: *See* antibody.

Antibody: Proteins produced by immune cells. They help the immune response by targeting specific antigens.

Anticholinergic medication: Group of medications typically prescribed for overactive bladder, which work by inhibiting the neurotransmitter acetylcholine at the level of the bladder and calming the bladder muscle. The side effects include dry mouth, blurred vision, rapid heart rate, constipation, and confusion.

Anticoagulant: Having properties that prevent blood-clot formation by inhibiting the coagulation of blood.

Anticoagulation: The act of hindering the clotting of blood or a class of medications that do the same. These medications are typically discontinued prior to surgery or changed to a short-acting form that can be stopped and re-started quickly.

Anticonvulsant: A class of medications used to treat seizures and seizure disorders that also plays a role in the treatment of neuropathic pain.

Antidepressant: A class of medications used to treat mood disorders, including depression, which also play a role in the treatment of neuropathic pain. This class includes tricyclic antidepressants (TCAs) and serotonin-norepinephrine reuptake inhibitors (SNRIs).

Antidiarrheal: Any medication that provides symptomatic relief of diarrhea.

Antifungal: A medication that works to stop the growth of a fungus, such as a vaginal yeast infection.

Antihistamine: A medication used to provide relief from allergies and often used in bladder pain syndrome.

Anti-inflammatory: A medication that helps to reduce inflammation, swelling, and pain caused by various mechanisms.

Antineutrophil cytoplasmic antibodies (ANCAs): Antibodies that target specific proteins within a type of white blood cell called a neutrophil.

Antinuclear antibodies (ANA): Antibodies that target proteins in a cell nucleus.

Antiplatelet medication therapy: Use of medication that prevents blood clot formation by inhibiting platelets from adhering to each other.

Anus: The opening on the perineum where the gastrointestinal tract ends as it exits the body.

Aorta: The main arterial trunk arising from the heart, which distributes blood to the whole body.

Apixaban (Eliquis®): A blood thinner (anticoagulant) medication that inhibits factor Xa, which is part of the coagulation cascade. It is typically be stopped 24–48 hours prior to surgery on the advice of the prescribing physician or surgeon.

Appendicitis: An inflammation of the appendix, which is a finger-shaped pouch that projects from the colon on the lower-right side of the abdomen.

Appendix: A finger-shaped pouch that projects from your colon on the lower-right side of your abdomen.

Arachnoid mater: The delicate, spider-like, middle lining (meninge) around the brain and spinal cord. Cerebrospinal fluid circulates in the subarachnoid space (between the arachnoid and pia mater).

Areflexia: Absence of neurological reflexes as demonstrated when a reflex hammer taps on a tendon to elicit a stretch reflex.

Aromatase inhibitor: A medication used to treat breast cancer that stops the production of the female hormone, estrogen. It works in women who have already passed menopause by blocking the enzyme "aromatase," which converts androgens to estrogen. The class includes anastrozole (Arimidex®), exemestane (Aromasin®) and letrozole (Femara®).

Arteries: Blood vessels that deliver blood from the heart to the rest of the body. This blood has received oxygen in the lungs.

Arthritis: A disorder involving inflammation of joints and tissue surrounding the joints.

Astrocytes: The supporting cells within the glia.

Asymmetric: Having two sides that are not the same.

Asymptomatic: Without symptoms.

Atherosclerosis/atherosclerotic plaque: Fatty deposits and fibrosis of the inner layer of blood vessels.

Augmentation cystoplasty: Surgical expansion of the bladder using a segment of the bowel.

Autoantibody: Antibody targeting a structure of the organism producing it.

Autoimmune disease process/condition/disease/disorder: A disorder in which the body's own cells are perceived as foreign irritants and are attacked by the immune system.

Autonomic nerves/nervous system: The part of the nervous system that supplies the internal organs (including the blood vessels, stomach, intestine, liver, kidneys, bladder, genitals, lungs, pupils, heart, and sweat, salivary, and digestive glands). The system has two main divisions: the sympathetic and parasympathetic plexuses.

Avulsion fracture: A fracture that breaks off small parts of the bone that are attached to tendons and ligaments.

Axial spondyloarthritis: The seronegative spondyloarthritis (see definition) very commonly associated with pelvic pain, affecting the sacroiliac joint, spine, and pelvis.

Axons: Nerve cell extensions that conduct impulses to and away from the cell body.

Azathiaprine (Azasan®, Imuran®): Medication used to reduce the function of the immune system, for example, in autoimmune disease and inflammatory bowel disease.

Baclofen (Lioresel®): Muscle relaxant/antispasmodic agent that works by inhibiting neurotransmitters at nerve junctions.

Bacteria: Single-celled organisms that are neither plant nor animal. Some are harmful and cause infections, some are benign (such as those that live in the mouth), and many serve a useful purpose (such as those in yogurt).

Balloon expulsion test: A functional test where a balloon is a flexible replacement for stool.

Barrier cream: A protective, non-irritating cream used to cover skin surfaces after cleaning to prevent irritation. Special barrier creams are made for the vulvar and the anal skin.

BCB-PMD (board-certified biofeedback pelvic muscle dysfunction): This distinction means that a practitioner has passed the requirements of the Biofeedback Certification International Alliance (BCIA) for biofeedback directed at pelvic floor muscle function.

Behavioral modification therapy: The techniques used to decrease or increase a type of behavior to promote healthy behaviors. Techniques include positive reinforcement, negative reinforcement, flooding, systematic desensitization, aversion therapy, and extinction.

Benign: Of a non-threatening or non-cancerous character.

Benzodiazepines (Valium®, Xanax®, Librium®, Klonopin®, Atavan®): Muscle relaxants and anti-anxiety medications that work by enhancing a neurotransmitter.

Beta-3 agonist medication (mirabegron, Myrbetriq®): A medication that causes relaxation of the bladder smooth muscle (detrusor) to help with urinary urgency, frequency, and urinary urge incontinence. The mechanism of action is different from the "anticholinergics."

Biofeedback: Training and a technique that increases one's awareness of muscle activity.

Biologically-based medications: Products found in nature to treat the body, such as vitamins, herbals, probiotics, and certain foods.

Biomechanical compensation: Altering movement patterns to adjust for a weak or painful area, such as limping in the case of a sprained ankle.

Biopsy: A diagnostic surgical procedure in which a doctor removes cells or tissue with a grasper or sharp blade to be sent for testing in a laboratory.

Biopsychosocial: A model of care that accounts for the relationship among biological (physical), psychological, and social/environmental factors.

Biopsychosocial factors: The biological (genetic and physical); psychological (mood, personality, and behavior); and social (educational, cultural, and socioeconomic) factors that contribute to overall health.

Birth control pills (BCPs): Hormonal medications with progesterone and usually estrogen that when taken orally will suppress the ovary's natural production of those hormones.

Bladder: A hollow muscular organ that collects and stores urine from the kidneys before disposal by urination.

Bladder biopsy: A diagnostic surgical procedure in which a doctor removes cells or tissue from your bladder or urethra with a grasper to be tested in a laboratory. This typically involves cystoscopy (insertion of a camera into the urethra and the bladder).

Bladder exstrophy: Exstrophy means "inside out." In bladder exstrophy in a newborn, the bladder is open and exposed on the lower abdominal wall because of incomplete fusion and formation of the structures of the lower abdominal wall during development. (The skin, muscle, and pelvic bones are not joined in the midline.)

Bladder incontinence: Leakage of urine through the urethra during times that urination is not desired.

Bladder neck obstruction: Blockage of the bladder and urinary flow at the level of the bladder neck.

Bladder outlet obstruction (BOO): A blockage at the base of the bladder that reduces or stops the flow of urine into the urethra.

Bladder re-training: Bladder re-training involves increasing the amount of time between emptying your bladder and increasing the amount the bladder can hold by following a fixed-urination schedule.

Bladder-relaxing medications: Medications that can decrease the sensation of the bladder or its quickness to contract, allowing one to hold more urine for longer.

Bladder symptom complex: A set of bladder symptoms such as overactive bladder (OAB) that is a collection of described symptoms, rather than being a specific disease. Bladder symptom complex involves urgency, frequency, nighttime urination, and/or urge incontinence.

Blockers of interleukin-1 (IL-1): Medications used for arthritis. They block the "cytokines" called "interleukins" that have a function in regulating the immune system—the effect is to reduce inflammation.

Blog: An article usually written for an internet website.

Board-certified: Having met the requirements of a recognized medical board for certification.

Board Certified Biofeedback Pelvic Muscle Dysfunction (BCB-PMD): A therapist certified through the Biofeedback Certification International Alliance, which specifically certifies therapists in the use of all forms of biofeedback.

Board-certified CAPP (Certificate of Achievement in Pelvic Physical Therapy): The Certificate of Achievement in Pelvic Health Physical Therapy (CAPP-Pelvic) is awarded by the American Physical Therapy Association after achieving certain standard training credentials.

Bones: The hard whitish tissue making up the skeleton.

Botox®: *See* botulinum toxin/onabotulinumtoxinA (Botox®).

Botulinum toxin/onabotulinumtoxinA (Botox®): Neurotoxic protein produced by the bacterium Clostridium botulinum and related species that prevents the release of the neurotransmitter acetylcholine from nerve endings and therefore, relaxes muscles. It is the same toxin that causes a life-threatening type of food poisoning called botulism when canning is performed improperly.

Botulinum toxin injections: Needle injection of botulinum toxin into specific muscles or tissues.

Bowel: The intestines—the small intestine, large intestine, and rectum—running from the stomach to the anus in one continuous tube.

Bowel ischemia: Lack of blood flow to the intestines, which can be a surgical emergency.

Bowel obstruction: Blockage of the bowel, which can be a surgical emergency.

Bowel preparation: Preparation of the bowel for colonoscopy or surgery by emptying the colon of stool. This is accomplished by avoiding solid food and by taking a medication that causes diarrhea. It is important to stay hydrated. Each provider has slightly different recommendations for timing of the preparation and the medication choice.

Brand name: Also known as a trade name, a brand name created by a pharmaceutical company as a means of marketing a medication. If more than one company markets the drug, there will be more than one brand name.

Bulbocavernosus muscles: Paired superficial (surface) muscles of the pelvic floor that originate from the perineal body and a midline tendon; these muscles travel along the urethra and erectile tissue in men and around the vagina over the major vestibular (Bartholin's) gland to the clitoris in women. In both genders, these muscles contribute to sexual function and to emptying the urethra in men.

Bulking agent: A material injected along the urethra, usually in women, to narrow the urethra's width and to prevent stress incontinence (leakage with coughing).

Bupivicaine (Marcaine®): Local anesthetic that blocks nerve impulses by decreasing permeability to sodium ions in nerve cell membranes.

Bursa: Fluid-filled pads (bursae) that act as cushions at the joints.

Bursitis: Inflammation of the bursa.

Calcium channel blocker (Norvasc®, Diltiazem®, Felodipine®, Verapamil®): Medication that causes smooth muscle relaxation by preventing calcium ion entry into excitable cells.

Carbamazepine (Tegretol®, Carbatrol®): An anticonvulsant used for the treatment of bipolar disorder and seizures that works by decreasing the nerve impulses that cause nerve pain.

Cardiovascular: Having to do with the heart and blood vessels.

Caregiver burnout: A state of fatigue that occurs when a person provides emotional or physical support for a loved one over an extended period, leading to neglect for his or her own health and needs, resulting in hopelessness, irritability, depression, and/or anxiety.

Cartilage: A smooth, strong, and elastic connective tissue in the body (composed of glycosaminoglycans, proteoglycans, collagen fibers, and elastin) that lines the ends of bones at the joints and contributes to structures of the ear, nose, trachea, bronchi in the lungs, intervertebral discs, and rib cage.

Catheter (urinary catheter): A soft pliable tube that enters the bladder to drain urine, via either the natural opening, the urethra, or through a tiny incision above the pubic bone (suprapubic catheter).

Cauda equina: The area in the lower spinal cord that has loose spinal nerve roots surrounded by cerebrospinal fluid. It consists of pairs of second through fifth lumbar nerves; first through fifth sacral nerves; and the coccygeal nerve, arising from the lumbar enlargement and the conus medullaris of the spinal cord. Cauda equina means "horse's tail" in Latin.

Cauda equina syndrome: Condition that occurs when the bundle of nerves below the end of the spinal cord are compressed and lead to a wide range of symptoms including bladder dysfunction, bowel incontinence, sexual dysfunction, numbness around the anus (saddle anesthesia), and pain radiating down the leg. This is often a surgical emergency.

Cauterize: To burn off or seal tissue using thermal or other energy (such as infra-red or laser).

Celiac disease: A hereditary disease characterized by a sensitivity to wheat that can result in inflammation and damage to the small intestine.

Cell bodies of neurons: Also called the soma, it is the spherical part of the neuron that contains the nucleus. The cell body connects to the dendrites, which bring information to the neuron and the axon; the axon sends information to other neurons.

Cell signaling pathways: Communication mechanisms that control the basic activities of cells and multi-cell coordination, which affects development, healing, immunity, and normal day-to-day cell function.

Central nervous system (CNS): Part of the nervous system, which consists of the brain and spinal cord.

Central nerve sensitization: A condition of the nervous system that is associated with the development and maintenance of chronic pain.

Cerebral palsy: A disorder that affects movement and muscle tone or posture caused by damage to the immature brain as it develops, most often before birth.

Cerebrospinal fluid (CSF): The fluid that flows around the hollow spaces of the spinal cord and brain for the purposes of nutrient supplementation, waste removal, and protection from trauma; it is enveloped by the thecal (dural) sac.

Cerebrovascular accident (CVA): A stroke.

Cervical myelopathy: A disorder of nerve impairment in the neck, that occurs after an injury or with a herniated disc.

Cervical radiculomyelopathy: Dysfunction of the cervical (neck), spinal cord (myelopathy), and its nerve roots (radiculopathy).

Cervical radiculopathy: Dysfunction of the nerve roots exiting the spine in the neck.

Chemodenervation: Blocking nerve signaling at the junction of nerves and muscles using the medication botulinum toxin (as opposed to destroying the nerve [neurolysis] with irritants or incisions).

Chemotherapeutic agents: The medications or treatments used in chemotherapy, usually for cancer or rheumatologic disease.

Chemotherapeutic/chemotherapy: Use of chemicals to treat disease, typically in cancer, but it is also applicable to inflammation.

Child and adolescent psychiatrist: A physician who specializes in the diagnosis and treatment of disorders of thinking, feeling, and behavior affecting children and adolescents (and their families).

Chiropractor: A licensed health care provider who treats disorders of the musculoskeletal system, focusing on the spine, through primarily hands-on physical manipulation.

Chlamydia trachomatis (Chlamydia): A common sexually transmitted bacteria that can cause pelvic pain and pelvic inflammatory disease.

Cholesterol: A waxy, fat-like sterol (modified steroid) made by the liver that is found in most body tissues. It is an important part of cell membranes and is a precursor for other steroid compounds, such as testosterone.

Chronic: Persisting or recurring for a long time.

Chronic demyelinating neuropathy/chronic inflammatory demyelinating polyneuropathy (CIDP): A neurological disorder of unclear cause that involves inflammation of nerves and nerve roots, which destroys myelin, the protective sheath around nerves. It is characterized by progressive weakness and impaired sensory function (numbness or pain) in the legs and arms.

Chronic ischemic vascular disease: Longstanding reduced blood flow caused by blood vessel constriction from waxy plaque build-up (atherosclerosis).

Chronic pain: Pain lasting more than (three to) six months.

Chronic pelvic pain (CPP): Pain in the area below your belly button and between your hips that lasts three to six months or longer.

Chronic pelvic pain syndrome (CPPS): Pain in the area below your belly button and between your hips that lasts three to six months or longer.

Churg Strauss syndrome: *See* eosinophilic granulomatosis with polyangitis (EGPA).

Claudication: Pain caused by too little blood flow, such as pain in the calves while walking. Someone with chronic ischemic vascular disease.

Claustrophobia: Abnormally strong fear of confined spaces.

Clean intermittent catheterization (CIC): A procedure performed several times a day to empty the bladder. CIC can expand treatment options for those with serious urinary symptoms and neurologic problems by emptying the bladder without the need to have an indwelling catheter.

Clitoris: The female erogenous organ that is well innervated. The glans, or head, lies under the pubic bone at the top of the labia minora, above the urethra. Its erectile tissue, which develops from the same structures as the penis, extends under the pubic bones (the superior pubic rami) on both sides.

Clopidogril (Plavix®): Blood thinner to prevent stroke and heart attacks and to treat other blood vessel diseases.

Coccyx: The tip of the tailbone on which the pelvic floor muscles insert.

Codeine (Tylenol #3®, Tylenol #4®, Vopac®): An opiate pain medication that can mitigate a cough.

Cognitive-behavioral therapy (CBT): A psychosocial intervention that focuses on correcting unhelpful cognitive distortions and behaviors.

Colibacillus (coliform bacilli): Bacteria of the genus Escherichia coli, which are the predominant bacteria in stool.

Collagen: A protein that provides structural support found in the connective tissue and skin; it is related to scarring.

Collagenase clostridium histolyticus (Xiaflex®): An injectable medication containing an enzyme that breaks down collagen in scar tissue; it is used in a series of injections to treat Peyronie's disease as well as a hand condition called Dupuytren's contracture.

Colonoscopy: An exam using a long flexible telescope to visualize the inside of the colon or rectum. A bowel preparation must be completed ahead of time to remove stool so that the examiner can visualize the inside of the colon.

Colorectal surgeon: A general surgeon who has undergone further training in the diagnosis and treatment of diseases of the colon, rectum, and anus.

Common and internal iliac arteries: The common iliac arteries are formed when the largest artery in the body, the aorta, divides in the pelvis. The internal iliac artery, also called the hypogastric artery, forms when the common iliac splits to form the external and internal iliac arteries. The internal iliac supplies the pelvis, its organs, the external genitalia, and surface of the pelvis.

Common femoral vein: The segment of the femoral vein (the vein that returns blood from each leg) between the branching of the deep femoral vein and the inguinal ligament (above which the common femoral vein becomes the external iliac vein).

Complex: In medicine, complex refers to either a complex medical situation (e.g., multiple diagnoses) or a symptom complex (a set of symptoms that are known to be associated with one another, such as overactive bladder).

Complex pelvic pain: Pelvic pain that is either not improving with standard interventions or that presents with other pain syndromes, such as migraine and heartburn.

Complex regional pain syndrome (CRPS): A chronic (lasting greater than six months) pain condition that most often affects one limb (arm, leg, hand, or foot) usually after an injury. CRPS is believed to be caused by damage to or malfunction of the peripheral and central nervous systems.

Compound medication: A medication in which the active drug ingredient is mixed into a base that allows for less irritation or a different way of delivering the medication.

Compound pharmacist: A pharmacist who identifies known potential allergens and/or irritants and creates a dosage form of a medication with drug concentrations that can focus on pain management without introducing unwanted additives. Also, compound pharmacists can create a different way of administering a medication through its carrier base, such as vaginally rather than by way of the mouth.

Computed tomography (CT, CAT) scan: An imaging modality using multiple X-ray films that align to provide a cross-sectional or 3D view of the body. There is some radiation exposure and sometimes a special form of iodine-based intravenous dye might be used to better delineate fine details.

Computed tomography angiography (CTA): An arteriogram (study highlighting the arterial anatomy) using CT scan imaging guidance.

Computer tomographic (CT) scan venogram: A venogram (study highlighting the vein anatomy) performed using CT scan imaging guidance.

Computerized tomographic (CT) myelogram: A diagnostic imaging test generally done by a radiologist. It uses a contrast dye and X-rays or computed tomography (CT) to look for problems in the spinal canal.

Congenital: Present from birth.

Congenital abnormality/congenital malformations: Structural or functional differences (anomalies) in development that occur in the fetus during intrauterine life. Some developmental differences have no effect on bodily function (such as a vein in an unexpected location); some could contribute to pain (such as Nutcracker syndrome); and some are incompatible with life.

Connective tissue: One of the four basic types of animal tissue (the other three are epithelial tissue, muscle tissue, and nervous tissue) found between other tissues everywhere in the body. It serves to bind, support, protect, insulate, store, and transport.

Connective tissue disorder: A disease involving the connective tissue, such as Ehlers-Danlos syndrome, which involves a genetic defect in collagen and connective tissue formation.

Contraceptive implant: A hormone (such as progesterone) that is delivered via a device implanted under the skin.

Contrast dye: A solution that is used to accentuate specific structures when looking at a body image. Radiocontrast agents are substances that are used in X-rays, fluoroscopy, and computed tomography (CT) scans can be inserted directly, e.g., into the bladder, or injected into a blood vessel.

Corpus luteum cyst: After an egg is released in the ovary, the corpus luteum, the area where the egg matured, usually absorbs back into the ovary. If it fills with fluid and persists, it can form a cyst.

Corticosteroids (Prednisone®, Methylprednisone®, Depo-medrol®, Solu-medrol®): Steroid hormones that reduce inflammation by suppressing certain functions of the immune system.

Couples therapy: A type of psychotherapy in which a professional helps a couple understand their relationship, resolve conflict, and gain satisfaction.

Crowdfunding: When a person asks for money (typically, small amounts from many people) to fund projects.

Cranial nerve palsy: Decrease or loss of function in one or more cranial (head) nerves, such as pain in the fifth cranial nerve (the trigeminal nerve), which provides, for example, the sensation of facial touch.

Cranial nerves: Pairs of nerves that arise in the brain and pass through the openings in the skull.

C-reactive protein (CRP): A protein produced by the liver that increases when the body is inflamed.

Crohn's disease: A type of inflammatory bowel disease that can affect any segment of the gastrointestinal tract, from the mouth to the anus. The cause of the inflammation involves a malfunctioning immune system.

Cryoablation: A minimally invasive technique in which a small needle is inserted next to a nerve or group of nerves; they are frozen, which kills them.

CT angiography (CTA): A test that uses X-rays and an intravenous dye to show detailed pictures of the heart and blood vessels. It can show narrowed or blocked areas of a blood vessel.

CT myelogram: A CT scan performed in conjunction with contrast material injected into the fluid around the spinal cord. This allows evaluation of the spinal cord, nerve roots, and spinal lining (meninges). It is an alternative to MRI for imaging these structures.

Cyclobenzaprine (Flexeril®, Fexmid®, Amrix®): A muscle relaxant medication that works at the level of the brain stem.

Cyclosporine A (Sandimmune®, Neoril®, Gengraf®, Restasis®): An anti-immune medication (immunosuppressant) that works by inhibiting cytokines that stimulate T cells, which are part of the immune system.

Cyst: A fluid-filled sac lined by a membrane.

Cystectomy: Surgical removal of a cyst or of the urinary bladder.

Cystitis: Inflammation of the bladder, often due to bacteria, less often due to a virus, parasite, or chemical exposure (e.g., ketamine), and sometimes in the absence of infection in an irritative condition called Interstitial Cystitis.

Cystocele (anterior pelvic organ prolapse): A condition in which the bladder drops (prolapses or herniates) into the space of the vagina through a weakening between these side-by-side organs. It can bulge out the vaginal entrance and obstruct the flow of urine by kinking the urethra.

Cystogram/voiding cystourethrogram (VCUG): A special imaging study to assess the bladder, urethra, and sometimes the ureters. It includes plain X-ray cystograms and computed tomography (CT) cystograms, while an iodine-based contrast (a liquid that is visible on X-rays) is injected to the bladder through a urethral catheter.

Cystogram: A procedure used to visualize the urinary bladder; using a urinary catheter, radiocontrast is instilled in the bladder, and X-ray imaging is performed.

Cystoscopy: A procedure using a small camera that allows your doctor to examine the bladder, urethra, ureter openings, (and prostate in males) from within the natural opening that starts at the urethral tip.

Cytokines: Immunomodulatory proteins secreted by the immune system.

Cytology: A test in which a pathologist looks for cancer cells under a microscope.

Dactylitis: Inflammation of a finger or toe (from the Greek word *dactylos*, meaning finger).

Deep breathing: Breathing with long breaths, especially as exercise or a method of relaxation.

Defecography: A type of medical radiological imaging in which the mechanics of a patient's defecation are visualized in real time using a fluoroscope.

Deficiency: A shortage of something the body needs, for example hormone deficiency.

Delorme's procedure: A surgical procedure performed for full-thickness rectal prolapse via the perineal approach. The mucosa (surface) is removed and the muscles of the rectal wall are plicated (stitched together).

Deoxyribonucleic acid (DNA): A long macromolecule that is the main component of chromosomes encoding genetic information. Four nucleotides containing the following bases make up DNA: adenine (A), guanine (G), cytosine (C), and thymine (T). DNA codes and transfers genetic traits in humans, and RNA (ribonucleic acid) is transcribed from it.

Depo progesterone injection: A commonly used term to refer to the medication medroxyprogesterone acetate (Depo-Provera®), which is an injection of progesterone that suppresses ovarian production of hormones.

Depression: A common mood disorder that interferes with daily function that can present with persistent sadness, loss of interest, disturbed sleep, impaired concentration ability, preoccupation of thought, guilt, disturbed appetite, and thoughts of suicide.

Dermatomal: Associated with a dermatome.

Dermatomes: Areas of skin supplied by a single spinal nerve. Mapping the dermatome can help determine whether there is a problem with a single spinal segment or root (radiculopathy) or with another neurological problem.

Dermis: The thick layer of skin below the surface (the epidermis) that contains capillaries, nerve endings, sweat glands, hair follicles, and other structures.

Dermoid teratoma: A benign ovarian cyst containing hair, fatty fluid, and sometimes cartilage or teeth.

Detrusor/detrusor muscle: The spherical muscle of the bladder that is made up of smooth muscle and is innervated by the autonomic nervous system. Relaxation (sympathetic) allows storage, and contraction (parasympathetic) allows for contraction and emptying.

Detrusor sphincter dyssynergia: In normal bladder function, the sphincters of the bladder neck (internal sphincter) and urethra (external sphincter) relax during bladder contraction to allow for emptying. When there is a problem in the spine (containing the upper motor neurons), the sphincters can be uncoordinated or dyssynergic and paradoxically contracting when the bladder is trying to empty.

Dextrose: A simple sugar that is sometimes used in a concentrated form in pain syndromes. It tricks the body into thinking it is injured to stimulate healing.

Diabetes/diabetes mellitus: A condition associated with a difficulty processing sugar, leading to high levels in the bloodstream. In diabetes, there can be insufficient insulin production, or the body may be blind to it (insulin resistance).

Diabetic neuropathy: Injury to the nerves caused by high blood sugar levels, including peripheral neuropathy, proximal neuropathy (diabetic amyotrophy), autonomic neuropathy, and focal (mono) neuropathy.

Diabetic peripheral neuropathy: *See* diabetic neuropathy.

Diagnostic injection: An injection designed to deliver medication directly to the site of pain or its nerve origin to determine whether the pain is relieved by targeting this location.

Diaphragm: A dome-shaped muscle that separates the chest (thorax) from the belly (abdomen). Its contraction increases the volume of the chest and draws air into the lungs.

Diclofenac (Voltaren®): A non-steroidal anti-inflammatory drug (NSAID).

Differential diagnosis: The list of diagnoses that could cause a set of symptoms and physical findings.

Digital rectal examination: Examination of the anus and rectum using a gloved finger (digit). This exam allows for identification of rectal masses, high or low muscle tone, and hemorrhoids in both women and men; in men, it allows for the identification of prostate growth, pain, or cancerous nodules.

Dilation and curettage (D&C): A surgical procedure performed without an incision in which the opening of the uterus is dilated from below and the lining of the uterus is scraped to remove tissue.

Discectomy: Partial or entire surgical removal of an intervertebral disc.

Disease-modifying anti-rheumatic drugs (DMARDs): Medications used for the treatment of rheumatic diseases; these medications reduce inflammation and slow down the damaging effects of inflammation of organs or joints.

Distal: Situated away from the center of the body or from the point of attachment.

Diverticulitis: An infection or inflammation of pouches that can form in your intestines.

Diverticulosis: A condition in which pockets, called diverticula, form in the walls of your digestive tract.

Diverticulum: A bulging pouch anywhere in the body, including the urethra, bladder, and bowel. If the neck of the pouch is narrow, the diverticulum might have a hard time emptying and become inflamed.

Dorsal horn: A part of the spinal cord where cell bodies (control centers) of the sensory nerves connect (in synapses) with other neurons (projection neurons).

Dorsal root ganglia (DRG): A cluster of neurons (a ganglion) in a dorsal root of a spinal nerve. The cell bodies of sensory neurons known as first-order neurons in the dorsal root ganglia.

Dorsal root ganglia (DRG) stimulation: Electrical stimulation at the dorsal root ganglion that is accessed through the neural foramen.

Duloxetine (Cymbalta®): An antidepressant in the serotonin-norepinephrine re-uptake inhibitor (SNRI) class, which helps restore the balance of serotonin and norepinephrine. It can also be used for the treatment of pain.

Dura: Synonym for dura mater.

Dura mater: The tough outermost membrane enveloping the brain and spinal cord.

Dysesthesia: Abnormal sensation that typically presents as painful burning, prickling, or aching feelings.

Dysmenorrhea: Pain during menses.

Dyspareunia: Persistent or recurrent genital pain that occurs before, during, or after sexual activity.

Dystonia: Abnormal muscle contraction and tone.

Dysuria: Painful urinary symptoms that are typically referable to the urethra.

E. coli: Escherichia coli, the most common bacteria naturally occurring in the stool.

Ectopic pregnancy: Also called an extrauterine pregnancy, an ectopic pregnancy occurs when a fertilized egg grows outside of a woman's uterus, somewhere else in her belly.

Ehlers-Danlos Syndrome (EDS): A heritable connective tissue disorder characterized by joint hypermobility, skin stretchiness, tissue fragility, and pelvic floor laxity, among other things. Chronic pain can be a component of the diagnosis.

Ejaculatory duct: The short duct (channel) that receives fluid from both the vas deferens (carrying sperm) and the duct from the seminal vesicle (which produces 70%–85% of ejaculate volume), passing through the prostate into the prostatic urethra at the level of the veru montanum.

Ejaculatory duct obstruction: Blockage of the ejaculatory duct (from a cyst or infection/scarring) and causing back-up of testicular and seminal vesicle fluid.

Ejaculatory dysfunction: Rapid (premature), delayed, retrograde (backward into the bladder caused by an open bladder neck), or painful ejaculation.

Elagolix (Orilissa®): An oral medication that competes with gonadotropin-releasing hormone, thereby suppressing ovarian production of hormones.

Electrodes: Thin electrical wires that deliver tiny electrical impulses.

Electrodiagnostic testing (EDX): Recording the response of a body structure to electrical stimulation.

Electrogalvanic stimulation: A means of over-stimulating and over-contracting a muscle to the point of fatigue and then relaxing it. This is carried out via a vaginal or rectal probe when applied to the pelvic floor muscles.

Electromyogram/electromyograph (EMG): A diagnostic technique that measures the electrical activity of muscles during stimulation to assess the function of muscles and nerve cells (motor neurons) that control them.

Embolization: When something such as a blood clot or an agent placed intentionally into a blood vessel blocks blood flow.

Emotional regulation: The ability to exert control over one's emotional state. It can involve rethinking or refocusing.

Endoanal ultrasound: An ultrasound performed via the anus.

Endogenous: Naturally made by the body.

Endometrioma: Blood-filled cysts created by endometriosis.

Endometriosis (cyclic pain): An often-painful disorder in which tissue, similar to the tissue that normally lines the inside of your uterus (the endometrium), grows outside your uterus.

Endometriosis nodules: Solid deposits of endometriosis.

Endometritis: An inflammation of the inner lining of the uterus (endometrium); symptoms include fever, lower abdominal pain, and abnormal vaginal bleeding or discharge.

Endometrium: Tissue that makes up the uterine lining.

Endorphins: A group of hormones secreted by the brain and nervous system that activate the body's opiate receptors and naturally reduce pain.

Endoscope: Instrument that can be inserted into body for visualization of internal parts.

Endovenous/endovascular stent: A metal mesh tube used to expand against blocked or narrowed vein walls, restoring blood flow. Reserved for the larger veins of the chest, abdomen, and pelvis.

Endovascular/endovascular technique: Administered or done within a blood vessel.

Enoxaparin sodium (Lovenox®): An anticoagulant related to a low-molecular weight heparin.

Enteric nervous system: The nervous system that is responsible for managing digestion.

Enterocele: The small bowel drops (prolapses or herniates) into another space—most commonly the vagina—through a weakening between these side-by-side organs. It can cause bowel symptoms if the bowel is narrowed or kinked.

Enteropathic: A condition that triggers problems with the small intestine.

Enteropathic spondyloarthritis: A seronegative spondyloarthritis occurring with IBD presenting with lower-back and pelvic pain and GI tract inflammation and diarrhea.

Enthesitis: Inflammation of the tendon and ligament insertion sites.

Enucleation: The surgical removal of an intact organ, especially of the eye and of cysts and tumors.

Eosinophilic granulomatosis with polyangiitis (EGPA) (Churg Strauss): Formerly known as Churg Strauss, EGPA is a disorder associated with asthma, nasal polyps, sinusitis, elevated eosinophil counts, and vasculitis. EGPA tends to involve the lungs, peripheral nerves, skin, kidneys, and heart.

Epididymis: A delicate winding tube that sperm traverses as it exits the testis, maturing as it proceeds.

Erectile dysfunction: Inability to get or maintain an erection for sexual activity, or a reduced erection, lasting at least six months.

Erythema: Surface-level reddening of the skin as a result of infection or irritation that causes dilation of the capillaries.

Erythrocyte sedimentation rate (ESR): A laboratory test measuring how quickly red blood cells (erythrocytes) settle at the bottom of a test tube containing blood. If it settles faster than normal, it might indicate inflammation.

Esophagus: The muscular tube connecting the throat (pharynx) with the stomach.

Estrogen: The female sex hormones, including estrone, estradiol, and estriol, which are important for sexual and reproductive development, vulvar health, and protection from urinary tract infection. Certain breast cancers are sensitive to estrogen.

Estrogen receptors (ERs): A group of proteins found on cell nuclei or membranes that are activated by the hormone estrogen (17β-estradiol).

Etiology: The cause of a disease or condition.

European Association of Urology: A non-profit organization committed to the representation of urology professionals worldwide.

Evaluated: To be evaluated is to have a chance to discuss symptoms and to undergo a relevant physical exam and testing, in order to get a medical opinion.

Evidence-based therapy: Therapy or treatment that is backed by scientific evidence.

Excision: A procedure of removing tissue, especially by cutting it out.

Excisional hemorrhoidectomy: Removal of hemorrhoidal tissue by incising and removing it.

External: On or toward the surface of the body, for example external urethral sphincter.

External hemorrhoid: A hemorrhoid located outside the anal sphincter and beneath the surface of the anal skin.

External iliac veins: Large paired veins within the pelvis that receive blood from the femoral veins coming from the legs and that run until they join with the internal iliac vein and form the common iliac veins.

Extra-articular: Outside of a joint.

Fallopian tube: The tube, either right or left, that carries an egg from the ovary to the uterus. It opens into the peritoneal cavity near the ovary.

Fallopian tube torsion: An abnormal twisting of the fallopian tube that can impair its blood supply.

Fascia: A layer of connective tissue made up primarily of collagen that attaches, stabilizes, encloses, and separates muscles and other internal organs.

FAST exam: Stands for focused assessment with sonography in trauma, and is a bedside ultrasound to look for evidence of bleeding in the abdomen.

Fear-avoidance model: A model of thought explaining why some pain becomes chronic. Pain-related fear may lead to avoidance of pain and chronic pain caused by disuse and disability.

Fecal calprotectin: A stool test to screen for inflammation.

Fecal incontinence: A disorder characterized by difficulty holding on to stool.

Federal Trade Commission (FTC): A federal office designed to prevent anti-competitive, deceptive, and unfair business practices to promote competition and consumer access to accurate information.

Female cystocele: *See* cystocele.

Femoral acetabular impingement (FAI) syndrome: A disorder in which a structure within the hip joint becomes pinched or impinged upon between bony structures.

Femoral acetabular joint: The large paired joint between the femur (thigh bone) and the acetabulum of the hip/pelvis.

Femoral canal: Passageway through which femoral structures travel from abdomen into the upper thigh.

Femoral hernia: A hernia, usually bowel or fatty tissue, pushes through a weak area of the groin at the top of the inner thigh within the femoral canal.

Femur: The large bone in the thigh.

Fentanyl (Duragesic®, Fentora®): A potent opiate medication used for severe pain with a high potential for abuse.

Fibroid: Non-cancerous, abnormal growths in the uterus.

Fibroid degeneration: A benign muscle wall tumor of the uterus that outgrows its blood supply.

Fibroid torsion: A benign muscle wall tumor of the uterus that twists on its blood supply, causing ischemia.

Fibroid tumor: *See* fibroid.

Fibromyalgia: A disorder characterized by widespread musculoskeletal pain accompanied by fatigue and disturbances of sleep, memory, and mood.

Fissure: A cut or tear in the thin, delicate lining of the anus.

Fissurectomy: Surgical cleaning up of an anal fissure floor and walls.

Fistula: Inflammatory tracts between neighboring organs.

Flame war: An internet fight among various individuals.

Fleet enema: A saline enema that works by increasing water in the intestine to soften the stool to produce a bowel movement and empty the rectum.

Focal neuropathies: Injuries to peripheral nerves at specific sites—often only one. In diabetes, diffuse peripheral or autonomic neuropathies are more common.

Foley catheter: A soft and flexible urinary drainage catheter with a balloon on the end of it to gently hold it in the bladder. It is the most common type of indwelling urinary catheter.

Food and Drug Administration (FDA): A federal agency in the United States that protects the public health by ensuring the safety, efficacy, and security of human and veterinary drugs, biological products, medical devices, the food supply, cosmetics, and products that emit radiation.

Frontal lobe: Each of the paired lobes of the brain lying immediately behind the forehead. Its functions include organization, sequencing, planning, and voluntary movement.

Fulguration: The use of heat or electric current to destroy abnormal tissue, such as a tumor or other lesion.

Functional obstruction: As opposed to anatomical obstruction, a functional obstruction has to do with a tight muscle, either due to a neurological cause or a muscle that is unable to relax out of habit.

Functional/functional disorder: A physical disorder in which a physical cause has not been identified; instead, attention has been turned toward psychological factors, such as emotional conflicts or stress.

Functional cyst: Ovarian cysts that are created as part of the natural menstrual cycle, in which the ovaries make a cyst and then release an egg each month.

Functional somatic syndrome: Refers to a group of chronic diagnoses with no identifiable organic causes.

Gabapentin (Neurontin®): Oral anti-seizure medication used also to treat neuropathic pain.

Gabapentinoid medications: Medications that are derivatives of the γ-aminobutyric acid (GABA) inhibitory neurotransmitter; these medications include gabapentin (Neurontin®), pregabalin (Lyrica®), mirogabalin, gabapentin enacarbil, and phenibut.

Gait deviations: Any variations of standard human gait that usually occur as compensation for pain, weakness, or anatomical or neurological abnormalities.

Gartner's duct cyst: A benign vaginal cyst originating from the mesonephric duct.

Gastrointestinal (GI) tract: A series of hollow organs that form a continuous passage between the mouth and anus.

Gastroenterologist: A physician who specializes in conditions and diseases of the gastrointestinal (digestive) tract, which includes the esophagus, stomach, small intestine, colon, liver, pancreas, gallbladder, and bile ducts.

Gel foam (Gelfoam®) embolization: A temporary blockage of blood flow using a gelatin sponge material; for example, gel foam embolization can be used to stop internal bleeding.

Gender-affirmation surgery (GAS): Gender-affirmation surgery is a collection of surgical procedures performed in those with gender dysphoria. These procedures include genital, facial, and body procedures required to create a body phenotype that best represents one's identity.

Gender dysphoria: Gender dysphoria involves a conflict between a person's physical or assigned gender and the gender with which he/she/they identifies.

Gene expression: The appearance of a characteristic associated with a segment of DNA known as a gene.

General anesthesia: A combination of inhaled and intravenous medications that allow for a state of unconsciousness during surgery.

Generic: An approved scientific or medical name that is decided by expert scientists to classify a drug.

Genetic studies: Genetic studies are sometimes referred to as "genetic testing" and are a type of medical test that identifies abnormalities in chromosomes, genes, or proteins. Also, genetic studies refer to publications that examine genetic diseases.

Genitals: The internal and external reproductive organs of any gender. Female sex internal genitalia include the ovaries, fallopian tubes, uterus, cervix, and vagina; external genitalia include the labia minora and majora (the vulva) and the clitoris. Male sex internal genitalia include the testes, epididymis, and vas deferens; external genitalia include the penis and scrotum.

Genitofemoral nerve: A nerve in the abdomen that supplies sensation to the upper anterior thigh, as well as the skin of the anterior scrotum in males and the mons pubis in females.

Genitourinary (urogenital) system: All organs involved in the production and excretion of urine, as well as all organs involved with reproduction. They are close to each other and share common embryological origins.

Genomic memory: The idea that the experiences of a species encode readiness to respond to stimuli in certain ways, which leads to a genetic memory that is present at birth. For example, the ability of horses to sense fear.

Giant cell arteritis (GCA): The most common form of vasculitis in adults, which is caused by inflammation of the lining of the arteries. It can cause headaches, joint pain, fever, and difficulties with vision.

Glia: Supporting tissue within the nervous system.

Glomerulations: Burst capillaries visible in the wall of the bladder, particularly after the stress of filling. These are associated with but not diagnostic of interstitial cystitis.

Glomerulus: A cluster of capillaries around the end of a kidney tubule, which filter waste from the blood.

Glucocorticoids: Any group of corticosteroids involved in carbohydrate metabolism and having anti-inflammatory properties.

Glucose-6-phosphate dehydrogenase (G6PD) deficiency: An enzyme disorder that affects red blood cell function, which can be affected by certain medications.

Gluten allergy: Allergy to a protein found in wheat, barley, and rye; not to be confused with celiac disease, or wheat allergy.

Gluten-containing foods: Foods containing gluten.

Gluteus medius muscle: This buttock muscle originates from the outer surface of the ilium (part of the pelvis) and attaches to the outside of the greater trochanter. It stabilizes the pelvis.

Gluteus muscles: Muscles of the buttocks.

Gonadotropin-releasing hormone agonist/analog: This class of medication mimics "gonadotropin-releasing hormone" and inhibits the upstream hormonal messages leading to formation of estrogen, progesterone, and testosterone in both women and men at the level of the brain.

Gonadotropin-releasing hormone antagonist: A medication that competes with gonadotropin-releasing hormone, thereby blocking ovarian follicular maturation and ovulation in women, as well as hormone production in both genders. Useful for prostate cancer and endometriosis.

Gonads: The testes (male anatomic sex) or ovaries (female anatomic sex). In rare intersex conditions, variations occur at birth.

Gonococcus: A common sexually transmitted bacteria that can cause pelvic pain and pelvic inflammatory disease.

Gonorrhea: The name of the infection caused by gonococcus.

Goserelin (Zoladex®): Hormonal treatment that reduces levels of estrogen, progesterone, and testosterone in women and men by tricking the system by mimicking gonadotropin-releasing hormone and therefore inhibiting the upstream hormonal messages at the level of the brain.

Gout: A crystal-induced arthritis that may present with hip pain. Pain occurs after high levels of uric acid concentrate and form crystals in the joints. Risk factors for gout include diets rich in red meat, alcohol, and seafood; obesity; hypertension (high blood pressure); diabetes; and being born male.

Granulomatosis with polyangiitis (GPA): Formerly known as Wegener's granulomatosis, GPA is systemic disease characterized by inflammation of the blood vessels in the lungs, kidneys, upper respiratory tract, and other organs. It is associated with the autoantibody known as ANCA.

Gross hematuria: Blood in the urine that is visible to the naked eye.

Growth factor: A substance—usually a vitamin or hormone—that stimulates growth in living cells.

Guided visualization: A relaxation technique in which guidance using words, sounds, and other stimuli are used to evoke positive images and feelings.

Gynecologic vasculitis: Diagnosis of vasculitis within the female genital tract.

Gynecologic: Related to the reproductive organs of women.

Gynecological examination: An exam of the external reproductive organs and anus; internal speculum exam of the vagina and cervix; manual exam of the bladder, urethra, pelvic floor muscles, and rectum; and a bimanual exam (compressing areas of the pelvis against the hand in the vagina through the abdominal wall) during the examination of a woman.

Gynecologist: A doctor who specializes in the medical and surgical care of the female reproductive system.

Hemi-laminectomy: Surgical removal of a portion of the vertebral lamina, which is a part of the vertebral arch.

Hemiplegia: Paralysis of one side of the body.

Hemi-walkers: Designed for people who have the use of only one arm, this walker is wide-based and more stable than a cane, though it serves only one side of the body.

Hemoglobin: Iron-containing molecule that plays a role in oxygen transport.

Hemorrhoid: A disorder characterized by dilated blood vessels at the level of the anus.

Hemorrhoidectomy: Surgical excision of hemorrhoids.

Heparin (Heparin Sodium®): Medication that interrupts clotting and thins the blood, sometimes instilled in the bladder via a catheter to treat interstitial cystitis.

Hernia: An abnormal opening or weak spot through which organs or tissue can protrude.

Herniated disc: Condition in which an intervertebral disc protrudes and pinches a nerve. Also called a bulged, slipped, or ruptured disc.

Heroin: A highly addictive street drug that is part of the opiate family. It was first created and marketed for common ailments as well as a cure for morphine addiction. It led to a new wave of addiction and was banned in 1924.

Herpes zoster (shingles) infection: A viral infection that occurs with re-activation of the varicella-zoster virus; it is usually a painful but self-limited dermatomal rash.

Higher-frequency pulses: Electromagnetic waves/signals transmitted at increased megahertz ranges (less perceptible when stimulated).

Hip abductors: The muscles that open your hips.

Hip extensors: Muscles that extend the hip, sending the thigh back behind the body.

Hip flexors: Muscles that flex the hip, drawing the knee up toward the chest.

Hip girdle weakness: Weakness of the muscles of the pelvic girdle (also known as the hip girdle).

Histopathologic: From the Greek words, histos, pathos, and logia meaning "study of tissue suffering," it refers to the microscopic examination of tissue to study the manifestations of disease.

Hives: An acute skin disorder characterized by big, flat rashes, typically as part of an allergic reaction.

HLA-B27: A protein, that if present on the surface of white blood cells on laboratory testing, suggests seronegative spondyloarthritis.

Hormone: A regulatory substance (amino acid, protein, fatty acid, or cholesterol [steroid] derivative), which is produced in an organism and transported in tissue fluids to stimulate specific cells or tissues into action.

Hormone therapy: Treatment with synthetic or naturally derived hormones, such as estrogen and progesterone.

Hormone replacement therapy (HRT): *See* hormone therapy.

Hunner's ulcer: Ulcerated patch on the surface of the bladder, identified via cystoscopy, suggestive of interstitial cystitis.

Hydrocodone (Lortab®, Vicodin®): Synthetic opioid pain medication that when combined with acetaminophen is marketed as Lortab® or Vicodin®.

Hydrodistention: A procedure in which the urinary bladder is filled through a cystoscope at higher pressure, and the bladder is left in the distended position for several minutes to stretch it. This procedure is typically used for interstitial cystitis.

Hydromorphone (Dilaudid®, Exalgo®): Potent opioid pain medication that has a high risk of addiction.

Hyperalgesia: Abnormally increased sensitivity to pain.

Hypercoagulable: Abnormally increased propensity of the blood to clotting.

Hyperesthesia: Disorder characterized by increased sensory sensitivity.

Hyperlipidemia: A state of having extra fats or lipids in the blood, such as high cholesterol.

Hyperlordosis: A condition in which there is an excessive spine curvature in the lower back.

Hypertension (high blood pressure): Persistent elevation of the blood pressure in the arteries.

Hypertonic/hypertonicity: Muscle tone that is too high.

Hypervigilant: Having increased sensitivity and reactivity.

Hypoareflexia: Weak reflexes.

Hypoesthesia: A disorder characterized by decreased sensory sensitivity.

Hyporeflexia: Low-response neurological reflexes, as can be seen when a reflex hammer taps on a tendon to elicit a stretch reflex.

Hypothalamic-pituitary-adrenal (HPA) axis: The central stress response system in which the central nervous system and the endocrine (hormone) system coordinate responses.

Hysterectomy: An operation in which a woman's uterus is surgically removed. This might include removal of the ovaries, fallopian tubes, and cervix.

Hysteroscopy: An operation in which a telescope is used to look inside the uterus.

Ibuprofen: An over-the-counter, non-steroidal anti-inflammatory medication that helps with pain and fever but can cause bleeding.

Iliac arteries: Arterial branches arising at the bifurcation of the aorta in the pelvis, becoming the common iliac arteries. They supply the lower limbs and pelvic region with blood.

Iliac venous outflow obstruction: A condition with blockage of venous outflow (blood returning to the heart in the blood vessels called veins).

Iliohypogastric nerve: A nerve of the abdominal wall that derives from the anterior division of the twelfth thoracic and first lumbar nerve roots. If injured, it can cause pelvic pain above the pubic bone and in the lateral gluteal (buttock) or thigh area.

Ilioinguinal nerve: A nerve of the abdominal wall that derives from the anterior division of the twelfth thoracic and first lumbar nerve roots. If injured, it can cause pelvic pain at the waist, at the root of the penis and upper scrotum in men and in the mons pubis (the skin overlying the pubic bone) or labia majora in women.

Iliopsoas muscle: A powerful hip flexor that runs on both sides along the inner trunk to the legs. It is both a major pelvic floor muscle as well as a major postural (standing) muscle that is responsible for dynamic stabilization of the lumbar spine of the pelvis.

Ilium: The large wing-like bone of the pelvis.

Immune system: The bodily system that protects the body from foreign organisms, substances, and cells.

Immunomodulator medication: A substance that affects the functioning of the immune system.

Immunomodulatory: Affecting the function of the immune system.

Immunosuppressant: A medication that dampens inflammation and the impact of the immune response, such as after organ transplantation.

Implantable pulse generator (IPG): An implantable device that provides timed electrical stimulation.

In utero: In the uterus or womb before birth.

Inactive ingredient: The material in which the drug is mixed to make a tablet, capsule, or cream that is responsible for things such as the color and the amount of time the medication takes to release.

Incarcerated hernia: Abdominal contents protruding through an abnormal opening or weak spot that is trapped and has lost blood flow, thereby leading to tissue death. It is a medical emergency.

Incomplete SCI: Incomplete spinal cord injury. In incomplete injuries of the spinal cord, some muscle or sensory function exists below the level of the injury.

Incontinence: Unwanted leakage, such as of urine or stool, that occurs when pressure is placed on your bladder; also, it can occur when coughing, sneezing, exercising, or lifting something heavy.

Indwelling suprapubic catheter (SPTube): A small tube, often a Foley catheter, is inserted through the lower abdominal wall above the pubic bone, into the bladder (rather than through the urethra).

Indwelling urethral catheter: A small tube called a "Foley catheter" is inserted through the urethra into the bladder. The catheter is held in place with a soft balloon.

Inferior cluneal nerves: Also called the gluteal branches of the posterior femoral cutaneous nerves. These nerves serve the skin of the lower buttocks.

Inferior hypogastric plexus: A network of nerves that supplies the organs of the pelvic cavity.

Inferior: Lower in position.

Inferior vena cava: The large vein carrying deoxygenated blood from the lower body, abdomen, and pelvis back to the heart.

Inflammation: Your body's way of protecting itself from infection, illness, or injury. As part of the inflammatory response, your body increases its production of white blood cells, immune cells, and substances called cytokines.

Inflammatory: Relating to or causing inflammation in the body.

Inflammatory arthritis: A group of conditions in which the body's immune system attacks one's own tissues.

Inflammatory bowel disease (IBD): A term referring to two conditions, Crohn's disease and ulcerative colitis, which are characterized by chronic inflammation of the gastrointestinal (GI) tract.

Inflammatory vasculitis: A group of disorders that destroy blood vessels (arteries and veins) by inflammation.

Infliximab (Remicade®): Immunosuppressant medication used to treat several autoimmune diseases. It is a monoclonal antibody, which is a lab-produced molecule serving as a substitute antibody to enhance the immune response.

Inguinal canal: Passageway for reproductive structures (vas deferens and spermatic cord in the male and the vestigial [remaining from development] round ligament in the female), as well as the ilioinguinal nerve and genital branch of the genitofemoral nerve, to travel from the lower abdominal cavity to the groin region.

Inguinal hernia: An abnormal opening or weak spot through which organs or tissue may protrude into the inguinal canal.

Innervate: *See* innervation.

Innervation: To innervate is to supply nerves to, to stimulate, or to supply with energy; nervous system supply/stimulation to a target tissue or organ.

Instrumentation: The use of tools for diagnostic or therapeutic purposes.

Insufficiency fracture: Fracture caused by the bone being unable to withstand the stresses of normal activities, such as in osteoporosis or when cancer has metastasized to the bone.

Interleukin (for example, IL-1 or IL-17): A medication related to proteins produced by white blood cells for regulating the immune response.

Intermittent claudication: Painful cramping of a limb that is associated with physical activity and is relieved by rest. It is caused by a poor blood supply.

Internal digital exam: An exam in which a finger is inserted into the body (such as the rectum or vagina).

Internal hemorrhoids: Hemorrhoids located inside the anal sphincter of the rectum and beneath the mucous membrane.

Internal jugular vein: A paired set of veins that collect blood from the brain and the surfaces of the face and neck, running within the carotid sheath alongside the common carotid artery and vagus nerve.

Internal pelvic exam: An exam in which a speculum is inserted in the vagina to see its inner surface.

International Continence Society (ICS): A leading organization for research and education about urinary, bowel and pelvic floor disorders.

International Pelvic Pain Society (IPPS): An organization of health care professionals whose primary mission is to disseminate educational resources for the management of chronic pelvic pain.

Interneuron: A neuron that transmits impulses between neurons as part of communication within the nervous system, especially as part of a reflex arc.

Interstitial cystitis (IC): A chronic condition causing bladder pressure, bladder pain, and sometimes pelvic pain.

Interstitial Cystitis Network (ICN): A worldwide health education company dedicated to interstitial cystitis and chronic pelvic pain syndrome.

Interventional radiologist: A physician trained in interventional radiology.

Interventional radiology: A radiologic specialty involving the performance of minimally invasive interventions guided by specialized imaging.

Intervertebral disc: Shock-absorbing structure found between each vertebra and comprised of nucleus pulposus and annulus fibrous.

Intestinal permeability: The ease of passage of material passing from inside the gastrointestinal tract, through the cells lining the gut wall, and into the rest of the body.

Intra-articular hip joint dysfunction: Problems within the hip joints, such as a labral tear.

Intraepidermal: Within the epidermis, which is the top-most surface level of the skin.

Intrathecal baclofen therapy: Delivering a liquid form of baclofen into the spinal fluid using a device called a baclofen pump.

Intrathecal: The intrathecal space—also known as the subarachnoid space—is the fluid-filled area located between the innermost layer covering of the spinal cord (the pia mater) and the middle layer (the arachnoid mater).

Intrathecal pain pump: A pain pump that works by inserting low doses of medicine into the intrathecal space surrounding the spinal cord.

Intravascular ultrasound (IVUS): A diagnostic test that uses small ultrasound probes inside blood vessels.

Intravenous sedation: Administration of medications through a vein that is typically done to help a person tolerate a procedure.

Intussusception: The inversion of one portion of the intestine within another that resembles a long sock folded within itself after hasty removal.

Invasive procedure: A medical procedure that enters the human body, either through a natural orifice (such as cystoscopy) or by incising the skin. Some invasive procedures have minimal to no pain, and some require general anesthesia.

Iodinated contrast: A form of radiographic contrast that can be injected in the vein or instilled in a hollow organ such as the bladder or rectum to improve visibility for diagnosis.

Ipsilateral: On the same side of the body.

Irritable bowel syndrome (IBS): A common disorder with abdominal pain, bloating, diarrhea, or constipation.

Irritant dermatitis: A form of contact dermatitis (skin irritation).

Ischemia/ischemic: A restriction of the blood supply to tissues, causing a shortage of oxygen that is needed for cellular metabolism (to keep tissue alive).

Ischial tuberosity: The "sit bones", located in the region of the crease of the buttocks.

Joint: Where bones connect to each other.

Kegel exercises: Exercises performed to strengthen the pelvic floor muscles, involving repeated contractions. Of note, these are often counterproductive in people who have pain caused by high tone of the pelvic floor muscles.

Ketoprofen (Frotek®): A non-steroidal medication that reduces inflammation, for example, in arthritis.

Ketorolac (Toradol®): Ketorolac tromethamine is a non-steroidal anti-inflammatory drug (NSAID) that is used to treat moderately severe pain and inflammation, usually after surgery.

Keyhole surgery: Laparoscopic or robotic-assisted laparoscopic surgery performed telescopically through a small incision.

Kidney (renal) insufficiency: A condition in which the kidneys have lost some ability to remove waste and balance fluids.

Kidney stones: Hard deposits of minerals and acid salts that stick together in concentrated urine; they can be painful when passing through the urinary tract but usually don't cause permanent damage.

Kidneys: The pair of organs sitting behind the upper abdomen under the rib cage that receive 25% of the blood pumped by the heart, filtering it and removing waste products, chemicals, medications, and unneeded water, thereby producing urine.

Labia (lips): The inner and outer folds of the vulva, paired on either side of the vagina.

Labral/labrum: A ring of fibrocartilage (fibrous cartilage) around the edge of the articular (joint) surface of a bone.

Lacrimal glands: Glands responsible for producing tears.

Lactose intolerance: The inability to digest lactose, a sugar component of milk and other dairy products.

Lambert Eaton Syndrome: Progressive muscle weakness mediated by autoimmune attacks on the neuromuscular junction; usually associated with malignancy.

Lamina: Flattened part of the vertebral arch that forms the roof of the spinal canal, directly posterior to spinal cord or nerves.

Laminectomy: Surgical removal of the entire vertebral lamina, which is a part of the vertebral arch.

Laparoscope: Instrument that can be inserted through the abdominal wall for visualization of organs in the abdomen.

Laparoscopy: Surgical procedure in which a laparoscope is inserted through abdominal wall for visualization of and access to organs in the abdomen.

Laparotomy: Surgical incision into the abdominal cavity.

Large intestine (large bowel): The last part of the gastrointestinal tract where water is absorbed, and the remaining waste material is stored until defecation can occur.

Lateral femoral cutaneous nerve: A nerve that supplies sensation to the outer thigh.

Left renal vein: The vein that drains the blood from the left kidney. The left gonadal vein (from the testis or ovary) drains into the left renal vein.

Left renal vein compression (nutcracker syndrome): This phenomenon occurs when the superior mesenteric artery compresses the left renal vein against the aorta, causing left flank pain. In some variants the aorta compresses the vein against the spine.

Leiomyoma: Another term for a fibroid.

Length-dependent polyneuropathy: A type of neuropathy affecting multiple nerves in which the longest nerves are most affected.

Lesion: Site of damage or change (or a tumor) in an organism that is usually caused by injury or disease.

Levator/levator ani muscles: Pelvic floor muscles. "Levator" means lift, so levator muscles also exist elsewhere in the body, such as in the eyelids.

Levator ani syndrome: A type of non-relaxing pelvic floor dysfunction with frequent dull pain in the rectum caused by a spasm in the levator ani muscle, which is near the anus.

Lichen sclerosis: An uncommon condition that creates patchy white skin that appears thinner than normal and usually affects the genital and anal areas.

Lichtenstein procedure: Open-abdomen surgery for inguinal hernias in which a mesh is placed to strengthen the abdominal wall after removing and/or returning herniated tissue back to the abdominal cavity.

Lidocaine (Xylocaine®, Lidoderm®, Recticare®, Urojet®): Local anesthetic (numbing medication) that works by blocking nerve signals in your body; it blocks sodium channels at the level of the cell membrane.

Ligament: Tissue connecting bones to bones.

Limbic system: A primal region of the brain concerned with instinct and mood which affects basic emotions (fear, pleasure, anger) and drives hunger, sex, dominance, and care of one's young.

Liver (hepatic) insufficiency: Malfunction of the liver.

Local anesthetics: A class of medications that cause temporary anesthesia (lack of sensation).

Low-frequency pulses: Electromagnetic waves/signals transmitted at decreased megahertz ranges, which might cause a perceptible sensation (paresthesia).

Lumbar spine: Part of the spine consisting of five vertebral bodies that extend from the lower thoracic spine (chest) to the sacrum (bottom of spine).

Lumbosacral spine: The part of the spine involving the small of the back (the five lumbar vertebrae) and the sacrum (the tailbone).

Lupron Depot®: The trade name for leuprolide acetate, which is an injection of "gonadotropin releasing hormone" that suppresses ovarian production of hormones.

Lyme disease: An inflammatory infectious disease transmitted by ticks.

Lymph nodes: Glands found throughout the body containing important components of the immune system that ward off infection.

Magnetic resonance imaging (MRI) scan: An advanced imaging study using a strong magnetic field and radio waves to create detailed images of the organs and tissues within the body. It is especially useful for brain, spine, and joint imaging.

Malar rash: A red "butterfly" facial rash commonly associated with lupus.

Malignant: Tending to be severe and progressively worse; it often applies to blood pressure or cancer.

Malingering: The act of exaggerating illness for secondary gain—either for attention or to avoid duties such as work.

Mandatory reporters: People (including all health care providers) who are mandated by law to report any known or suspected child abuse to the proper authorities.

Marplan® (isocarbaxazid): An antidepressant medication in the monoamine oxidase inhibitor class.

Martius flap: A surgical technique in which a labia majora fat pad flap is tunneled into the vagina to help support the tissues after complicated surgical repair (such as the repair of a fistula or urethral diverticulum).

Massage therapist: A trained practitioner who is certified to therapeutically manipulate the muscles or other soft tissues of the body using hands or special instruments.

Mature teratoma: Benign ovarian cyst containing hair, fatty fluid, and sometimes cartilage or teeth.

May-Thurner syndrome: A vascular condition in which the (usually) left common iliac vein is compressed by the right common iliac artery. This can lead to painful congestion of the pelvic veins and even deep venous thrombosis.

Meatus: From the Latin word for "passage," the meatus is an opening leading into the interior of the body, as in the urethral or external auditory meatus.

Mechanoreceptors: In the sensory organs, a receptor whose nerves respond to mechanical displacement, such as touch, pressure, vibration, and sound.

Medical release form: A document that gives health care professionals permission to share a patient's medical information with other parties.

Meditation: A practice of relaxation that encourages focus and quieting. Focus can be on breathing, an image, a phrase, a relaxing location, or other focal points.

Medroxyprogesterone acetate (MPA [Depo-Provera®] injection): Progestin-based female hormone shot given every three months. Works as birth control or control of menopausal symptoms. Inhibits gonadotropin production, which blocks follicular maturation and ovulation as well as hormone production.

Meninges: The three membranes (the dura mater, arachnoid, and pia mater) that line the skull and vertebral canal and enclose the brain and spinal cord.

Menopause: The time in life when menstruation stops (usually around age 50). During and after this time, estrogen levels drop. Surgery that removes both ovaries can lead to earlier menopause.

Mesalamine (Pentasa®, Asacol®, Apriso®, Delzicol®, Lialda®): Anti-inflammatory medication in the aminosalicylates class that is used for decreasing colon swelling from ulcerative colitis.

Mesonephric duct: Also known as the Wolffian duct or nephric duct, the mesonephric duct is present on both the left and right during formation of the fetus *in utero*. In both sexes, it develops into the trigone of urinary bladder, which surrounds the entrance of the ureters. In males, the mesonephric duct forms the epididymis, vas deferens, and seminal vesicles, and it usually recedes in females. If it persists, there can be a Gartner's duct cyst, which is present in the vagina but can lead into the pelvis.

Metabolic syndrome: A group of diagnoses (high blood pressure, elevated blood sugar, excess fat at the waistline, and high cholesterol or triglyceride levels) that, together, increase the risk of stroke, heart disease, and diabetes.

Metal coil embolization: A small metal coil that can be placed from within a blood vessel to allow for directed, precise clotting of that blood vessel, that will be permanent once a scar develops.

Metastatic lesions: Cancer cells that have broken away from the original (primary) tumor and traveled through the blood or lymph vessels to grow in a new area of the body.

Methotrexate (Otrexup®, Rasuvo®, Rheumatrex®, and Trexall®): A chemotherapy agent that prevents cell division/growth and therefore can be used to treat an ectopic pregnancy.

Methylation: A biochemical reaction that adds a methyl group (with one carbon and three hydrogen atoms) from a molecule, helping to regulate gene expression and to detoxify substances.

Microcolony: A minute colony (usually bacterial) growing under suboptimal conditions.

Microsurgical targeted denervation: A minor outpatient procedure in which a surgeon makes a small incision and makes a few specific cuts in abnormal nerve tissue to reduce function of the nerve.

Microbiome: The natural mix of bacteria that co-exists with our bodies.

Microglia: Cells scattered throughout the central nervous system (CNS) that act as the first form of active immune defense in the CNS.

Microscopic exam: Looking at a substance under the microscope. For example, in urine, the sample is spun and viewed under 40x magnification. This can confirm and quantify any suspicion of blood, pus, bacteria, or other substances suspected from the history.

Microscopic hematuria: Blood in the urine that is not visible to the naked eye. The presence of at least three red blood cells (RBCs) per 40x magnification under a microscope in the absence of a urinary tract infection qualifies for the diagnosis according to the American Urological Association guidelines.

Microscopic polyangiitis: A systemic vasculitis affecting small- and medium-sized blood vessels associated with the autoantibody, ANCA.

Migraine headache: A type of headache that can cause throbbing pain, often accompanied by nausea, vomiting, and extreme sensitivity to light or sound.

Mindfulness: A therapeutic strategy of focusing one's awareness on the present moment, acknowledging and accepting one's feelings, thoughts, and bodily sensations.

Mindfulness-based therapy/training/treatment: Therapy building non-judgmental awareness of thoughts and feelings.

Minimally invasive procedures: Surgical techniques that either use natural orifices or access the surgical site using small incisions (or shallow incisions in dermatologic surgery).

Mirror therapy: A rehabilitation technique typically used when a limb is impaired after a stroke. A mirror is placed between the arms or legs giving the illusion of normal movement in the affected limb, which allows stimulation of different brain regions for movement, sensation, and pain.

Mittelschmerz: Pain that occurs at the time of ovarian cyst rupture during natural ovulation.

Mnemonic: A memory aid.

Molecular level: The structure and function of biology at the level of DNA, RNA, and protein molecules.

Monoamine oxidase inhibitors (MAOIs): Class of drugs that include certain antidepressant medications whose mechanism involves inhibiting the activity of monoamine oxidase enzymes.

Monoclonal antibody therapy: A form of immunotherapy that uses monoclonal antibodies to bind specifically to certain cells or proteins in the hopes that a person's immune system will now attack those cells.

Monoclonal gammopathy: A condition in which a person makes an abnormal amount of a certain protein, which is then stored in the bone marrow.

Morphine (MS Contin®, Roxanol®): Potent opioid (narcotic) pain medication; highly addictive and typically used only in acute pain.

Magnetic resonance angiography (MRA): A magnetic resonance imaging (MRI) study looking at the blood vessels, often including intravenous dye injected to better delineate the vessels.

Mucinous: Containing mucus.

Mucopexy: Excision of anal lining tissue (mucosal surface) that has moved outward through the anus.

Multi-modal therapy: Taking advantage of the properties of different classes of medications in combination with behavior changes, physical therapy, and/or procedures, if indicated, to target pain or other problems.

Multi-modal treatment: Using more than one modality for treatment (such as physical therapy, medications, or behavioral therapy).

Multi-molecular immunofluorescent analysis: A technique to detect antibodies.

Multiple sclerosis: A potentially disabling disease of the brain and spinal cord in which the immune system attacks the protective sheath (myelin) that covers nerve fibers and causes communication problems between your brain and the rest of your body.

Muscles: Tissue in the body that functions to contract. The three types of muscle are cardiac (heart) muscle, skeletal muscle (e.g., arms and legs), and smooth muscle (e.g., in bowel bladder and blood vessels).

Muscle biopsy: Sampling of a small piece of muscle taken for microscopic analysis.

Muscle relaxant: A class of medications used to treat muscle spasms.

Muscle spasm: A sudden, involuntary contraction of one or more muscles.

Muscular dystrophy: A group of diseases in which abnormal genes affect the production of proteins needed for healthy muscle. This causes progressive weakness and loss of muscle function.

Musculoskeletal: *See* musculoskeletal system.

Musculoskeletal pain: Pain in the muscles, bones, ligaments, tendons, and nerves.

Musculoskeletal problem: A problem with muscles, bones, joints, connective tissue, skin, or nerves that leads to altered movements that adversely affect the body's function.

Musculoskeletal system: Body system relating to the muscles and skeleton and including muscles, joints, tendons, and bones.

Myalgia: Muscle pain, ache, or spasm.

Myasthenia gravis: An autoimmune disorder affecting nerve and muscle connections (receptors), which can be affected by certain medications. It is characterized by progressive voluntary muscle weakness.

Mycoplasma: *See* mycoplasma genitalium.

Mycoplasma genitalium: A genus of bacteria that lack a cell wall; this characteristic makes them naturally resistant to antibiotics that target cell wall synthesis (like the beta-lactam antibiotics).

Myelinated A-delta fibers: Known as the "fast pain fibers," these are thin, 2- to 5-μm diameter nerves that have a thin layer of myelin, which is an insulating material. They carry cold, pressure, and acute pain signals to the spinal cord and brain.

Myelomeningocele: The most serious form of spina bifida (divided spine) in which a baby is born with the spinal cord and nerves developing in a fluid-filled sac outside the body overlying the spine. Below the level of the sac, the baby will have loss of muscle strength and sensation.

Myofascial pain/myofascial dysfunction: A chronic and painful condition that affects the fascia (connective tissue that covers the muscles).

Myofascial release: A specialized massage to treat pain by stretching scars, muscles, and skin.

Myomectomy: Surgical procedure to remove uterine fibroids.

Myopathy: A disease of muscle in which the muscle fibers do not function properly, resulting in weakness.

Myotomes: A group of muscles innervated by the ventral (front) root of a single spinal nerve. Examining muscle function can help determine the level of a nerve problem.

Naproxen (Aleve®, Anaprox®, Naprelan®, Naprosyn®): Non-steroidal anti-inflammatory medication used to relieve pain and swelling and to reduce joint stiffness. It works by blocking prostaglandin production, which plays a role in pain and inflammation.

National Institutes of Health (NIH): A part of the United States Department of Health and Human Services; the nation's medical research agency, which funds a great deal of research in the United States to improve health. (*See* https://www.nih.gov/about-nih.)

Nerves: Bundles of fibers that carry messages (nerve impulses) toward the brain and spinal cord and out toward the extremities, skin, and organs.

Nerve block: Infiltration (placement) of a local anesthetic around a peripheral nerve to produce anesthesia in the area supplied by the nerve.

Nerve conduction studies: Testing that measures the conduction of electrical impulses through a specific nerve.

Nerve entrapment: Compression of a nerve by the surrounding tissues that can lead to abnormal functioning of the nerve.

Nerve radiculopathy: Pain, weakness, numbness, and tingling from pinching of a nerve root as it exits the spinal column.

Nerve root: A nerve root is the part of the nerve that branches off from the spinal cord and enters the intervertebral foramen (the bony opening between adjacent vertebrae). Most spinal levels have two paired nerve roots on each side per level: The anterior (ventral, front) root carries motor (movement) signals from the brain out to the muscles, and the posterior (dorsal, back) root carries sensory signals from the skin and other structures to the brain. The anterior root and posterior root combine at each spinal level to form the spinal nerve, which exits the spinal canal through the intervertebral foramen.

Neural tissue: The components of the peripheral and central nervous system.

Neurectomy: Partial or complete surgical removal of a nerve.

Neurogenic pelvic pain: Pelvic pain caused by nervous system dysfunction.

Neuroinflammatory disease: Inflammation of the nervous system.

Neurologic/neurological: Referring to the brain, spinal cord, and peripheral (somatic and autonomic) nerves.

Neurological obstruction: Obstruction (blockage) that is due to abnormal nerve impulses to a muscle, for example the external urethral sphincter at the exit of the bladder.

Neurologist: A physician who specializes in diseases and function of the brain, spinal cord, and peripheral (somatic and autonomic) nerves.

Neurology: The field of medicine having to do with diseases and function of the brain, spinal cord, and peripheral (somatic and autonomic) nerves.

Neurolytic: Deliberately injuring a nerve.

Neurolytic injection: An injection intended to decrease function of a nerve by applying an irritant.

Neuroma: A tumor, tangle, or mass growing from a nerve that usually consists of nerve fibers and often is painful.

Neuromodulator/neuromodulatory: Anything that alters the transmission of a nerve impulse. This can be a medication, an internally produced hormone or peptide, or an electrical stimulator.

Neuromuscular junction: The union of a nerve fiber and the muscle fiber membrane.

Neurons: Nerve cells; the functional units of nervous tissue, which transmit and receive electrical and chemical impulses.

Neuropathic pain: A complex, chronic pain state that usually is accompanied by tissue injury. With neuropathic pain, the nerve fibers themselves might be damaged, dysfunctional, or injured. These damaged nerve fibers of the somatosensory nervous system send incorrect signals to other pain centers.

Neuropathy/neuropathies: Disease or dysfunction of one or more nerves causing pain, weakness, or numbness.

Neurophysiological: Relating to the study of nervous system function.

Neuroplasticity: The ability of the brain to make new connections and continually adapt to new information.

Neurosurgeon: A surgeon who, after rigorous training, specializes in surgery on the nervous system, especially the brain and spinal cord.

Neurotoxin: A poison that is destructive to nerve tissue.

Neurotransmitter: A natural chemical substance, such as acetylcholine or norepinephrine, that is released at the end of a nerve terminal, traveling across the synapse or junction to a nerve or muscle cell to transmit a signal.

Nociception: The processing of information about one's environment, starting from peripheral nerves and moving to the spinal cord and then to the brain.

Nocturia: Waking up to urinate one or more times per night.

Non-pharmacologic approaches: Approaches to a health problem that do not involve taking a medication.

Non-pharmacologic treatments: Treatments that do not involve taking a medication.

Non-steroidal anti-inflammatory drugs (NSAIDs): Aspirin-like medications that reduce inflammation, and therefore pain related to inflammation, which can arise from injured tissue.

Non-union: A rare case in which a fracture does not heal at all.

Norethindrone: An oral progesterone-only hormonal medication that is used to suppress the ovaries, such as for birth control.

Nortriptyline (Pamelor®): A tricyclic antidepressant and nerve pain medication.

Nucleus pulposus: Inner core of intervertebral disc.

Neuro-inflammation/neuroinflammation: Inflammation of nervous tissue, especially within the brain or spinal cord that occurs secondary to nerve injury, infection, trauma, autoimmune disorders, or toxic agents.

Nutcracker syndrome: A rare disorder that results from the compression of the left renal (kidney) vein, most commonly between the superior mesenteric artery and aorta. Less commonly, the left renal vein can be compressed between the aorta and the vertebral body.

Obesity: A disease in which the body accumulates too much body fat because of sustained overeating, underactivity, pregnancy, genetic, or other conditions. Obesity increases the risk of diseases, such as diabetes, heart disease, stroke, hypertension, osteoarthritis, infertility, some cancers, and sleep apnea.

Obstetrician/gynecologist (obstetrics/gynecology, OB-GYN): A doctor who specializes in female reproductive health including cancers of the female reproductive organs, sex, pregnancy, childbirth, lactation, sexually transmitted infections, and infertility.

Obturator hernia: A rare but serious condition characterized by the protrusion of the bowel through the obturator canal; reaching a correct diagnosis is difficult because of non-specific symptoms.

Obturator internus muscle (internal obturator muscle): A hip rotator muscle. It originates on the inner surface of the obturator membrane, which lines the inner surface of the pelvis (as well as other pelvic structures) and then exits the pelvis; it stabilizes the hip during flexion and extension.

Obturator nerve: Nerve originating from the second, third, and fourth lumbar levels of the spinal cord, which runs through the pelvis down the medial aspect of the thigh to the knee. It innervates the leg adductors, gracilis muscles, hip joint, and knee joint. Impingement or injury of the obturator nerve often presents as pain, numbness, or allodynia of the inner thigh as well as some hip instability.

Occupational therapists: The professionals who practice occupational therapy (OTs).

Occupational therapy (OT): Professional, personalized guidance aimed at improving a patient's ability to participate in everyday activities when his/her ability might be limited because of injury, illness, or disability.

Off-label: Prescription of a drug or treatment option for a condition other than for which it was officially approved.

OnabotulinumtoxinA (Botox®): One form of botulinum toxin, which is a medication injected directly into muscles to prevent muscle contraction.

Oophorectomy: The surgical removal of an ovary or ovaries.

Opioids: The word "opioid" comes from "opium," as this class of prescription pain medications stimulates the same receptors on brain cells as do opium and heroin. These are natural, semi-synthetic, and synthetic medications. Prescribed opiates include oxycodone (OxyContin®), hydrocodone (Vicodin®), codeine, morphine, hydromorphone, tramadol, fentanyl, and many others.

Opium (Paregoric®, B and O Suppositories): Potent narcotic pain medication. This was traditionally an illegal drug of the old world.

Oral: Related to the mouth. In medicine, it refers to method of delivery; for example, medicine taken orally is ingested through the mouth.

Oral contraceptive pills (OCPs): Hormonal medication with progesterone (and usually estrogen) that when taken orally will suppress the ovary's natural production of those hormones.

Orchitis: Testis infection, which might be accompanied by redness, enlargement, and fever.

Organic compound: Compound containing carbon and bonding via covalent bonds to at least one non-carbon atom (hydrogen, oxygen, and nitrogen). Historically, organic compounds referred to compounds with living origins. Some carbon-containing compounds, such as carbides, carbonates, and cyanides, are considered inorganic.

Orgasm: A feeling of intense pleasure that happens at the peak of sexual activity; also referred to as "climax." Physiologically, the heart might beat faster, breathing might change, and the genital muscles contract rhythmically. In anatomic males, this is often accompanied by ejaculation. In anatomic females, clear fluid may be released from the Skene's glands next to the urethra during orgasm.

Orthopedic: Related to the disease or treatment of the musculoskeletal system, including through surgery.

Orthopedic certified specialist: Board certification in orthopedic physical therapy with advanced knowledge and experience in orthopedic health.

Orthopedist: A physician who corrects congenital or functional abnormalities of the bones with surgery, casting, and bracing.

Osteitis: Inflammation of a bone.

Osteitis condensans ilii: A condition that commonly presents with chronic pelvic pain and lower-back pain. It is thought to result from mechanical stress across the pelvic joints causing inflammation, especially in women before and/or after childbirth. The condition is usually self-limiting and resolves on its own.

Osteoarthritis (OA): A chronic condition in which the cartilage capping and cushioning the bone wears down because of overuse.

Osteomyelitis: An infection of the bone.

Osteopath: A doctor of osteopathy (DO) who practices a branch of medicine that addresses all disease, but emphasizes the treatment of medical disorders through the manipulation and massage of the bones, joints, and muscles.

Osteoporosis: A chronic, treatable, condition characterized by low bone density and quality, which increases the risk of fractures. Osteoporosis most commonly affects older white and Asian women.

Ostium: A small opening.

Ovarian cyst: Fluid-filled structures (sac or pockets) found in or on the surface of the ovaries.

Ovarian cyst rupture: The bursting of an ovarian cyst, releasing its fluid, often associated with sudden pain.

Ovarian cystectomy: Surgical removal of ovarian cysts while preserving the rest of the ovary.

Ovarian torsion: An abnormal twisting of the ovary that can cause acute pain and ischemia (lack of blood flow). Without intervention, the ovary can die.

Ovarian vein reflux: A disorder in which blood in the ovarian vein flows opposite its normal upward direction, downward from the renal vein or inferior vena cava toward the pelvis. Ovarian vein reflux is one cause of pelvic pain from venous varicosities.

Ovarian venous abnormality: A disturbance of the vasculature of the ovaries.

Ovaries: Pair of female reproductive organs that produce sex hormones, eggs, and fertilization.

Ovary: *See* ovaries.

Overactive bladder syndrome (OAB): Urinary diagnosis based on symptoms (in the absence of infection or other explanation) of urinary urgency accompanied by daytime frequency and/or nocturia or urinary incontinence.

Ovulation: Discharge of ova or ovules from the ovary. This occurs mid-cycle and allows for conception of pregnancy.

Oxycodone (Oxycontin®): An oral opiate and habit-forming pain medication.

Oxygenated blood: Also known as arterial blood, oxygenated blood is bright red because of oxygen bound to iron on the heme protein subunit of red blood cells. Oxygenated blood exits the lungs via the pulmonary vein into the left atrium of the heart before being pumped into arteries throughout the body from the left ventricle of the heart.

Paget's disease: A disease of the bones, which most commonly occurs in the pelvis, skull, spine, and legs and in which bones can become fragile and misshapen.

Pain catastrophizing: Engaging in a set of negative thoughts or emotions during an actual or anticipated painful experience. People who have high levels of pain catastrophizing tend to ruminate (think over and over about) about the pain and feel helpless when attempting to cope with their pain.

Pain diary: The daily recording of activities and descriptions of pain experienced, used to analyze patterns and assess treatment effectiveness.

Pain psychologist: Since pain is defined as both a negative sensory and emotional experience, the pain psychologist works with the emotional side of pain, coping with thoughts, feelings and behaviors that accompany pain.

Pain signals: The sensory nervous system transmission pathways in the brain, spinal cord, and periphery.

Pain specialist: A provider who specializes in preventing, treating, reducing, and managing pain.

Palpation: Examination by the touch of hands.

Palpitations: Feeling of a briefly irregular heartbeat, especially one that feels too hard or too fast, like the heart "skipping a beat."

Pap smear: Abbreviation for the Papanicolaou test, in which cells are collected from the cervix (the tip of the uterus at the top of the vagina) to look for cancer.

Papules: A small, elevated area of skin that is often inflamed or accompanies a rash. Papules do not contain pus.

Parabens: A class of widely used preservatives in cosmetic and pharmaceutical products.

Parasympathetic nervous system: The nervous system that innervates the digestive system.

Paresthesia: A dermal sensation on the skin, such as a tingling, pricking, chilling, burning, or numb sensation.

Parkinson's disease: A neurological disorder, often accompanied by tremors, which can progress to severe stiffness and loss of balance requiring around-the-clock care.

Pediatric pain physician: A provider who specializes in preventing, treating, reducing, and managing pain in children.

Pediatrics: The field of medicine related to the care of those 18 or younger.

Pediatrician: A medical provider who practices the field of medicine related to the care of children, typically people 18 or younger.

Pelvic/genitourinary examination: An exam of the external reproductive organs and anus, and internal exam of the vagina, cervix, and rectum in those with female anatomy, and an internal exam of the rectum and prostate in those with male anatomy.

Pelvic congestion syndrome (PCS): Dilated veins in the pelvis that cause pooling of blood in pelvic organs.

Pelvic floor/pelvic floor muscles (PFMs): A complex group of muscles in the pelvis that both support the organs of the pelvis and abdomen and help one control the bladder and bowels. The PFMs include the levator ani muscles (pubococcygeus, puborectalis, and iliococcygeus), coccygeus muscles. The urethral and anal sphincters, the more surface-level urogenital diaphragm, and the piriformis muscles are intimately related.

Pelvic floor physical therapy/physiotherapy (PFPT): Physical therapy related to the pelvic floor muscles, often employed as a strategy to treat chronic pelvic pain, incontinence, difficulty urinating or defecating, and painful intercourse.

Pelvic girdle: The combination of bones, joints, and ligaments of the pelvis.

Pelvic girdle pain (PGP)/pregnancy-related pelvic girdle pain (PRPGP): Pain related to pregnancy felt in the three pelvic joints, lower back, hips, or thighs. PRPGP is often complex and hard to diagnose. It can begin in the first trimester and it affects one in four women during pregnancy.

Pelvic inflammatory disease (PID): Pelvic infections of the uterus, fallopian tubes, and ovaries that usually begin with bacteria entering the uterus through the vagina.

Pelvic pain: An unpleasant sensory and emotional experience associated with actual or potential tissue damage. This pain affects the lower abdomen and pelvis and the area between the belly button and the pubic bone down to the tailbone.

Pelvic rehabilitation practitioner certificate (PRPC): Special training for physical therapists, doctors of osteopathy, occupational therapists, and other professions that identifies the bearer as a specialist in the pelvic health field, covering both women's and men's pelvic health throughout the life cycle.

Pelvic ring fracture: A very serious injury with fractures to two or more parts of the pelvic ring. In unstable, compound fractures, the mortality rate approaches 50%.

Pelvic venous disorder/disease: Pelvic pain of venous vascular origin, such as pelvic congestion syndrome caused by venous insufficiency, nutcracker syndrome, and May-Thurner Syndrome. Pelvic venous disorders are often hard to diagnose because of their non-specific symptoms and they are affected by levels of female hormones.

Pelvic venous hypertension: Increased venous pressure in the pelvic veins. Pelvic venous hypertension is a potential cause of chronic pelvic pain.

Penile-brachial index (PBI): A test that compares the blood pressure in the dorsal penile arteries to the blood pressure in the brachial arteries (blood pressure in the arm) that can predict vascular (blood vessel) disease elsewhere in the body when the ratio is low.

Penis: The external male organ (also called "prick", "dick", "cock", "willy", "dong" and other colloquial terms) with two erectile chambers—the corpora cavernosa—surrounded by the tunica albuginea, nerves, veins, arteries, and one urinary channel leading from the bladder to the glans (head), called the urethra. Foreskin covers the glans in men who have not been circumcised.

Perianal Paget's disease: A slow growing rare cancer of the skin around the anus, sometimes resembling a rash. It can become thickened, scaled, and itchy.

Perineal: The area between the anus and the scrotum or vulva.

Perineal approach: Surgical treatment of pelvic surgical disease, such as rectal prolapse, via an incision on the perineum (the area between the anus and the vulva or scrotum). In rectal prolapse, the perineal approach trades higher recurrence rate for lower perioperative and postoperative morbidity.

Perineum: The area between the anus and the scrotum or vulva.

Peripheral artery disease (PAD): Narrowing of the arteries far (peripheral) from the heart, most commonly caused by atherosclerosis.

Peripheral nerves: The nerves that connect the spinal cord and brain (central nervous system) to the limbs and organs.

Peripheral nervous system (PNS): Every part of the nervous system outside the central nervous system, such as the spinal nerves.

Peripheral neuropathy: Problems with the small peripheral nerves.

Peripheral sensitization: A natural protective process that increases local pain sensitivity after an injury.

Peripheral spondyloarthritis (pSpA): A type of spondyloarthritic (SpA) disorder presenting with joint inflammation other than in the spine or sacroiliac joint, especially in the arms and legs. This can lead to pelvic pain if a gait abnormality leads to pelvic floor muscle tension.

Perirectal fissure: *See* anal fissure.

Perirectal fistula: *See* anal fistula.

Peritoneal cavity: Abdominal space bound by thin membranes that contains the intestines, stomach, and liver.

Peritoneum: Membrane lining the abdominal cavity and covering the abdominal organs.

Peyronie's disease: A scarring of the elastic sheath surrounding the erectile tissue (the tunica albuginea) that is usually secondary to penile trauma.

Pfannensteil (Cesarean section) incision: A horizontal bikini-line incision along the top of the pubic hair. Under the surface, the incision is vertical to prevent cutting of the rectus muscles.

PFM biofeedback: Training that increases awareness of pelvic floor muscle (PFM) activity and how to contract and relax them.

Phantom limb pain (PLP): Pain that persists in the location of a limb even after it is no longer attached.

Phantom pain: Pain that persists in the location of an organ after it has been removed.

Phenazopyridine (Pyridium®): A urinary anesthetic that turns the urine orange. It can mask the symptoms of a urinary tract infection. Long-term use can discolor the skin and nails and can cause organ dysfunction.

Phenelzine (Nardil®): A monoamine oxidase inhibitor antidepressant medication.

Physiatrist/physical medicine and rehabilitation (PMR, Physiatry) specialist: Practitioner of physiatry, a branch of medicine that aims to enhance and restore functional ability and quality of life to people with physical impairments or disabilities.

Physical Medicine and Rehabilitation (PMR): Also known as Physiatry, a branch of medicine that aims to enhance and restore functional ability and quality of life to people with physical impairments or disabilities.

Physical therapist (PT): Movement expert who performs hands-on care and who educates and prescribes exercise.

Physical therapy (PT): Hands-on treatment and education techniques designed to promote the ability to move, reduce pain, restore function, and prevent disability.

Physical therapy (PT) exam: The physical exam performed by a physical therapist. The exam will be tailored to the parts of the body involved.

Physiologic changes: Natural changes to the body based on the way it works.

Physiological: Related to normal bodily function.

Physiotherapy: *See* physical therapy.

Pia mater: The delicate innermost membrane enveloping the brain and spinal cord.

Piriformis: A hip rotator muscle.

Piroxicam (Feldene®): Non-steroidal anti-inflammatory medication used for pain that is typically associated with arthritis or inflammation.

Plasticity: Capacity for adaptation or change.

Platelet: Tiny blood cells that form clots to stop bleeding.

Platelet-rich plasma (PRP): Also known as autologous conditioned plasma, PRP is a concentrate of protein from whole blood with the red blood cells removed by a centrifuge; it is used to accelerate healing.

Platelets: *See* platelet.

Plicated: In surgery, this refers to tissue narrowed or folded like a fan using sutures.

Podcast: A live or recorded event available only in audio format.

Polyarteritis nodosa (PAN): A rare, systemic, vasculitis that is characterized by necrotizing (rotting) inflammation through the entire arterial wall, which can result in a "rosary sign." Early treatment greatly reduces the five-year mortality rate. Advanced cases can result in heart attack, stroke, and kidney failure.

Polycystic ovarian syndrome (PCOS): A condition in women in which a hormonal imbalance—often an overproduction of male hormones—leads to improper maturation of eggs or failed ovulation. PCOS can lead to infertility, growth of ovarian cysts, acne, male-pattern hair growth, baldness, diabetes, and heart disease, among other things.

Polymyalgia rheumatica (PMR): An inflammatory disorder that causes widespread aching, stiffness, and flu-like symptoms.

Polyp: An abnormal, usually benign, growth on mucus membranes.

Polyradiculopathy: Damage to multiple nerve roots emanating from the spinal cord. *See* radiculopathy.

Positive: In medicine, a "positive" test means one that demonstrates the condition or marker for which it is testing.

Positive pregnancy test: A test of the urine or blood that shows the presence of hormone beta human chorionic gonadotropic (HCG), which indicates pregnancy.

Posterior femoral cutaneous nerve/inferior cluneal nerve: A sensory branch of the sacral plexus arising from the sacral first, second, and third nerves. It supplies the skin of the posterior thigh, buttocks, and the posterior scrotum/labia. The inferior cluneal nerve is a gluteal (buttocks) branch of this nerve.

Posterior pelvic pain provocation test: A test that looks for sacroiliac joint dysfunction. The examiner's hand supports the sacrum while the leg is bent and the femur is pushed downward, which places force on the sacroiliac joint.

Posterior tibial nerve stimulator (PTNS): A device that allows indirect stimulation to the nerves of the bladder and pelvic floor by stimulating the posterior tibial nerve at the level of the ankle.

Post-laminectomy syndrome: The situation in which a person continues to feel back pain after undergoing a laminectomy (removal of part of a vertebra to reduce pressure on the nerves in the spinal cord).

Post-menopausal: The stage of life of the adult woman after menopause.

Post-partum: The state of the mother after the birth of a child.

Post-void residual: The amount of urine in the bladder after voiding measurable by ultrasound or a quick passage of a catheter.

Pranayama: Conscious breathing in yoga that helps to decrease heart rate and blood pressure and relax pelvic floor muscles (PFMs).

Prednisone (Deltasone®, Rayos®, Orasone®): A corticosteroid medication that reduces inflammation in the body and suppresses the immune system.

Pregabalin (Lyrica®): A pain medication used to treat nerve and muscle pain (for example, neuropathic pain, fibromyalgia) as well as seizures. It works by preventing the release of neurotransmitters.

Primary care physician/provider (PCP): A physician who provides both the first contact for a person with an undiagnosed health concern as well as continuing care of varied medical conditions, not limited by cause, organ system, or diagnosis.

Probiotics: Live microorganisms that can provide health benefits when consumed, generally by improving the gut flora.

Proctalgia fugax: A functional anorectal disorder characterized by severe, intermittent, self-limited episodes of rectal pain.

Proctodynia: Episodic rectal pain caused by spasm of the levator ani muscles, also known as "levator syndrome."

Proctoscope: A smooth instrument used to allow a view into the rectum through the anus.

Proctoscopy: A procedure in which the examiner looks into the rectum through the anus using a smooth instrument.

Progesterone/progestine: A female hormone, the principal hormone that prepares the uterus to receive and sustain fertilized eggs.

Progesterone-only birth control: This hormonal medication works by preventing the release of eggs from the ovaries (ovulation) and by changing the cervical mucus and the lining of the uterus. It suppresses estrogen production and can reduce the growth of endometriosis.

Progesterone-releasing intrauterine device (IUD): An implanted, removable device that delivers progesterone directly to the lining of the uterus, preventing pregnancy and lessening the symptoms of endometriosis.

Progressive muscle relaxation training: A muscle relaxation technique often employed with other forms of therapy that involves alternating tension and relaxation in all the body's major muscle groups.

Progressive neuromuscular disorders: Disorders that affect the nerves serving the skeletal (voluntary) muscles.

Prolapse: A condition in which organs fall or slip out of place.

Prolotherapy: A regenerative medicine injection technique in which small volumes of an irritant solution, such as dextrose, are injected to the site of painful muscles, tendon insertions, joints, and ligaments to promote the growth of normal cells and tissues.

Propylene glycol: A substance commonly used as a food additive in cosmetic or hygiene products. It can be used as anti-freeze. It can be found in creams and lotions and can be irritating to some people.

Prostaglandins: A hormone-like substance that participates in functions such as the contraction and relaxation of smooth muscle, dilation and constriction of blood vessels, control of blood pressure, and control of inflammation.

Prostate: The prostate is an organ specific to male anatomy at the base the bladder and surrounding the urethra (the tube that expels urine). The prostate contributes to the fluid contents of semen and contains nerves that aid in sexual pleasure.

Prostatitis: Inflammation of the prostate, which can be caused by infection.

Prostatodynia: Prostate pain.

Proximal: Situated nearer to the center of the body or the point of attachment.

Pruritis ani: Intense chronic itching affecting peri-anal skin.

Psoas dysfunction: Injury or spasm of the psoas muscle, a long muscle stabilizing the spine through the pelvis to the femur. It can lead to dysfunction of the diaphragm, which must compensate for its abnormal contractions.

Psoriasis: An immune-mediated disease that causes skin cells to multiply at an abnormally fast rate. This leads to bumpy red patches with white scales.

Psoriatic arthritis: An inflammatory disease of the joints and sites of tendon/ligament connection to bone in people who also have psoriasis, a skin condition involving red patches of skin topped with silvery scales.

Psychiatrist: A medical doctor (an MD or DO) who specializes in mental health, including substance use disorders.

Psychologist: A health care provider who studies normal and abnormal mental states and perceptual, cognitive, emotional, and social processes, and behavior; psychologists experiment with and observe, interpret, and record how individuals relate to one another and to their environments. They assess, diagnose, and treat individuals suffering from chronic pain, psychological distress, and mental illness. They perform psychotherapy and develop treatment plans.

Psychosocial: Having to do with the interrelationship of social factors and individual thoughts and behaviors.

Psychosocial history: Information about the interrelationship of social factors and individual thoughts and behaviors.

Psychotherapy: Treatment of psychological distress and mental illness by talking with a psychiatrist, psychologist, or other mental health professional.

Pubic bone: The very front part of the pelvic bone that can be felt at the lowest part of the pelvis under the pubic hair.

Pubic symphysis: Anterior joint of the pelvis where the right and left hemi-pelvis meet.

Pubic symphysis diastasis: A disorder of the widening of the pubic symphysis, sometimes occurring during vaginal delivery.

Pubococcygeal muscle: Part of the levator ani muscle that starts at the pubic bone and ends (inserts) at the coccyx. It helps to support the pelvic organs.

Pudendal nerve: A nerve that supplies the external genitalia, the skin of the perineum, and the anal sphincters. It derives from the second, third, and fourth sacral nerves and can be entrapped at various points, leading to pain.

Pudendal nerve stimulator: Experimental pain-reduction treatment targeting the pudendal nerve by producing a gentle vibration that acts like "white noise." While not approved by the Food and Drug Administration (FDA) for the treatment of pain, small studies have shown some benefit for people with chronic pelvic pain. (Sacral nerve stimulators are FDA-approved for urinary problems and fecal incontinence.)

Pudendal neuralgia/neuropathy: A disorder of the pudendal nerve that can lead to chronic pelvic pain.

Pulse generator: An electronic circuit or a piece of electronic test equipment used to generate electrical signals.

Purpura: Patchy purplish discoloration of the skin, which arises from extravasation of blood into the skin or mucous membranes.

Pustules: A blister or pimple on the skin containing pus.

Quadratus lumborum: A deep abdominal muscle; it is found in your lower back between the top of your pelvis and your lowest rib.

Questionnaires: Standardized questionnaires, validated measures, and patient-reported outcome measures (PROMs) are all ways of describing a questionnaire that has been tested for assessing symptoms based on patient report.

Radiate: To spread.

Radiculopathy: Irritation or injury of a nerve root emanating from the spinal cord that can cause pain, numbness, or weakness.

Radiofrequency ablation/lesioning (RFA/RFL): An interventional procedure performed on nerves including peripheral and central nerves to relieve pain by permanent disruption of nerve pathways.

Radiology: The field employing imaging methodologies to diagnose and manage patients and provide therapeutic options. Physicians practicing in the field of radiology specialize in diagnostic radiology, interventional radiology, or radiation oncology.

Range of motion: The extent of movement of a joint.

Range-of-motion exercises: Exercises aimed at improving movement of a specific joint, which is dependent on bone surfaces, ligaments, tendons, and muscles.

Raynaud's phenomenon: A disorder in which blood vessels constrict when encountering cold temperatures (or high stress), which leads to painful decreased blood flow to the skin. Fingertips and/or toes change in color from normal skin tone to white, blue, and red.

Reactive arthritis: Inflammation (such as joint pain, eye irritation, and swelling) that is reacting to an infection in another part of the body, such as the intestines, genitals, or urinary tract.

Receptor: A molecule, such as a protein, on or inside a cell that has an affinity for a specific chemical group, molecule, or organism.

Rectal cancer: A malignant growth of the tissues of the rectum.

Rectal prolapse: A condition in which the structures of the anal canal or rectum slip outward through the anus. It can involve the lining (mucosal prolapse) or the complete rectal wall (full-thickness rectal prolapse). It is not to be confused with a rectocele, which is a vaginal prolapse involving the rectal wall.

Rectocele (posterior pelvic organ prolapse): A condition in which the rectum drops (prolapses or herniates) into the space of the vagina through a weakening between these side-by-side organs. It can bulge out the vaginal entrance and obstruct defecation by kinking the rectum. Rectocele should not be confused with rectal prolapse, in which the structures of the anal canal or rectum slip outward through the anus.

Rectovaginal fistula: An abnormal epithelialized connection between the rectum and the vagina that is often accompanied by stool or flatus passing into the vagina.

Rectum: The distal (closest to the anus and perineum) portion of the large intestine.

Rectus femoris muscle: Straight quadriceps muscle of the thigh that helps with knee and hip flexion.

Red blood cells (RBCs): Cells containing hemoglobin that are the main transporter of oxygen in vertebrates.

Referred pain: Pain perceived at a location other than the site of the painful stimulus/origin.

Reflux: Abnormal backward passage of fluid—for example from the bladder into the ureter or from the stomach into the esophagus.

Rehabilitation specialist: A health care professional (for example a physical or occupational therapist) who helps people recover from an illness or injury, with the goal of recovering prior functions.

Reinnervation: Restoration of nerve supply to a part of the body where it has been lost. Sometime this happens with time after an injury and sometimes it is facilitated by surgery.

Reiter's syndrome: A seronegative spondyloarthritis (see definition) usually triggered by a bacterial infection presenting with a classic triad of inflammation in the eyes, joints, and urethra.

Relaxation therapist: Someone who knows how to quiet the mind for the purpose of relaxation and stress relief.

Relaxation training: A method or set of strategies taught to help a person relax, reduce stress, anxiety, or pain.

Renal vein: Veins carrying filtered blood from the kidney into the inferior vena cava.

Resectoscope: A tubular endoscope (surgical scope) through which bladder tumors or bulky prostates can be worked on with special resecting/removing instruments.

Response-focused emotion regulation: A form of emotion management performed during an emotional experience by intensifying, diminishing, or prolonging the emotional response.

Retrograde ejaculation: Flow of ejaculate back into the bladder during ejaculation that is caused by a relaxed bladder neck.

Retrograde pyelogram: In this procedure, contrast is injected into the ureter through a telescope, allowing an "inside X-ray" of the ureter. The contrast allows the ureters and kidneys to be seen more easily on X-rays.

Revascularization: Surgical procedure done to improve blood flow to a body part.

Rheumatoid arthritis (RA): A systemic, autoimmune disorder in which the immune system attacks the synovium (tissue lining the joints). RA can present with joint pain, lung disease, rheumatoid nodules, and elevated levels of rheumatoid factor (RF) in the blood.

Rheumatoid factor (RF): Autoantibodies produced by the immune system. Usually, they are composed of immunoglobulin M (IgM) and are associated with various autoimmune diseases, such as rheumatoid arthritis. A positive or negative test is insufficient to diagnose rheumatoid arthritis.

Rheumatoid nodules: Firm lumps that form beneath the skin as a common symptom of rheumatoid arthritis.

Rheumatologic disease/disorder: Medical conditions of the joints, muscles, ligaments, and tendons. Most rheumatologic diseases present with pain due to inflammation.

Rheumatologic testing: A variety of tests to identify the underlying cause of a person's symptoms, and to diagnose systemic inflammatory diseases and musculoskeletal conditions.

Rheumatologic: Related to the diagnosis and management of rheumatic diseases, such as the joints, soft tissues, and connective tissues.

Rheumatologist: A doctor who specializes in musculoskeletal and rheumatologic diseases, such as rheumatoid arthritis.

S1 nerve root: Compression or injury to the S1 nerve root can present as pain or numbness on the external aspect of the posterior thigh, calf, leg, and the exterior aspect of the foot. S1 nerve root entrapments can cause gait disturbances and loss of ankle stability.

S2 nerve root: Compression or injury to the S2 nerve root may present as pain or numbness on the internal half of the posterior thigh, calf, leg, internal surface of the foot, vulva, clitoris (female), penis and scrotum (male), as well as urinary urgency and frequency, genital arousal disorders, erectile dysfunction, or lack of vaginal lubrication.

Sacral: Relating to the sacrum (triangular portion of the spine) found in the lower back.

Sacral nerve stimulator (SNS): Experimental pain-reduction treatment targeting the sacral nerve by producing a gentle vibration that acts like "white noise." While not approved by the Food and Drug Administration (FDA) for the treatment of pain, small studies have shown some benefit for people with chronic pelvic pain. (Sacral nerve stimulators are FDA-approved for urinary problems and fecal incontinence.)

Sacral neuromodulation: *See* sacral nerve stimulator.

Sacral plexus: A network of nerve fibers that supplies the skin and muscles of the pelvis and lower limbs.

Sacral tumor: Tumor found in the sacral region.

Sacroiliac joints (SIJs): The points at which the spine connects to the left and right pelvic bones where the lowest part of your back contact a chair.

Sacrum: The area above the tail bone.

Saddle anesthesia/dysesthesia: Loss of or abnormal sensation in buttock and groin regions. If sudden, this requires urgent evaluation.

Salivary gland: Gland responsible for producing saliva.

Salpingectomy: Surgical removal of the fallopian tubes.

Saphenous-femoral junction/Saphenofemoral junction (SFJ): Where the saphenous vein and common femoral vein meet.

Sarcoidosis: A systemic and inflammatory disease in which granulomas form in the body, most typically in the lungs and lymph glands. It is a potential cause for small fiber polyneuropathy (SFPN).

Schistosomiasis: Schistosomiasis, also known as bilharzia, is a disease caused by parasitic worms that live in certain freshwater snails. It can be contracted from contact with contaminated freshwater. These worms are not found in the United States, but the infection has a significant effect on health worldwide, affecting the intestine, liver, lungs, nerves, prostate, seminal vesicles, and urinary bladder.

Schnitzler syndrome: A rheumatic condition that often presents with pelvic pain, hives, joint pain, fever, and enlarged lymph nodes. On a molecular level, Schnitzler syndrome is associated with a "monoclonal gammopathy."

Sciatic nerve: A pair of nerves running from the spinal cord in the lower back to the feet. Entrapment can cause pain, hip muscle weakness, difficulty walking, and a foot drop.

Scleroderma: A disorder in which the body is triggered by the immune system to produce and deposit too much collagen. This can cause skin tightening of the hands, especially the fingers, and kidney dysfunction, lung disease, difficulty swallowing, red thread-like lines in the skin, and Raynaud's phenomenon.

Sclerosants: Clotting agents and scarring materials used to treat venous diseases. Sclerosants can also be used to block venous reflux.

Sclerotherapy: A minimally invasive procedure where a sclerosant is injected into the vein or lymph vessel. Sclerotherapy is typically used to treat varicose veins and less serious hemorrhoids.

Scoliosis: A sideways curvature of the spine that occurs most often during the growth spurt just before puberty.

Scrotum: Sac of skin containing testes in men.

Sedative: A substance that depresses (slows down) central nervous system activity, reducing anxiety and inducing sleep.

Selective serotonin re-uptake inhibitors (SSRIs): A class of antidepressant medications that works by increasing levels of serotonin in the brain by blocking or delaying its re-uptake/re-absorption by nerves.

Self-catheterization: A small tube called a *"straight catheter"* is inserted via the urethra to empty the bladder. If performed by the person him or herself it is called self-catheterization. If by the clinic staff, provider, or caregiver, then intermittent straight catheterization. Abbreviations include CIC (clean intermittent catheterization) IC (intermittent catheterization), ISC (intermittent straight or self-catheterization), and SC (self-catheterization).

Self-efficacy: An individual's confidence in his or her ability to exert control over her motivation, behavior, and environment.

Semen: The thick whitish liquid elicited during ejaculation in men that is made up of sperm and fluid from the prostate, Cowper's glands, and seminal vesicles.

Seminal vesicles: Paired glands behind the prostate that produce 70%–85% of ejaculate, consisting of proteins, enzymes, fructose, mucus, vitamin C, flavins, phosphorylcholine, and prostaglandins. The fluid is alkaline and is thought to neutralize the acidic vaginal pH. The fluid follows the sperm and zinc-containing prostate fluid through the ejaculatory duct during ejaculation.

Sensory nerves: Also called afferent nerves, these nerves carry sensory information (pain, heat, temperature) toward the central nervous system.

Sensory neuropathies: Nerve malfunction affecting the small sensory nerves, for example diabetic neuropathy.

Sensory symptoms: A feeling of altered bodily sensation.

Sensory system: The system of nerves that carries sensory information (pain, heat, temperature) toward the central nervous system.

Sensory-discriminative component of pain: The location, nature, and intensity of a painful stimulus.

Septum: A dividing wall or membrane between bodily spaces—this can be normal as in the nasal septum or abnormal as in a vaginal septum.

Seronegative: In rheumatic diseases, seronegative refers to diseases where blood (serum) tests are negative for rheumatoid factor and ANA.

Seronegative Spondyloarthritis: A family of rheumatologic diseases that causes arthritis, involving inflammation at the site that ligaments and tendons attach to bones. They are called "seronegative" because the blood (serum) tests are negative for rheumatoid factor and ANA.

Serotonin: A monoamine neurotransmitter that contributes to feelings of well-being and happiness.

Serotonin norepinephrine re-uptake inhibitors (SNRIs): A class of antidepressant medications that works by increasing levels of serotonin and norepinephrine in the brain by blocking or delaying their re-uptake/re-absorption by nerves.

Serous adenomas: A benign cystic tumor which can occur in the ovary or other organs. Serous refers to the serosa or lining of the cyst, which produces a thin clear yellow fluid.

Serum: The yellow fluid portion of blood that does not contribute to blood clotting, including all non-clotting proteins, electrolytes, antibodies, antigens, and hormones, and excluding white blood cells (leukocytes), red blood cells (erythrocytes), platelets, and clotting factors.

Sex therapy: A psychiatrist, marriage or family therapist, psychologist, or clinical social worker specially trained in sex therapy methods. A "specialist" in sexual issues affecting psychological health or deriving from dynamics earlier in life.

Sexual abuse: Unwanted sexual activity, with perpetrators using force, making threats, or taking advantage of victims who are unable to give full consent.

Sexually transmitted infections (STIs): Infections that are passed from one person to another through genital contact with another's genitals or mouth.

Sexually transmitted infection (STI) testing: These tests look for infections that are sexually transmitted. They include blood tests, urine tests, and sometimes swab specimens taken from the genitals or suspicious lesions in the urogenital area.

Side effect profile: The secondary, unintended effects of a medication, usually referring to adverse effects.

Sigmoid colon (pelvic colon): The part of the large intestine that is closest to the anus.

Sigmoidoscopy: A procedure akin to colonoscopy in that it uses a thin flexible tube with a camera at the end. In sigmoidoscopy only the anus, rectum, and sigmoid colon are seen, as the scope is shorter.

Sign: Objective evidence of disease, such as an elevated temperature, redness, bleeding, or mass found by observation or a physical exam.

Single leg stance: The phase of walking in which the weight is on one leg.

Sitzmark study: A test that indicates whether a sluggish colon could be the cause of constipation.

Sjögren's syndrome: A disorder characterized by autoimmune destruction of the lacrimal (tear) and salivary (saliva) glands. The immune system may also attack joints, the thyroid gland, the kidneys, liver, lung, skin, and nerves. Sjögren's syndrome often presents with dry eyes and mouth, as well as with vaginal dryness and nerve pain.

Skeletal muscles: One of three major muscle types, the others being cardiac muscle and smooth muscle. It is a form of striated muscle tissue, which is under the voluntary control of the somatic nervous system. Most skeletal muscles are attached to bones by bundles of collagen fibers known as tendons.

Skene's glands: Glands located on the anterior surface of the vagina around the lower end of the urethra.

Skin barrier: Primarily the outer layers of the skin, the epidermis and its stratum corneum, use dead skin cells to form a barrier and protect against external threats, such as infectious agents, chemicals, and allergens. Internally, the skin helps to protects from loss of water from the body.

Small fiber neuropathy/small fiber polyneuropathy (SFPN): A condition characterized by severe pain that typically begins in the feet or hands.

Small intestine: Also called the small bowel, it is an organ in the gastrointestinal tract where most of the absorption of nutrients and minerals from food takes place. It lies between the stomach and large intestine and receives bile and pancreatic juice through the pancreatic duct to aid in digestion. It is typically 20 feet long and 1 inch in diameter.

Smooth muscle anatomy: Muscle that shows no cross stripes under microscopic magnification. It consists of narrow spindle-shaped cells with a single, centrally located nucleus. Unlike striated muscle, smooth muscle tissue contracts slowly and automatically.

Social media: Websites that allow users to share information (videos, text, images), including Facebook, Twitter, Instagram, Pinterest, and others.

Social network: A dedicated website that enables users to interact with each other by posting information, comments, messages, and images.

Soft tissue: Tissues such as muscles, fascia, fat, and joint membranes that connect, support, or surround other structures in the body.

Somatic nervous system: The part of the peripheral nervous system that carries motor (movement) and sensory information to and from the central nervous system. This system is made up of nerves that connect to the skin, the sensory organs (such as the eye), and the skeletal (voluntary) muscles.

Somatic pain: Pain that is characterized as well-localized, intermittent, or constant, and described as aching, gnawing, throbbing, or cramping.

Somatosensory: A part of the nervous system having to do with conscious perception within the muscles, joints, skin, and fascia of touch, pressure, pain, temperature, position, movement, and vibration.

Spastic diplegia: A disorder characterized by tightness of the hip adductors on both sides.

Spastic hemiplegia: A disorder characterized by tightness of the hip adductors on one side.

Spasticity: A disorder of increased muscle tone.

Specific identifiable causes: A cause for symptoms that can be identified and potentially treated, for example nutcracker syndrome causing blockage of pelvic veins and therefore pelvic pain.

Sperm: The small male reproductive cell that is contained in semen.

Spermatic cord: The structure in the male groin that runs from the deep inguinal ring to each testis. Each cord contains the vas deferens, testicular artery, artery of the ductus deferens, cremasteric artery, pampiniform plexus, genital branch of the genitofemoral nerve, parasympathetic and sympathetic nerves, lymphatic vessels, and layers of tissue, most notably the tunica vaginalis, an extension of the peritoneum.

Sphincterotomy: A surgical procedure designed to divide the sphincter muscles under anesthesia.

Spina bifida occulta: A disorder characterized by a hidden gap in the spine due to its not fully forming *in utero*. It may be identified at any point in life, and sometimes it is associated with neurological problems.

Spinal anesthesia: Also called a spinal block, is a form of neuraxial anesthesia involving the injection of a local anesthetic or opioid into the subarachnoid space, generally through a fine needle.

Spinal canal: Cavity containing the spinal cord that runs successively through each of the vertebrae.

Spinal cord: A long, thin, tubular, structure made up of nervous tissue, which extends from the medulla oblongata in the brainstem to the lumbar region of the vertebral column. It encloses the central canal of the spinal cord, which contains cerebrospinal fluid.

Spinal cord injury (SCI): Damage to the spinal cord from injury or disease that can result in loss of function, such as mobility or sensation.

Spinal cord stimulation (SCS): A technique that delivers mild electrical stimulation to nerves along the spinal column, modifying nerve activity to minimize the sensation of pain reaching the brain.

Spinal fluid: A clear, colorless body fluid found in the brain and spinal cord.

Spinal nerves: Pairs of nerves originating from the spinal cord that carry motor, sensory, and autonomic signals between the spinal cord and body.

Spinal stenosis: Narrowing of the spinal canal, which contains nerve roots and the spinal cord, leading to pain, cramping, weakness, or numbness.

Spine: A structure made up of small bones, called vertebrae, which are stacked on top of one another and create the natural curves of your back and neck. These bones connect to create a canal that protects the spinal cord.

Spondyloarthritis: A type of arthritis that attacks the spine, and in some people, the joints of the arms and legs; it can also involve the skin, intestines, and eyes.

Spondylolisthesis: A spinal condition that affects the lower vertebrae (spinal bones). This disease causes one of the lower vertebrae to slip forward onto the bone directly beneath it.

Stent: A tubular support placed temporarily inside a blood vessel, canal, or duct to aid healing or to relieve an obstruction.

Steroid: A natural or pharmacologic chemical substance classified by a specific carbon structure. Steroids include cholesterol, and drugs used to relieve swelling and inflammation, such as prednisone and cortisone; vitamin D, and some sex hormones, such as testosterone and estradiol.

Steroid injection: Injection of a steroid, used to control local inflammation.

Steroid-induced myopathy: An excess of steroids, either made by the body or taken as a medication, can result in muscle weakness and atrophy.

Stomach: The pear-shaped enlargement after the esophagus, where the major part of food digestion occurs.

Stool test: A test of the fecal matter (stool) for infection or blood.

Straddle injury: An injury to the groin sustained when falling on a hard object, such as a bicycle bar.

Straight catheter: *See* Straight catheterization.

Straight catheterization: A small tube called a *"straight catheter"* is inserted to empty the bladder, to get a sterile urine sample, or to feel how tight the urethra and its sphincter muscles are. In straight catheterization, the catheter is removed after the bladder is emptied.

Strangulated hernia: Abdominal contents protruding through an abnormal opening or weak spot that is trapped and cannot be reduced or pushed back into the abdominal cavity. A strangulated hernia is a medical emergency.

Streaming: A live event being broadcast over the internet.

Stricture: Narrowed passage that is often caused by scarring.

Stroke: A sudden interruption of the blood supply to the brain.

Submucosal fibroids: Fibroids (non-cancerous, abnormal growths in the uterus) located near the cavity of the uterus under the lining, which is called the mucosal surface.

Supplement: A pill, vitamin, or food taken to improve health.

Suprapubic catheter: A catheter (a soft pliable tube) that enters the bladder above the pubic bone in order to drain urine.

SP Tube: *See* suprapubic catheter.

Stress urinary incontinence: Urinary leakage that occurs when the pressure within the abdomen increases, for example during coughing or jumping.

Surface electromyogram (sEMG)/surface electromyographic feedback: Use of surface (stick-on) electrodes to measure the electrical activity of certain muscles and to show the individual being trained about their contractions in relation to the electrode reading.

Surgeon: A medical practitioner credentialed to practice surgery after a long training after medical school called residency, which is like an apprenticeship. There are many different types or surgeons with varying levels of sub-specialization.

Surgery: The treatment of illness, injury, or disorders of the body by incision (cutting) with instruments.

Sutures: Surgical stitches. Sutures can be made as absorbable or permanent material, both of which are left inside the body, and are chosen based on the needs of the tissue. When permanent sutures are used on the skin surface, for example after a facial laceration (cut), they are later removed.

Suture rectopexy: A procedure designed to treat rectal prolapse, suturing the rectum to the ligamentum flavum, the tough tissue anterior to (in front of) the sacrum within the pelvis.

Sympathetic nerves/sympathetic nervous system: Part of the autonomic nervous system that activates what is often termed the "fight or flight response" and can be involved in the transmission of pain signals.

Sympathetic plexus: An aggregation of nerves and ganglia. Situated in the thoracic, abdominal, and pelvic cavities, and named the cardiac, celiac, and hypogastric plexuses.

Symptoms: Subjective awareness of bodily sensations, experienced and reported by the person who has them.

Synapse: Point at which a nervous impulse moves from one neuron to another cell.

Syndrome: A set of medical signs and symptoms that are correlated with each other and often associated with a disease or disorder.

Synovitis acne periostitis hyperostosis and osteitis (SAPHO): A syndrome that includes five different entities: synovitis (inflammation of the joint lining), acne (blemishes that occur when dead skin cells and oil from the skin clog hair follicles), pustulosis (blister-like inflammation of the skin), hyperostosis (excessive growth of bone), and osteitis (inflammation of bone); this syndrome is characterized by periodic exacerbations, remissions, and variable severity.

Synovium: A type of soft tissue that lines the joints as well as other areas of the body.

Systematic desensitization: A therapeutic technique in which one works their way up a hierarchy of stressful, reflex-provoking or painful sensations to reduce the response.

Systemic disease: A disease that affects many body parts or the whole body.

Systemic lupus erythematosus (SLE): An autoimmune disorder that affects multiple organs and joints in the body. SLE is commonly associated with fever, joint pain, and malar rashes, as well as sensitivity to light, kidney dysfunction, neurologic dysfunction (in the form of seizures and/or mood disorders), mouth ulcers (that are generally painless), and inflammation of the membranes that line the heart and lungs.

Tai chi: An ancient Chinese discipline of meditative movements practiced as a system of exercises, aimed at integrating the mind and body.

Takayasu's arteritis: A large-vessel vasculitis that affects the aorta, its major branches to the extremities, and sometimes internal organs. It usually occurs in young women (under 50 years old).

Tamsulosin (Flomax®): A medication that works by inhibiting the alpha receptor of smooth muscle cells, such as at the bladder neck or in the prostate. This medication is referred to as an "alpha blocker" and can cause dizziness (especially when rising to a standing position after sitting,) and floppy iris syndrome.

Tarlov cyst: CSF-filled sac found at the level of the sacral vertebral bodies; these cysts are often associated with sensory symptoms.

Temporal artery: A branch of the maxillary artery. It supplies the temporalis muscle in the head with blood.

Tendon: Tissue connecting muscles to bones.

Testes/testis/testicles: Male reproductive organs located in the scrotum; they produce reproductive cells known as spermatozoa, and sex hormones.

Testicular torsion: A (typically) acute event that occurs when the testis twists on its blood supply. It is usually sudden, accompanied by pain, nausea, and change in position of the testis. It is a surgical emergency, as de-torsion within six hours will restore blood supply and save the testis.

Testis infarction: Interruption of blood blow to the testis. This can occur if a clot or other embolus enters the artery or if the artery wall is injured, thereby clotting.

Testosterone: The primary male sex hormone and an anabolic steroid. In males, it plays a key role in reproduction. It is present in smaller concentrations in women.

Tethered cord syndrome/tethered cord/tethered spinal cord: A rare condition that occurs when tissue attachments limit the movement of the spinal cord within the spinal column. The lower tip of the spinal cord can be tethered, leading to a slow tension on the cord as a person grows.

Tetracaine (Kovanaze®, Pontocaine®, Ametop®, Dicaine®): An intermediate- to long-acting local anesthetic that reduces the ability of nerves to generate a pain impulse, by blocking intracellular sodium channels.

Thecal sac: The thecal sac or dural sac is the membranous sheath (theca, dura) that surrounds the spinal cord and the cauda equina. The thecal sac is the same as the dural sac.

Therapeutic injection: A treatment targeting a nerve or group of nerves with medications to reduce pain or inflammation for a longer duration (months or even years) than diagnostic injections. Therapeutic injections frequently include a local anesthetic and a steroid.

Therapeutic ultrasound: A treatment modality commonly used in physical therapy. It is used to provide deep heating to soft tissues of the body. These tissues include muscles, tendons, joints, and ligaments.

Thoracic radiculomyelopathy: Dysfunction (myelopathy) of the thoracic (chest) spinal cord and its nerve roots (radiculopathy).

Thromboembolism: Embolization, or movement, of a blood clot through the blood vessels after dislodging from one area, then plugging another. It may cause, for example, a pulmonary embolism in the lungs or a stroke in the brain.

Thrombosis: A blood clot.

Thyroid disease: Any disorder affecting the thyroid gland. Abnormal high production of hormones is called hyperthyroidism (too much hormone), while hypothyroidism is the result of too little thyroid hormone.

Tibial nerve stimulator/percutaneous tibial nerve stimulator (TNS/PTNS): A device that allows indirect stimulation to the nerves of the bladder and pelvic floor by stimulating the posterior tibial nerve at the level of the ankle.

Tizanidine (Zanaflex®): A muscle relaxant that blocks nerve impulses and can be used to treat spasticity of muscles. It is referred to as an alpha-adrenergic agonist.

Topical: On the surface, as in a medication applied topically.

Torsed uterine fibroids: Fibroids (non-cancerous, abnormal growths in the uterus) that grow on the surface of the uterus then can twist on a stalk.

Torsion: The action of twisting or being twisted.

Totally extraperitoneal (TEP): A laparoscopic procedure to repair hernias in which entrance into the abdominal (peritoneal) cavity is avoided, staying superficial to this cavity. Placement of mesh is typically employed to strengthen the abdominal wall after the herniated tissue is removed or returned to the abdominal cavity.

Touchdown weight-bearing (TDWB): An instruction one receives after a leg or hip injury that means one can put one's foot on the ground for balance, but no weight should be placed through that leg.

Toxic neuropathy: Neuropathy (disease or dysfunction of one or more nerves) caused by drug ingestion, drug or chemical abuse, or industrial chemical exposure from the workplace or the environment.

Tramadol (Ultram®): Opioid pain medication used to treat moderate to moderately severe pain. In 1994, it was initially classified as a non-scheduled (non-controlled) drug and therefore, consumers have been confused about the fact that it is still addictive.

Transabdominal approach: Any evaluation with an ultrasound transducer overlying the abdominal wall.

Transabdominal preperitoneal (TAPP): A laparoscopic procedure to repair inguinal hernias in which the peritoneal cavity is entered for placement of mesh to strengthen the abdominal wall after the herniated tissue is removed or returned to the abdominal cavity.

Transcutaneous electrical nerve stimulation (TENS): *See* transcutaneous nerve stimulator.

Transcutaneous nerve stimulator (TENS): The device used in transcutaneous electrical nerve stimulation, a therapy that uses low voltage electrical current to provide pain relief.

Transdermal: Delivery of medication by applying it to the skin and having it absorb and work directly on the site as needed, or even absorbed into the blood stream for systemic benefit, depending on the formulation.

Transrectal ultrasound: Imaging using a special ultrasound probe placed gently in the rectum to image the prostate.

Transurethral resection of the ejaculatory duct (TURED): A therapeutic option for partially or completely obstructed ejaculatory ducts.

Tranylcypromine (Parnate®): An antidepressant in the class of medications called monoamine oxidase inhibitors.

Traumatic pelvic fracture: Pelvic injuries that occur in conjunction with trauma.

Trendelenburg gait: An abnormal gait resulting from weak gluteal (medius and minimus) musculature, which normally abduct (draw out) the hip. The weakness leads to drooping of the pelvis to the contralateral side while walking.

Trial: A temporary test to assess the potential efficacy of an intervention.

Tricyclic antidepressant: A type of antidepressant medication that works by blocking the serotonin and norepinephrine transporters.

Trigeminal neuralgia: A chronic pain condition involving pain derived from the fifth cranial nerve known as the trigeminal nerve. Severe pain can be experienced with touching the face, chewing, speaking, or brushing the teeth.

Trigger points: Small points of tightly contracted muscles, which are painful when pressure is applied.

Trochanteric bursitis: Inflammation of the bursa (fluid-filled cushion) at the interface of the hip with the greater trochanter.

Trochanters: The two protuberances (tubercles) of the femur near its joint with the hip bone to which the hip and thigh muscles attach.

Tuberculosis: A potentially serious infectious disease caused by the bacteria Mycobacterium tuberculosis. These are spread through tiny droplets released into the air via coughs and sneezes. The lungs are involved in 90% of cases, but it can also involve the brain, lymph vessels, bones, and the genitourinary system (in which case it can cause infertility).

Tubo-ovarian abscess: An infection of the tubes and ovaries, usually due to Chlamydia or Gonococcus (related to pelvic inflammatory disease).

Tumor: An abnormal mass or lump of tissue in the body, which can be due to cancer or can be benign (non cancerous).

Tumor necrosis factor-alpha (TNF-α): A protein released by cell membranes; it functions like a cytokine.

Tunica albuginea: The white elastic sheath surrounding the chambers of erectile tissue (the corpus cavernosum) in the penis and clitoris.

Ulcerative colitis (UC): An inflammatory bowel disorder characterized by severe and sometimes bloody diarrhea, crampy abdominal pain, and often fever, weight loss, and generalized fatigue. It typically spares the colon.

Ultrasound/ultrasound imaging: A painless surface-level imaging tool that uses high frequency sound waves to assess different internal organs. Sometimes transrectal or transvaginal ultrasound provides better images. Also called sonography or diagnostic medical sonography.

Ultrasonic imaging biofeedback: A means of imaging the pelvic floor muscles during rehabilitation.

Umbilicus: The depression in the center of the surface of the abdomen indicating the point of attachment of the umbilical cord to the embryo—navel or belly button.

Underactive bladder (UAB): Low-strength bladder muscle (detrusor) contraction versus normal. Symptoms are typically characterized by prolonged urination time, usually with hesitancy, and often incomplete bladder emptying.

Unmyelinated C-fibers: A type of nerve fiber that does not have a myelin sheath and therefore transmits messages more slowly. Examples of these fibers are the autonomic nerves and the "afferent" (ingoing) messages of the peripheral nervous system. Damage to these fibers can cause dysfunction of the viscera and neuropathic pain.

Ureaplasma: A group of tiny bacteria that inhabit the respiratory and urogenital (urinary and reproductive) tracts.

Ureter: The paired tubes through which urine passes from the kidneys to the bladder. Rarely, there can be congenital differences (anomalies) in the formation of the ureter, such as duplication.

Ureteral endometriosis: Endometriosis involving the ureter, which can cause scarring and narrowing (stricture).

Ureteral stent/ureteric stent: A flexible tube inserted into the ureter to heal it, dilate it, or to bypass a stone and allow for drainage of the kidney.

Ureterocele: Developmental abnormality involving slippage of the lining of the ureter that can lead to blockage of the kidney or bladder neck with resulting pain.

Ureteroscopy: A procedure to visualize the ureters and the lining of the kidney (the renal pelvis or "collecting system") with a telescope to look for stones, abnormal growths, or strictures. The tiny camera and scope are narrower than those used for a cystoscopy.

Urethra: A narrow tube made of muscles, connective tissue, and vessels, which conducts urine from the bladder to the tip of the penis or to an opening between the vagina and the clitoris.

Urethral biopsy: A biopsy is a diagnostic surgical procedure in which a doctor removes cells or tissue with a grasper from your bladder or urethra to be tested in a laboratory. This typically involves cystoscopy (inserting a camera into the urethra and the bladder).

Urethral swab: A laboratory test performed typically in male patients to check for infection-causing germs in the urethra, collected with a cotton swab.

Urethral caruncle: A benign, fleshy, outgrowth of the posterior urethral meatus.

Urethral diverticulum: A pocket or out-pouching in the urethra thought to be due to dilated glands or injury, which can fill with stagnant urine, causing pain, infection, post-void dribbling, and inflammation.

Urethral mucosal prolapse: A circumferential loosening and slippage of the lining of the urethra, like the lining of a pant leg which elongates and stretches beyond the pant leg.

Urethritis: Common condition affecting people of all ages characterized by inflammation of the urethra.

Urethritis urine sediment: *See* urine sediment.

Urethrogram: A special X-ray in which iodinated contrast is injected through the urethra to show urethral abnormalities. It is used primarily for characterizing urethral strictures or injuries in men.

Urethroplasty: Surgical reconstruction or replacement of the urethra, usually as a correction to scarring and narrowing (stricture).

Urinalysis: Simple instant "dip" chemical test strip of your urine that suggests, but does not confirm, inflammatory cells, blood, hydration status, and sugar and protein content of urine.

Urinary frequency: Urination occurring more frequently than deemed normal by the individual.

Urinary incontinence: The involuntary leakage of urine.

Urinary retention: A condition in which one's bladder does not empty completely, even when trying to urinate. If the event is acute (sudden) it is likely to cause significant pain. Chronic urinary retention can cause a dull pelvic ache, or no pain at all, due to the gradual process.

Urinary tract: The urinary system (kidneys, ureters, bladder, and urethra).

Urinary tract infection (UTI): An infection in any part of your urinary system (kidneys, ureters, bladder, and urethra).

Urinary urgency: A sudden, compelling, urge to urinate.

Urine: Also referred to as "pee", the watery yellow waste removed from the blood by the kidneys, and passed via the ureters, bladder, and urethra.

Urine culture (including Mycoplasma and Ureaplasma): A test to find germs (such as bacteria) in the urine that can cause an infection. In this test urine is "plated" in a petri dish with nutrients that will allow bacteria to grow. It takes two to three days for the result to be final, as the bacteria needs time to grow. "Susceptibilities" or "sensitivities" should be run to identify which antibiotics will be effective.

Urine cytology: This is a urine test in which a pathologist looks for cancer cells in urine under microscopic view.

Urine sediment: Definitive microscopic analysis of the actual types and number of cells and content in the urine. The sediment is the best way to know if there is truly blood or pus in the urine. The term also refers to visible flaky precipitates in the urine.

Ureaplasma: A group of tiny bacteria that inhabit the respiratory and urogenital (urinary and reproductive) tract.

Urodynamic evaluation/testing/urodynamics: A test performed in a specially equipped private room in which a tiny catheter is placed in your bladder and another in the rectum or vagina to balance the pressures, and your bladder is slowly filled with a sterile liquid. You are asked to report bladder sensation then empty your bladder (urinate) while measurements are made. Video urodynamics include X-rays. This study assesses how the bladder and urethra are performing their job of storing and releasing urine.

Uroflowmetry: A test using a special toilet with a funnel that records how much urine you pass per second and how strong your stream is.

Urogynecologist: A gynecologic physician with special training in the diagnosis and treatment of pelvic floor disorders, also known as female pelvic medicine and reconstructive surgery (FPMRS).

Urologic: Related to the diseases of the male and female geniturinary tract (kidneys, ureters, bladder, and urethra and genitalia).

Urologist: A physician who specializes in diseases of the urinary tract and the male reproductive system. Some urologists undertake further subspecialized training in female pelvic medicine and reconstructive surgery (FPMRS), the treatment of pelvic floor disorders, and neurourology.

Urology: A specialty dealing with the genitourinary tract (the kidneys, urinary bladder, adrenal glands, urethra, and male reproductive organs), and male fertility, as well as the surgical and medical treatment of diseases that affect these organs. "Female urology" involves further training in female pelvic medicine and reconstructive surgery (FPMRS).

Ustekinumab (Stelara®): An immunosuppressant drug that interferes with the body's inflammatory response by interfering with certain cytokines (inflammatory proteins).

Uterine fibroids: Non-cancerous growths of the uterus that often appear during childbearing years.

Uterine prolapse: A condition that occurs when pelvic floor muscles and ligaments stretch and weaken and no longer provide enough support for the uterus; as a result, the uterus slips down or protrudes out of the vagina.

Uterus: A hollow, muscular, pear-shaped organ found in a woman's lower abdomen. It contains the fetus during pregnancy.

Uveitis: Inflammation of the eye membrane, the middle layer (consisting of the iris, ciliary body and choroid).

Vagina: The internal female organ (also called "va-jj", "girl", "box", "muff", "pussy", "hoo-haw", "cooch," and other colloquial terms) consisting of an elastic, muscular tract from the vulva to the cervix lined by a soft mucus membrane. During sexual arousal, the Bartholin glands situated at the vaginal vestibule (vaginal opening) secrete lubricating mucus.

Vaginal dilation/vaginal dilator therapy/dilator therapy: A self-administered procedure for females to improve vaginal capacity and elasticity (which can be reduced due to surgery, age, and lower estrogen levels), and to treat pelvic floor muscle pain. Applying pressure on the pelvic floor muscles with the aid of a dilator can help relax them and decrease or eliminate spasms.

Vaginal discharge: A normal bodily function in which fluids, shed cells, and bacteria exit the vagina to help keep it clean. Vaginal discharge will have minor variances in quantity, color, viscosity, and odor due to the menstrual cycle and level of sexual arousal. Abnormal discharge, however, especially in concert with pain or itching, can be a sign of infection or other disorders.

Vaginal prolapse/vaginal vault prolapse: A condition in which the top of the vagina falls out of place. This condition often co-exists with a cystocele or rectocele and is more common in post-menopausal women, after hysterectomy, and in those who have had multiple and/or complicated vaginal deliveries.

Vaginal swab: A laboratory test obtained in female patients by using a cotton swab to check for infection-causing germs in the vagina.

Vaginismus: A disorder characterized by strong muscle tension of the surface-level (superficial) or deep pelvic floor muscles in women; it leads to painful constriction of the vaginal opening and pain or difficulty during vaginal penetration.

Varicocele: Dilated veins serving the testis, which can be seen as blue or purple lumps under the scrotal skin.

Varicose veins: Dilated enlarged veins, often appearing blue or purple.

Vasculitis: A condition involving inflammation of a blood vessel or lymph vessel.

Vasectomy: A male surgical sterilization in which the vas deferens are cut, interrupting passage of sperm out of the testes.

Vasectomy reversal: A surgery performed to undo a vasectomy, typically by rejoining severed ends of the vas deferens. This procedure is sometimes used in men who experience pain after vasectomy.

Vedolizumab (Entyvio®): An immunosuppressant medication in the monoclonal antibody family. It blocks $\alpha 4\beta 7$ integrin and reduces inflammation specifically in the gut. Used for moderate to severe inflammatory bowel disease (ulcerative colitis or Crohn's disease).

Vehicle: The substance that carries the active part of a medication, for example, the cream base or whatever holds a tablet together.

Veins: Vessels returning blood to the heart after it has circulated through the body.

Venography: An X-ray procedure completed with the aid of a contrast dye injection to image the veins. Imaging the insides of veins directly can help diagnose venous disease, can determine the volume of clotting agents (sclerosants) needed to treat certain types of venous disease, and can provide directed roadmaps for the treatment of varices (dilated veins).

Venous duplex ultrasound: A diagnostic imaging test that can evaluate the surface and internal veins of the veins of interest, as well as the varicose vein connections to these venous systems.

Ventral rectopexy (VR)/ventral mesh rectopexy: A surgical procedure usually performed to correct rectal prolapse and sometimes a rectocele. A sterile mesh is sewn into place along the front wall of the rectum and the back wall of the vagina, then attached to the surface of the sacrum (the ligamentum flavum) to provide structural support.

Vertebra: Each of the series of small bones forming the spine.

Vertebral arch: Posterior part of the vertebra consisting of a pair of pedicles and a pair of laminae.

Vertebral body: Anterior part of the vertebra. Stacked in between each vertebral body are intervertebral discs.

Vertebral discs: Intervertebral fibrocartilage between adjacent vertebrae that function like shock absorbers.

Verumontanum: A rise of tissue within the urethra of the prostate, that holds the prostatic utricle (the male homologue of the uterus and vagina, a duct which contracts to open the ejaculatory ducts during ejaculation), and the paired ejaculatory ducts.

Vesicovaginal fistula: Fistula (abnormal epithelialized connection) between the bladder and vagina, commonly resulting in an involuntary leakage of urine through the vagina.

Vestibulectomy: Surgical removal of painful vulvar tissues at the vaginal entrance (a very rarely recommended surgery).

Vestibulodynia: Recurrent and localized vulvovaginal pain.

Video urodynamic study: *See* urodynamic evaluation/testing/urodynamics.

Visceral: Referring to the viscera, the internal organs of the body. In pain, it refers to internal organ pain.

Visceral nervous system: *See* autonomic nervous system.

Visceral pain: Pain that results from the activation of nociceptors of the thoracic, pelvic, or abdominal viscera (organs); it might be described as sickening, deep, squeezing, and dull.

Vitamin B_{12} deficiency: A shortage of vitamin B_{12} (cobalamin), a critical molecule in various bodily functions. Since vitamin B_{12} is water-soluble, excess can be stored in the liver for years, so diagnosis of its deficiency can be delayed. Vitamin B_{12} deficiency is a potential cause for small fiber polyneuropathy among other conditions.

Voiding diary: A chart on which one records voided urine volume with each void, amount and type of fluid drunk, and events such as leakage and time slept for 24–72 hours.

Volvulus: A loop of intestine twirls around its blood supply (like twisting a plastic bag to close it). This results in ischemia and bowel obstruction. Symptoms include abdominal pain, abdominal bloating, vomiting, constipation, and bloody stool.

Vulva: The vulva makes up most of the external portion of the female genitalia. There are the labia majora (the fatty hair bearing "lips"), the labia minora (the thin velvety inner lips), and the clitoral prepuce (the hood of the clitoris).

Vulvar atrophy: Thinning, drying, and inflammation of the vaginal walls that may occur when the tissue has less estrogen; it occurs most often after menopause.

Vulvar vestibulitis syndrome (VVS): A condition characterized by pain at the vaginal entrance upon penetration (or on touch in more severe cases). VVS is a common cause of dyspareunia (pain during sex) in pre-menopausal women.

Vulvodynia: Pain that is specifically located in a female's external genital (vulvar) area.

Vulvovaginal atrophy: A common and under-reported condition associated with less estrogen in the vaginal tissue.

Warfarin (Coumadin®, Jantoven®): A blood thinner (anticoagulant) that decreases the clotting ability of the blood. It inhibits vitamin K epoxide reductase which has multiple effects in the clotting cascade.

Wegener's granulomatosis: *See* granulomatosis with polyangiitis (GPA).

Weight-bear as tolerated (WBAT): After an injury, a doctor may prescribe that the injured person is to weight-bear as tolerated—that is, to put as much on the leg as one is able to tolerate, and to gradually increase this amount until the muscles strengthen and one is able to resume normal life without experiencing pain.

White blood cells (WBCs): Also called leukocytes or leucocytes, these are cells of the immune system that are involved in protecting the body against infectious disease and foreign invaders; produced and derived from cells in the bone marrow. WBCs make up 1% of blood, and can also be found in lymph tissue. They envelop and kill foreign microbes and also increase at the site of injury. Their presence, if increased above normal, may indicate a disorder; for example elevated WBC count in the urine may suggest infection.

Wikipedia: An online encyclopedia located at www.wikipedia.org.

Women's health clinical specialist (WCS): Board certification by the American Board of Physical Therapy Specialties with high level of knowledge and experience in all of women's health, including pelvic pain.

X-ray: A painless radiology imaging study used for non-invasive diagnostics and monitoring. X-rays can be used in combination with other materials, such as iodinated contrast dyes, to increase the visibility of areas of interest.

Yoga: A physical activity involving the adoption and holding of various poses. Yoga can increase the flexibility of muscles and connective tissue and the soft tissues in the pelvis and trunk. This allows nerves to move more freely, reducing irritation. Yoga can be effective for pain management, retraining the brain to be comfortable with various motions.

Zipper injury: An injury in which the foreskin or penile skin is trapped when closing a zipper. It is a potential cause of urethral stricture.

REFERENCES

1. Abrams P, Cardozo L, Fall M, et al: The standardisation of terminology of lower urinary tract function: Report from the Standardisation Subcommittee of the International Continence Society. *Neurourology and Urodynamics.* 2002; 21: 167–178.

2. Absinta M, Rocca MA, Colombo B, et al: Selective decreased grey matter volume of the pain-matrix network in cluster headache. *Cephalalgia.* 2012; 32(2): 109–115.

3. Aitken RCB: Measurement of feelings using visual analogue scales. *Proceedings of the Royal Society of Medicine.* 1969; 62: 989–993.

4. Altarac S, Papeš D: Use of D-mannose in prophylaxis of recurrent urinary tract infections (UTIs) in women. *BJU International.* 2014; 113(1): 9–10.

5. American College of Obstetrics and Gynecology Committee Opinion No. 651: Menstruation in girls and adolescents: Using the menstrual cycle as a vital sign. *Obstetrics and Gynecology.* 2015; 126(6): e143–146.

6. American Heart Association: Silent ischemia and ischemic heart disease. (2019). https://www.heart.org/en/health-topics/heart-attack/about-heart-attacks/silent-ischemia-and-ischemic-heart-disease. Accessed June 6, 2020.

7. Anderson RU, Wise D, Sawyer T, et al: Integration of myofascial trigger point release and paradoxical relaxation training treatment of chronic pelvic pain in men. *Journal of Urology.* 2005; 174(1): 155–160.

8. Antunes-Lopes T, Vasconcelos A, Costa D, et al: The impact of chronic pelvic ischemia on LUTS and urinary levels of neuroinflammatory, inflammatory, and oxidative stress markers in elderly men: A case-control study. *Urology.* 2019; 123: 230–234.

9. Applegate WV: Abdominal cutaneous nerve entrapment syndrome (ACNES): A commonly overlooked cause of abdominal pain. *Permanente Journal.* 2002; 6(3): 20–27.

10. As-Sanie S, Clevenger LA, Geisser ME, et al: History of abuse and its relationship to pain experience and depression in women with chronic pelvic pain *American Journal of Obstetrics and Gynecology*. 2014; 210(4): 317e1–317e8.

11. Bair MJ, Robinson RL, Katon W, et al: Depression and pain comorbidity: A literature review. *Archives of Internal Medicine*. 2003; 163(20): 2433–2345.

12. Ballweg M: Impact of endometriosis on women's health: Comparative historical data show that the earlier the onset, the more severe the disease. Best Practice and Research. *Clinical Obstetrics and Gynaecology*. 2004; 18(2): 201–218.

13. Beal MC: Viscerosomatic reflexes: A review. *The Journal of the American Osteopathic Association*. 1985; 85(12): 786–801.

14. Beckman H, Widenbrant M, Bohm-Starke N, et al: Combined physical and psychosexual therapy for provoked vestibulodynia: An evaluation of a multidisciplinary treatment model. *Journal of Sex Research*. 2008; 45(4): 378–385.

15. Bergeron S, Amsel R, Binik YM, et al: A randomized comparison of group cognitive-behavioral therapy, surface electromyographic biofeedback, and vestibulectomy in the treatment of dyspareunia resulting from vulvar vestibulitis. *Pain*. 2001; 91(3): 297–306.

16. Bergeron S, Corsini-Munt S, Aerts L, et al: Female sexual pain disorders: A review of the literature on etiology and treatment. *Current Sexual Health Reports*. 2015; 7(3): 159–169.

17. Bergeron S, Rosen NO, Pukall CF: Genital pain in women and men: It can hurt more than your sex life. In: Binik Y and Hall KSK, eds. Principles and Practice of Sex Therapy. New York City: *The Guilford Press*. 2014; 159–176.

18. Bharucha AE, Dorn SD, Lembo A, et al: American Gastroenterological Association medical position statement on constipation. *Gastroenterology*. 2013; 144(1): 211–217.

19. Bhatt D: What is vasculitis? Harvard Heart Letter 2017; Available at: https://www.health.harvard.edu/heart-health/what-is-vasculitis. Accessed June 6, 2020.

20. Bibi S, Zutshi M, Gurland B, et al: Is Botox for anal pain an effective treatment option? *Postgraduate Medicine*. 2016; 128(1): 41–45.

21. Biswas S, Konala VM, Adapa S, et al: Osteitis condensans ilii: An uncommon cause of back pain. *Cureus*. 2019; 11(4): e4518.

22. Blair KL, Pukall CF, Smith KB, et al: Differential associations of communication and love in heterosexual, lesbian, and bisexual women's perceptions and experiences of chronic vulvar and pelvic pain. *Journal of Sex and Marital Therapy*. 2015; 41(5): 498–524.

23. Bliss TV, Collingridge GL: A synaptic model of memory: Long-term potentiation in the hippocampus. *Nature*. 1993; 361(6407): 31–39.

24. Borre YE, Moloney RD, Clarke G, et al: The impact of microbiota on brain and behavior: Mechanisms and therapeutic potential. *Advances in Experimental Medicine and Biology*. 2014; 817: 373–403.

25. Brauer M, ter Kuile MM, Laan E, et al: Cognitive-affective correlates and predictors of superficial dyspareunia. *Journal of Sex and Martial Therapy*. 2008; 35(1): 1–24.

26. Braun J, Baraliakos X, Buehring B, et al: Imaging of axial spondyloarthritis. New aspects and differential diagnoses. *Clinical and Experimental Rheumatology*. 2018; 36 (Suppl 114[5]): 35–42.

27. Brotto LA, Bergeron S, Zdaniuk B, et al: A comparison of mindfulness-based cognitive therapy vs cognitive behavioral therapy for the treatment of provoked vestibulodynia in a hospital clinic setting. *The Journal of Sexual Medicine*. 2019; 16(6): 909–923.

28. Brotto LA, Yong P, Smith KB, et al: Impact of a multidisciplinary vulvodynia program on sexual functioning and dyspareunia. *Journal of Sexual Medicine*. 2015; 12(1): 238–247.

29. Brown B: The Gifts of Imperfection. Center City, MN: *Hazelton*; 2010: p. 6.

30. Bryant C, Cockburn R, Plante AF, et al: The psychological profile of women presenting to a multidisciplinary clinic for chronic pelvic pain: High levels of psychological dysfunction and implications for practice. *Journal of Pain Research*. 2016; 9: 1049–1056.

31. Buchheit T, Van de Ven T, Shaw A: Epigenetics and the transition from acute to chronic pain. *Pain Medicine*. 2012; 13(11): 1474–1490.

32. Bushnell MC, Case LK, Ceko M, et al: Effect of environment on the long-term consequences of chronic pain. *Pain*. 2015; 156 (Suppl 1): S42–49.

33. Caldarella MP, Giamberardino MA, Sacco F, et al: Sensitivity disturbances in patients with irritable bowel syndrome and fibromyalgia. *The American Journal of Gastroenterology*. 2006; 101(12): 2782–2789.

34. Calixte N, Kartal IG, Tojuola B, et al: Salvage ultrasound guided targeted cryoablation of the peri-spermatic cord for persistent chronic scrotal content pain after microsurgical denervation of the spermatic cord. *Urology*. 2019; 130: 181–185.

35. Calixte N, Tojuola B, Kartal I, et al: Targeted robotic assisted microsurgical denervation of the spermatic cord for the treatment of chronic orchialgia or groin pain: A single center, large series review. *The Journal of Urology*. 2018; 199: 1015–1022.

36. Camellino D, Giusti A, Girasole G, et al: Pathogenesis, diagnosis and management of polymyalgia rheumatica. *Drugs Aging*. 2019; 36(11): 1015–1026.

37. Carter JE: A systematic history for the patient with chronic pelvic pain. *Journal of the Society of Laparoendoscopic Surgeons*. 1999; 3(4): 245–252.

38. Chang FY, Chey WY, Ouyang A: Effect of transcutaneous nerve stimulation on esophageal function in normal subjects—evidence for a somatovisceral reflex. *The American Journal of Chinese Medicine*. 1996; 24(2): 185–192.

39. Chapple CR, Osman NI, Birder L, et al: Terminology report from the International Continence Society (ICS) working group on underactive bladder (UAB). *Neurourology and Urodynamics*. 2018; 37: 2928–2931.

40. Chen A, De E, Argoff C: Small fiber polyneuropathy is prevalent in patients experiencing complex chronic pelvic pain. Pain Medicine. 2019; 20(3): 521–527.

41. Cherner RA, Reissing ED: A comparative study of sexual function, behavior, and cognitions of women with lifelong vaginismus. *Archives of Sexual Behavior*. 2013; 42(8): 1605–1614.

42. Chiarioni G, Nardo A, Vantini I, et al: Biofeedback is superior to electrogalvanic stimulation and massage for treatment of levator ani syndrome. *Gastroenterology*. 2010; 138(4): 1321–1329.

43. Chou R, Fanciullo GJ, Fine PG, et al: Clinical guidelines for the use of chronic opioid therapy in chronic noncancer pain. *The Journal of Pain*. 2009; 10(2): 113–130.

44. Chronic pelvic pain: Patient Education FAQ099. ACOG: 2011. https://www.acog.org/Patients/FAQs/Chronic-Pelvic-Pain?IsMobileSet=false. Accessed July 8, 2019.

45. Cleveland Clinic: Caregiver burnout. January 13, 2019; retrieved from https://my.clevelandclinic.org/health/diseases/9225-caregiver-burnout.

46. Coakley R: When your child hurts: Effective strategies to increase comfort, reduce stress, and break the cycle of chronic pain. *Yale University Press Health and Wellness*. 2016.

47. Colwell JC, Rattiff CR, Goldberg M, et al: MASD part 3: Peristomal moisture—associated dermatitis and periwound moisture associated dermatitis: A consensus. *Journal of Wound, Ostomy, and Continence Nursing*. 2011; 38(5): 541–553.

48. Conces MR, Williamson SR, Montironi R, et al: Urethral caruncle: Clinicopathologic features of 41 cases. *Human Pathology*. 2012; 43: 1400–1404.

49. Corsini-Munt S, Bergeron S, Rosen NO, et al: Feasibility and preliminary effectiveness of a novel cognitive-behavioral couple therapy for provoked vestibulodynia: A pilot study. *The Journal of Sexual Medicine*. 2014; 11(10): 2515–2527.

50. Costantini R, Affaitati G, Wesselmann U, et al: Visceral pain as a triggering factor for fibromyalgia symptoms in comorbid patients. *Pain*. 2017; 158(10): 1925–1937.

51. Craig AD: How do you feel? Interoception: The sense of the physiological condition of the body. Nature Reviews. *Neuroscience*. 2002; 3(8): 655–666.

52. Crean PM, Tirupathi S: Essentials of neurology and neuromuscular disorders. In: Cote CJ, Lerman L, Anderson BJ, eds. *A Practice of Anesthesia for Infants and Children* 6th ed. Philadelphia: Elsevier; 2019: 561–580.

53. Creswell JD: Mindfulness interventions. *Annual Review of Psychology*. 2017; 68(1): 491–516.

54. Damasio A, Carvalho GB: The nature of feelings: Evolutionary and neurobiological origins. Nature Reviews. *Neuroscience*. 2013; 14(2): 143–152.

55. Daugherty SF, Gillespie DL: Venous angioplasty and stenting improve pelvic congestion syndrome caused by venous outflow obstruction. *Journal of Vascular Surgery*. 2015; 3: 283–289.

56. Davies MG: Patient education: Peripheral artery disease and claudication (beyond the basics). https://www.uptodate.com/contents/peripheral-artery-disease-and-claudication-beyond-the-basics/print. Accessed June 6, 2020.

57. Davis BR, Lee-Kong SA, Migaly J, et al: The American Society of Colon and Rectal Surgeons clinical practice guidelines for the management of hemorrhoids. *Diseases of the Colon and Rectum*. 2018; 61(3): 284–292.

58. Davis R, Jones JS, Barocas DA, et al: Diagnosis, evaluation and follow-up of asymptomatic microhematuria (AMH) in adults: AUA Guideline. *The Journal of Urology*. 2012; 188: 2473–2481. Updated in 2016: Guideline can be found at https://www.auanet.org/guidelines/asymptomatic-microhematuria-(amh)-guideline.

59. Davis SN, Morin M, Binik YM, et al: Use of pelvic floor ultrasound to assess pelvic floor muscle function in urological chronic pelvic pain syndrome in men. *Journal of Sexual Medicine*. 2011; 8(11): 3173–3180.

60. de C Williams AC, Chambers C, Flor H, et al: International Association for the Study of Pain Curriculum Outline on Pain for Psychology. 2018; retrieved from https://www.iasp-pain.org/Education/CurriculumDetail.aspx?ItemNumber=2054.

61. Descalzi G, Ikegami D, Ushijima T, et al: Epigenetic mechanisms of chronic pain. *Trends in Neurosciences*. 2015; 38(4): 237–246.

62. Desrochers G, Bergeron S, Khalife S, et al: Fear avoidance and self-efficacy in relation to pain and sexual impairment in women with provoked vestibulodynia. *Clinical Journal of Pain*. 2009; 25(6): 520–527.

63. Desrochers G, Bergeron S, Landry T, et al: Do psychosexual factors play a role in the etiology of provoked vestibulodynia? A critical review. *Journal of Sex and Marital Therapy*. 2008; 34(3): 198–226.

64. DiSabato DJ, Quan N, Godbout JP: Neuroinflammation: The devil is in the details. *Journal of Neurochemistry*. 2016; 136–153.

65. Doggweiler R, Whitmore KE, Meijlink JM, et al: A standard for terminology in chronic pelvic pain syndromes: A report from the chronic pelvic pain working group of the international continence society. *Neurourology and Urodynamics*. 2017; 36: 984–1008.

66. Dong Q, Jacobson JA, Jamadar DA, et al: Entrapment neuropathies in the upper and lower limbs: Anatomy and MRI features. *Radiology Research and Practice*. 2012; 230679. doi: 10.1155/2012/230679.

67. Doughty D, Junkin J, Kurz P, et al: Incontinence—associated dermatitis. Consensus statements, evidence-based guideline for prevention and treatment, and current challenges. *Journal of Wound, Ostomy, and Continence Nursing*. 2012; 39(3): 303–315.

68. Drake RL, Vogl AW, Mitchell A, eds.: Dermatomes and cutaneous nerves of perineum in men. Dermatomes and cutaneous nerves of perineum in women. In: Gray's Atlas of Anatomy. Philadelphia, PA: Elsevier Limited. 2021; 213–292.

69. Drake RL, Vogl AW, Mitchell A, eds.: Meninges. In: Gray's Atlas of Anatomy. Philadelphia, PA: Elsevier Limited. 2021; 19–60.

70. Drossman DA, Li Z, Andruzzi E, et al: U.S. householder survey of functional gastrointestinal disorders. Prevalence, sociodemography, and health impact. *Digestive Disease and Sciences*. 1993; 38(9): 1569–1580.

71. DSM-5: American Psychiatric Association: *Diagnostic and Statistical Manual of Mental Disorders* (5th ed.). Arlington, VA. 2013.

72. Dubin, A: Elucidating the cause of pelvic pain. Physical Medicine and Rehabilitation Clinics of North America: V*alue-Added Electrodiagnostics*. 2018; 29(4): 777–782.

73. Eckardt VF, Dodt O, Kanzler G, et al: Treatment of proctalgia fugax with salbutamol inhalation. *The American Journal of Gastroenterology*. 1996; 91(4): 686–689.

74. Edwards IS: Vasectomy reversal for treatment of the post-vasectomy pain syndrome. *The Journal of Urology*. 1997; 158: 2252.

75. Els C, Jackson T, Kunyk D, et al: Adverse events associated with medium- and long-term use of opioids for chronic non-cancer pain: An overview of Cochrane Reviews. *Cochrane Database of Systematic Reviews*. 2017.

76. Engeler D, Baranowski AP, Berghmans B, et al: European Association of Urology Guidelines. 2016; retrieved from https://uroweb.org/guideline/chronic-pelvic-pain/.

77. Engeler DS, Baranowski AP, Dinis-Oliveira P, et al: The 2013 EAU guidelines on chronic pelvic pain: Is management of chronic pelvic pain a habit, a philosophy, or a science? 10 years of development. *European Urology*. 2013; 64(3): 431–439.

78. Engman M, Wijma K, Wijma B: Long-term coital behaviour in women treated with cognitive behaviour therapy for superficial coital pain and vaginismus. *Cognitive Behaviour Therapy*. 2010; 39(3): 193–202.

79. Erben Y, Gloviczki P, Kalra M, et al: Treatment of nutcracker syndrome with open and endovascular interventions. *Journal of Vascular Surgery*. 2015; 3: 389–396.

80. Fall M, Baranowski AP, Elneil S, et al: EAU guidelines on chronic pelvic pain. *European Urology*. 2010; 57(1): 35–48.

81. Farmer MA, Meston CM: Predictors of genital pain in young women. *Archives of Sexual Behavior*. 2007; 36(6): 831–843.

82. Feagins LA, Kane SV: Caring for women with inflammatory bowel disease. *Gastroenterology Clinics of North America*. 2016; 45(2): 303–315.

83. Federal Trade Commission: How to donate wisely and avoid charity scams. *Federal Trade Commission Consumer Information*. https://www.consumer.ftc.gov/features/how-donate-wisely-and-avoid-charity-scams. Accessed June 14, 2019.

84. Fitzgerald CM, Neville CE, Mallinson T, et al: Pelvic floor muscle examination in female chronic pelvic pain. *Journal of Reproductive Medicine*. 2011; 56: 117–122.

85. Fitzgerald MP, Anderson RU, Potts J, et al: Randomized multicenter feasibility trial of myofascial physical therapy for the treatment of urological chronic pelvic pain syndromes. *Journal of Urology*. 2013; 189(1 Suppl): S75–S85.

86. Fitzgerald MP, Brubaker L: Variability of 24-hour voiding diary variables among asymptomatic women. *The Journal of Urology*. 2003; 169: 207–209.

87. FitzGerald MP, Koch D, Senka J: Visceral and cutaneous sensory testing in patients with painful bladder syndrome. *Neurourology and Urodynamics*. 2005; 24: 627–632.

88. Fleming-Dutra K, Hersh AL, Shapiro DJ, et al: Prevalence of inappropriate antibiotic prescriptions among US ambulatory care visits, 2010–2011. *Journal of the American Medical Association*. 2016; 315(17): 1864–1873.

89. Fletcher C, Bradnam L, Barr C: The relationship between knowledge of pain neurophysiology and fear avoidance in people with chronic pain: A point in time, observational study. *Physiotherapy Theory and Practice*. 2016; 32(4): 271–276.

90. Flor H, Fydrich T, Turk DC: Efficacy of multidisciplinary pain treatment centers: A meta-analytic review. *Pain*. 1992; 49(2): 221–230.

91. Fuentes IM, Christianson JA: The influence of early life experience on visceral pain. *Frontiers in Systems Neuroscience*. 2018; 12: 2.

92. Gart M: Medical Economics 2017: Blog. https://www.medicaleconomics.com/medical-economics-blog/why-do-we-keep-prescribing-heroin-patients.

93. Gates EA, Galask RP: Psychological and sexual functioning in women with vulvar vestibulitis. *Journal of Psychosomatic Obstetrics and Gynecology*. 2001; 22(4): 221–228.

94. Gellrich FF, Gunther C: Schnitzler syndrome, Der Hautarzt, 2019; doi: 10.1007/s00105-019-4434-4.

95. Gerbershagen HJ, Dagtekin O, Isenberg J, et al: Chronic pain and disability after pelvic and acetabular fractures assessment with the Mainz Pain Staging System. *The Journal of Trauma*. 2010; 69(1): 128–136.

96. Giger U, Wente MN, Buchler MW, et al: Endoscopic retroperitoneal neurectomy for chronic pain after groin surgery. *British Journal of Surgery*. 2009; 96: 1076–1081.

97. GoFraudMe: Ten of GoFundMe's Worst Fake Scammers to Date. http://gofraudme.com/ten-gofundmes-worst-fake-cancer-scammers-date/. Accessed June 12, 2019.

98. Gormley EA, Lightner DJ, Faraday M, et al: Diagnosis and treatment of overactive bladder (non-neurogenic) in adults: AUA/SUFU guideline amendment. *The Journal of Urology*. 2015; 193: 1572–1580.

99. Greene IC, Cohen SL, Finkenzeller D, et al: Interventional therapies for controlling pelvic pain: What is the evidence? *Current Pain and Headache Reports*. 2010; 14: 22–32.

100. Gross JJ: Antecedent- and response-focused emotion regulation: Divergent consequences of experience, expression, and physiology. *Journal of Personality and Social Psychology*. 1998: 74(1): 224–237.

101. Grundy Q, Chiu K, Held F, et al: Data sharing practices of medicines related apps and the mobile ecosystem: Traffic, content, and network analysis. *The BMJ*. 2019; 364: 1920.

102. Gyang A, Hartman M, Lamvu G, et al: Musculoskeletal causes of chronic pelvic pain: What a gynecologist should know. *Obstetrics and Gynecology*. 2013; 121(3): 645–650.

103. Hallam-Jones R, Wylie KR, Osborne-Cribb J, et al: Sexual difficulties within a group of patients with vulvodynia. *Sexual and Relationship Therapy*. 2001; 16(2): 113–126.

104. Hanno PM, Burks DA, Clemens JQ, et al: AUA guideline for the diagnosis and treatment of interstitial cystitis/bladder pain syndrome. *The Journal of Urology*. 2011; 185: 2162–2170.

105. Hanno PM, Erickson D, Moldwin R, et al: Diagnosis and treatment of interstitial cystitis/bladder pain syndrome: AUA guideline amendment. *The Journal of Urology*. 2015; 193: 1545–1553.

106. Hernández-Rodríguez J, Tan CD, Rodriguez ER, et al: Gynecologic vasculitis: An analysis of 163 patients. *Medicine*. 2009; 88(3): 169–181.

107. HIPAA Journal: Facebook accused of privacy violations and exposure of sensitive health information disclosed in private groups. https://www.hipaajournal.com/facebook-accused-privacy-violations-phi-private-groups/. Accessed February 21, 2019.

108. Hoag N, Gani J: Underactive bladder: Clinical features, urodynamic parameters, and treatment. *International Neurourology Journal*. 2015; 19: 185–189.

109. Hodge CJ, Jr., Apkarian AV: The spinothalamic tract. *Critical Reviews in Neurobiology*. 1990; 5(4): 363–397.

110. Hoebeke P, Van Laecke E, Renson C, et al: Pelvic floor spasms in children: An unknown condition responding well to pelvic floor therapy. *European Urology*. 2004; 46(5): 651–654; discussion 654.

111. Holloran-Schwartz MB: Surgical evaluation and treatment of the patient with chronic pelvic pain. *Obstetrics and Gynecology Clinics of North America*. 2014; 41: 357–369.

112. Howell AB, Botto H, Combescure C, et al: Dosage effect on uropathogenic Escherichia coli anti-adhesion activity in urine following consumption of cranberry powder standardized for proanthocyanidin content: A multicentric randomized double blind study. *BMC Infectious Diseases*. 2010; 10: 94.

113. Hunt MG, Marx R, Lipson C, et al: No more FOMO: Limiting social media decreases loneliness and depression. *Journal of Social and Clinical Psychology*. 2018; 37(10): 751–768.

114. Hyman N: Incontinence after lateral internal sphincterotomy: A prospective study and quality of life assessment. *Diseases of the Colon and Rectum*. 2004; 47(1): 35–38.

115. Ivo R, Nicklas A, Dargel J, et al: Brain structural and psychometric alterations in chronic low back pain. *European Spine Journal*. 2013; 22(9): 1958–1964.

116. Jain N, Li AL, Yu Y, et al: Association of macular disease with long-term use of pentosan polysulfate sodium: Findings from a U.S. cohort. *The British Journal of Ophthalmology*. 2019; pii: bjophthalmol-2019-314765. doi: 10.1136/bjophthalmol-2019-314765. (Epub ahead of print).

117. James W: Discussion: The physical basis of emotion. *Psychological Review*. 1894; 1: 13.

118. Janssen EB, Rijkers AC, Hoppenbrouwers K, et al: Prevalence of endometriosis diagnosed by laparoscopy in adolescents with dysmenorrhea or chronic pelvic pain: A systematic review. *Human Reproduction Update*. 2013; 19(5): 570–582.

119. Jensen KB, Loitoile R, Kosek E, et al: Patients with fibromyalgia display less functional connectivity in the brain's pain inhibitory network. *Molecular Pain*. 2012; 8(1): 32.

120. Jenson MC, Brant-Zawadzki MN, Obuchowski N, et al: Magnetic resonance imaging of the lumbar spine in people without back pain. *New England Journal of Medicine*. 1994; 331(2): 69–73.

121. Ji RR, Kohno T, Moore KA: Central sensitization and LTP: Do pain and memory share similar mechanisms? *Trends in Neurosciences*. 2003; 26(12): 696–705.

122. Ji RR, Nackley A, Huh Y, et al: Neuroinflammation and central sensitization in chronic and widespread pain. *Anesthesiology*. 2018; 129(2): 343–366.

123. Johanson JF, Sonnenberg A: The prevalence of hemorrhoids and chronic constipation. An epidemiologic study. *Gastroenterology*. 1990; 98(2): 380–386.

124. Jones MP, Dilley JB, Drossman D: Brain-gut connections in functional GI disorders: Anatomic and physiologic relationships. *Neurogastroenterology and Motility*. 2006; 18(2): 91–103.

125. Kavic SM, Kavic SM: Adhesions and adhesiolysis: The role of laparoscopy. *Journal of the Society of Laparoendoscopic Surgeons*. 2002; 6: 99–109.

126. Khandker M, Brady SS, Stewart EG, et al: Is chronic stress during childhood associated with adult-onset Vulvodynia? *Journal of Women's Health*. 2014; 23(8): 649–656.

127. Klein JR, Litt IF: Epidemiology of adolescent dysmenorrhea. *Pediatrics*. 1981; 68(5): 661–664.

128. Knowles CH, Aziz Q: Basic and clinical aspects of gastrointestinal pain. *Pain*. 2009; 141(3): 191–209.

129. Kockerling F, Simons MP: Current concepts of inguinal hernia repair. *Visceral Medicine*. 2018; 34145–34150.

130. Koechlin H, Coakley R, Schechter N, et al: The role of emotion regulation in chronic pain: A systematic literature review. *Journal of Psychosomatic Research*. 2018; 107: 38–45.

131. Kokubo Y, Oki H, Sugita D, et al: Functional outcome of patients with unstable pelvic ring fracture. Hong Kong: *Journal of Orthopaedic Surgery*. 2017; 25(1): 2309499016684322. doi: 10.1177/2309499016684322.

132. Kuchinad A, Schweinhardt P, Seminowicz DA, et al: Accelerated brain gray matter loss in fibromyalgia patients: Premature aging of the brain? *The Journal of Neurosciences*. 2007; 27(15): 4004–4007.

133. Labat JJ, Riant T, Robert R, et al: Diagnostic criterial for pudendal neuralgia by pudendal nerve entrapment (Nantes criteria). *Neurourology and Urodynamics*. 2008; 27(4): 306–310.

134. Labropoulos N, Jasinski PT, Adrahtas D, et al: A standardized ultrasound approach to pelvic congestion syndrome. *Phlebology*. 2017; 32: 608–619.

135. Lake L: Avoid crowdfunding scams. *Federal Trade Commission Consumer Information*. https://www.consumer.ftc.gov/blog/2019/05/avoid-crowdfunding-scams. Accessed June 14, 2019.

136. Landi, H: Privacy experts skeptical of Facebook's moves to protect sensitive health information. *Fierce Healthcare*. https://www.fiercehealthcare.com/tech/privacy-experts-skeptical-facebook-s-moves-to-protect-sensitive-health-information. Accessed June 12, 2019.

137. Landry T, Bergeron S: Biopsychosocial factors associated with dyspareunia in a community sample of adolescent girls. *Archives of Sexual Behavior*. 2011; 40(5): 877–889.

138. Latthe P, Latthe M, Say L, et al: WHO systematic review of prevalence of chronic pelvic pain: A neglected reproductive health morbidity. *BMC Public Health*. 2006; 6: 177.

139. Laufer M, Sanfilippo J, Rose G: Adolescent endometriosis: Diagnosis and treatment approaches. *Journal of Pediatric and Adolescent Gynecology*. 2003; 16(Suppl 3): S3–11.

140. Le Bars D: The whole body receptive field of dorsal horn multireceptive neurones. Brain Research. *Brain Research Reviews*. 2002; 40(1–3): 29–44.

141. Lee MH, Chang KM, Wu SL, et al: A cohort study of interstitial/bladder pain syndrome and hysterectomy. *International Urogynecology Journal*. 2016; 27(9): 1401–1407.

142. Leitl MD, Onvani S, Bowers MS, et al: Pain-related depression of the mesolimbic dopamine system in rats: Expression, blockade by analgesics, and role of endogenous κ-opioids. *Neuropsychopharmacology*. 2014; 39(3): 614–624.

143. Lemos N, Possover M: Laparoscopic approach to intrapelvic nerve entrapments. *Journal of Hip Preservation Surgery*. 2015; 2(2): 92–98.

144. Lexicomp Website. https://online-lexi-com.ezproxymcp.flo.org/lco/action/home. Accessed August 26, 2019.

145. Lightner DJ, Gomelsky A, Souter L, et al: Diagnosis and treatment of overactive bladder (non-neurogenic) in adults: AUA/SUFU guideline amendment 2019. *The Journal of Urology*. 2019; 202: 558–563.

146. Lundeberg T, Bondesson L, Lundstrom V: Relief of primary dysmenorrhea by transcutaneous electrical nerve stimulation. *Acta Obstetricia Gynecologica Scandinavica.* 1985; 64(6): 491–497.

147. Luqmani RA, Suppiah R, Grayson PC, et al: Nomenclature and classification of vasculitis update on the ACR/EULAR diagnosis and classification of vasculitis study (DCVAS). *Clinical and Experimental Immunology.* 2011; 164 (Suppl 1): 11–13.

148. Magistro G, Wagenlehner FM, Grabe M, et al: Contemporary Management of Chronic Prostatitis/Chronic Pelvic Pain Syndrome. *European Urology.* 2016; 69(2): 286–297.

149. Magistro G, Wagenlehner FM, Grabe M, et al: Contemporary management of chronic prostatitis/chronic pelvic pain syndrome. *European Urology.* 2016; 69(2): 286–297.

150. Maillé DL, Bergeron S, Lambert B: Body image in women with primary and secondary provoked vestibulodynia: A controlled study. *Journal of Sexual Medicine.* 2015; 12(2): 505–515.

151. Malde S, Solomon E, Spilotros M, et al: Female bladder outlet obstruction: Common symptoms masking an uncommon cause. *Lower Urinary Tract Symptoms.* 2019; 11: 72–77.

152. Marques CF, Nahas SC, Nahas CS, et al: Early results of the treatment of internal hemorrhoid disease by infrared coagulation and elastic banding: A prospective randomized cross-over trial. *Techniques in Coloproctology.* 2006; 10: 312–317.

153. Masheb RM, Brondolo E, Kerns RD: A multidimensional, case-control study of women with self-identified chronic vulvar pain. *Pain Medicine.* 2002; 3(3): 253–259.

154. Mathias SD, Kuppermann M, Liberman RF, et al: Chronic pelvic pain: Prevalence, health-related quality of life, and economic correlates. *Obstetrics and Gynecology.* 1996; 87(3): 321–327.

155. McCracken LM: "Attention" to pain in persons with chronic pain: A behavioral approach. *Behavior Therapy.* 1997; 28(2): 271–284.

156. McNichol LL, Ayello EA, Phearman LA, et al: Incontinence-associated dermatitis: State of the science and knowledge translation. *Advances in Skin and Wound Care Journal.* 2018; 31(11): 502–513.

157. Meana M, Binik Y, Khalife S, et al: Biopsychosocial profile of women with dyspareunia. *Obstetrics and Gynecology.* 1997; 90(4): 583–589.

158. MedicineNet: https://www.medicinenet.com/script/main/hp.asp ©1996–2020 MedicineNet, Inc.

159. MedlinePlus: [Internet]. Bethesda (MD): National Library of Medicine (U.S.); [updated 2019 Aug 27; cited 2019 Aug 30]. Available from: https://medlineplus.gov/.

160. Mehedintu C, Plotogea MN, Ionescu S, et al: Endometriosis still a challenge. *Journal of Medicine and Life*. 2014; 7: 349–357.

161. Mei-Dan, O: The use of platelet-rich plasma to augment conservative and surgical treatment of hip and pelvic disorders. *Muscles, Ligaments and Tendons Journal*. 2016; 6(3): 410–419.

162. Meissner MH, Gibson K: Clinical outcome after treatment of pelvic congestion syndrome: Sense and nonsense. *Phlebology*. 2015; 30(Suppl 1): 73–80.

163. Merkel PA: Overview of and approach to the vasculitides in adults. *UpToDate*, 2019. https://www.uptodate.com/contents/overview-of-and-approach-to-the-vasculitides-in-adults. Accessed June 6, 2020.

164. Merriam-Webster's Medical Dictionary. Merriam-Webster, Inc.; Martinsburg WV. Newest edition, 2016.

165. Merskey HD, Bogduk N (Eds): Classification of chronic pain: Descriptions of chronic pain syndromes and definition of pain terms 2nd ed. Washington, DC: IASP Press; 1994. https://www.iasp-pain.org/PublicationsNews/Content.aspx?ItemNumber=1673&navItemNumber=677. Accessed June 16, 2020.

166. Micromedex Website. https://www-micromedexsolutions-com.ezproxymcp.flo.org. Accessed August 26, 2019.

167. Miriam Webster Medical Dictionary: Merriam-Webster Online (www.Merriam-Webster.com) © 2015 by Merriam-Webster, Incorporated.

168. Modirian E, Pirouzi P, Soroush M, et al: Chronic pain after spinal cord injury: Results of a long-term study. *Pain Medicine*. 2010; 11(7): 1037–1043.

169. Moleski SM, Choudhary C: Special considerations for women with IBD. *Gastroenterology Clinics of North America*. 2011; 40(2): 387–398, viii–ix.

170. Moseley GL, Gallace A, Spence C: Is mirror therapy all it is cracked up to be? Current evidence and future directions. *Pain*. 2008; 138(1): 7–10.

171. Nangia AK, Myles JL, Thomas AJ: Vasectomy reversal for the post-vasectomy pain syndrome: A clinical and histological evaluation. *The Journal of Urology*. 2000; 164: 1939–1942.

172. National Heart, Lung and Blood Institute: Atherosclerosis. 2019; https://www.nhlbi.nih.gov/health-topics/atherosclerosis. Accessed June 6, 2020.

173. National Heart, Lung and Blood Institute: Peripheral artery disease. 2019; https://www.nhlbi.nih.gov/health-topics/peripheral-artery-disease. Accessed June 6, 2020.

174. National Institute of Neurological Disorders and Stroke: Vasculitis syndromes of the central and peripheral nervous systems fact sheet. 2020; https://www.ninds.nih.gov/disorders/patient-caregiver-education/fact-sheets/vasculitis-syndromes-central-and-peripheral. Accessed June 6, 2020.

175. National Register of Health Service Psychologists. 2019, June 10; retrieved from www.findapsychologist.org.

176. Nelson RL, Thomas K, Morgan J, et al: Non-surgical therapy for anal fissure. *Cochrane Database Systematic Review.* 2012; (2): CD003431.

177. Neville CE, Fitzgerald CM, Mallinson T, et al: A preliminary report of musculoskeletal dysfunction in female chronic pelvic pain: A blinded study of examination findings. *Journal of Bodywork and Movement Therapies.* 2012; 16(1): 50–56.

178. Nickel JC, Tripp DA: International Interstitial Cystitis Study G. Clinical and psychological parameters associated with pain pattern phenotypes in women with interstitial cystitis/bladder pain syndrome. *Journal of Urology.* 2015; 193(1): 138–144.

179. Nielsen CS, Stubhaug A, Price DD, et al: Individual differences in pain sensitivity: Genetic and environmental contributions. *Pain.* 2008; 136(1–2): 21–29.

180. Oaklander AL, Nolano M: Scientific advances in and clinical approaches to small-fiber polyneuropathy: A review. *JAMA Neurology.* 2019; doi: 10.1001/jamaneurol.2019.2917.

181. Obara H: Acute limb ischemia. *Annals of Vascular Diseases.* 2018; 11(4): 443–448.

182. Obrien MT, Gillespie Dl: Diagnosis and treatment of the pelvic congestion syndrome. *Journal of Vascular Surgery.* Venous and Lymphatic Disorders. 2015; 3(1): 96.

183. Oen AC, Felt-Bersma RJ, Cuesta MA, et al: A randomized controlled trial of rubber band ligation versus infra-red coagulation in the treatment of internal haemorrhoids. *European Journal of Gastroenterology and Hepatology.* 2000; 12: 535–539.

184. Ooijevaar RE, Felt-Bersma RJF, Han-Geurts IJ, et al: Botox treatment in patients with chronic functional anorectal pain: Experiences of a tertiary referral proctology clinic. *Techniques in Coloproctology.* 2019; 23(3): 239–244.

185. Oyama IA, Rejba A, Lukban JC, et al: Modified Thiele massage as therapeutic intervention for female patients with interstitial cystitis and high-tone pelvic floor dysfunction. *Urology.* 2004; 64(5): 862–865.

186. O'Brien MT, Gillespie DL: Diagnosis and treatment of the pelvic congestion syndrome. *Journal of Vascular Surgery.* 2015; 3: 96–106.

187. Pagé MG, Fortier M, Ware MA, et al: As if one pain problem was not enough: Prevalence and patterns of coexisting chronic pain conditions and their impact on treatment outcomes. *Journal of Pain Research.* 2018; 11: 237–254.

188. Palsson OS, Whitehead WE: Psychological treatments in functional gastrointestinal disorders: A primer for the gastroenterologist. *Clinical Gastroenterology and Hepatology*. 2013; 11(3): 208–216.

189. Parekattil SJ, Gudeloglu A, Brahmbhatt JV, et al: Trifecta nerve complex—potential anatomic basis for microsurgical denervation of the spermatic cord for chronic orchialgia. *The Journal of Urology*. 2013; 190: 265–270.

190. Payne KA, Binik YM, Amsel R, et al: When sex hurts, anxiety and fear orient attention towards pain. *European Journal of Pain*. 2005; 9(4): 427–436.

191. Payne KA, Binik YM, Pukall CF, et al: Effects of sexual arousal on genital and non-genital sensation: A comparison of women with vulvar vestibulitis syndrome and healthy controls. *Archives of Sexual Behavior*. 2007; 36(2): 289–300.

192. Pazmany E, Bergeron S, Verhaeghe J, et al: Sexual communication, dyadic adjustment, and psychosexual well-being in premenopausal women with self-reported dyspareunia and their partners: A controlled study. *The Journal of Sexual Medicine*. 2014; 11(7): 1786–1797.

193. Pedersen KV, Drewes AM, Frimodt-Møller PC, et al: Visceral pain originating from the upper urinary tract. *Urological Research*. 2010; 38: 345–355.

194. Pelvic Health History Form: 2019; retrieved from https://pelvicpain.org/IPPS/Professional/Documents-Forms/IPPS/Content/Professional/Documents_and_Forms.aspx?hkey=2597ab99-df83-40ee-89cd-7bd384efed19.

195. Perry CP, Echeverri JD: Hernias as a cause of chronic pelvic pain in women. *Journal of the Society of Laparoendoscopic Surgeons*. 2006; 10(2): 212–215.

196. Pew Charitable Trust: Trends in U.S. antibiotic use, 2018. https://www.pewtrusts.org/en/research-and-analysis/issue-briefs/2018/08/trends-in-us-antibiotic-use-2018. Accessed August 1, 2018.

197. Potts JM, Moritz N, Everson D, et al: Chronic abacterial prostatitis: A functional somatic syndrome? [abstract]. Presented at: Annual Meeting of the American Urological Association; June 2, 2001; Anaheim, CA. Abstract 2005; 126.

198. Potts JM: Male pelvic pain: Beyond Urology and chronic prostatitis. *Current Rheumatology Reviews*. Bentham Science Publishers; 2016: 12(1): 27–39.

199. Prather H, Hunt D, Fournie A, et al: Early intra-articular hip disease presenting with posterior pelvic and groin pain. PM&R: *The Journal of Injury, Function, and Rehabilitation*. 2009; 1(19): 809–815.

200. Price DD: Psychological and neural mechanisms of the affective dimension of pain. *Science*. 2000; 288(5472): 1769–1772.

201. Price TJ, Inyang KE: Commonalities between pain and memory mechanisms and their meaning for understanding chronic pain. *Progress in Molecular Biology and Translational Science.* 2015; 131: 409–434.

202. Pukall CF, Binik YM, Khalifé S, et al: Vestibular tactile and pain thresholds in women with vulvar vestibulitis syndrome. *Pain.* 2002; 96(1–2): 163–175.

203. Quartana PJ, Campbell CM, Edwards RR: Pain catastrophizing: A critical review. *Expert Review of Neurotherapeutics.* 2009; 9(5): 745–758.

204. Ramachandran VS, Rogers-Ramachandran D: Synaesthesia in phantom limbs induced with mirrors. Proceedings. *Biological Sciences.* 1996; 263(1369): 377–386.

205. Randall ET, Smith KR, Conroy C, et al: Back to living: Long-term functional status of pediatric patients who completed intensive interdisciplinary pain treatment. *The Clinical Journal of Pain.* 2018; 34(10): 890–899.

206. Rao SS, Paulson J, Mata M, et al: Clinical trial: Effects of botulinum toxin on Levator ani syndrome: A double-blind, placebo-controlled study. *Alimentary Pharmacology and Therapeutics.* 2009; 29(9): 985–991.

207. Rees J, Abrahams M, Doble A, et al: Diagnosis and treatment of chronic bacterial prostatitis and chronic prostatitis/chronic pelvic pain syndrome: A consensus guideline. *BJU International.* 2015; 116(4): 509–525.

208. Reichard CA, Makovey I, Shoskes DA: Phenotype, symptom severity and treatment in a 'cured' cohort of chronic pelvic pain syndrome patients. *The Canadian Journal of Urology.* 2015; 22(1): 7623–7626.

209. Roane DW, Griger DR: An approach to diagnosis and initial management of systemic vasculitis. *American Family Physician.* 1999; 60(5): 1421–1430.

210. Rosenbaum TY: An integrated mindfulness-based approach to the treatment of women with sexual pain and anxiety: Promoting autonomy and mind/body connection. *Sexual and Relationship Therapy.* 2013; 28: 20–28.

211. Rosen NO, Bergeron S, Glowacka M, et al: Harmful or helpful: Perceived solicitous and facilitative partner responses are differentially associated with pain and sexual satisfaction in women with provoked vestibulodynia. *The Journal of Sexual Medicine.* 2012; 9(9): 2351–2360.

212. Rosen NO, Muise A, Bergeron S, et al: Daily associations between partner responses and sexual and relationship satisfaction in couples coping with provoked vestibulodynia. *Journal of Sexual Medicine.* 2015; 12(4): 1028–1039.

213. Rovner ES: Urethral Diverticula. In: Raz S, Rodriguez L, eds. Female Urology. 3rd ed. Philadelphia: Saunders; 2008: 815–834.

214. Rukavina I: SAPHO syndrome: A review. *Journal of Children's Orthopaedics.* 2015; 9(1): 19–27.

215. Rutkove SB: Differential diagnosis of peripheral nerve and muscle disease. *UpToDate.* 2018; https://www.uptodate.com/contents/differential-diagnosis-of-peripheral-nerve-and-muscle-disease. Accessed June 6, 2020.

216. Safavi-Abbasi S, Mapstone TB, Archer JB, et al: History of the current understanding and management of tethered spinal cord. *Journal of Neurosurgery.* 2016; 25: 78–87.

217. Sanderson J: Electrical neurostimulators for pain relief in angina—Reply. *British Heart Journal.* 1991; 65: 234–235.

218. Sandkuhler J, Lee J: How to erase memory traces of pain and fear. *Trends in Neurosciences.* 2013; 36(6): 343–352.

219. Sandkuhler J: Understanding LTP in pain pathways. *Molecular Pain.* 2007; 3: 9.

220. Sato A: Somatovisceral reflexes. *Journal of Manipulative and Physiological Therapeutics.* 1995; 18(9): 597–602.

221. Schreiner L, Nygaard CC, Anschau F: Urethral prolapse in premenopausal, healthy adult woman. *International Urogynecology Journal.* 2013; 24: 353–354.

222. Schroeder B, Sanfilippo JS, Hertweck SP: Musculoskeletal pelvic pain in a pediatric and adolescent gynecology practice. *Journal of Pediatric and Adolescent Gynecology.* 2000; 13(2): 90.

223. Seidman LC, Brennan KM, Rapkin AJ, et al: Rates of anovulation in adolescents and young adults with moderate to severe primary dysmenorrhea and those without primary dysmenorrhea. *Journal of Pediatric and Adolescent Gynecology.* 2018; 31(2): 94–101.

224. Seminowicz DA, Wideman TH, Naso L, et al: Effective treatment of chronic low back pain in humans reverses abnormal brain anatomy and function. *The Journal of Neuroscience.* 2011; 31(20): 7540–7550.

225. Senapati S, Atashroo D, Carey E, et al: Surgical interventions for chronic pelvic pain. *Current Opinion in Obstetrics and Gynecology.* 2016; 28: 290–296.

226. Sherrington CS: The integrative action of the nervous system. *Scribner's.* Yale University Press; 1906.

227. Shoskes DA, Altemus J, Polackwich AS: The urinary microbiome differs significantly between patients with chronic prostatitis/chronic pelvic pain syndrome and controls as well as between patients with different clinical phenotypes. *Urology.* 2016.

228. Shoskes DA, Landis JR, Wang Y, et al: Chronic Prostatitis Collaborative Research Network Study Group. Impact of post-ejaculatory pain in men with category III chronic prostatitis/chronic pelvic pain syndrome. *Journal of Urology*. 2004; 172: 542–547.

229. Siddiqi S, Vijay V, Ward M, et al: Pruritus ani. *Annals of the Royal College of Surgeons of England*. 2008; 90(6): 457–463.

230. Sieper J, Poddubnyy D: Axial spondyloarthritis. *Lancet*. 2017; 390: 73–84.

231. Silvis ML, Mosher TJ, Smentana BS, et al: High prevalence of pelvic and hip magnetic resonance imaging findings in asymptomatic collegiate and professional hockey players. *American Journal of Sports Medicine*. 2011, 201; 39(4): 715–721.

232. Singer T, Seymour B, O'Doherty J, et al: Empathy for pain involves the affective but not sensory components of pain. *Science*. 2004; 303(5661): 1157–1162.

233. Smith KB, Pukall CF: A systematic review of relationship adjustment and sexual satisfaction among women with provoked vestibulodynia. *Journal of Sex Research*. 2011; 48(2–3): 166–191.

234. Spiegel DR, Shaukat AM, McCroskey AL, et al: Conceptualizing a subtype of patients with chronic pain: The necessity of obtaining a history of sexual abuse. *The International Journal of Psychiatry in Medicine*. 2016; 51(1): 84–103.

235. Spierings EL, Padamsee A: Menstrual-cycle and menstruation disorders in episodic vs chronic migraine: An exploratory study. *Pain Medicine*. 2015; 16(7): 1426–1432.

236. Standring S, ed.: Figure 16.11. Efferent pathways of the autonomic nervous system In: Gray's Anatomy. *The Anatomical Basis of Clinical Practice*. 41st Edition. Philadelphia, PA: Elsevier Limited. 2016; 225–237.e3.

237. Standring S, ed.: Figure 16.13. Outflow from preganglionic sympathetic neurones in the lateral horn of the spinal cord. In: Gray's Atlas of Anatomy. *The Anatomical Basis of Clinical Practice*. 41st Edition. Philadelphia, PA: Elsevier Limited. 2016; 225–237.e3.

238. Standring S, ed.: Figure 61.5. The cutaneous branches of the lower intercostal and lumbar nerves. In: Gray's Atlas of Anatomy. *The Anatomical Basis of Clinical Practice*. 41st ed Philadelphia, PA: Elsevier Limited. 2015; 1069–1082 .e2.

239. Standring S, ed.: Figure 62.14. Muscles and nerves of the posterior abdominal wall. In: Gray's Atlas of Anatomy. *The Anatomical Basis of Clinical Practice*. 41st ed. Philadelphia, PA: Elsevier, Limited. 2016; 1083–1097.e2.

240. Standring S, ed.: Figure 62.15. The lumbar plexus and its branches. In: Gray's Atlas of Anatomy. *The Anatomical Basis of Clinical Practice*. 41st ed. Philadelphia, PA: Elsevier, Limited. 2016; 1083–1097.e2.

241. Standring S, ed.: Figure 61.5. The cutaneous branches of the lower intercostal and lumbar nerves. In: Gray's Atlas of Anatomy. *The Anatomical Basis of Clinical Practice.* 41st ed Philadelphia, PA: Elsevier Limited. 2015; 1069–1082.e2.

242. Standring S, ed.: A) Figure 73.3. Muscles of the female pelvis viewed from above. B) Figure 77.4. The muscles, vessels and nerves of the female perineum: Inferior view. In: Gray's Anatomy. *The Anatomical Basis of Clinical Practice.* 41st Edition. Philadelphia, PA: Elsevier Limited. 2016; A) 1221–1236.e1. B) 1288–1313.e1.

243. Standring S, ed.: Figure 77.3. A: The vessels of the female pelvis: Sagittal view. In: Gray's Atlas of Anatomy. *The Anatomical Basis of Clinical Practice.* 41st ed. Philadelphia, PA: Elsevier, Limited. 2016; 1288–1313.e1.

244. Steele A: Opioid use and depression in chronic pelvic pain. *Obstetrics and Gynecology Clinics of North America.* 2014; 41(3): 491–501.

245. Stein SL: Chronic pelvic pain. *Gastroenterology Clinics of North America.* 2013; 42(4): 785–800.

246. Sutton KS, Pukall CF, Chamberlain S: Pain ratings, sensory thresholds, and psychosocial functioning in women with provoked vestibulodynia. *Journal of Sex and Marital Therapy.* 2009; 35(4): 262–281.

247. Suvitie PA, Hallamaa MK, Matomaki JM, et al: Prevalence of pain symptoms suggestive of endometriosis among Finnish adolescent girls (TEENMAPS Study). *Journal of Pediatric and Adolescent Gynecology.* 2016; 29(2): 97–103.

248. Swiergiel AH, Juszczak GR, Stankiewicz AM: Genetic and epigenetic mechanisms linking pain and psychiatric disorders. *Modern Trends in Pharmacopsychiatry.* 2015; 30: 120–137.

249. Tahir H: Therapies in ankylosing spondylitis-from clinical trials to clinical practice. Rheumatology (Oxford). 2018; 57 (Suppl 6): vi23–vi28.

250. ter Kuile MM, Both S, Van Lankveld JJDM: Cognitive behavioral therapy for sexual dysfunctions in women. *Psychiatric Clinics of North America.* 2010; 33(3): 595–610.

251. ter Kuile MM, Melles R, De Groot HE, et al: Therapist-aided exposure for women with lifelong vaginismus: A randomized waiting-list control trial of efficacy. *Journal of Consulting and Clinical Psychology.* 2013; 81(6): 1127–1136.

252. The Foundation for Peripheral Neuropathy: What is Peripheral Neuropathy? https://www.foundationforpn.org/what-is-peripheral-neuropathy/. Accessed November 20, 2019.

253. The New Oxford American Dictionary (3rd Edition) Publisher: Oxford University Press. Print Publication Date: 2010 Print ISBN-13: 9780195392883. Published online: 2011. Current Online Version: 2015. doi: 10.1093/acref/9780195392883.001.0001.

254. The Oxford Dictionary of English 3rd edition. Publisher: Oxford University Press. Print Publication Date: 2010 Print ISBN-13: 9780199571123. Published online: 2010. Current Online Version: 2015. doi: 10.1093/acref/9780199571123.001.0001.

255. Tillisch K: The effects of gut microbiota on CNS function in humans. *Gut Microbes.* 2014; 5(3): 404–410.

256. Tincello DG, Walker AC: Interstitial cystitis in the UK: Results of a questionnaire survey of members of the Interstitial Cystitis Support Group. *European Journal of Obstetrics & Gynecology and Reproductive Biology.* 2005; 118: 91–95.

257. Traisak P, Basnyat S, Eid H, et al: A unique case of systemic lupus erythematosus pelvic vasculitis. *Case Reports in Rheumathology.* 2016; doi: 10.1155/2016/6347901.

258. Tripp DA, Nickel JC, Katz L: A feasibility trial of cognitive behavioural symptom management program for chronic pelvic pain for men with refractory chronic prostatitis/chronic pelvic pain syndrome. *Canadian Urologic Association Journal.* 2011; 5(5): 328–332.

259. Tripp DA, Nickel JC, Shoskes D, et al: A 2-year follow-up of quality of life, pain, and psychosocial factors in patients with chronic prostatitis/chronic pelvic pain syndrome and their spouses. *World Journal of Urology.* 2013; 31(4): 733–739.

260. Tugay N, Akbayrak T, Demirturk F, et al: Effectiveness of transcutaneous electrical nerve stimulation and interferential current in primary dysmenorrhea. *Pain Medicine.* 2007; 8(4): 295–300.

261. Turk DC, Okifuji A: Psychological factors in chronic pain: Evolution and revolution. *Journal of Consulting and Clinical Psychology.* 2002; 70(3): 678–690.

262. Ulmer WD, Gilbert JL, De EJB: Urethritis in women—considerations beyond urinary tract infection. *Current Bladder Dysfunction Reports.* 2014; 9: 181–187.

263. Valentine LN, Deimling TA: Opioids and alternatives in female chronic pelvic pain. *Seminars in Reproductive Medicine.* 2018; 36: 164–172.

264. Valovska A: Pelvic pain management. 1st ed. New York: Oxford: 2016.

265. Vandyken C, Hilton S: The puzzles of pelvic pain: A rehabilitation framework for balancing tissue dysfunction and centralization II: A review of treatment consideration. *Journal of Women's Health Physical Therapy.* 2012; 36(1): 44–54.

266. Vassilopoulou L, Matalliotakis M, Zervou MI, et al: Defining the genetic profile of endometriosis. *Experimental and Therapeutic Medicine.* 2019; 17(5): 3267–3281.

267. Velasquez CA, Saeyeldin A, Zafar MA, et al: A systematic review on management of nutcracker syndrome. *Journal of Vascular Surgery.* 2018; 6: 271–278.

268. Verne GN, Robinson ME, Vase L, et al: Reversal of visceral and cutaneous hyperalgesia by local rectal anesthesia in irritable bowel syndrome (IBS) patients. *Pain.* 2003; 105(1–2): 223–230.

269. Vernez SL, Okhunov Z, Wikenheiser J, et al: Precise characterization and 3-dimensional reconstruction of the autonomic nerve distribution of the human ureter. *The Journal of Urology.* 2017; 197: 723–729.

270. Vierck E: American Psychological Association: Coping with stress and anxiety. 2019; retrieved from https://www.apa.org/pi/about/publications/caregivers/consumers/common-problems.

271. Vlaeyen JW, Linton SJ: Fear-avoidance and its consequences in chronic musculoskeletal pain: A state of the art. *Pain.* 2000; 85(3): 317–332.

272. Warren JW, Brown J, Tracy JK, et al: Evidence-based criteria for pain of interstitial cystitis/painful bladder syndrome in women. *Urology.* 2008; 71: 444–448.

273. Weiss JM: Pelvic floor myofascial trigger points: Manual therapy for interstitial cystitis and the urgency-frequency syndrome. *Journal of Urology.* 2001; 166(6): 2226–2231.

274. Wessely S, Nimnuin C, Sharpe M: Functional somatic syndromes: One or many? *Lancet.* 1999; 354: 936–939.

275. West K, Williamson J: Wikipedia: Friend or foe? *Reference Services Review.* 2009; 37(3): 260–271.

276. Wiech K, Lin CS, Brodersen KH, et al: Anterior insula integrates information about salience into perceptual decisions about pain. *The Journal of Neuroscience: The Official Journal of the Society for Neuroscience.* 2010; 30(48): 16324–16331.

277. Wikipedia: https://www.wikipedia.org/. Wikipedia® is a registered trademark of the Wikimedia Foundation, Inc., a non-profit organization.

278. Williams FM, Scollen S, Cao D, et al: Genes contributing to pain sensitivity in the normal population: An exome sequencing study. *PLoS Genetics.* 2012; 8(12): e1003095.

279. Woolf CJ: Central sensitization: Implications for the diagnosis and treatment of pain. *Pain.* 2011; 152(3 Suppl): S2–15.

280. www.mayo.edu © 1998–2020 Mayo Foundation for Medical Education and Research (MFMER).

281. Zhao Y, Zhang J: Consumer health information seeking in social media: A literature review. *Health Information and Libraries Journal.* 2017; 34(4): 268–283.

INDEX

A

abdominal wall dysfunction, 104
acute pelvic pain, 2
acute prostatitis/infection, 39–40
adenomyosis, 25–26, 28, 154
adolescent patients. *See* pediatric and adolescent patients
anal fissures, 40, 76, 79–80, 92, 127, 258
anal skin irritation, 90
ankylosing spondylitis, 147, 258
arthritis, 144–145
axial spondyloarthritis, 149

B

benign prostatic hyperplasia (BPH), 39, 61
bladder biopsy, 70
bladder diaries, 65
bladder outlet obstruction (BOO), 42, 55, 60–61, 228
bladder pain, 55–57, 179, 229
bladder pain syndrome (BPS), 56–58
bladder symptom complex, 55–56
bone and ligament problems. *See also* musculoskeletal conditions
  assessment of spine and hip issues, 113–118
  bone and soft tissue tumors, 122
  imaging studies for, 118
  injuries to ligaments and tendons, 122
  pelvic fractures, 118–122
  pelvic pain originating in hips, 123
  physical evaluation for, 113
  treatment by bone specialists, 112–113
bursitis, 150

C

cancer
  abdominal, 79
  anorectal, 76–77, 231
  asymptomatic, 16
  bladder and urethral, 64–65, 69
  bone and soft tissue, 122, 138, 237
  breast, 34, 195, 202
  colon, 76, 78, 80, 85, 88
  gynecologic, 26, 35, 82, 201
  hormone-receptive, 203
  prostate, 39
caregivers, stress and coping in, 248, 288–290
catheterization
  clean intermittent, 63, 229
  indwelling suprapubic, 54, 63, 70
  indwelling urethral, 69
  injury due to, 64
  straight, 69
central sensitization, 4, 15, 127, 138, 247, 282, 284–285, 295
children and adolescents. *See* pediatric and adolescent patients

chronic pelvic pain (CPP)
  versus acute pelvic pain, 2
  challenges of diagnosis and treatment, 127
  costs of, 4
  pain sensitization and, 278–285
  potential causes of, 4–7, 14, 24–35, 54, 244, 266, 295
chronic pelvic pain syndrome (CPPS), 2, 14, 40, 49
clitoral pain, 34, 215
computerized tomography (CT), 13, 22, 71, 81, 119–120, 140, 158, 220
coping skills
  effect of past experiences on pelvic pain, 266
  effect of pelvic pain on relationships, 265
  emotional reactions to pelvic pain, 262–263
  evidence-based treatments and, 268
  mindfulness interventions, 268
  psychological factors associated with pelvic pain, 263–264
  psychological interventions and, 266–268
Crohn's disease, 76, 81, 83–85, 149
cystograms, 72–73
cystoscopy, 40, 54–57, 60, 62, 70

D

diagnostic injections, 212
digital rectal examination, 40–41, 80

E

educational resources
  articles, videos, podcasts, CDs, and DVDs, 301–303
  finding reliable internet sources, 297–300, 304
  importance of self-education, 294–295
  local libraries, 297
  professional organizations and support groups, 300–303
  second opinions, 295
  social media, 304–305
  specialized care, 296
  Treatment Map, 306–316
ejaculatory duct pain, 43, 228
emotional stress
  associated with IBS, 82–83
  associated with proctalgia fugax, 94
  caused by gynecological pain, 24
  caused by male pelvic pain, 38
  in children with pelvic pain, 242, 248–249
  developing coping skills, 250, 262–269
  due to sexual activity, 272, 274
  of family and friends, 288–289
  increased pelvic pain due to, 179
  leading to PFM dysfunction, 98
  psychological health and, 4
endometriosis, 21–22, 24–26, 28, 56, 63, 245
enlarged prostate, 39, 61
enteropathic spondyloarthritis, 149
epididymal and vas deferens pain, 42, 228
evaluation
  bladder or urethral biopsy, 70
  cystoscopy, 70
  diagnostic process, 14–15
  health care records, 11
  health care team members, 14
  history and physical, 10–12
  indwelling suprapubic catheters (SP tubes), 70
  indwelling urethral catheters, 69
  laboratory and imaging studies, 12–13, 71–73
  of musculoskeletal conditions, 106–108
  patient's role in, 16–17
  for pediatric and adolescent patients, 242
  pelvic/genitourinary examinations, 68–70
  potential outcomes of, 17
  sexually transmitted infection (STI) testing, 68
  of spine and hip conditions, 113–118

evaluation *(continued)*
  standardized questionnaires, 65
  straight catheterization, 69
  ureteroscopy, 70
  urethral culture, 71
  urinalysis, 68
  urine culture, 68
  urine cytology, 69
  urodynamic evaluation, 71
  uroflowmetry, 70
  vaginal culture, 71
  voiding diaries, 65–67
evidence-based treatments, 268
exercise, 170–172

F

family and friends, stress and coping among, 288–291
fear-avoidance model of pain, 262
female genital mutilation/cutting, 34
female pelvic anatomy, 3, 20. *See also* gynecologic conditions
forced FABERs (Flexion, Abduction, External Rotation) Test, 117
functional somatic syndromes (FSS), 15

G

gait deviations, 254–256
gastrointestinal-related pelvic pain
  anal fissures, 76, 80, 92, 127, 258
  anal skin irritation, 90–91
  diagnostic possibilities, 77
  hemorrhoids, 88–90, 225, 232, 258, 295
  hernias, 49, 87–88, 233–234, 238
  inflammatory bowel disease (IBD), 83–85, 149, 154
  intra-abdominal adhesions, 87
  irritable bowel syndrome (IBS), 82–83, 280
  levator ani syndrome, 94–95, 98, 231
  medical history concerning, 77–78
  overview of, 76
  physical examination for, 79–81
  physical or emotional trauma leading to, 83–84
  proctalgia fugax, 94, 100
  pruritis ani, 92
  rectal prolapse, 93–94, 233
  refractory constipation, 85–86
  symptoms of, 78–79
  testing for, 80–81
gout, 149
gynecologic cancer, 35, 82, 201
gynecologic conditions
  causes of acute pelvic pain, 20–21
  causes of chronic pelvic pain, 24–35
  diagnostic tests for, 22–23
  emergent care for, 22
  female pelvic anatomy, 20
  treatments for, 24

H

health care team, 14–16
hemorrhoids, 88–89, 225, 232, 258, 295
hernias, 49, 87, 233–234, 238
hips
  evaluating pelvic pain involving, 113–118
  gait abnormalities and, 258
  gout pain and, 149
  lumbo-pelvic-hip pain, 100–104
  pelvic pain originating in, 15, 35, 123
  polymyalgia rheumatica (PMR) and, 16
  relaxing overactive hip adductors, 257
Hunner's ulcer, 56–57, 299
hypervigilance, 262

I

imaging studies, 12–13, 71–72
indwelling suprapubic catheters (SP tubes), 70
indwelling urethral catheters, 69
inflammatory bowel disease (IBD), 83–85, 149, 154

internal vaginal exams
　ability to tolerate, 107
　assessing pelvic pain through, 16
　in pediatric and adolescent patients, 244
International Pelvic Pain Society (IPPS), 2, 296, 298, 300–301
interstitial cystitis (IC), 16, 56–58, 229, 302–303
intra-abdominal adhesions, 87
intrathecal pain pumps, 221
irritable bowel syndrome (IBS), 82–83, 280
ischemic pelvic disease, 163–165

L

laboratory tests, 12–13, 56, 59, 70–71
levator ani syndrome, 94, 98, 231
ligament injuries, 118, 122
low-back pain (LBP), 101
lumbo-pelvic-hip pain, 100–102

M

magnetic resonance imaging (MRI), 72
male pelvic anatomy, 3, 38. *See also* urogenital conditions (male)
medications
　antifungals, 194–195
　for bladder pain, 188–190
　bladder-relaxing medications, 187
　blood thinners, 205
　compound medications, 185
　general pain medications, 205–208
　generic versus brand name drugs, 184–185
　for GI and anal pain, 193–194
　hormonal medications, other, 203
　hormonal medications, systemic, 201–203
　immune and anti-inflammatory medications, 203–204
　injected Botulinum Toxin, 191
　injected irritants, 191
　injected neurolytics, 191
　injected steroids, 191
　local anesthetics, 190
　medication classes used to treat pain, 186
　medications that open bladder outlet, 188
　muscle relaxants, 208–209
　opioids, 209
　penile injections, 192
　skin barriers, 194
　stool softeners, 194
　transdermal or topical pain management, 185
　for urinary tract infections, 192–193
　vulvar/vaginal treatments for atrophy, inflammation or infection, 195–197
　vulvar/vaginal treatments for spasm or pain, 198–201
mindfulness interventions, 268
minimally invasive interventions
　as part of multi-modal treatment, 212
　diagnostic injections, 212
　intrathecal pain pumps, 221
　peripheral nerve blocks, 215–217
　pudendal nerve stimulators, 221
　sacral nerve stimulators, 221
　spinal cord stimulation (SCS), 218–221, 237, 246
　therapeutic injections, 213–214
mobility issues and pain
　ankylosing spondylitis, 258
　gait deviations, 254–257
　myopathy and stroke, 257
　neuropathies, 258–259
　rheumatologic disorders, 258
　spinal cord injury (SCI), 257–258
　treatment for, 259
multi-modal therapy, 127, 141, 184, 212, 225, 232, 294
muscle relaxation, 172–175
musculoskeletal conditions. *See also* bone and ligament problems
　abdominal wall dysfunction, 104–105
　evaluation of, 106–109

musculoskeletal conditions. *See also* bone and ligament problems *(continued)*
  lumbo-pelvic-hip pain, 100–103
  nerve entrapment, 104–105
  pelvic floor muscle (PFM) dysfunction, 98–100
myofascial pelvic pain, 15, 28–29, 245–246
myopathy, 257

N

nerve blocks
  diagnostic, 140, 212, 246
  in pediatric and adolescent patients, 246
  peripheral, 134, 215
nerve entrapment, 104–105
nerve sensitivity, 55
neuroinflammatory conditions, 151–153
neurological conditions
  chronic pain defined, 127
  diagnosis and treatment of, 139–141
  evaluation for causes of pelvic pain, 127–129
  nervous system overview, 126, 134
  peripheral nerves and pain, 129–134
  peripheral neuropathy, 134–136
  role of CNS in pain, 137–138
neuropathies
  causes of, 152
  defined, 15
  diagnosis, 10
  due to amyloidosis, 149
  due to spinal cord injury, 257–258
  peripheral, 114, 134–136
  resulting in pelvic pain, 2
  small fiber polyneuropathy (SFPN), 15, 55, 136, 284–285, 295
  treatment for, 185, 218, 237, 258–259
non-specific low-back pain (LBP), 101

O

osteitis condensans ilii, 150
ovarian cysts/masses, 26–27
overactive bladder syndrome (OAB), 59–60

P

pain catastrophizing, 263–264
painful bladder syndrome (PBS), 56–58
pain sensitization
  brain-based pain treatments, 284–285
  central sensitization, 284
  communication between the spinal cord and brain, 282
  effect of brain and emotions on, 282
  neurological (neurophysiological) mechanisms of, 278
  nociceptive stimuli and pain perception, 279
  overview of, 285
  pain messaging in the brain, 282
  predisposition to pain, 278–279
  somatic and autonomic nervous systems, 279–281
  visceral pain, 282
pain, types of, 14–15. *See also* pain sensitization; pelvic pain
Patrick Test, 117
pediatric and adolescent patients
  causes of pelvic pain in, 242–243
  central sensitization in, 247
  endometriosis, 245
  evaluation of pelvic pain in, 242
  internal vaginal exams, 244
  menstrual pain and irregular periods, 244
  multidisciplinary approach to pain management in, 250
  myofascial pelvic pain in, 245–246
  nerve blocks in, 246
  neuroplasticity in, 247
  pain in patients with developmental delays, 247–248
  pelvic floor physical therapists and, 246
  pelvic pain in girls versus boys, 244
  psychological support and treatment for, 250
  sexual abuse among, 249–250
  supporting children experiencing pain, 248–249

pelvic congestion syndrome, 34–35
pelvic examinations, 12, 22–23, 68
pelvic floor muscle (PFM) dysfunction, 98–100, 134
pelvic floor muscles (PFMs)
  bladder outlet obstruction due to, 55
  evaluating, 107–108, 118, 168
  nerve blocks for, 246
  physical therapy for, 41, 49
  rectal prolapse and, 93
  in refractory constipation, 85–86
  relationship to posture and pain, 254, 257
  relaxing, 174–176
  spasms leading to pain, 28, 94, 98, 244
pelvic fractures, 118–122
pelvic inflammatory disease (PID), 21, 28
pelvic organ prolapse, 29–30
pelvic pain
  acute versus chronic, 2
  causes of, 4–7, 14
  coping with, 262–269, 290
  diagnosis. *See* evaluation
  incidence and cost of, 2
  relationship to psychological health, 4
  symptoms of, 2, 7
  treatment. *See* treatment
pelvic physical therapists, 106–109
pelvic structures, 2
pelvic ultrasound, 22–23
pelvic venous disorders, 154–160
penile pain, 47
peripheral nerve blocks, 215–216
peripheral sensitization, 127, 282
peripheral spondyloarthritis, 149
physical disabilities. *See* mobility issues and pain
physical therapy (PT)
  biofeedback, 175
  breathing exercises, 174–175
  finding specialized therapists, 179–181
  goals of, 170
  good posture and ergonomics, 176–178
  healthy bowel and bladder habits, 178–181

muscle relaxation, 172–174
pelvic floor muscle relaxation, 174
pelvic physical therapists, evaluation by, 106–109
pelvic physical therapists, for children and adolescents, 246
role in reducing pelvic pain, 168–169
role of aerobic exercise in pain reduction, 171–172
role of exercise in improving or worsening pain, 170–171
role of yoga and stretching in pain management, 172–173
polymyalgia rheumatica, 150
Posterior Pelvic Pain Provocation Test, 118
proctalgia fugax, 94, 100
prostate gland conditions
  acute prostatitis/infection, 39–40
  chronic pelvic pain syndrome (CPPS), 40
  enlarged prostate (benign prostatic hyperplasia/BPH), 39
  function of prostate gland, 39
  pelvic pain caused by, 40–41
  treatment for prostate problems, 41–42
prostatitis, 39, 100
pruritis ani, 92
psoriatic arthritis, 147
psychological issues
  depression, 264
  effect of pelvic pain on relationships, 265
  emotion regulation, 263
  evidence-based treatments, 268–269
  fear-avoidance model of pain, 262
  hypervigilant approach to pain, 262
  mindfulness interventions, 268
  pain catastrophizing, 263–264
  pelvic pain in women versus men, 262
  psychological interventions, 266–268
  sexual abuse, 266
  support for pediatric and adolescent patients, 250
pudendal neuralgia, 100

R

rectal examination, 80, 128
rectal prolapse, 93, 233
refractory constipation, 85
Reiter's syndrome, 149
retrograde pyelograms, 73
rheumatologic conditions
  ankylosing spondylitis, 147
  arthritis, 144–145
  axial spondyloarthritis, 149
  bursitis, 150
  diagnosing, 151
  enteropathic spondyloarthritis, 149
  gout, 149
  osteitis condensans ilii, 150
  overview of, 144
  peripheral spondyloarthritis, 149
  polymyalgia rheumatica, 150
  psoriatic arthritis, 147
  Reiter's syndrome, 149
  Schnitzler syndrome, 149
  scleroderma, 146
  seronegative spondyloarthritis, 147
  Sjögren's syndrome, 147
  symptoms of, 144
  synovitis acne periostitis hyperostosis and osteitis (SAPHO), 150
  systemic lupus erythematosus (SLE), 146
  treatment for, 151
rheumatologic disorders, 258

S

sacral nerve stimulators, 221
Schnitzler syndrome, 149
scleroderma, 146
second opinions, 221, 225, 295–296
seminal vesicle pain, 43
seronegative spondyloarthritis, 147
sexual abuse
  among pediatric and adolescent patients, 249
  relationship to pelvic pain, 266

sexual activity and pain
  alternate strategies to manage pain, 273
  based on sexual orientation or gender identity, 272
  causes in males, 49
  continuing intimacy and sex, 273
  dealing with emotional reactions to, 274
  decreasing pain during sexual acts, 272–273
  effects of pelvic pain on sexual function, 273–274
  male versus female experience, 272
  managing sexual pain, 275
sexually transmitted infections (STIs)
  diagnosing, 49, 54, 68
  epididymal infections due to, 42
Sjögren's syndrome, 147
small fiber polyneuropathy (SFPN), 15, 55, 136, 284–285, 295
smoking, 179
social media, 304–305
somatic pain, 14
spinal cord injury (SCI), 257
spinal cord stimulation (SCS), 218–220, 237, 246
straight catheterization, 69
stroke, 257
surgical interventions
  for abdominal hernias, 233–234
  for anorectal problems, 231–233
  for gynecological conditions, 226–229
  for herniated discs, 235–236
  for male anatomy conditions, 228–229
  medications to discontinue prior to, 238
  for musculoskeletal, bone, and ligament problems, 237
  for nerve entrapment, 235
  for neurological pelvic pain, 235
  options available prior to surgery, 225
  for other neurological pain problems, 237
  overview of, 224
  potential drawbacks of, 238–239
  questions to ask prior to surgery, 225

for urinary tract conditions, 229–231
for vascular problems, 238
symptoms
　of gastrointestinal-related pain, 78–79
　of pelvic pain, 2, 7
　of rheumatologic diseases, 144
　of vasculitis, 162
synovitis acne periostitis hyperostosis and osteitis (SAPHO), 150
systemic lupus erythematosus (SLE), 146

T

tendon injuries, 122
testicular pain, 44–46
therapeutic injections, 213
treatment
　advances in, 294–295
　importance of communication and self-education in, 294–295
　medications, 184–209
　minimally invasive, 212–221
　multi-modal therapy, 127, 141, 184, 212, 225, 232
　for neuropathies, 185, 218, 237, 258
　second opinions, 221, 225, 295–296
　specialized care, 296–297
　surgical interventions, 224–239
Treatment Map, 10, 306–316
Trendelenburg gait, 113–114
tumors, 122

U

ulcerative colitis, 83–85
ultrasound examinations, 71
underactive bladder (UAB), 62–63
ureteral endometriosis, 63
ureteroscopy, 70
ureter pain, 63
urethral biopsy, 70
urethral caruncles, 55
urethral culture, 71
urethral diverticulum, 54–55
urethral mucosal prolapse, 55
urethral pain, 53–54
urethritis, 54
urethrograms, 72
urinalysis, 68
urinary tract infections (UTIs), 54, 65
urine cultures, 68
urine cytology, 69
urodynamic evaluation, 71
uroflowmetry, 70
urogenital conditions (male)
　epididymal and vas deferens pain, 42–43
　incidence of male pelvic pain, 38
　pain during intercourse and sexual activity, 49
　penile pain, 47–48
　prostate problems, 39–42
　seminal vesicles and ejaculatory duct pain, 43–44
　testicular pain, 44–47
urogenital conditions (unisex)
　bladder outlet obstruction (BOO), 60–62
　bladder pain, 55–58
　cancer, 64–65
　evaluation of, 65–73
　infection, 65–66
　overactive bladder syndrome (OAB), 59–60
　underactive bladder (UAB), 62–63
　ureter pain, 63–64
　urethral pain, 53–55
urologists, 38
uterine fibroids, 27–28

V

vaginal pain, 30–31
vasculitis, 161–163
videos, 299–300
visceral pain, 14, 282
voiding cystourethrograms (VCUGs), 72–73
voiding diaries, 65–66
vulvar pain, 31–34

Y

yoga, 172–173, 250, 258, 279, 303

Made in the USA
Middletown, DE
07 November 2023